The Mormons' War on Poverty

The Mormons' War on Poverty
A History of LDS Welfare
1830–1990

Garth Mangum and Bruce Blumell

University of Utah Press
Salt Lake City

Volume Eight, Publications in Mormon Studies
Linda King Newell, editor

Publications in Mormon Studies was established to encourage creation and sub-
mission of work on Mormon-related topics that would be of interest to scholars
and the general public. The initiation of the series represents an acknowledgment
by the Press and the editor of the region's rich historical and literary heritage and
of the quality of work being done in various areas of Mormon studies today.

Financial assistance by The Mormon History Trust Fund in the publication of this
work is gratefully acknowledged.

∞ This symbol indicates books printed on paper that meets the minimum
requirements of American National Standard for Information Services—
Permanence of Paper for Printed Library Materials, ANSI A39.38–1984.

Library of Congress Cataloging-in-Publication Data

Mangum, Garth L.
    The Mormons' war on poverty : a history of LDS welfare, 1830–1990 /
Garth Mangum and Bruce Blumell.
        p.   cm. — (Publications in Mormon studies, ISSN 0893-4916 ; v. 8)
    Includes bibliographical references and index.
    ISBN 0-87480-414-0 (alk. paper)
        1. Church of Jesus Christ of Latter-Day Saints—Charities—
History.   2. Mormon Church—Charities—History.   I. Blumell, Bruce D.
(Bruce Dudley), 1943–   . II. Title. III. Series.
    BX8643.W4M36   1993
    261.8'325'088283—dc20
                                                            92-35616
                                                            CIP

CONTENTS

TABLES

FOREWORD BY LEONARD J. ARRINGTON

IN ONE OF HIS earliest revelations, one that came to him in December 1830 just a few months after the organization of the Church of Jesus Christ of Latter-day Saints, Joseph Smith, founding prophet of the Mormons, gave a description of the ideal city, the City of Enoch of biblical times:

> And the Lord called his people Zion, because they were of one heart and one mind, and dwelt in righteousness; and there was no poor among them." (Pearl of Great Price, Moses 7:18)

The youthful prophet also held before his people the frequent statements in the Book of Mormon, first published earlier in 1830, regarding the obligation of God's people to care for the poor. One passage refers to the perfect society created through the ministry of Jesus Christ, in which the people "had all things common...therefore there were not rich and poor, bond and free, but they were all made free, and partakers of the heavenly gift." (Book of Mormon, Fourth Nephi 31.)

Readers of *The Mormons' War on Poverty* will discover that the doctrines promulgated by Joseph Smith and his successors have gone far beyond the traditional practice of charitable giving common among most religions. The saving of the physical body has been seen as an obligation in the same sense as the saving of the soul. Programs have varied over time, but the goals of preventing poverty and improving the lives of members have remained. Loyal church members have made generous gifts to maintain programs designed to provide short-term emergency help for those in dire need, support for those unable to become self-supporting, and reinforcement to all others in achiev-

ing self-reliance—believing that all should live frugally and be ever-
ready to respond to any request for assistance in building the kingdom
of God.

During its first one hundred years the church functioned in a land-
based economy. In Ohio local members with land were induced to
share with converts migrating from New York. In Missouri, those in
the more settled East were required to contribute to the purchase of
western lands. In Nauvoo, Illinois, the Missouri refugees were expected to be settled and prepared to assimilate the growing number of
convert-immigrants from the East and the British Isles. In 1847 the
church was propelled to the Great Basin, beyond the frontier, where
land was plentiful. The new task, along with assisting immigrants,
was to create the infrastructure to make the marginal land in the Great
Basin fruitful. In the absence of outside capital, the Mormon people,
until late in the nineteenth century, created their own economy.
By the twentieth century they had to learn how to apply their economic principles within a broader economy over which they had little
control.

The challenge of the 1930s was what to do for city-dwellers when
the external economy upon which they depended had become criti-
cally depressed. A means was developed for them to draw sustenance
from local farmers who were at least able to provide their own food.
From 1940 onward, the church in the United States and other developed nations functioned in a setting of general prosperity accompanied by an emerging set of governmental social welfare programs to
care for the poor. The challenge for the church was to sort out its responsibilities relative to those of government for the elderly, the temporarily unemployed, the victims of natural disasters, and the few unable to meet the rigors of an industrial society in which most members
had little difficulty providing for themselves.

The primary challenge since the 1970s has been the economic status of the multiplying membership in less-developed countries, where
only a few were able to rise above abject poverty and where Latter-
day Saints were a tiny minority in nations with their own laws, customs, economic realities, and social welfare programs.

For years, short-term emergency assistance has come from "fast
offerings," monthly cash donations by faithful members intended
only for support of the poor. From 1930 to 1960 in perhaps two hundred localities there were also welfare production projects that contributed food and other commodities for those in need of emergency
aid and long-term support. But the goal has always been to promote

self-reliance. Whether in the less-developed lands, the newly industrializing countries, or the advanced developed nations, the church has promoted and assisted:

1. Subsistence extraction from farming, fishing, or grazing.
2. Self-employment in individual and small family enterprises.
3. Commercial agriculture.
4. Entrepreneurship in the promotion of larger enterprises.
5. Jobs in private and public organizations.

Every democratic nation also has its own set of social welfare programs, all inadequate to the task and of varying degrees of effectiveness. Most of these, including those in the United States, are seeking improved ways of promoting self-reliance. To what extent the church should go it alone and to what extent it should tap community resources is a continuing issue. The enhancement of the economic well-being of the Latter-day Saints by strengthening self-reliance is a never-ending goal.

The challenge is particularly acute in 1992 as a substantial proportion of the 8.4 million Latter-day Saints reside in third world countries where the battle against poverty is unending. Once limited to a philosophy of "we take care of our own," the church is now reaching out with projects similar to those of United Jewish Appeal, the Catholic Relief Fund, and the American Friends Service Committee. That is the praiseworthy story this volume tells.

Although several economists and historians began to write articles and books on Mormon economic programs, particularly in the 1930s, a need still existed for a comprehensive and thorough treatment of church welfare programs, both historical and contemporary. In 1974, Elder Joseph Anderson, managing director of the Historical Department of the Church, after consulting with advisors to the Council of Twelve Apostles and the First Presidency of the church, directed me as Church Historian and one of our staff members, Dr. Bruce Blumell, to prepare a carefully researched history of the church's welfare programs. Dr. Blumell had full access to all of the material in the Church Archives and in the individual offices of welfare agencies. After three years of research and writing, Dr. Blumell completed a book-length manuscript, "Remember the Poor: A History of Welfare in the Church of Jesus Christ of Latter-day Saints, 1830–1980." Some parts of that study were published, but most of it remained in manuscript form when Dr. Blumell left the Historical Department to engage in a legal career in Calgary, Alberta.

With the approval of Dr. Blumell and my own encouragement,

Dr. Garth Mangum, a consultant to the LDS Welfare Services Department, agreed in 1987 to update the manuscript and revise it for publication in its present form. Dr. Mangum introduced the broader economic context within which church welfare was operating, indicating some of the challenges being faced during each time period; better identified the target groups within the church—employables or unemployables, aged, widows and orphans, and the socially disoriented; gave a more realistic assessment of the extent to which need was met; provided more information on the geographical areas of the church that were served as the church spread out from its Salt Lake City base; and, above all, wrote chapters describing current challenges—internationalization, third world growth, varied cultures and legal systems, the feminization of poverty, and the fragmentation of values.

Solidly based on the mass of materials in the Church Archives in Salt Lake City, reference to some of which have had to be omitted in footnotes, this is a comprehensive, accurate, informative history of Mormon efforts to provide assistance to its less-fortunate members, develop self-reliance, induce a spirit of oneness and selflessness, and help victims of famine and natural disaster around the world. The authors have taken pains to place the book within the ambience of American history and economics, and indeed within the conditions and experiences of other nations where there are substantial numbers of Mormons, including Mexico, Brazil, Chile, The Philippines, Japan, and Nigeria. The book is fascinating for its insights into local cultures and problems. A particular challenge is the decline in public funding, the moral deterioration and the consequent need for social services, and the spread of the church to places where everyone is poor.

The detail of this study and its scope, and the amount of attention it gives to post-World War II programs puts it in a class by itself. This is a major contribution toward an understanding of the rapid and vast expansion of the Mormon Church in recent years. The church's changing attitude of assistance to its members—from economic assistance to health care, counseling, educational opportunity, and employment preparation—is new and illuminating. Whereas the traditional approach in the nineteenth-century was to provide food for less-fortunate members, the church in this century has been concerned with all the social needs of its members. And whereas it was traditionally concerned with its own members, it has become in recent decades a major provider of assistance to victims of famine and disaster throughout the world.

The Mormon's War on Poverty is an exciting story and a dependable analysis of the church's efforts to ameliorate the conditions of life—for Mormons and for others. Joseph Smith's dream of the City of Zion has not been realized, but it has been a potent force in the development and maintenance of programs that have significantly improved the lives of his followers.

PREFACE

FEW DISCUSSIONS of anti-poverty efforts or of the doctrines and policies of the Church of Jesus Christ of Latter-day Saints occur in an environment free of controversy. This religious history of the economic welfare principles and programs will surely be no exception. Although our goal as scholars has been to gather and state the facts as accurately as possible, our selection and interpretation of those facts has certainly been shaped by training, preference, and personality. Consequently, we feel it important to disclose relevant facts about ourselves and about the shaping of this history.

Garth Mangum is partially retired as Max McGraw Professor of Economics and Management at the University of Utah. He is the son of a sharecropper, whose family's income was multiplied by half a dozen of the New Deal's work relief programs during the 1930s. He observed, from the grassroots, the introduction and unfolding of the LDS Church Welfare Plan of the 1930s. After military service and a number of years as a steelworker, miner, trucker, and construction worker, he belatedly served an LDS mission and, following the counsel of his mission president, enrolled in college as a twenty-seven-year-old freshman. He earned a bachelor's degree in economics from Brigham Young University, a Master of Public Administration and a Ph.D. in economics from Harvard University, and a J.D. from the University of Utah, and has taught economics, management, and law at Harvard University, Brigham Young University, George Washington University, and the University of Utah.

The title of this book reflects his service in the federal administrations of John F. Kennedy and Lyndon B. Johnson where he was engaged in the design and administration of the antipoverty programs of

that era. He served as a consultant or participant in every federal administration from Dwight D. Eisenhower to Jimmy Carter. As a consultant to the World Bank, the International Labor Organization, the
U.S. Agency for International Development, and a number of foreign
governments, he has been involved in antipoverty and economic development efforts in over thirty countries in Eastern Europe, Africa,
the Middle East, the Far East, and Latin America. In all of those and in
other countries of more casual travel, he has attended and observed
whatever LDS Church activities were under way and has also conducted studies for the LDS Church Welfare Services Department as a
church-service (unpaid volunteer) assignment in several countries.
Publications include nearly fifty books and monographs and more
than two hundred articles on economic development, labor, human
resource development, and antipoverty measures.

Bruce Blumell, a practicing attorney in Calgary, Alberta, began
his professional career as a historian. He grew up in the largely Mormon settlement of Magrath in southwestern Alberta and served an
LDS mission in Montreal, Quebec. He earned a B.A. and an M.A. in
history at the University of Alberta and his Ph.D. in the same discipline at the University of Washington. His master's thesis was a study
of the 1930s Federal Emergency Relief Administration in Montana
and his dissertation dealt with the development of public assistance in
the state of Washington during the 1930s. His interest in the LDS
Church Welfare Program had been earlier sparked when, as a bishop's
son, he had worked on the ward welfare farm and helped his father
deliver commodities from the bishop's storehouse to needy members
of the congregation.

From 1973 to 1979, Blumell was a Senior Historical Associate in
the LDS Church's Historical Department, working with Leonard J.
Arrington, then Church Historian. Blumell's major effort was a review of archival materials on the church's attempts to alleviate poverty among its members from its beginnings in 1830 to 1980, with
emphasis on the twentieth century. He drafted a book-length manuscript, "Remember the Poor: A History of Welfare in the Church of
Jesus Christ of Latter-day Saints, 1830–1980," which was never published. While working on that volume, he published "The Latter-day
Saints' Response to the Teton, Idaho, Flood, 1976," *Task Papers in
LDS History, No. 16* (Salt Lake City: LDS Church Historical Department, 1976). Summaries and sections of specific focus were published
in *Sunstone* and in the *Journal of Mormon History* 6 (1979): 80–106, as
"Welfare before Welfare: Twentieth-century LDS Church Charity be-

fore the Great Depression." In 1979, Blumell returned to Canada where he obtained his bachelor of laws degree and commenced his legal career.

As of 1987, we had never met or even heard of each other. The connecting link between us was Leonard J. Arrington, dean of LDS historians, LDS Church Historian from 1972 to 1982 and director of the Joseph Fielding Smith Institute until his retirement in 1987. Mangum's choice of research topics has always stemmed from wanting to know more about a particular subject. In a casual conversation with Arrington in 1987, he asked why no one had ever done a history of the LDS Church Welfare Program. Arrington replied that it had been done but never published. He loaned Mangum a copy of Blumell's unpublished work as a matter of interest and, when Mangum returned it, asked if he would be interested in bringing it up to date as a coauthor. As Mangum evaluated Blumell's carefully researched and illuminating manuscript, he concluded that it would benefit from three additional elements: (1) the context of the national economic conditions against which the church struggled to assist its members, (2) new historical works that had appeared in the 1980s, and (3) an updating to 1990, particularly the international challenge accompanying the church's highly successful proselyting efforts in poverty-stricken third-world countries, with many of which Mangum had some familiarity. With Arrington's blessing, our serial collaboration began with correspondence, then coauthorship, and finally, midway through the enterprise, a meeting.

Although our scholarly training and experience enable us, we believe, to research dispassionately, evaluate objectively, and avoid special pleading, it is still true that where one stands depends, to some extent, on where one sits. We recognize that the selection of facts for coherence and their interpretation for meaning are inevitably colored by our predispositions and predilections. Perhaps the most significant is that we are, simultaneously with our scholarly credentials, fully active and committed Mormons. Both of us served full-time unpaid proselyting missions, endeavoring to persuade others to investigate and accept the truth claims of the church. Both of us have served as officers in the church's unpaid, lay organization all of our adult lives. As a consequence, both of us have seen the church as insiders, functioning at its very best as a loving, nurturing community in caring for the needs of its poor. As insiders, we honor and revere LDS leaders, considering ourselves bound not only by duty but by respect to accept their authority.

However, like all insiders, we know that even organizations with divine claims must make do with human efforts. Even inspired decisions usually come after long struggle and experimentation, rather than springing ready-made to mind. The Mormon quip, "Revelation is usually one-third desperation, one third perspiration, and one-third inspiration," has certainly been true of LDS welfare efforts. This history is a history of trial-and-error experimentation, all prompted by good motives, all buttressed by sincere efforts, but not all equally successful.

Sources for this work present an unexpectedly complicated problem. During the era in which Leonard Arrington, a professional academic historian, headed the Church Historical Department, the archives were, for all practical purposes, open to all reputable researchers with the exception of such confidential items as tithing and excommunication records. Blumell's research drew freely on all archival sources. It is regrettable that it was not published during that era. Later administrators, with institutional rather than academic values, have maintained more restrictive policies due to their greater sensitivity to criticism and conflict. Many sources open to Blumell are no longer accessible to researchers. Furthermore, these administrators have judged his previously unpublished work to be proprietary, since he performed the research as an employee of the Church Historical Department.

In parallel fashion, research that Mangum conducted and studies that he wrote for the Church Welfare Services Department between 1988 and 1990 have been adjudged proprietary by that department, unavailable for direct citation. As academics, we regret these decisions even though we acknowledge the authority of the respective departments to make them. No one in either department who has read this work either objects to or endorses what we have said. No one has made any effort to influence our judgments or restrain us from publishing.

Our research shaped our hypotheses, undergirded our judgments, and is reflected in what we have written; but our citations are, in some cases, sparser than we, as academics, are comfortable with. In other cases, we have used personal material in our files that contains parallel information rather than the full documentary references that the conventions of scholarship would suggest. In such cases, we offer our apologies and our assurances that, when policies become less restrictive, the documentation will not contradict our conclusions, even if another generation of scholars, looking at the same evidence with new orientations, might form different interpretations.

INTRODUCTION

IN THE DEPTHS of the Great Depression, amidst the barrage of federal programs emanating from Franklin D. Roosevelt's "New Deal" and the accompanying controversy, a flurry of headlines appeared in the national press. The Mormons had introduced a new program which would take care of their poor and point the way for other private organizations. As the *Reader's Digest* had it: "A year and a half ago, . . . one-sixth of the entire church membership were on direct relief. Today none of them are. The church is taking care of its own. . . . Within a year [every Mormon] was removed from the government relief rolls all over the country."[1] The report was exaggerated but the program and the excitement were real.

IN NOVEMBER 1945, George Albert Smith, president of the Church of Jesus Christ of Latter-day Saints, called on Harry S Truman, president of the United States of America. People across the devastated continent of Europe faced a bitter winter and implacable hunger. The church asked for authorization to send food and clothing to its members there. "When will the supplies be ready?" President Truman reportedly asked. "Loaded and ready to roll," responded President Smith. And 140 railroad carloads followed the order.[2]

DAM BREAK! The fracturing of the Teton Dam in the summer of 1976 released the pent-up waters of the Snake River, inundated 90,000 acres of Idaho farmland, and destroyed over 4,000 homes. Almost before the flood waters ended their eighty-five-mile rampage, trucks were rolling out of Salt Lake City and other LDS storehouses with food and clothing, followed by busloads of workers and trucks hauling heavy equipment to clean up the debris.[3] That story could be duplicated for earthquakes, hurricanes, and other natural disasters throughout the United States and abroad.

IN LATE 1984 as the pinched faces and bloated bodies of starving Ethiopian children filled American television screens, the First Presidency called upon members of the LDS Church to forego two meals on Sunday, 24 January 1985, and contribute a generous estimate of the value of those meals to famine relief. Money flowed in quietly and out with no fanfare. Another special fast dedicated to the same purpose was undertaken in November of the same year. Some $11 million aided the Ethiopian refugees and others in similar straits in African and other third world countries, launching a new Humanitarian Services effort which became a permanent addition to the roster of LDS welfare services.[4]

Those were spectacular responses to need; but the real story of economic welfare activities within the Church of Jesus Christ of Latter-day Saints occurs within LDS congregations throughout the world in their day-to-day operations. The 1936 publicity and the centralized welfare structure which emerged with the definition of a formal welfare program have led the general public, church members, and even some LDS scholars to see it as a new departure. In reality, surprisingly little was new except that certain local experiments within the Salt Lake Valley were now sufficiently mature to be endorsed and extended throughout the Mormon core area. Succoring the European Saints during 1945–47 and responding to the Teton flood were merely applications of supplies and administrative machinery held in readiness for such cataclysmic events as well as individual daily need. The Ethiopian fast was only an extension to nonmember needy of the monthly practice, typical in devout homes, of foregoing two meals and contributing their value for the support of the poor.

Even the seven-year experimentation preceding the 1936 announcement had not been the beginning. That was only one major skirmish in an organized "war on poverty" which had been waged from Mormonism's beginnings in 1830. In fact, the economic concerns of the church had been even broader, encompassing the economic well-being of all of its members, not just those who happened to be poor or victims of calamities at any point in time. Though time, place, circumstance, and application had changed repeatedly, these efforts had been tied together by a consistent set of principles integral to what the church, its leaders, and members had always conceived to be the very reason for its existence.

The Theological Base

The Mormon Church defines its primary mission as "bring[ing] to pass the immortality and eternal life of [humankind]" (Moses 1:39); yet Mormon attentiveness to the poor has theological, historical, and social roots. The chapters which follow place Mormon anti-poverty efforts in their historical, economic, and social context; but the accompanying policies and decisions will not be understood without some familiarity with LDS theology.

The basic premise of Mormon theology is that all human beings had a pre-earthly existence as literal spirit children of divine parents who themselves had achieved exaltation after successful completion of a life not unlike this one. Agency, or the possession of the capacity for independent choice, is inseparably associated with identity. This world, among others, was created for the purposes of allowing these spirits to inhabit mortal bodies and exercise options of choice for good or evil. A rebellious spirit son, Lucifer, tempted Adam and Eve and their descendants to disobedience while chosen prophets preached Christ's redemptive sacrifice.

Thus, the universal fatherhood of God and the universal brotherhood and sisterhood of all human beings are accepted as literal by Latter-day Saints. They accept the ideal of Christian love and service, though like all humans, they fall short of their ideals. Because temporal conditions have an inevitable impact upon moral choice and spiritual progress, that mutual responsibility includes material well-being. As Joseph F. Smith, sixth church president, stated: "It has always been a cardinal teaching with the Latter-day Saints that a religion that has not the power to save people temporally and make them prosperous and happy here cannot be depended upon to save them spiritually and to exalt them in the life to come."[5]

Theologically, the Mormons accept an unsparing ideal: Family obligations of brotherhood and sisterhood will never be fulfilled as long as one has less of this world's goods than another. Nevertheless, the theology which combines both grace and works stresses the necessity of making a full effort toward self-sufficiency, rather than simply accepting charity. The idler—whether rich or poor—may not eat the bread nor wear the garments of the laborer (D&C 42:42), not only to lessen the burden on the laborer, but also to strengthen the spiritual character of the idler. Hence, Mormonism encourages self-reliance for all, while the affluent are encouraged to devote economic surplus, energies, and abilities to the practical building of God's kingdom. Such a program is a formula for approaching equality from both directions without jealousy or lust.

The Perceived Church Mission

The Church of Jesus Christ of Latter-day Saints defines itself as a restoration of a church established by Jesus Christ, lost in its authorized form through apostasy, and restored through the prophetic calling of Joseph Smith in New York State in 1830. They call themselves Saints or Mormons (after the Book of Mormon, a record of the ancient Christian inhabitants of the Americas translated by Joseph Smith). To prepare themselves for the second coming of Christ, Mormons believe themselves charged with responsibility for both the spiritual and temporal salvation of all humankind by establishing and maintaining a kingdom of God on earth. This kingdom, they believe, is destined to become Zion, sometimes interpreted literally as a place but more often as a condition of pure-heartedness in which Saints who are "of one heart" will share until they have all things in common and, therefore, have no poor among them.

The LDS Church defines its mission as tripartite:

1. To perfect the Saints—to constantly urge church members to improve their capabilities and conduct.
2. To proclaim the gospel—to proselyte in both organized and individualized fashion wherever the opportunity arises.
3. To redeem the dead—to perform certain essential ordinances on behalf of those who died without hearing the gospel message but who retain both identity and choice in the post-mortal sphere.[6]

The only resources with which the church may accomplish those tasks are the time, talents, and surplus income of its members. Obviously, it is to the church's advantage to enlist members with, or help them attain, an economic status in which they can not only support themselves and their families but contribute time, energy, and financial resources to church service. Thus, among other facets distinctive to Mormonism are its reciprocal economic commitments—the economic commitment of member to church required for full fellowship and the historically demonstrated commitment of the church to the economic well-being of its members. This bilateral pact has three components:

1. Short-term emergency help to those in need.
2. A continuing concern for member self-sufficiency which in turn has two sources:

a. The principle of gathering which dominated the first century of Mormon history. The church had an obligation to see that those who forsook their homes had the means to sustain themselves in Zion.

b. The continuing principle of consecration which binds the member to devote, when called upon, all of his or her time, talent, and means to the church.

3. The theological yearning for Zion, an earthly society in which no economic inequality mars the essential unity of those who are to be of one heart and one mind.

Therefore, a dominant theme throughout the history of the Church of Jesus Christ of Latter-day Saints has been a persistent effort to eradicate poverty and encourage economic self-reliance among its members while looking forward to and periodically attempting what has always proven to be a premature social and economic utopia. Geography, social conditions, and economic realities have changed constantly; but that triple commitment has never wavered, though its intensity has waxed and waned with need. Tracing those three interwoven threads through some 160 years of history in order to focus on current economic challenges confronting the LDS Church is the purpose of this book.

The Dictates of History

History also imposed immediate and practical reasons for becoming involved with the care of the poor. The nineteenth-century concept of gathering to a central place—successively Kirtland, Ohio; Jackson County, Missouri; Nauvoo, Illinois; and the valley of the Great Salt Lake in what is now Utah—reinforced unity and mutual concern economically as well as spiritually. The restored gospel was meant to encompass all of life's activities. In contrast to the secularizing and individualizing trends of early nineteenth-century America, Mormonism envisioned a more organic social order. Thus, LDS history reinforced LDS theology and doctrine. As a practical side-effect, Mormon history also gave the Saints limited opportunities for accumulation well into the twentieth century, making members more nearly equal in their material possessions.

The Mormons of the nineteenth century were community developers and colonizers. Nationally, care of the poor had been a civic responsibility since colonial times; and Mormons accepted responsibility for their own poor as a civic, social, and ecclesiastical duty. During the last half of the nineteenth century, church leaders directed much of the economic development of the immense geographical area marked by the Colorado

River and its tributaries and the Basin and Range Province between the Rockies and the Sierras, lapping over at the north and south into Canada and Mexico. The cooperative nature of Mormon economic policy and institutions made possible the survival of the Saints on this difficult frontier.

Nationally, social work became a profession after the turn of the century; the LDS Relief Society women led out in this effort in Utah. Public welfare entered a centralized phase with the New Deal of the 1930s, just as the church simultaneously created its own centralized program, not in opposition to the government's, but apprehensive that the government would cease its relief efforts. Mormon commitment to welfare became so intense that, paradoxically, it maintained its centralized program even while it largely abandoned its historical assumption of civic and even governmental responsibility.

Now, in the closing years of the twentieth century, Mormons, wherever they live, are subjects of their prevailing nations and participants in national and world economies. Every democracy and some nations which are not democracies have become welfare states. The differences among such nations are only matters of degree. Since most Mormons are citizens of democracies, their welfare system generally functions within the context of and in parallel with systems of public welfare.

It is not enough, therefore, to trace in isolation Mormon efforts to care for their poor. Those activities must be reviewed in the broader social context. What were the economic conditions with which the society struggled and in which the poor lost the battle? What was society doing for the bulk of the poor and how did the LDS efforts compare? How well has the 1936 Welfare Program, which emerged in the Mountain West during the Great Depression, met the needs of a drastically changed economy and society since then? How well has the welfare program adapted to internationalization as membership has skyrocketed in developing nations since the 1960s? When members develop personal mental or emotional problems, can the untrained lay clergy of the Church of Jesus Christ of Latter-day Saints adequately perform that function? What social services can and should the church maintain?

Throughout its history, the LDS Church Welfare Program has been shaped by response to such pressing practical questions. Leaders have sought answers in the doctrine, and new doctrine has emerged out of the experience. This interaction between doctrinal principle and practical economic issues is the theme of LDS welfare history. The path ahead has never been clear in prospect; but in retrospect, the pursuit has been persistent and consistent.

Organizational Structure

The history of LDS welfare decisions requires some familiarity with its completely lay but emphatically hierarchical structure, duplicated identically in congregations all over the world. Although this structure also evolved over time, its main priesthood organization remained essentially unchanged between the 1840s and the 1970s. The central male hierarchy is collectively called General Authorities. A president, also accepted as a prophet, is assisted by two counselors selected from the Quorum of the Twelve Apostles; together they comprise the First Presidency. The Quorum of the Twelve has a president (its senior apostle) who serves without counselors. The succeeding president of the church has always been the senior apostle. Three men, also General Authorities but not apostles, form the Presiding Bishopric, responsible for the temporal and business affairs of the church under the supervision of the First Presidency and the Twelve. The Presiding Bishopric, however, is the fourth, not the third, echelon of leadership.

The third level of the hierarchy is Quorums of the Seventy, administrators rather than policy-makers. Until 1941, Seven Presidents of the Seventy, largely responsible for proselyting, represented the Seventies. In 1941, Assistants to the Twelve were called to aid those administrators. In 1976, the assistants were redesignated members of the First Quorum of the Seventy, and many additional men were called to their ranks. In 1989, a Second Quorum of the Seventy was created.

Apostles serve for life. The Presiding Bishopric and First Quorum of the Seventy serve until released or placed on emeritus status, usually at age seventy, or earlier if they have health problems. The Second Quorum of the Seventy serve five-year terms.

The First Presidency, Twelve, and Presiding Bishopric are headquartered in Salt Lake City, Utah. The Seventy are administrators rather than policy-makers. The worldwide membership of the church experienced explosive growth after 1960. To accommodate that growth, those parts of the world with substantial membership were divided into areas in 1975; in 1977, members of the Quorums of the Seventy were designated as area supervisors and, in 1984, they became resident in the areas they supervise, usually on three-year rotating assignments. There were eighteen such areas and area presidencies in 1991. Those not under such assignment or assigned to areas within commuting distance of Salt Lake City serve simultaneously as managing directors of various church programs. Other church programs are directed by church civil servants who constitute a growing body, most of them at high-rise church headquarters at 50

East South Temple in Salt Lake City, but others in area offices throughout the world.

These bodies constitute the priesthood line of authority at the general church level. All General Authorities and the presidents of the church's 256 missions worldwide (1991), each of whom serves as a volunteer for a three-year term, receive a living allowance; no other general or local officers do. Forty-four thousand (1991) full-time missionaries (young single men and women, mature couples, or single women of retirement age) are supported during their eighteen-to-twenty-four months of service by their own savings, or by their families, friends, and neighbors.

Also on the general level are auxiliary organizations, all founded between 1867 and 1880: a Relief Society for the adult women of the church (founded in 1842), a young women's and young men's program for youth twelve to approximately eighteen, a Primary for children three through eleven, and a Sunday School (ages twelve through adult). Each has a three-person presidency and a general board. The presidents for the young men's and Sunday School programs are drawn from the Seventy. General officers for the others are women, called by the First Presidency, who live within commuting distance of Salt Lake City. General board members are unpaid volunteers who accept the assignment as a "calling."

The three-man priesthood presidency structure is duplicated for, in descending order, areas, regions, and stakes (a simile from Isaiah visualizing outlying stakes supporting the tent of Zion; Isaiah 54:2), and wards (individual congregations). Auxiliary structure exists only in stakes and wards. Each ward, consisting of approximately three hundred to a thousand members, is headed by a three-man bishopric.

The lay priesthood of the LDS Church is divided between an Aaronic Priesthood, comprising age groupings with different responsibilities designated deacon, teacher, and priest for young men ages twelve to eighteen, and the Melchizedek Priesthood, consisting of adult men grouped as elders, seventies, and high priests. Each of these groupings in a ward or (for high priests) stake is known as a "quorum." Pairs of priesthood representatives called "home teachers" visit every home each month, both to teach and encourage and to report personal or family problems requiring church assistance back to quorum leaders. Two "visiting teachers" from the Relief Society fill a parallel function for the women of the church.

LDS scriptures, often called "standard works," consist of the King James Version of the Bible, the Book of Mormon (writings of ancient American prophets, translated by Joseph Smith), the Doctrine and Covenants (abbreviated textually as D&C, first called the Book of Commandments, revelations received by Joseph Smith and others), and the Pearl of

Great Price (writings of Abraham, Moses, and Joseph Smith, revealed by Joseph Smith).

A Synopsis

Chapter 1 identifies factors in Joseph Smith's family background, early religious experiences, and social and economic environment that prepared him for the economic component of his prophetic mission. It then illustrates the application of those foundational Mormon economic doctrines amid the chaotic events of the church's first decade, absorbing a continuous flow of impecunious converts while it moved from New York to Ohio and Missouri. Stakes emerged during this period.

Chapter 2 describes a period of relative stability and prosperity in Illinois and Iowa, characterized by land speculation and enormous in-migration from British converts, 1839–43. Wards headed by lay bishops responsible for the temporal and spiritual well-being of their members emerged during the Nauvoo period; so did the Relief Society and temple worship with a series of covenants that included consecration as a mark of devoutness.[7] The Nauvoo interlude ended with the assassination of Joseph Smith and his brother (1844), the expulsion of the Saints from Nauvoo (1846), and their trek to the territory that would become Utah (1847) (Chapter 3). Unity and cooperative action became hallmarks of the church during the physical and psychic initiation of crossing the plains, a march that never stopped during the nineteenth century, though mechanized by the completion of the transcontinental railroad in 1869.

Chapter 4 describes the collective action essential to creation of an irrigation, transportation, communication, and "home industry" infrastructure in the harsh and arid West. That collective style, plus the "repugnant" institution of plural marriage, collided sharply with the individualistic and *laissez-faire* philosophy developing in the rest of the nation. This chapter describes how the ward structure under the bishops served joint ecclesiastical and socioeconomic functions while the reestablished women's Relief Society undertook a variety of social services. Experimentation with a variety of mostly short-lived cooperative and joint-property "united orders" constitutes the last efforts to date to recreate a communal "Zion." Statehood in 1896 and accommodation to the larger national economy at the turn of the century followed.

Chapter 5 discusses the national transition into commercialized agriculture and industry during the early twentieth century. The emergence of a cash economy brought a new form of economic dependence and made welfare issues more pressing in urban than in rural areas. Between

1900 and 1915, bishops stressed self-reliance while using cash donations to relieve acute poverty or long-term illness. The church's espousal of the progressive movement for civic betterment found its most distinctive institutional manifestation in the Church Social Service Department, which offered professionalized social work under the joint sponsorship of the Relief Society and Presiding Bishopric. World War I added patriotism to community betterment. Then the postwar depression descended upon western mining and agriculture, not to lift until World War II.

The church, like the nation, was overwhelmed by the sheer numbers of unemployed created by the disastrous Great Depression of the 1930s (Chapter 6). Anticipating an early recovery, government response lagged, but the church actively cooperated with city, county, and federal relief agencies to meet short-term needs and provide employment, primarily for city dwellers. Simultaneously, six stakes in the Salt Lake Valley innovated decentralized anti-poverty activities which became the basis for the 1936 churchwide welfare program. The evolution of these fragmented efforts occurred against a backdrop of intensifying governmental activity, primarily of a direct relief nature.

As implemented in 1936, the Church Welfare Program emphasized the traditional values of work, sacrifice, and cooperation, motivated in part by fears of demoralization if a government "dole" became pervasive (Chapter 7). Ironically, the federal government abandoned direct relief for work relief, but the "dole" image was already firmly implanted in the consciousness of many LDS leaders, who adopted agricultural production, food and clothing distribution, job finding, and cash contributions for its churchwide program—all elements developed in the Salt Lake stakes. Between then and World War II, further refinements were added: implementation in rural areas, sheltered employment in second-hand stores (Deseret Industries), a renewed emphasis on home food storage, and the construction of major processing and storage facilities. This program, continued through the prosperous war years, poised the church to ship impressive quantities of food and clothing to Europe at the war's end.

In subsequent years in the United States and Western Europe, an increasingly complex safety net of social security and welfare legislation guaranteed many basic needs for families and individuals. As Chapter 8 records, the church relinquished some activities which were in direct competition with government counterparts but found the Welfare Program too important in teaching discipline and spiritual values to abandon, even after physical needs had been met. Urban employment, as contrasted with the earlier agricultural self-reliance, became the mainstay and major economic concern of welfare efforts. At the same time, Mormons suffered the personal and social ills of modern urban life and Church Welfare Services added LDS Social Services, a professional counseling arm, to its roster.

By 1980, the Church Welfare Program could be declared mature for members in the United States and Canada. The church's contemporary economic program is a bilateral pact. Members are to achieve self-reliance through six areas of personal and family preparedness: literacy and education, career development, financial and resource management, home production and storage, physical health, and social-emotional and spiritual strength. In turn, the church stands ready to help during large-scale disasters or when the individual and family resources fail with its "storehouse system," which likewise has six components: employment centers, production projects, bishops' storehouses, LDS Social Services, Deseret Industries, and fast-offering cash.

But despite the stability in principle, the 1970s and 1980s were times of rapid change in the welfare system as the church expanded and then contracted its numbers of welfare farms, health care institutions, and schools, experimented briefly with career guidance, and assumed more responsibility for special populations like the handicapped, the institutionalized, and the chronically ill. Chapter 8 chronicles those developments and summarizes the personal and socioeconomic characteristics of families receiving church welfare assistance in the United States during the 1980s.

The greatest contemporary challenge to the LDS Church in all areas of administration is the dramatic shift in proportions of international members between 1960 (16 percent) and 1990 (44 percent), most of them in impoverished third world countries. Chapter 9 analyzes the economic status and prospects of the nation and the welfare needs of LDS members in Asia, Latin America, the Caribbean, Africa, and Eastern Europe. It then describes the experimental welfare efforts currently under way, efforts that parallel experimentation in Utah between 1930 and 1936.

Varied conditions require decentralized response, but principles of historic importance in Mormon welfare still seem applicable. A short menu of services appears to be emerging for differential packaging according to condition and need. Employability preparation, placement services, self-employment support, and agricultural development seem to be most promising. The church cannot hope to change the economies of the nations in which its members reside, but it can help its members maximize their economic opportunities. Accompanying that internationalization of welfare has been an impressive first-time LDS Church involvement in humanitarian relief among nonmembers, not only in the United States but especially in third-world and Eastern European countries.

It is our view that programs and projects have come and gone over 160 years, but principles have remained constant. There is no more reason to

expect programmatic stability in the future and no less reason to expect
principle continuity. The history manifests a remarkable consistency of
principle and purpose: a Christian compassion in caring for the poor, a vision of a Zion society in which poverty would be eliminated, a sense of
stewardship in productivity and the management of resources, and a
spirit of consecration so that the achievements of a self-reliant individual
or family are available to the broader community.

Despite the consistency of principle, the programs and projects have
taken shape through trial and error. Little has worked as well as its spon-
sors initially hoped; but with perseverance and flexibility, success has
generally come. Leaders continually admonish Latter-day Saints to avoid
materialism, and Mormons have no special immunity to temptation; but
a remarkable proportion appear to take the struggle toward sainthood
seriously.[8]

One sign is their generosity in sharing their sometimes meager resources. With the vast membership expansion in poverty-stricken countries, there is some internal concern that the church is not moving fast
enough to alleviate want among its members. Yet its resources are limited, and proselyting has always been its first priority. The laws of economic scarcity dictate that every new or expanded activity means abandoning or curtailing some other function.

Chapter 10 summarizes this history and its lessons and speculates
about the future, both in direction and accomplishment. The past promises to the future constant new challenges, perpetual trial-and-error
experimentation, frequent failure and human shortcoming, but also continued visionary idealism, adherence to well-tried principle, uncommon
persistence and endurance—and more than a little triumph.

CHAPTER 1

Economic Welfare in Ohio and Missouri

1831–1839

JOSEPH SMITH, Mormonism's founding prophet, was accepted by his followers as God's mouthpiece on earth; but that fact burdened him with, rather than shielding him from, worldly affairs. The first practical economic issue which confronted the twenty-five-year-old leader was his decision to move the headquarters of the church and its approximately two hundred members from New York to Ohio in the spring of 1831. The challenge continued as he sent others on to Missouri, then resettled them after they were driven by mob violence from their first Missouri homes. That same scenario would be repeated with variations for the entire decade of the 1830s.

A Prophet's Preparation

Joseph Smith's personal preparation for succoring the poor was a family life of poverty and insecurity along the frontiers of New England and New York.[1] The examples available to him were the rudiments of social welfare as practiced in the United States at that time and a burst of communitarian experiments in surrounding regions, though there is no way of knowing how familiar Joseph Smith was with either.[2]

The young religious leader's more sure guides were ancient scripture and current revelation. But even these must have been confusing, instructing him and his followers to abandon human economic systems in favor of a revealed radical departure, while simultaneously charging them within the existing system to support the poor and guide resettling migrants of varied economic abilities. The challenge, with all its social and religious elements, was primarily economic; and whatever Smith undertook had to be accomplished within the realities of the existing economy and with the resources at hand. From that spring of 1831 until his death by assassination in June 1844, Joseph Smith was continuously beset by the interacting economic problems of "gathering" converts from their points of origin, helping them earn a living in those new surroundings, caring for the indigenous and incoming poor at the successive gathering sites, and seeking to establish an independent economic system to remove his followers from the perceived evils of the surrounding society.

Familiarity with Joseph Smith's economic background, exposure to his pre-1831 scriptural guidance, and exploration of the current economic conditions are essential to understanding the economic policies of Mormonism in Ohio and Missouri.

Smith Family Fortunes

Despite Joseph Smith's limited knowledge of the economic forces around him, all that was new to him in the New York-to-Ohio move was the number of people for whom he was responsible. His childhood had been spent, generally in penury, on a series of tenant farms in Vermont and New Hampshire. The Smith family had arrived in Palmyra, in western New York, in 1816 with a team, a wagon, a few provisions, and nine cents in cash.[3] Unable to afford land, even at two to three dollars per acre, they rented acreage and supplemented its produce by huckstering handpainted oil tablecloths and refreshments and by hiring out as day laborers for more prosperous farmers. By 1818, they were able to contract to buy a hundred acres of uncleared land, only to lose it in 1825 after clearing it of timber, nearly paying for it, and building both a cabin and then a substantial frame home upon it. Joseph Smith, Sr., was briefly incarcerated in debtor's prison in Canandaigua, New York, for a fourteen-dollar debt.[4]

Joseph, Jr., had labored for a treasure hunter, worked for surrounding farmers, then tried his hand at tenant farming after his marriage in 1827, while translating the Book of Mormon (1827–30).[5] That economic background certainly had its impact on his economic policies as a church leader.

Scriptural Admonition

A boy who knew, at fourteen, that the apostle James had admonished those who lacked wisdom to ask of God (James 1:5–6), leading to the vision which launched his prophetic career, would certainly have known that the New Testament saints temporarily sought to abolish poverty by having all things in common (Acts 2:44–45). He might also have been forewarned of coming problems by the account of Ananias and Sapphira, who held back part of their property, lied about their actions, and were struck down by God on the spot for their deceit (Acts 5:1–11).

Reinforcing these New Testament teachings were those of the Book of Mormon. One example of its economic tenets is a sermon on social justice delivered by an ancient king about 100 B.C., which must have weighed heavily on Joseph Smith's mind:

> And also, ye yourselves will succor those that stand in need of your succor; ye will administer of your substance unto him that standeth in need; and ye will not suffer that the beggar putteth up his petition to you in vain, and turn him out to perish.
>
> Perhaps thou shalt say: The man has brought upon himself his own misery; therefore I will stay my hand, and will not give him of my food, nor impart unto him of my substance that he may not suffer, for his punishments are just—
>
> But I say unto you, O man, whosoever doeth this the same hath great cause to repent; and except he repenteth of that which he hath done he perisheth forever, and hath no interest in the kingdom of God.
>
> For behold, are we not all beggars? Do we not all depend upon the same Being, even God, for all the substance which we have, for both food and raiment, and for gold, and for silver, and for all the riches we have of every kind? . . .
>
> And now if God who has created you, on whom you are dependent for your lives and for all that ye have and are, doth grant unto you whatsoever you ask that is right, in faith, believing that ye shall receive, O then, how ye ought to impart of the substance that ye have one to another. (Mosiah 4:16–19, 21)

After a visitation by the resurrected Christ, whom these ancient Americans accepted as their savior, the Book of Mormon describes them as achieving an ideal existence for over two centuries: they had "no contentions and disputations among them, and every man did deal justly one with another. And they had all things common among them; therefore there were not rich and poor, bond and free, but they were all made free, and partakers of the heavenly gift" (4 Nephi 1:2–3).

In addition to these two ideal religious communities of New Testament times, one in the Old World and another in the New, Joseph Smith in a December 1830 revelation described a third. Enoch, a patriarch five generations after Adam, established a city in which the people "were of one heart and one mind, and dwelt in righteousness; and there was no poor among them." So righteous was this city, Zion, that "God received it up into his own bosom" (Moses 7:18, 69).

A few years later in what he characterized as an "inspired revision" of the King James Bible, Smith attributed an equally successful communal society to Abraham's mentor Melchizedek (JST Genesis 14:25–40). These scriptural models established clearly for Mormonism's converts the ideal of forsaking the Babylon of secular economies and establishing a divinely guided Zion society of economic justice and equity.

Caring for the poor was firmly linked to spiritual leadership in a parable Joseph Smith received on 2 January 1831:

> And for your salvation I give unto you a commandment, for I have heard your prayers, and the poor have complained before me, and the rich have I made, and all flesh is mine, and I am no respecter of persons.
>
> For what man among you having twelve sons, and is no respecter of them, and they serve him obediently, and he saith to the one: Be thou clothed in robes and sit thou here; and to the other: Be thou clothed in rags and sit thou there—and looketh upon his sons and saith I am just?
>
> Behold, this I have given unto you as a parable, and it is even as I am. I say unto you be one, and if ye are not one ye are not mine (D&C 38:16, 26–27).

But these scriptural guides only instructed the young prophet that establishing a compassionate community should and could be done—not how to do it. Nevertheless, Smith was not left long without guidance. For him, revelation was a very practical process. Doctrine and philosophy often appeared to be more the by-products, than the purposes, of his communications with Deity. Rarely also was the answer delivered by heavenly messenger or written on his mind as on a blank slate, but he was instructed to search for an answer himself, then take it to the Lord for divine confirmation or refutation (D&C 9:8–9). So it was with economic principles. How to handle economic deprivation among his followers was a constant issue. The extant scriptural guides affixed the obligation but did not execute it. In the context of Mormon belief, modern economic revelation was a process of gradual unfolding.

The Economic Setting

This background of personal experience and the scriptural record was the intellectual baggage Joseph Smith carried with him from New York to Ohio and on to Missouri in the spring of 1831. And his economic tasks had to be accomplished within the existing national and regional economic environment.

The United States, then in its forty-second constitutional year, was changing rapidly from a subsistence economy of self-sufficient frontier dwellers to a cash-and-jobs economy of mercantile traders, commercialized agriculture, and the beginnings of manufacturing. America's rudimentary factories could not compete for European markets against transportation costs and European protectionism; they concentrated on domestic markets behind high tariff walls of their own. The United States had a strong comparative advantage in agriculture and its exports were swelling, but this condition increased its dependence on foreign markets. During this transition, small farmers and independent tradesmen along the frontier suffered from a chronic cash shortage. They could no longer rely totally on barter to acquire such manufactured essentials as guns, hand tools, and wagon parts. Yet they raised few products attractive to urban markets where the necessary cash could be earned and had limited means for transporting the few products that were marketable. This dilemma had caused the Whiskey Rebellion which George Washington had faced a generation earlier as he tried to control frontier farmers who turned corn and wheat into liquor, which they could carry to market on their backs.

However, the 1820s had seen the extension of national roads into the interior and the development of a canal system. Most of the New York Saints moved to Ohio on the Erie Canal. Settlers in the Ohio Valley and others west of the Appalachians and Alleghenies could now get their produce directly to Eastern and European markets without the long flatboat trip to New Orleans. But transportation was still costly in time and effort.

By 1830, the American frontier had pushed beyond the Ohio and, at some points, even beyond the Mississippi to the Missouri River. Though a rural people throughout the 1830s, the Mormons never crossed an actual frontier until their exodus to the Mountain West in 1847. Neither New York nor Ohio had lands available for the taking. Missouri was actually at the frontier of settlement; but earlier settlers were already there, a fact which ultimately destroyed the Mormon dream of an early Zion in America. Homesteading was not a legal activity until the Homestead Act of 1862. Initially, each colony or state distributed land under its own laws, usually by selling large tracts to land speculators or by giving grants to political favorites who sought to profit from resale rather than settlement. The U.S. Congress looked to the public domain primarily as a source of revenue. Eastern interests also wanted to slow the access to western lands to preserve their labor force.

Thus, the Ordinance of 1785 restricted land sales to surveyed areas and required a minimum cash sale of 640 acres at one dollar per acre, raised to two dollars in 1796. By 1820, this price had been gradually reduced to a minimum of 40 acres at $1.25 with up to four years for payment. The settlement restraint was constantly thwarted, however, by the adventurous who bypassed the less attractive surveyed land and illegally squatted on more attractive land beyond. Congress sympathetically sanctioned such preemptions in 1841 by opening the land to purchase after the fact of settlement.[6]

In Missouri, there would be both new and repurchasable land, but Ohio was already closed to new purchases. Northeastern Ohio, formerly Connecticut's Western Reserve, had been opened to sale and settlement about 1800, becoming part of Ohio, the sixteenth state, in 1803. By 1830, Ohio was the fourth most populous state in the union with over one million inhabitants and no unclaimed lands. Kirtland, located ten miles from Fairport Harbor on Lake Erie, was a town of over a thousand people, serving a substantial farming region with its stores, mills, and factories. Land and other property could only be purchased at settled rates or shared with the current owners. Missouri lands would also have to be purchased, some from the government and some from current owners and speculators, but at prices consistent with new settlements.

Nevertheless, 1831 was a favorable time for resettlement in both Ohio and Missouri. Agricultural exports made the U.S. economy subject to fluctuations in European demand. Open unemployment was not yet a problem for residents of the hinterlands, but fluctuations in prices and credit were. Such upheavals had caused depressions in 1808–09 and 1819–21, but the years between 1821 and 1837 were a general time of prosperity. Home manufacture was giving way to factory production with rapid expansion in the small-manufacturing sector—iron, tools, leather, shoes, and textiles. Construction boomed with canals, steamboats, turnpikes, housing, and the beginning of railroads. The population was growing from both immigration and natural increase. A money economy was rapidly emerging; but since the money supply was not increasing as rapidly as production, prices were tending downward.

But this prosperity had within it the seeds of its own destruction. Real economic growth began to give way to speculative ventures as prosperity became accepted and presumed. Small farmers and large landholders all speculated on increases in land values, usually on credit. Many of the new manufacturing firms were undercapitalized. Many canals, constructed in the expectations of heavy traffic, failed when tolls did not generate the required income. And all of this speculation was financed by an unregulated banking system.

In 1836, when Mormons were actively colonizing both Kirtland and Missouri, the balance of trade turned sharply against the United States as exports fell. In 1837 gold flowed to Britain as English merchants tightened their credit to southern planters. Bank reserves fell and with them, inadequately liquid banks. One-third of New York City's labor force was unemployed, and its almshouse was full to overflowing. More significant to the Latter-day Saints, as land prices plunged, rural banks based on them collapsed. The economy seemed to recover in 1838 and early 1839, but a new crisis developed from the same causes in late 1839, settling into a major depression and unemployment which continued until 1843. Prosperity then prevailed until 1857.[7] It was into this economic environment that Joseph Smith led his followers in 1831 and beyond.

Economic Experimentation and Collapse in Ohio

By the close of 1830, the fledgling church claimed some two hundred members in New York and adjacent Pennsylvania.[8] Other churches were responding with increasing pressure to claims that the Book of Mormon was new scripture and that a restoration was necessary because all other churches were unauthorized corruptions. Both mutual support and centralized direction were difficult to provide with members scattered through many communities, and ardent proselyting was rapidly producing new converts, thus increasing the problem of supervision. In September 1830, these practical problems were resolved by the revelatory enunciation of the "gathering," a concept that dominated the Mormon movement for the remainder of the nineteenth century: "Ye are called to bring to pass the gathering of mine elect.... Wherefore the decree hath gone forth from the Father that they shall be gathered in unto one place upon the face of this land (D&C 29:7–8).[9]

Kirtland as Gathering Place

In October 1830, only six months after the organization of the Church, four missionaries to the Native Americans beyond the Missouri

River stopped off in northeastern Ohio so that one of them, Parley P. Pratt, could visit Sidney Rigdon, his former Disciples of Christ mentor (D&C 32:1–3).[10] The visit was fruitful; 130 members of Rigdon's congregation, including Rigdon himself and his family, were baptized. Ohio membership reached approximately three hundred by the following spring.[11] Kirtland, Ohio, had become the demographic center of the new church. In December 1830, another revelation designated Kirtland as a gathering place, though not yet the promised location where the Saints would recreate Enoch's City of Zion (D&C 37:3).

But that only intensified the economic issue. The New York Saints were, for the most part, subsistence farmers. By the same intense labor as the Smiths, they had acquired and cleared land sufficient to support their families. They had hardly any cash or liquid assets. Their only resources to finance the move were clothing, tools, and livestock and what little they could realize from selling their lands and houses in the cash-short communities they were leaving. Martin Harris, who mortgaged his farm for three thousand dollars to print the Book of Mormon, was considered relatively wealthy—an indicator of the general lack of liquidity. But the instructions to "gather" came with instructions to care for each other in the process:

> And now I give the church in these parts a commandment that certain men among them shall be appointed by the voice of the church.
>
> And they shall look to the poor and needy, and administer to their relief that they shall not suffer; and send them forth to the place which I have commanded them;
>
> And this shall be their work, to govern the affairs of the property of this church.
>
> And they that have farms that cannot be sold, let them be left or rented as seemeth them good. (D&C 38:34–37)

Abandonment would be no loss in the long run:

> And if ye seek the riches which it is the will of the Father to give unto you, ye shall be the richest of all people, for ye shall have the riches of eternity; and it must be that the riches of the earth are mine to give. (D&C 38:39)

The pressing economic challenge was to relocate these approximately two hundred New York members, most of them farmers, integrate them with Kirtland's members, and enable them to support their families, contribute enough of a surplus to sustain the missionaries and church leaders, welcome an influx of converts, and build meetinghouses, including, as it turned out, an ambitious temple. Yet simultaneously, there was little incentive for long-term investment, because revelation warned from the beginning that Kirtland was a temporary resting place (D&C 38:13, 42:62, 51:16, 64:21).

The Law of Consecration and Stewardship

The New York migration to Ohio lasted from January through June 1831. Settlement would have forced the makings of an economic policy, but an even more pressing decision confronted Joseph Smith as he preceded the rest of the New York members to Kirtland early in February. Among Parley P. Pratt's Kirtland converts were eight families—some fifty members—who had earlier organized themselves as a communal order patterned after the New Testament on land belonging to Isaac Morley.[12] Strife had already marred their efforts to share personal effects and produce. Joseph Smith needed a home; so did Sidney Rigdon, who had lost his parish house as a result of his conversion. The incoming Saints would also need homes and means of livelihood. Should Smith encourage them to unite their possessions in common, be individually self-sufficient, or adopt some third option? That issue spoke not only to the costs of resettlement or the care of the poor but also to the basic nature of the economy in which "Saints" should participate.

The answer came on 9 February 1831 in a revelation designated as the "law of the church":

> If thou lovest me, thou shalt serve me and keep all of my commandments; and behold, thou shalt consecrate all of thy properties, that which thou hast unto me, with a covenant and a deed which cannot be broken; and they shall be laid before the bishop of my church, . . .
>
> [Who] after he has received the properties of my church, that it cannot be taken from my church, he shall appoint every man a steward over his own property, or that which he has received, inasmuch as shall be sufficient for himself and family:
>
> And the residue shall be kept to administer to him who has not, that every man may receive according as he stands in need:
>
> And the residue shall be kept in my storehouse to administer to the poor and needy, as appointed by the elders of the church and the bishop; and for the purpose of purchasing lands, and the building up of the New Jerusalem, which is hereafter to be revealed; that my covenant people may be gathered in one, in the day that I shall come to my temple. . . .
>
> Let all of your garments be plain, and their beauty the beauty of the work of thine own hands. . . . Thou shalt not be idle; for he that is idle shall not eat the bread, nor wear the garments of the laborer. . . .
>
> Thou shalt not take thy brother's garment; thou shalt pay for

that thou shall receive of thy brother. And if thou obtainest more than that which would be for thy support, thou shalt give it unto my storehouse, that all things may be done according to that which I have spoken. . . .

The priests and teachers, shall have their stewardship given them even as the members; and the elders are to assist the bishop in all things, and he is to see that their families are supported out of the property which is consecrated to the Lord, either a steward-ship, or otherwise, as may be thought best by the elders and bishop.

There shall be as many appointed as must needs be necessary to assist the bishop in obtaining places for the brethren from New York, that they may be together as much as can be, and as they are directed by the Holy Spirit; and every family shall have a place, that they may live by themselves. (The Book of Commandments, chap. 44:26–29, 33–34, 41–42, 54, 57)

As initially conceived, therefore, it was expected that each family, through the father, would consecrate all that they had—land, tools, livestock, or liquid capital—each receiving as a "stewardship" only the productive resources needed to sustain themselves.[13] From this re-source base, the thrifty and hardworking household would generate further surpluses which would also be consecrated. Such surpluses would support widows and orphans, the incoming poor, newly mar-ried couples (if their parents could not provide the needed resources, D&C 83:1–6), temporary support or a new start for those who failed in their stewardships, and the cash with which to purchase church lands, construct buildings, provide education, publish, support missionaries, and maintain full-time church leaders. All consumers, whether poor or rich, were to be laborers. The plan was intriguing but workable only if the resources, when shared, were adequate to support the total burden, if the owners were willing to share, and if the stewards were diligent enough to produce a surplus.

Of the original Ohio members, only Isaac Morley and Leman Copley are historically identified as consecrating land; the situation is not clear, but perhaps they were the only property owners with lands substantially beyond their immediate needs. Copley agreed to make part of his thousand-acre farm available for the May 1831 arrival of twenty-three adults and thirty-eight children from Colesville, New York.[14] However, he reneged after two months, used the courts to reclaim his property, and forced the Colesville group in June to move on to Missouri, which, by then, had been designated as the location of the future Zion (D&C 54:1–10). Had that thousand acres been distributed in "stewardships," it should have made a significant difference in the viability of the LDS community. Instead, the church apparently purchased part of the Copley farm with borrowed funds and maintained it as a "church farm" upon which Joseph Smith's parents, among others, lived.[15]

The less-landed Morley was more saintly, perhaps predictably since the 1830 communal "family" had largely resided on his land. Upon emigrating to Missouri in October 1831, he sold fifty acres to a nonmember and left eighty acres in church hands. This land became the major reception area for new arrivals from New York and the staging ground for Missouri-bound immigrants during the early Kirtland period (1831–33).[16] That eighty acres was also apparently the only substantial plot of land ever consecrated under the law of consecration and stewardship. The remaining land acquired in Kirtland was purchased, either by the church or by individuals. Even the substantial farm of the Johnson family at Hiram, Ohio, with whom Joseph Smith and his family spent the winter of 1831–32 while he revised the King James version of the Bible and received numerous revelations, was never consecrated. Nor were the lands of other Ohio converts, despite the efforts of Edward Partridge, the church's first Presiding Bishop, to persuade the Saints.[17]

Settling Immigrants

The problems of land shortage had been presaged as early as March 1831, the month following the original consecration and stewardship revelation, when the Kirtland members were told, through Joseph Smith:

> And inasmuch as ye have lands, ye shall impart to the eastern brethren; And inasmuch as ye have not lands, let them buy for the present time in those regions round about, as seemeth them good, for it must needs be necessary that they have places to live for the present time. It must needs be necessary that ye save all the money that ye can, and that ye obtain all that ye can in righteousness, that in time ye may be enabled to purchase lands for an inheritance.... (Book of Commandments, chap. 51:1–4; compare D&C 48:2–3).

Though the revelatory document simultaneously warned that "it is not given that one man should have that which is above another, wherefore the whole world lieth in sin" (D&C 49:20), apparently equality was a goal to be pursued with patience.

In April 1832, Frederick G. Williams, a counselor to Joseph Smith, purchased 144 acres of land for two thousand dollars and turned it over to the church; in April 1833 the church purchased an additional 103 acres for five thousand dollars.[18] None of this land was assigned as individual stewardships, but those who lived on it paid rent if they could. A few immigrants who were better off purchased land privately from nonmembers.

The church now owned two farms in Kirtland (three by 1833), a printing and publishing operation, a store, a tannery, a sawmill, and an ashery. Consequently, church leaders established an administrative body of their number called the United Firm or United Order in April 1832 with the responsibility of overseeing properties in both Ohio and Missouri. However, with an average of a little over five acres compared to the fifty acres farmed by the typical non-Mormon in the area, the amount of land could not produce more than subsistence, and none of the industries produced a surplus to sell outside the community for imported necessities.[19]

Caring for the Poor

As a result, poverty was persistent among the potentially self-reliant as well as among the inevitable widows, orphans, and aged that any community accumulates. With all of the attention required by resettlement and the innovative economic system, additional revelations repeatedly reminded the new church of its special responsibilities to the poor. In June 1831, a revelation admonished the relatively well-off to "give of your substance to the poor" and also rebuked the poor "whose eyes are filled with greediness, and who will not labor with your own hands" (D&C 56:16–17). Six months later in December 1831, another revelation appointed Newel K. Whitney, a Kirtland merchant, as bishop to be "keeper of the storehouse" and receive funds for the poor and needy (D&C 72:8, 10, 12). In March 1832 a third revelation declared that a "storehouse for the poor of my people" was essential, for "if ye are not equal in earthly things ye cannot be equal in obtaining heavenly things" (D&C 78:3–7). In April 1832, at the inauguration of the United Firm, a fourth revelation identified its primary purpose as to "manage the affairs of the poor" (D&C 82:11–12). Four days later, a fifth revelation explained that widows, fatherless children, and orphans "have claim . . . upon the Lord's storehouse" which was to be maintained by "consecrations" (D&C 83:1, 6). In September 1832, a sixth revelation counseled Whitney to seek out the poor and "administer to their wants by humbling the rich and proud" (D&C 84:112).

The following summer, in June 1833, the First Presidency reminded Whitney in Kirtland and Edward Partridge, then bishop in Missouri, that "when the Bishops are appointed according to our recommendation, it will devolve upon them to see to the poor, according to the laws of the Church."[20] Even as the formal stewardship system was breaking up the following year, a seventh revelation reiterated the church's continuing responsibility for the poor in the strongest terms. The earth contained an abundance, and "if any man shall take of the abundance which I have made, and impart not his portion, according to the law of my gospel, unto the poor and needy, he shall, with the wicked, lift up his eyes in hell, being in torment" (D&C 104:18).

Spreading the news of the restoration—proselyting—was first priority but caring for the poor among those who gathered in response to the message was a close second.

Ominous Developments in Ohio

Despite the Kirtland community's limited resources, it survived because its membership remained small. Usually they came to Kirtland only to continue on to Missouri. When the Missouri Saints were expelled from their homes in 1833, Kirtland's conditions worsened sharply. Proselyting continued, and converts gathered; but there was no longer anywhere for them to go.

In 1832, Kirtland township contained an estimated 1,200 non-Mormons and 100 members. While the non-Mormon population remained stable, the Mormon population rose to 1,100 members by 1835 and 2,000 in 1838.[21] From mid-1833 to the spring of 1836, Kirtland's Mormons benefited from the general national prosperity and the construction of the Kirtland Temple, the primary source of employment. Constructing housing for the newcomers was a secondary source of economic activity.

In 1836, the church obtained an additional 240 acres of land in the township but did not distribute it for farmland. Rather, it sold half-acre lots ranging from $55 to $200 to members who could afford them. By 1837, Kirtland had 300 homes, three churches, and one tavern. Latter-day Saints had added several new enterprises: a brickyard, a forge, a carriage shop, a pottery, and such small individual businesses as dressmaking, furniture making, shoe repair, and so forth. Non-Mormons owned mercantile firms, a sawmill, a gristmill, a carding mill, and a clothing and shoe factory.[22] All of this economic development rested upon what the surrounding farmers could produce, sell, and buy, plus the purchasing power of incoming converts and the contributions of members outside of the area.

Kirtland was a heavily burdened community. Its Mormon residents had to support missionaries and church leaders, build the temple, and assist the dislocated membership in Missouri. In addition to their own poor, they had to care for those sent from other branches. In December 1836, weary church leaders assigned each congregation the responsibility

of caring for its own poor and counseled members not to gather to Kirtland unless they could send money ahead to purchase land and prepare to
establish homes.[23] Kirtland was clearly a concerned Christian community,
but it had never become, as was originally contemplated, an experimental
communitarian utopia.

Rethinking the Law of Consecration

Between 1833 and 1835, a rethinking of the law of consecration
and stewardship must have occurred. The Book of Commandments,
containing the revelation establishing the law of consecration and stewardship, would have been printed in Independence, Missouri, in 1833;
but the printing press was destroyed by mob violence. Although proof-
sheets were rescued and some copies were bound, the renamed, revised,
and reissued Doctrine and Covenants, published in Kirtland in 1835, contained some significant changes in this revelation, now Section 42:

> And behold, thou wilt remember the poor, and consecrate of
> thy properties for their support that which thou hast to impart
> unto them, with a covenant and deed which cannot be broken.
> And inasmuch as ye impart of your substance unto the poor, ye
> will do it unto me; and they shall be laid before the bishop of my
> church
> . . . and after he has secured these testimonies concerning the
> consecration of the properties of my church . . . every man shall be
> made accountable unto me, a steward over his own property, or
> that which he has received by consecration, as much as is sufficient
> for himself and family. (D&C 42:30–32)

In this revision, consecration was redefined as support for the poor
rather than as a general social structure. In a sermon, Joseph Smith
added this explanation: "Now for a man to consecrate his property . . . to the Lord is nothing more nor less than to feed the hungry,
clothe the naked, visit the widow and the fatherless, the sick and the
afflicted, and do all he can to administer to their relief in their afflic-
tions, and for him and his house to serve the Lord."[24]

No longer must members consecrate all of their property; the portion to be consecrated was apparently an individual judgment. The
church would not assign stewardships; rather, stewardship became
the owners' attitude toward the portion of their property they chose
not to consecrate. What remained unchanged was the directive to continue consecrating surpluses to the Lord's storehouse. The United

Firm was dissolved; various church leaders took over the management of its community enterprises as individual stewardships for the support of their families (D&C 104:19–66).

The revised revelation was now a more accurate description of what had actually happened in Kirtland. Contribution-supported construction and rising land values, rather than agricultural production, had become the temporary economic base. Employment was plentiful, as long as there was an adequate flow of temple contributions, land purchases, and home building to support it. Mormon farmers could be called on to contribute foodstuffs and their wives homespun clothing to temple workers; but the problem lay in obtaining goods they could not produce themselves when the economy was money-scarce. The effort to solve this problem—one shared with other Ohio communities—proved Kirtland's undoing.

The Kirtland Debacle

Times were prosperous in 1836. The Ohio Canal was being rapidly expanded, offering both construction jobs and an augmented route to markets. The state's population was growing at double the rate of the burgeoning nation, driving up land values. Throughout the state there was growing demand for loanable funds with which to purchase land and farming tools, establish factories, and found retail enterprises to serve the expanded population. The tax-assessed value of land in Kirtland had multiplied from seven dollars an acre in 1830 to thirty-four in 1837, even controlled for inflation.[25] Using land as the basis for a money supply was an obvious answer in a nation without a central bank or a national currency. The only problem for the Mormons was that they came to that solution too late.

As three historians of the Kirtland period point out, the number of banks established in Ohio increased from eleven in 1830 to thirty-one in 1835, some with capitalization as low as twenty thousand dollars, the amount the Kirtland Latter-day Saints invested in their Kirtland Safety Society bank two years later.[26] However, it was November 1836 before Orson Hyde was sent to the capital in Columbus, Ohio, to obtain a bank charter while Oliver Cowdery traveled to Philadelphia to purchase engraved plates to print bank notes. They both returned 1 January 1837. Cowdery had been successful but Hyde reported that the "hard money" wing of the Democratic Party had won control of the state legislature and was consistently turning down all requests for bank charters.

Defiantly, the members of the Kirtland Safety Society added "Anti-

Banking Company" to their printed notes and began issuing them. By mid-January, newspapers in surrounding communities warned against accepting notes from Kirtland and other unchartered banks. Therefore, the Kirtland banknotes could be circulated outside the community only at a large discount, and their redemption in specie ceased within two weeks.

This mistrust was typical of other rural banks throughout the country. Land mortgages were not liquid. Even if the landholders met their obligations, the payments came in on a long-term, infrequent, and seasonal basis, while the demands for specie payment of banknotes was continuous. And, of course, those commitments were not always met. The new nation was learning what the savings and loan debacle of the 1980s and the banking crisis of the early 1990s would demonstrate again: nonliquid land and home mortgages are not an adequate base for commercial banking. In May 1837, all Ohio banks suspended specie payments as a banking panic spread west from New York City. Joseph Smith disassociated himself from the anti-banking society in June and denounced the practices of those still operating the anti-bank, which continued to function until November.

In that "wildcat banking" era, half the banks organized in the United States between 1830 and 1845 failed. However, other Ohio banks, sharing much the same 1837 experience, rode out the panic and resumed specie payment in August 1838. But by then, the Kirtland Mormon community had disintegrated. Land values there had dropped to less than 60 percent of their 1837 peak in 1838 and 40 percent by 1839.[27] Thwarted financial expectations were a major factor in a spirit of apostasy which swept the community and even invaded its temple. The other banks experiencing similar difficulties did not have as their presidents prophets who could be blamed for failing to predict national economic crises. Joseph Smith fled for his life on the night of 12 January 1838, his family soon joining him in Missouri. The remaining faithful, who were able, followed by June. A few believers remained in Kirtland until calls to gather to Nauvoo in the mid-1840s finally drew the line between the committed and the uncommitted.[28]

The Missouri Experience

Jackson County

The settlement in Jackson County was simultaneous in time but different in circumstance from the initial migration to Kirtland. Though Missouri was less thickly settled than Ohio, the Mormons were still relative latecomers. Washington Irving had visited western Missouri in 1812, declaring it to be the site of the Garden of Eden.[29] Missouri had become a state in 1821, and Jackson County had sufficient population to be incorporated in 1825.

However, unlike Kirtland, the area had no Latter-day Saints to share houses or land with Mormon newcomers in the summer of 1831. The settlers had to purchase land as they arrived, either from earlier residents or from the federal land office. The availability of federal land kept resold land near the federal price of $1.25 per acre, about one-fifth the price of Kirtland land, but money was still scarce.[30]

A few of the LDS immigrants arrived with sufficient wealth to buy adequate land, but most were indigent. Had the LDS settlers been left to their own resources to buy land, the contrast between rich and poor would have been divisive. Also, individual purchases might have bid up land prices to the detriment of all newcomers. Within the group, those who were well off might have been tempted to buy larger tracts than they needed, then profit by subdividing and selling them to their fellows—a pattern not considered saintly in any subsequent LDS settlement. However, it was a moot question. The new arrivals did not have the financial resources to purchase the necessary lands. Church members elsewhere had to be persuaded to contribute funds to buy land for the New Jerusalem.

Hence, all Saints immigrating to Missouri were instructed to put all their money, tools, livestock, and other mobile capital in the hands of the church leaders, to be pooled with other contributions so that church agents could buy land. These real estate holdings were then divided among new arrivals according to their "wants and needs." As a result, the 1831 consecration and stewardship model was applied in the Jackson County settlement as it never was in Kirtland.

Bishop Edward Partridge was assigned to receive consecrations, make land purchases, and assign stewardships. According to historian Max Parkin, during the Jackson County period, Partridge purchased in his own name, but for the church, a total of 2,260 acres, largely on credit.[31] A few members purchased small acreages in their own names. Still, at the peak of Mormon ownership, the estimated ratio of Mormon to non-member land was one to thirty.[32] Since an estimated thousand Mormon families were expelled from Jackson County in November 1833, Partridge was forced to divide the available land into twenty-acre plots, a size that non-Mormons ridiculed as outrageously noneconomic.[33] Even so, there was not enough land to go around, and some LDS residents were relegated to working as day laborers and laundresses.

Caldwell County

Fear of political domination by the clannish northern and anti-slavery Mormons, along with a distaste for their religion, led the predominantly southern and frequently slave-holding Missourians to drive the Latter-day Saint settlers from Jackson County in November 1833. Some of the displaced Saints scattered in Ray and Van Buren counties but most crossed the Missouri River into Clay County. There they camped throughout the winter, surviving on provisions they had carried or could recover surreptitiously from their farms, risking discovery by pillaging mobs. At first, Clay County residents sympathetically received the refugees, hiring them as day laborers, domestics, and schoolteachers.

The Mormons made unsuccessful efforts to recover their Jackson County properties, then many rented and some purchased Clay County lands, and other LDS immigrants began to gather there. Again, the sudden influx frightened and antagonized the original settlers. By mid-1836, hostilities flared.[34] A compromise was reached when the Saints agreed to move into northwestern Missouri, a prairie area largely ignored by earlier settlers. A few Latter-day Saints had settled there as early as 1833, rather than remain with the main body in troubled Jackson County, and Jacob Haun had built a mill there in 1835.[35] Church authorities resolved to appeal for funds from members in other states to buy out the area's few non-Mormons and to request the state legislature to charter a separate county. Church agents collected $1,450 in Tennessee, and the first purchases were made in May 1836. The state legislature quickly formed Caldwell County with Far West as its seat.

In addition to the private purchases, the church purchased large tracts from the federal government at the standard $1.25 an acre, beginning in August 1836.[36] After a year, according to the church-owned *Times and Seasons,* over three hundred farms consisting of several thousand acres were under cultivation, and Far West was a city of between a hundred and a hundred and fifty dwellings, stores, and shops.[37] Kirtland's conflicts increased the rate of Mormons moving to Missouri, culminating in the major exodus that followed Joseph Smith in 1838. Historian Leland Gentry reports that by 1839, the Mormons had bought 250,000 acres from the federal government for $318,000 and established two thousand farms.[38] Newcomers were encouraged to purchase land whenever possible, but needy families received farms, usually about forty acres, from church-owned land.

The Jackson County practices of consecration and stewardship were not revived, nor did Joseph Smith raise the issue when he arrived in the spring of 1838. He did, however, establish three agricultural companies

called Big Field United Firms, each cooperatively farming twelve sections of land or 7,780 acres.[39] Cooperatives of mechanics, shopkeepers,
and laborers were planned but never implemented.[40]

The existing structure had no provision for meeting the costs of either
church administration or social infrastructure. It was this problem and
the need to assimilate the remaining faithful who would soon follow
from Kirtland that led Joseph Smith to seek a revelatory answer. The answer was the law of tithing, a biblical principle which had received some
attention in Kirtland. Now church members were instructed to donate
whatever they currently had in surplus, followed thereafter by 10 percent
of their annual increase (D&C 119). Church members have since generally
interpreted this initiation of tithing as replacing the higher law of consecration with a less exalted practice that recognizes human weakness yet
promises an eventual return to the former "eternal law." Another alternative interpretation is a clarification and specification of "surplus," the
family or enterprise able to produce more than 10 percent above subsistence being a rarity under the prevailing conditions.

Expulsion from Missouri, 1838–39

All available land in Caldwell County was soon taken up, and the
Mormon leaders began seeking more land for the Kirtland emigrés.
Apostle Lyman Wight had already settled with others on an attractive site
in Daviess County, which Joseph Smith would soon designate as Adam-
ondi-Ahman. DeWitt in Carroll County was another appealing site for
church expansion. However, unlike Caldwell County, Daviess and Carroll were already substantially settled by non-Mormons. When Mormons began purchasing land for settlements, the specter of Mormon political domination rose again. Almost immediately strife erupted. By the
winter of 1838–39, Joseph Smith and several other church leaders were
imprisoned, and the governor had ordered the Saints to leave the state or
be exterminated.

The last exercise of Mormon economic principles in Missouri was the
collective commitment to see every family out, regardless of means.
With Smith in jail, the responsibility for evacuating the Saints fell upon
Brigham Young as president of the Quorum of the Twelve. In two public meetings at Far West, the General Authorities appointed a committee
of seven (later eleven) to superintend the move. On the motion of Brigham Young, the men assembled passed a resolution:

We whose names are hereunder written, do for ourselves individually hereby covenant to stand by and assist one another, to the ut-

most of our abilities, in removing from this state in compliance
with the authority of the state; and we do hereby acknowledge
ourselves firmly bound to the extent of all of our available property, to be disposed of by a committee who shall be appointed for
the purpose of providing means for the removing from this state of
the poor and destitute who shall be considered worthy, till there
shall not be one left who desires to remove from the state: with this
proviso, that no individual shall be deprived of the right of the dis-
posal of his own property for the above purpose, or of having the
control of it, or as much of it as shall be necessary for the removing
of his own family, and to be entitled to the over-plus, after the
work is effected; and furthermore, said committee shall give receipts for all property and an account of the expenditures of the
same.[41]

Eighty signed the first day and three hundred the second. Church
agents returned to Jackson County to sell what Mormon properties
they could, raising about two thousand dollars. This sum, along with
forced sales in more recent settlements, allowed the supervisory committee to buy, trade for, and hire teams and wagons for the 170-mile
trek through Missouri's harsh winter to Illinois. One family reported
trading forty acres of Missouri land for a blind mare and a clock. The
more fortunate got fifty cents per acre. Many had not been on their
lands long enough to receive patents and thus could only abandon
promising farms.[42]

Throughout the entire winter of 1838–39 and into the spring, an
estimated eight thousand men, women, and children of all ages
slogged eastward through the snow, ice, and mud, without shelter
and inadequately clothed, giving birth and dying on the way.[43] When
the wagons arrived at the icy Mississippi, across from Quincy, Illinois, the teamsters resolutely returned to transport other refugees. It
was a rigorous test of dedication.

The Ohio/Missouri Message

The language of the April 1834 revelation was stern, directing
the breakup of the Ohio/Missouri United Firm:

> For it is expedient that I, the Lord, should make every man ac-
> countable, as a steward over earthly blessings, which I have made
> and prepared for my creatures.
> I, the Lord, stretched out the heavens, and built the earth, my
> very handiwork; and all things therein are mine.

And it is my purpose to provide for my saints, for all things are mine.

But it must needs be done in mine own way; and behold this is the way that I, the Lord, have decreed to provide for my saints, that the poor shall be exalted, in that the rich are made low.

For the earth is full, and there is enough and to spare; yea, I prepared all things, and have given unto the children of men to be agents unto themselves.

Therefore, if any man shall take of the abundance which I have made, and impart not his portion, according to the law of my gospel, unto the poor and the needy, he shall, with the wicked, lift up his eyes in hell, being in torment. (D&C 104:13–18)

But that condemnation could hardly have included those who followed Joseph Smith from Kirtland to Far West, those of the Jackson County refugees they joined there, or any of those who survived the Missouri "war" and endured the exodus to become refugees again in Illinois. These survivors had demonstrated their willingness to abandon property, risk their lives, and serve each other unstintingly.

That the law of consecration and stewardship would not again be applied in the same form did not signal its abrogation. The Latter-day Saint belief then and now is that it was an eternal principle, to be applied in varying forms as circumstances demanded. The earth was still the Lord's; human beings were his stewards (D&C 104:11–15). Covenants of consecration designate time, talent, effort, financial resources, and even life as gifts held ready to offer for the Lord's work when recognized authority calls.

As literal children of the same Heavenly Father and therefore as siblings in spirit, all human beings are under common obligation to share until equal in both earthly and heavenly things (D&C 49:20; 78:5–6). Those who have must always be concerned to lift up those who have not, but in ways that dignify, rather than abase, them. Labor is inherently worthy. Neither the idle rich nor the idle poor shall "eat the bread nor wear the garments of the laborer" (D&C 42:42). Self-reliance is expected of all and made possible for all.

Thus, the pattern for LDS welfare had been clearly established by the end of the Ohio/Missouri period: aid to the poor, self-reliance for all, the shining goal of Zion for motivation.

CHAPTER 2

Resettlement and Relief in Nauvoo

1839–1846

THE CITIZENS in and around Quincy, Illinois, welcomed some eight thousand refugee Saints as they made their way from Missouri during the first six months of 1839.[1] The population of Illinois had trebled during each decade between 1820 and 1840, reaching approximately one-half million in the latter year. Adams and Hancock counties, where the Mormons would settle, had been developed out of the Illinois Military Bounty Tract, an area Congress granted to the veterans of the War of 1812.[2] By 1839, the entire area was in private ownership, though some of the undeveloped lands were still available for near the standard federal price of $1.25 per acre. Developed farms were going from $4 to $40 an acre and lots in some towns had sold for as much as $1,000. Land speculation was a major enterprise here as well as elsewhere in the state. However, the effects of the Panic of 1837 still lingered and new settlers and potential land buyers were at a premium. The new settlers, though impoverished, were not unwelcome.

Locating Nauvoo

Land speculator Isaac Galland offered in February to sell the new arrivals some twenty thousand acres, fifty miles upriver on the Iowa side, for two dollars an acre on long-term credit. The offer was attractive, though, as the Saints later learned, Galland lacked clear title.[3] However, with Joseph Smith still imprisoned at Liberty, Missouri, and Brigham Young and Sidney Rigdon just arriving in mid-February, the group's leadership was in disarray and no decision could be made. Galland was even more eager to sell Commerce, a speculator's "paper town" on the Illinois side, and Joseph Smith's uncertain subordinate Mormon leaders hesitated over both hopeful proposals.

By the time Joseph Smith rejoined his destitute followers at the end of April, he had little choice—find a new gathering place or see his flock disperse. Crops would have to be planted almost immediately or there would be no food for the following winter. Therefore, he expeditiously completed both the Iowa and Commerce negotiations with Galland, then began to purchase the rest of the Commerce peninsula from various owners. The total purchase involved no down payment, long-term notes, and substantial annual payments. Realistic about the purchase but optimistic about the future, Joseph Smith wrote in his journal on 11 June 1839:

> The place was literally a wilderness. The land was mostly covered with trees and bushes, and much of it was so wet that it was with utmost difficulty a footman could get through, and totally impossible for teams. Commerce was so unhealthy, very few could live there; but believing it might become a healthful place by the blessing of heaven to the Saints, and no more eligible place presenting itself, I considered it wisdom to make an attempt to build up a city.[4]

Though Commerce, soon designated as Nauvoo, was the most advantageous site for a capital city, the Iowa properties offered more extensive farm lands. All of the Missouri emigrés were destitute except for a few teams, wagons, and tools. They had scraped by during the spring with temporary employment and contributions from the Illinois settlers. Now they could commence farming for survival on both sides of the river; but the leaders surely were haunted by the awareness of payments due on their numerous separate purchases, beginning at various dates throughout 1840.[5]

The Economic Base

Joseph Smith suggested no communal pattern for the new settlements. In fact he had written from Liberty Jail with implied self-criticism:

> We further suggest . . . that there be no organization of large bodies upon common stock principles, in property, or of large companies of firms, until the Lord shall signify it in a proper manner, as it opens such a dreadful field for the avaricious, the indolent, and the corrupt hearted to prey upon the innocent and virtuous and honest. We have reason to believe that many things were introduced among the Saints before God had signified the times; and notwith-

standing the principles and plans may have been good, yet as aspiring men . . . who had not the substance of godliness about them, perhaps undertook to handle edged tools. Children, you know are fond of tools, while they are not yet able to use them.[6]

When some of the Saints settling on the Iowa side attempted to inaugurate consecration practices, Joseph Smith crossed the river to stop them, reportedly saying, "It was the will of the Lord that we should desist from trying to keep it; and if we persisted in it would produce a perfect defeat of its object."[7]

Nevertheless, the basic principles which had undergirded the law of consecration and stewardship were still in force. Available lands were divided equitably among the Missouri refugees. In a public letter of 1 July 1839, Joseph Smith encouraged church members to gather to the new settlements.[8] Those with means were expected to pay for their new lands to provide cash for Galland's payments and other purposes, but those who could not were not denied. New converts with property were encouraged to sell out and forward the money to purchase new homes. Smith also tried to arrange for holders of church land notes to accept immigrating members' lands elsewhere in payment, the members receiving Nauvoo lots in compensation. Charity for the poor was an oft-sounded theme. In several conferences, church leaders asked those assembled to contribute toward church lands beyond their own needs so that the poor could have "inheritances." A surprising number did so.[9]

Although the law of tithing had been instituted in July 1838, there had been little opportunity to implement it in the turmoil of Missouri. Now, as work began on the Nauvoo Temple, a December 1841 epistle from the Quorum of the Twelve directed each member to give one-tenth of his current possessions and one-tenth of the annual increase thereafter. Those who had no funds or possessions could donate a day's labor in ten to the temple or other church projects. The ill, disabled, or elderly were exempt from the law.[10]

This directive coincided with a rapid shift in the occupations of church membership. Previous converts had been predominantly farmers from the eastern United States and Canada; but now a flood of eventually five thousand British converts began swelling the ranks. At the young church's darkest hour during the spring of 1839, Smith, imprisoned in Missouri, had dispatched most of the Twelve to England. There residents of factory towns plagued by economic depression flocked to the new American religion. The apostles also oversaw the migration, denying those with greater means permission to emigrate unless they assisted poorer emigrants.[11] With a factory-skilled population and the river's potential for transportation and power, when harnessed by millraces and dams, Nauvoo might have become an early industrial center.[12] At a general Sunday service in June 1842, Brigham Young, by then back from Great Britain, "preached upon the law of consecration and union of action in building up the city and providing labor and food for the poor."[13] On 15 August 1844 in a general epistle to the church, the Twelve encouraged those with capital to gather to Nauvoo and use their wealth "for the erection of every branch of industry and manufacture which is necessary for the employment and support of the poor, or those who depend wholly on their labor."[14] An 1844 letter of Brigham Young to church business representative Reuben Hedlock in England stressed the need for funds to build a dam for water power and establish textile mills.[15] But there were so few with capital and so many without that the overwhelming need to house the rapidly growing population absorbed all that was available and more. Nauvoo had its grist mills and sawmills, its cabinetmakers, shoemakers, seamstresses, milliners, and tailors, but only for local consumption.

Instead, as in the earlier settlements, the Nauvoo economy rested upon agriculture, the sale or rental of land, and upon the construction of homes, public buildings, and a temple. Some Missouri refugees had individual farms, while others worked several cooperatively held farms, one of which, organized in 1843 and known as the "Big Field," comprised almost four thousand acres.[16] John Taylor reported in 1845 that the Big Field had produced sixty thousand bushels of wheat and corn that season along with "an abundance of oats, barley, buck wheat, potatoes and other vegetables."[17] Those who were not farmers had gardens on their sizable city lots.

Joseph Smith's plat for the city of Zion, originally designed for Jackson County, projected a vision of an agricultural economy with urban dwellers enjoying the cultural amenities possible only in a city but working suburban farms daily.[18] This view contemplated numerous small population centers; but if they grew very large, as Nauvoo promised to do, speculation would almost certainly drive up the price of the encircling land. Without commercial agriculture or manufacture, Nauvoo could never support itself at more than a subsistence level and could never produce the surplus necessary to support major missionary efforts or other significant church demands. Certainly, it could raise the food to feed itself. It could and did provide employment. Joseph Smith, as chairman of public works on the city council, took a personal interest in seeing that every person had employment;

and one traveler through Nauvoo claimed there was no pauperism because the church made work for those without subsistence.[19] Furthermore, it could create much of the needed infrastructure of roads and public buildings through tithing labor. In addition to homes and the temple, construction on which began in the spring of 1841, building projects included the Nauvoo House, the Seventies' Hall, stores, and other public buildings. These in turn generated a lumber-producing project up the river in Wisconsin and brick kilns and quarries in and near the city. In Nauvoo's barter economy, workmen on public projects were paid in contributed produce with which they could feed their families; and sometimes they boarded with other church members, who contributed that service.

Inevitably, some people complained that resources being used to build the temple could be better given directly to the poor. Others protested that the temple should have total priority over other construction projects. Joseph Smith held a more balanced view: in addition to spiritual values, the construction provided employment for those in need; however, he complained that the city had too many merchants and not enough manufacturers, who could provide employment, goods for consumption, and items that could be marketed for cash in other communities.[20]

Still, the crucial economic problem was that the community lacked the exports necessary to exchange for items the community could not produce for itself. It was ultimately dependent upon the limited cash of new arrivals and contributions which could be attracted from members elsewhere, primarily for building the temple. And cash was a problem—not only to pay for imported goods but to make payments on the land notes held by Isaac Galland and others.

As examples of the need for cash or exchange, in early May 1844 the church-owned *Maid of Iowa* was sent to Rock River, Illinois, and returned two weeks later with four hundred bushels of corn and two hundred bushels of wheat, primarily to feed temple builders.[21] Behind this evidence of the church's willingness to meet the needs of its public workers lies the fact that the settlement was not even agriculturally self-sufficient at this late date. The temple and other public buildings under construction voraciously consumed not only labor but also materials, not all of which could be produced within the LDS community.

Since nearly all immigrants were poor, it was a general practice to give them city lots at no cost. Others received lots during the early 1840s under the provision that repayment need not commence until as late as 1850. Three categories of Saints were eligible for free lots: the poor, widows, and those who had rendered such services as transporting destitute refugees from Missouri. Those who purchased lots could usually get them cheaper from the church than from private speculators; and even when privately held lots were less expensive, church leaders encouraged members to buy from the church to enable it to meet its obligations. During the spring of 1842, the Quorum of the Twelve inaugurated a debt-forgiveness program to relieve those who had arrived destitute from Missouri, Great Britain, or elsewhere, and found it necessary to borrow from the church or fellow members to survive.[22]

Because town plots were generally about an acre in size, many Nauvoo residents provided the greater part of their basic food from extensive gardens and such domestic animals as chickens, pigs, and milk cows. They frequently earned these animals by day labor. However, as the gathering quickened, it became necessary to subdivide lots of church-owned land, giving or selling smaller plots and thus lessening the subsistence base for each family. The church itself purchased land with tithes, contributions, profits from such enterprises as the *Maid of Iowa,* and borrowed funds. Most land, of course, was purchasable with long-term notes. Church leaders also continued to encourage members who had not yet gathered to Nauvoo to consecrate their properties to the church in exchange for Nauvoo lots; by selling those external lands, they were able to liquidate some of the land debts.[23] But to put the matter briefly, most of the commitments were simply beyond the capacity of the church, its people, and its leaders to manage. What saved them was that holders of church notes usually were not in any position to foreclose.

Joseph Smith faced a particular problem in supporting his family. He held important civic and ecclesiastical positions with heavy time demands. As church land agent, he had some income but it was limited and sporadic. He operated a store, beginning in December 1841; but that project involved him in buying and selling on credit, and he could not simultaneously care for the poor as their prophet and press them for payment.[24] His home served as a hotel while the new hotel, the Nauvoo House, was being built (it was never finished), but hospitality apparently took priority over profit there as well.

The prophet's personal finances were only a microcosm of economic issues never satisfactorily solved during Nauvoo's brief history as the largest city in Illinois. From 1841 until his death in 1844, Joseph Smith urged the creation of a water power system using water diverted from the Mississippi to drive machinery for manufacturing.[25] Nauvoo was unquestionably magnificent and had been built in an amazingly short period of time; but it was haunted by the temporary.

Conceived not as a permanent location for the Latter-day Saints but as an interlude before the expected return to Missouri, it actually turned out to be a six-year respite before the assassination of Joseph Smith and his brother in 1844 and the departure of those who formed the Utah-based Church of Jesus Christ of Latter-day Saints toward the unsettled West in 1846.

The Ward, the Bishop, and the Poor

At Nauvoo's October general conference in 1839, about six months after most of the membership had arrived from Missouri, stakes were organized for Nauvoo and Iowa, with a stake presidency and high council for each. One bishop was appointed in the Iowa stake with three in Nauvoo, each with a specified geographical jurisdiction called a ward. This distribution may indicate a more settled and agricultural base for Iowa with a greater immigrant population and town residency for Nauvoo. These wards were a new development in church administration. The stakes in Ohio and Missouri had never been subdivided; each had a single bishop who served as the welfare and financial officer for all of the Mormons in the entire area. The two earlier bishops, Newel K. Whitney in Kirtland and Edward Partridge in Missouri, had positions that were more the equivalent of the Presiding Bishop, a position introduced in Utah.

In August 1842, Nauvoo Stake's three wards were subdivided into thirteen, ten in the city and three in the surrounding rural area, each with its own bishop.[26] These Nauvoo bishops were charged directly with the welfare of the poor, and their burdens were heavy. They were responsible for seeing that ward members had housing, fuel, food, land, and work. They also collected the tithing and other donations and helped organize the labor for public works. One harried bishop, George Miller, wrote of his responsibilities in 1841:

Early this spring the English emigrants (late converts of the Apostles and Elders in the Vineyard) began to come in, in apparent poverty and in considerable numbers. Besides those, they were crowding in from the states, all poor; as the rich did not generally respond to the proclamation of the prophet to come with their effects, and assist in building the temple and Nauvoo House. The poor had to be cared for, and labor created that they might at least earn part of their subsistence, there not being one in ten persons that could set themselves to work to earn those indispensable things for the comfort of their families.

My brethren of the committee of the Nauvoo House Association, and the committee of the temple, all bore a part in the employment of laborers, and the providing of food for them, but I had a burden aside from theirs that rested heavily upon me, growing out of my Bishoprick. The poor, the blind, the lame, the widows and the fatherless all looked to me for their daily wants; and, but for the fact of some private property I had on hand, they must have starved, for I could not possibly by soliciting gratuitous contributions to bury the dead obtain them, let alone feeding the living. I was here thrown into straits unlooked for; no tithing in store; the rich among us pretended to be too poor to barely feed themselves and nurse their speculations, which they were all more or less engaged in, and those that were really poor could not help themselves.

I was now in the midst of a sickly season, filled with anxiety for the suffering, with multiplied labors crowding upon me, and hundreds of mouths to feed. My days were filled with trial and care, and the nights were not spent with the giddy and mirthful, but with sleepless anxiety in waiting on the suffering of the poor and sick of the city. Perhaps, I am saying too much, but I praise God of Heaven that he gave me shoulders to bear and patience to endure the burdens placed upon me....

The remainder of the summer and fall was taken up in providing the means for feeding and paying the wages of the laborers engaged on the temple and Nauvoo House, which was done abundantly for the time being, mainly by the exertions of Lyman Wight and myself, for both houses. The workmen were kept all winter, as we necessarily had to feed them whether we discharged them from work or not, they having no means of buying the winter's food without our aid.[27]

George Miller and Vinson Knight had been called as bishops in a revelation 19 January 1841 to Joseph Smith which declared Miller was to "receive the consecrations of mine house, that he may administer blessings upon the heads of the poor of my people, saith the Lord" (D&C 124:20–21). That spring, he was sent to Kentucky to preach and "obtain means for the early spring operations." He returned with "a hundred head of cattle, some horses and other effects."[28] The January revelation also exhorted Bishop Knight to "lift up his voice long and loud, in the midst of the people, to plead the cause of the poor and the needy; and let him not fail, neither let his heart faint." True to these instructions, Knight placed a notice six weeks later in the 1 March 1842 issue of the church-owned *Times and Seasons:* "Proclamation: To saints coming to the conf[erence], Forget not your tithes and your offerings, for we have in this place the blind, the halt, the widow and the orphan." At a special conference held in Nauvoo 16 August 1841, Bishops Miller and Knight "presented . . . the situation of the poor . . . and a collection [was then] taken for their benefit."[29]

On 31 January 1984, Bishop Daniel Carn of Nauvoo Sixth Ward placed the following request in the *Nauvoo Neighbor:*

> I take this opportunity of notifying all those that feel an interest in getting wood for the poor of the 6th Ward, that on Monday, the 5th of February, I shall meet all those at the upper steam mill to conduct them to the Big Island, as I have permission of the Messrs. Law to get all the wood I want for the poor.
>
> Come on neighbors, with your axes and teams, for the ice is good, the weather is cold, and many of the poor are without wood; come on brethren and don't neglect the poor.[30]

Though the practice of fasting one day each month and contributing the cost of the meals for relief did not begin until the mid-1850s in Utah, there is a reference to a combination of fasting and poor relief as early as January 1843. When Missouri's legal effort to have Joseph Smith extradited was defeated in court, Brigham Young and the Quorum of Twelve invited Nauvoo residents to participate in a day of "fastings, humiliations and thanksgivings," adding, "Let us not forget the poor and destitute, to minister to their necessities."[31] Another more specific link between fasting and poor relief occurred on 15 May 1845 when Bishop Edward Hunter of the Fifth Ward reported: "All works were stopped. Meetings were held in the several wards and donations made to the bishops for the poor; enough was contributed to supply the wants of the poor until harvest."[32]

Although the structure of organized relief is not clear, obviously a bishop was inadequate to the task alone. The assignment included canvassing the ward for contributions, most of them in kind, organizing work parties to fish, harvest, and store provisions, repair shelters, and otherwise meet the needs of ward members. During 1844–46 Brigham Young urged men ordained to the Aaronic Priesthood to visit regularly the homes of members and urged the deacons—today twelve-to-fourteen-year-olds but then adult males—to help bishops care for the needy. In October 1844, the St. Louis Conference voted to divide the city into wards to help the priests and teachers easily perform their duties, "that the poor and sick may be attended to."[33] On 13 December 1844, at a meeting of Aaronic Priesthood members in Nauvoo, Bishop Newel K. Whitney addressed them "on the subject of furnishing employment for the poor."[34] From these examples, it seems apparent that the policy of using Aaronic Priesthood members to assist the bishops in caring for the poor was quite general, at least after 1844.

The Relief Society and Other Institutionalized and Private Relief Efforts

A completely new institution designed to help the needy, the Female Relief Society of Nauvoo, was organized 17 March 1842. During January and February of that year, Sarah M. Kimball and her seamstress, Margaret A. Cook, decided to make shirts for the temple workmen. They asked several neighbors to join them in forming a women's society for that purpose. Upon being consulted, Joseph Smith offered to assist them in organizing "under the priesthood after the order of the priesthood." At the organizational meeting, Joseph Smith's wife, Emma Hale Smith, was elected president, the name was chosen, and Joseph Smith counseled members of the new association to "provoke the brethren to good works in looking to the wants of the poor, searching after objects of charity and in administering to their wants—to assist by correcting the morals and strengthening the virtues of the community."[35] At a later meeting in April, Joseph Smith added, "This is the beginning of better days for the poor and needy, who shall be made to rejoice and pour forth blessings on your heads."[36]

The society met about three times a month from March through September 1842, during which time its membership grew to 1,189, just short of the 1,341 members it would ultimately attain in Nauvoo. It did not meet during the winter, partly because no indoor facility could house a group of this size, though its members individually continued their charitable efforts. During the first year, the society collected about five hundred dollars and disbursed approximately four hundred of it.

In the second year, because of its size, the Relief Society decided to hold its meetings by rotation in each of the city wards, with the same general officers serving all wards. At these meetings, the officers correlated needs and resources. To increase effectiveness, the leadership organized four-member committees in each ward to identify the poor and solicit donations. When a woman in Second Ward resigned from the committee because she believed it was infringing upon the bishop's stewardship, Joseph Smith sent a representative to explain that this was not so. However, the minutes do not reveal how the bishops and the Relief Society correlated their efforts.

The last recorded meetings of the Nauvoo Relief Society were held in March 1844, two months before Joseph Smith's death; and the society recommenced its activities in Utah, first as an ad hoc effort to relieve poverty among local Indian tribes in 1857, and then as a formal institution in each ward beginning in 1866.[37] Voluntary benevolence extended beyond the women during the Nauvoo period as well. In January 1843, Heber C. Kimball, then an apostle and later a counselor to Brigham Young, invited a large group of young men and women to begin regular meetings which he addressed. Joseph Smith addressed the fifth such meeting, challenging them to help a lame English immigrant build a house.[38] In March 1843 they formalized themselves as the Young Gentlemen and Ladies Relief Society of Nauvoo. They drew up a constitution, chose presiding officers, and appointed a five-member committee of vigilance "to search out the poor of our city, and make known to the society the wants of those whom they, in their judgement, shall consider most deserving of our assistance." There are no records for this society beyond the spring of 1843.

There was little if any distinction between church and state in Nauvoo since almost all of its ten thousand residents were Latter-day Saints. The same people served in both civil and ecclesiastical organizations; ultimately both took their direction from Joseph Smith and other church leaders. Consequently, it was natural for both the city and the church to aid the destitute. The city created a "poor fund," and several city councilmen, who were paid per meeting, contributed their pay to this fund. The city council met in a special session on 2 July 1844 to devise and implement ways of "supplying the wants of the destitute." They organized committees to systematically canvass the city and countryside for donations, provisions, or loans.[39] Available records do not report this program's success, but the attempt shows the city's involvement.

One 1844 traveler through Nauvoo claimed there were no class distinctions, as "there were no men of leisure among them, and all were on the same dead level socially."[40] This was undoubtedly an exaggeration, but Nauvoo may have genuinely given that impression compared to other socially and economically structured American cities of the time. Class differences based upon economics were probably quite small; Nauvoo was a new community, its people were all generally poor, and Mormonism definitely stressed both cooperation and generosity. As a result, Nauvoo had no poorhouse or almshouse where paupers were forced to live. This device, popular elsewhere in contemporary America, was instituted at least partially to discourage the poor from asking for help and to goad them to find work.[41]

In Nauvoo, in contrast, leaders taught and used the general principles of consecration and stewardship to organize economic life and help those in need, even though the Ohio and Missouri consecration practices were never introduced in Nauvoo. Private property remained private, but church leaders did not hesitate to ask that it be shared with the destitute; and members complied. Before departing from Nauvoo, most of the Mormons who followed Brigham Young participated in the endowment ceremony in the barely completed temple. These instructions and covenants committed them to obedience, sacrifice, premarital chastity, postmarital fidelity, and a willingness to consecrate time, talent, and substance, if called upon, to the spread of the gospel message, the practical building of God's kingdom on earth, and, ultimately, to the establishment of a Zion society.[42] The Nauvoo period institutionalized both individual self-reliance and a commitment to poor relief. Both were to be cornerstones of welfare activity in the Mountain West.

CHAPTER 3

The Economics of the Exodus
1846–1887

BOTH THE EXODUS from Nauvoo and the relocation in Utah of Saints from within the nation and abroad until near the end of the nineteenth century was a cooperative endeavor with dual demands: self-reliance and caring for the poor. The departure from Nauvoo was governed by essentially the same covenant under which the church had left Missouri: "... that we take all the saints with us, to the extent of our ability, that is our influence and property."[1] Brigham Young added his personal comment that all of those making the westward trek must "come upon the apostles doctrine: no man say ought that he has is his own but all things are the Lord's and we his stewards."[2] Hence all three themes of Mormon economics are illustrated repeatedly during the forty-year exercise of church-supported emigration to the new Zion.

The Nauvoo Exodus

Though most Nauvoo residents may have paid little attention to the warning, it had been generally known to the leadership, at least since 1842, that Nauvoo was a temporary home and that the Rocky Mountains were likely to be the ultimate destination. In fact, Joseph Smith had been making such references since 1831.[3] Next to completing the temple, the most intensive activity following the June 1844 deaths of Joseph and Hyrum Smith became searching for a destination and planning for departure. Throughout the winter of 1844–45, the Quorum of the Twelve studied the journals of fur trappers and the reports of government exploring and surveying parties, interviewing as many western travelers as possible.[4] By mid-1845, the Valley of the Great Salt Lake had been chosen as the destination and only the time of departure was uncertain.

The escalation of violence in the fall truncated plans for a preliminary exploration as first April, then February, of 1846 were imposed upon the Saints as departure dates. Therefore, the winter of 1845–46 was an intensive time of selling property, building wagons, and gathering supplies. Most were able to sell or trade their properties but received very little in return. As a typical example, the wife of Apostle Franklin D. Richards traded a two-story brick house, occupied only three months, for "two yoke of half broken cattle and an old wagon."[5] However, those who exploited the desperate Saints suffered when they, along with the handful of ill and otherwise incapacitated Mormons left behind, were attacked by mobs in the "rape of Nauvoo" in September of 1846.[6] The church sold some two thousand acres of undeveloped land and 260 town lots to land speculators at similar prices, some of whom also lost that land when the federal government foreclosed in pursuit of compensation for church debts.[7]

As a result of evacuations begun in February 1846, by September there were spread between the Mississippi and Missouri rivers without shelter "15,000 Saints, 3,000 wagons, 30,000 head of cattle, a great number of mules and horses, and immense flocks of sheep."[8] Almost all Saints willingly shared their meager provisions, but the abrupt changes of departure dates and the rock-bottom prices their property fetched meant that there was little to share. At Sugar Creek, Iowa, the first encampment, only nine miles from Nauvoo, historian B. H. Roberts records that over eight hundred families arrived during the first two weeks of February with no more than two weeks' supplies for themselves and their teams.[9] In September, that same camp received several hundred of the poorest and feeblest who had been expelled from Nauvoo only during the final stages of mob violence.[10] By the time the advance camp, including Brigham Young and other leaders, had traveled a hundred and fifty miles into Iowa, they had given away the year's supply of necessities they had accumulated for their own families.[11]

Clearly the winter of 1846–47 would spell an emergency. On assignment from the Twelve and also as individuals, men traveled through Missouri and Iowa, as far away as St. Louis, to find employment, to barter their labor for commodities, or to sell household possessions both to meet family needs and to sustain the encampments. Church representatives also canvassed whatever branches they could contact, including St. Louis's, seeking contributions to sustain the exiles.[12]

With the arrival of spring, church leaders stressed self-reliance. Realizing that the Rocky Mountains were out of reach for the 1846 season, they encouraged the Saints to plant generous acreages, not only for themselves but for the needy and for those who would follow them. Church leaders negotiated permission from government and Indian landowners to establish semi-permanent settlements at Garden Grove, Mt. Pisgah, and Winter Quarters in western Iowa and eastern Nebraska.[13] Based probably on the "big field" model of Far West and Nauvoo, church leaders supervised the fencing, plowing, and planting of several thousands of acres of fertile prairie. They assigned land according to a family's need and ability to produce. A man could have as much land as he wanted, but he had to farm it all.[14] Those who planted might move on before harvest, just as those who harvested might have arrived after the planting. Cooperative labor also produced shelter—enough housing in Winter Quarters alone for 3,200 families plus public buildings.[15] In these circumstances, it was a godsend when the u.s. Army recruited approximately five hundred Mormon men for the Mormon Battalion. Most men turned their funds over to church leaders in exchange for the promise that their families would be transported west; amounting to twenty-one thousand dollars for the clothing allowance and eventually over fifty thousand dollars in pay, these sums were crucial in the Saints' survival.[16]

The organizational structure for these semi-permanent settlements consisted of presidencies and high councils in major settlements, which were then subdivided into wards. At Winter Quarters (which actually consisted of some fifty-five settlements) thirteen wards were created in mid-1846 and then subdivided to form twenty-two by the end of that year, each under a bishop.[17] Perhaps because most of the General Authorities resided there, more plentiful records exist for that community, but practices would have been similar in Mt. Pisgah and Garden Grove, the other two long-term Iowa camps. Bishops surveyed their wards to see who needed provisions, housing, or other help, marshalled people for community building and welfare projects, built roads and established a postal service, recorded contributions, and distributed goods to the needy and to those who were spending their full time caring for the poor and sick. If a bishop needed extra supplies, he could ask another bishop for help or draw from a central storehouse. The bishops also obtained such services as medical care for the needy, paying for them in barter or tithing credit.

Bishops took care of some of the poor by assigning certain families to be responsible for them. For example, Apostle George A. Smith took some orphans into his care, receiving some goods from his bishop. During the fall of 1846, Orson Spencer left his motherless family of six in a one-room cabin while he served an English mission. The neighboring Thomas Bullock family had general responsibility for their care until they developed problems as well. Then Brigham Young assumed responsibility for the Spencer children.[18]

Brigham Young met periodically with the high council and bishops about relief. The high councilors were instructed "to call bishops to account from time to time," and weekly meetings and written reports were introduced to implement that supervision.[19] Brigham Young also instructed the high council to "see that those under [the bishop's] charge have work and that none suffer through want."

The Trek, 1847

The 143-person advance company of 1847 was well-organized and well-supplied and reached the Salt Lake Valley in July without undue difficulty. That all of the seventy thousand Saints who followed over the next twenty-two years before the completion of the transcontinental railroad did not travel so expeditiously was not for want of organization.[20] A Perpetual Emigrating Fund was launched in the fall of 1849 to bring the remaining poor from the Midwest, supported by gold contributed by Mormon Battalion members who had reached Utah late in 1847. By 1852, that task had been largely completed, twenty thousand Saints were building new homes in the West, and the Iowa way stations were closed.[21] After that point, church leaders turned their attention to the thirty thousand Latter-day Saints living in England. A majority of immigrants from that point were Europeans who arrived at the successive staging points by boat or rail.

Three kinds of "companies" made the typically nine-month trip from England to the Salt Lake Valley between 1852 and 1869: the PEF companies, too poor to make their own way and totally financed by donations to the fund; the Ten-Pound companies, whose costs above that level were subsidized; and cash emigrant companies who were organized and dispatched by Perpetual Emigrating Company agents but who paid their own way. Of the 2,312 who came under PEF auspices in 1853, for instance, 400 were in totally subsidized companies, 1,000 in Ten-Pound companies, and 995 in self-supporting companies.[22] By the time the transcontinental railroad reached Utah in 1869, 51,000 emigrants had been thus assisted, 38,000 from the British Isles and 13,000 from Scandinavia and the Continent.

This fund was conceptualized as perpetual because the costs of emigration were a loan which the recipients would repay from their earnings after settling in the Great Basin. However, subsistence pioneering rarely produced sufficient surplus to repay these sums. The best new arrivals could often do was to contribute their labor to public works. At the 1880 Golden Jubilee of the church, half of the accumulated indebtedness to the PEF was cancelled and bishops were authorized to cancel the remainder for worthy members unable to pay.

Prospective emigrants were encouraged to deposit savings with the PEF. Most European tithing went into the fund, as did donations from the few wealthy European converts. This system helped the cash flow, but it did not generate a surplus to assist others. The principal source of revenues, therefore, was the labor, produce, livestock, equipment, and cash contributed by church members in U.S. settlements, with tithing making up the shortfall.[23] The church thus faced a dual challenge: continually generating a flow of contributions, then turning them into cash for use outside Utah Territory. Because applicants for PEF funds exceeded the money available, church-sponsored emigration served the secondary economic function of human resource allocation. Agents often allocated priorities according to skills needed in the new settlements.[24]

Until 1854, the emigrant companies came by ship to New Orleans, took steamboats up the Mississippi and Missouri rivers to Kanesville, Iowa, or similar outfitting points, then started across the plains by wagon. After 1854, the Central Pacific Railroad crept across the prairie month by month; Saints would take it as far as possible, disembark at the railheads, and continue by wagon. The picturesque but ultimately unsatisfactory and even tragic handcart experiments of 1856–57 were the direct consequences of the devastating crop failures of 1855 and 1856 on donations and tithing.[25] The Utah War interrupted immigration in 1858. Then hard economics in 1859 prompted another experiment in cooperation and group self-sufficiency. To avoid buying wagons and draft animals in the Missouri Valley, the church sent ox trains loaded with Utah produce to the railheads to sell their goods, purchase needed supplies, and pick up immigrants. This system was used with great success every year but two between 1861 and 1868.[26]

Although the convenience and speed of the railroad overrode other considerations, from an economic point of view it inflicted a hardship on the Saints because fares had to be paid in cash. However, the advent of the railroad coincided with slowing immigration caused by improved economic conditions in Europe and the diminishing availability of good locations in the Great Basin. Nevertheless, the total sum channeled through the PEF from 1849 until its funds were escheated to the federal government in 1887 by the Edmunds-Tucker Act has been estimated at eight million dollars. By then, according to Leonard J. Arrington, a hundred thousand immigrants had been aided directly or indirectly, half of them receiving direct financial assistance. If commercial services had been used, the estimated total cost of 1849–87 immigration, would have been twenty-five million dollars, with half of it contributed by the church.[27]

PEF activity is a forceful illustration of the LDS commitment to the poor. In numerous speeches, Brigham Young vividly urged the Saints accept their obligation to bring the poor to Zion. He and other church leaders apparently did not agree with the growing national opinion that the poor had defective characters. Rather they believed the poor had been oppressed—that proper opportunity and instruction would enable them to earn adequate livings. In 1855, a general epistle by the First Presidency stated that the Perpetual Emigrating Fund was:

> designed [to rescue] . . . the honest poor, the pauper, if you please, from the thraldom of the ages, from localities where poverty is a crime and beggary an offense against the law, where every avenue to rise in the scale of being to any degree of respectable joyous existence is forever closed, and [to] place them in a land where honest labor and industry meet a suitable reward, where the higher walks of life are open to the humblest and poorest.[28]

Still Mormons did not consider poverty a state of grace, nor did it guarantee sainthood. Church leaders expected the poor to become self-supporting, given the proper social environment and adequate opportunities. The PEF, wrote apostle and future church president Wilford Woodruff in 1856, represents the "hoisting of the flag of deliverance to the oppressed millions. We can say to the poor and honest in heart, come to Zion, for the way is prepared."[29]

CHAPTER 4

Economic Welfare
in the Mountain West
1847–1900

By TREKKING to the Rocky Mountains, the Latter-day Saints hoped to establish a base for their new Zion—a religious commonwealth where, after the tribulations of New York, Ohio, Missouri, and Illinois, they could worship and develop their society unmolested. Previously they had always lived just within the frontier, contending with the elements of a frontier society. Now by choice they would be alone, contending instead with a hostile physical environment. In addition to conquering geography and climate, they would have to build their own political and economic system. When Congress rejected their proposed state called Deseret, church leaders accepted territorial status as "Utah" but still tried to maintain a modicum of political independence and also promoted a cooperative, self-sufficient group economy. In this they were relatively successful until the coming of the railroad in 1869. Thereafter they struggled against great—and finally overwhelming—odds to maintain their political autonomy, economic self sufficiency, and peculiar family configuration of plural marriage. Within this context, then, the Mormons pursued self-reliance for their people and relief for the poor, applying Zion concepts but only sporadically experimenting with forms of Zion societies.

The Mormon economy was primarily based upon agriculture, but its leaders also promoted both large- and small-scale industry and mining in the effort to achieve self-sufficiency. Self-sufficiency was the objective of the "cooperative movement," under which Zion's Cooperative Mercantile Institution was founded in 1868, with more than two hundred local cooperative general stores and industries following during the next decade.[1]

While church leadership provided the direction for both spiritual and temporal affairs, the church as such did not own most of the economic resources. There was a brief attempt in the 1870s to organize each community as a "United Order," some of which lasted for several years; but throughout most of the nineteenth century, individuals honored the law of consecration and stewardship by the degree to which they consecrated their abilities, efforts, and income to the church and considered their property ownership as a stewardship. In addition, such economic activities as driving a team to Nebraska or Iowa to pick up new immigrants or colonizing a new area were given the same status as proselyting missions. This "spiritualization of temporal activity" accounts largely for the Mormon success in colonizing the inhospitable Great Basin.[2] Spiritual idealism infused temporal activities. And while there were backsliders and apostates, this union of the temporal and the spiritual gave most Saints the conviction that they were helping to build the kingdom of God. As a consequence, their zeal, diligence, and determination survived remarkable hardships and setbacks.

The National Economic Setting

Except for the California gold rush, the Latter-day Saints were largely shielded from the impact of national economic events until the arrival of the railroad. The effects of the gold rush were strongly positive, at least in the short run, and may have saved the vulnerable colony during its first two years in the Salt Lake Valley. For example, Mormon Battalion members, who were actually present at the discovery of gold in Sutter's Mill, brought small but crucial amounts of bullion to the valley when it was desperately needed to purchase essential goods and underwrite the poverty-parched immigration program.[3] While a few Mormons were tempted away to the gold fields by dreams of wealth—despite Brigham Young's thunderous warnings—various church leaders, including Young himself, called significant numbers of men on "gold missions" to mine the precious ore, both for the church and to supply the personal needs of various ecclesiastical leaders.[4] Visiting apostles made periodic visits to California, collecting the tithing of Mormon miners. Another direct benefit came from California-bound gold-seekers who purchased Mormon produce and either traded or abandoned livestock, equipment, and wagons that the Saints badly needed.[5] Historian Eugene Campbell points out that the gold rush, in the long run, ended Mormon isolation and defeated dreams of political autonomy.[6] But those negatives are irrelevant if the infant colony could not have survived without the short-term benefits.

The Mormon settlements concentrated on subsistence agriculture, producing few marketable commodities besides livestock which could be herded to California or eastern markets. External events, such as the relatively mild Panic of 1857, hardly registered in the isolated territory. The Mormon emphasis on subsistence and economic equality discouraged merchandising which, along with imports and exports, was left largely to non-Mormons. In any case, the internal market was too small to be of much interest. When President James Buchanan, inflamed by sensationalized reports of "rebellion" from federal officials who had alienated the Mormons and abandoned their posts, ordered an army into the territory in 1857–58, its arrival created a market for Mormon produce which did not require costly transportation. But it also created a target for non-Mormon merchandisers and encouragement for Mormons to become merchants. The soldiers turned miners during the late 1850s and early 1860s, exploiting mineral deposits which, except for useful coal, iron, and lead, the Mormons had largely ignored. However, the long, expensive overland haul restricted profitable mining to high-grade precious metals. Utah had little compared to California, Nevada, and Colorado. Utah's important minerals were coal, iron, and copper, which required railroad transportation, available only after 1869 and the much-later development of a western market.

The national economy was growing rapidly but not booming during the two decades of Utah's relative isolation, 1847–69. During this period, the foundation was being laid nationally for the post–Civil War industrial revolution, from which Utah would remain isolated. Both Utah and the nation as a whole absorbed a large number of immigrants; but Mormon immigrants came largely from Northern Europe, peaking before the Civil War. Nationally, the immigration boom came between the Civil War and World War I and stemmed largely from Southern and Eastern Europe. Lands surrounding Utah in all directions, which the Saints could have had for the taking during the forties and fifties, were settled by others under the combined forces of mineral exploration, ranching, and homesteading during the sixties and seventies. All became states before Utah except for Arizona and New Mexico.

National, state, and local government had played a major role in U.S. economic development from the beginning. But after mid-century, the ideal (though not necessarily the reality) became *laissez faire*—the view that government should keep its hands off private business's economic activities. The defeat of the South during the Civil War reduced the political influence of agriculture and exalted industry. It was an age of financial buccaneering. During the last quarter of the nineteenth century, the new concepts of biological selection grafted themselves to the economic sphere as "Social Darwinism" or the survival of the fittest.[7] To assist the weak was, in that view, to encourage and perpetuate weakness, hardly a philosophy compatible with Mormon social organization.

With the completion of the transcontinental railroad in 1869, eastern manufactured goods flooded the territory, competing with undercapitalized and expensive home manufactures, attracting non-Mormon merchants, turning ambitious Saints to merchandising, and creating noticeable economic inequality. The Mormons first attempted to reinforce group self-sufficiency and maintain a separate economy but ultimately they accepted a subordinate role of producing raw materials. By the Panic of 1873, the Utah economy had become vulnerable to national economic events; and the long depression of the 1890s compelled the church to make one last attempt at economic intervention by subsidizing several regional industries. This was the economic background against which the Saints sought personal self-reliance, group self-sufficiency, care for the poor, and the dream of Zion during the last half of the nineteenth century.

Early Years in Mormon Country

Survival was precarious during the first decade. The Saints had brought comparatively few resources with them; there were no easy ways to replace broken tools, weapons, or vehicles. Winters and summers were harsh. Stinging and biting insects irritated humans and animals, while locusts leveled tender crops. Toward the end of each summer, significant numbers of new settlers arrived, usually with few provisions left. Sixteen hundred reached the Salt Lake Valley during the first year and became the basis for the population which had expanded to approximately twenty thousand by 1852.[8] New arrivals had been unable to plant and cultivate but still needed to share the harvest for a full year. Church leaders maintained a vigorous agricultural program for newcomers, authorizing and encouraging an ever-lengthening chain of farming villages supplied by cooperatively maintained irrigation systems.

The village system hypothesized families—diligent and hard-working couples whose labor would make the earth yield harvests to sustain their dependent children and, sometimes, elderly parents. Embedded in this structural base of self-sufficient families, however, were those who, for one reason or another, could not make their own way. That was a challenge for the ecclesiastical organization. Presiding at a general level was the First Presidency, consisting of Brigham Young and his two counselors, the Council of the Twelve Apostles, the Salt Lake High Council (from 1847 until 1904, the entire Salt Lake Valley was a single stake), and the Council of Fifty, a quasi-political body.[9] But the immediate responsibility for aiding the poor and helping the Saints achieve self-reliance rested, as it had in Nauvoo, upon the ward bishops.

During the winter of 1847–48, the captains of fifties and hundreds, who had led wagon units of those sizes during the trek, continued to look after those same families as acting bishops, rotating responsibility for those without supplies from captain to captain on a regular basis. As the difficult first winter wore on, the Salt Lake High Council appointed a special committee "to act in behalf of the destitute and to receive donations, buy, sell, exchange and distribute, according to circumstances for that purpose." The committee turned these donations over to the acting bishops, who distributed them to the poor, asking them to repay these contributions when they were established. Church leaders also instituted a voluntary rationing system and placed price controls on necessities to prevent those who were well-off from taking advantage of shortages.[10]

The second winter, 1848–49, was even more trying. By then there had been but a single harvest, and the population had more than doubled to 4,200. Brigham Young preached strongly against hoarding and reselling at high prices, threatening, with obvious hyperbole, "If those who have do not sell to those who have not, we will just take it and distribute [it] among the poor, and those that have and will not divide willingly may be thankful that their heads are not found wallowing in the snow."[11] He had Salt Lake City divided into nineteen wards, each with a bishopric composed of three men who resided within its boundaries; their duties included responsibility for the ward's poor. He specified that the bishops should inventory each family's food supplies, solicit donations from those with surpluses, and use these surpluses to relieve those most in want.

In the spring of 1849, Brigham Young dispatched Apostle Amasa M. Lyman to the California gold fields to collect tithing from "gold missionaries," independent gold-seekers, and those who had lingered after arriving with the *Brooklyn* or with the Mormon Battalion.[12] After the harvest that year, Young instituted a campaign for full payment of tithing, which, in that cash-short economy, meant in-kind receipts, most of which were transmitted to the poor.[13]

During the winter of 1849–50, Brigham Young directed the establishment of a Church Public Works Department to provide employment (especially for new immigrants), construct public buildings and facilities, and establish manufacturing enterprises. Daniel H. Wells, one of Brigham Young's counselors, was appointed superintendent and held that position until public works responsibility was transferred to the Presiding Bishop in 1870. Requisitions for much of the labor and some of the provisions went from Wells to the ward bishops who then recruited manpower and found the necessary supplies. Brigham Young estimated in 1863 that the department had employed as many as two thousand men at one time, but the average number during the 1850s was between two and five hundred.[14] In March 1860, Brigham Young responded to criticism of the adobe wall these laborers had constructed part way around the city, asserting that he was willing to spend thousands of dollars to employ people who needed employment, even if the work performed was of no direct benefit.[15] Seven years later he counseled:

> My experience has taught me, and it has become a principle with me, that it is never any benefit to give, out and out, to man or woman, money, food, clothing, or anything else, if they are able-bodied and can work and earn what they need, when there is anything on earth for them to do. This is my principle, and I try to act upon it. To pursue a contrary course would ruin any community in the world and make them idlers.[16]

Men perceived as idle might well be called to settle outlying areas, drive wagons to railheads in the Midwest to help transport immigrants, or serve as Indian or proselyting missionaries. On the other hand, when there were pressing public works to be done, all were expected to do their share with each ward providing requisitioned manpower. Roads, canals, public buildings, railroads, and telegraph lines enriched the economic and social life of Utah, thanks to this system.[17]

Within the first few years after entering the Salt Lake Valley, the Mormons established an intricate system of requisitioning, storing, and using tithing goods and labor. The General Tithing Office or Bishop's Central Storehouse, established in Salt Lake City in 1850, served the entire church. Each settlement or ward also maintained a tithing office, often called a bishop's storehouse. Most tithing was in kind: one-tenth of the produce and often one day's labor in ten. About two-thirds of the produce donated locally was forwarded to the central storehouse for general church needs. These ward storehouses became so involved in local economic affairs that they served as community warehouses, general stores, banks, weighing stations, and relief and employment agencies throughout the 1850s and 1860s. During the 1850s, tithing houses added postal services to their duties, receiving and forwarding mail by tithing labor. The central storehouse looked after great numbers of poor, not only because of its church-wide function but also because Salt Lake City was the largest urban center in the territory. Still the prevailing philosophy was to care for the poor locally and with local resources to the extent possible, thus maintaining a policy of personalized and face-to-face service.

An excellent harvest in 1849 tipped the anxious balance by assuring the struggling pioneers that the Great Basin could be settled. Although over six thousand Mormons had already reached the Salt Lake Valley, some ten thousand were waiting in Iowa, on the Missouri River at Kanesville, and in adjacent settlements; approximately thirty thousand Saints had been baptized in Europe. The economics of migration, described in Chapter 3, were complex and challenging; but they paled before the task of developing an economy capable of supporting them.

The Settlement Process

In Utah, no attempt was made to reinstate the formal law of consecration and stewardship; however, its basic concepts had, by this time, assumed the status of both theology and social organization. The earth was the Lord's. Human beings held whatever portion of resources they controlled in stewardship. At any time, they could be called upon to consecrate their time, talent, wealth, or income to the demands of the church, including caring for the poor. William H. Dixon, a journalist with the *Atheneum* in London, observed this process and philosophy at work on a visit in 1866. The Saints, he observed, were a very industrious people for whom "work...[was] considered holy." He concluded:

> The Saints, as a rule, are not poor in the sense which the Irish are poor; not needy as a race, a body, and a church; indeed, for a new society, starting with nothing, and having its fortunes to make by labor, they are rich. Utah is sprinkled with farms and gardens; the

hillsides are pictured with flocks and herds; and the capital city, the
New Jerusalem, is finely laid out and nobly built. Every man labors with his hand and brain; the people are frugal; their fields cost
them nothing; and the wealth created by their industry is great. To
multiply flocks and herds, to lay up corn and wheat, is with them
to obey the commands of God.[18]

He was not with the Saints long enough to note the inevitable examples of neglect or deviance from this norm nor, perhaps, did he
give sufficient credit to nearly two decades of intensive effort. A
closer look at that settlement process, particularly during the early
years when economic theory had not yet met the realities that inevitably required adaptation, is instructive. Private ownership existed, but
for the public good. A family could own land but no more than it
could productively use. There was to be no buying and selling of farm
land. Grazing land, water, timber, and mineral resources were to be
public property. It is difficult to know how closely these principles
were followed in practice, because there was no means for legally re-
cording transfers of land until the first federal land office was established in 1869; but that was the intent.[19]

Joseph Smith's plat for the City of Zion, created for the Mormon
settlement in Jackson County, provided the first urban images. Salt
Lake City provided the working model after which other settlements
were patterned, though with substantial departures as time passed and
circumstances altered.[20] Around a ten-acre site set aside for a temple,
ten-acre surveyed blocks contained eight lots of one and one-quarter
acres each. These lots were distributed by a series of lotteries as portions of the new city were surveyed, beginning in the autumn of 1848.
Unmarried men were not eligible for lots, but one was allocated to
each polygamous wife and her children. Upon each of these lots, the
families were limited to one house, necessary outbuildings, and a
garden. Beyond the original 177 blocks divided into 19 wards were
five-acre farm plots allocated to mechanics and artisans who would
support their families in part from their trades and in part from their
farms. Farther out were ten- and twenty-acre farms for those whose
primary activity would be farming. The farm land was jointly developed and fenced in 1848 as an immense field of 11,000 acres, and its irrigation system was cooperatively developed even before the land was
subdivided and distributed by lottery.

Originally, according to Leonard Arrington, no one was to be
allowed to subdivide or sell either city or farm plots. Furthermore,
improving a plot was a condition of retaining it.[21] Undoubtedly, unau-

thorized land-trading and -selling developed almost immediately; nevertheless, a number of cases exist during the 1850s when people took control of more land than they needed. The bishops, petitioned to, appropriated the surplus and allocated it to others.[22] In one case, when the holder of excess land refused to sell part of it, Brigham Young ordered the surveyor to plot out the portion and deliver the certificate to the new owner without cost. In another case, a resident in a central Utah town found that the bishop had authorized a fellow member to build a house on some of his idle land. Not unnaturally, he demanded, "By what authority, Bishop, do you give away my property?" The bishop responded, "By the authority of the Priesthood of God." As late as the 1880s, a family could obtain land free in some areas by applying to the bishop and working on the cooperative irrigation canal.[23]

Irrigation systems were cooperatively built and maintained, beginning in the Salt Lake Valley and continuing throughout most of the settlements. All able-bodied males helped build, maintain, clean, and repair canals and ditches. Every family who benefited contributed to the support of the "ditch rider" or "watermaster" who supervised the system.[24] Families took regular turns at using the water, with the bishop negotiating differences. Roads, public buildings, and other public works were also cooperatively created, often by "tithing days" of contributed labor.

That same basic pattern of settlement prevailed throughout the Great Basin in pursuit of family self-reliance and group self-sufficiency for the largest population possible. Church leaders, first on the general, then on the stake level, normally planned activities, then delegated authority to others to supervise and direct the establishment and operation of each colony. At all stages of the process, cooperation and cohesion were essential tools in supporting a large population in the Mountain West's harsh climate and fragile ecology. Each colonizing venture became a group stewardship. All were ultimately responsible to God for the success of the colony, and each endeavor was viewed as part of the cooperative building of the kingdom of God.

The centrally directed pattern was typical of, though not exclusive to, the approximately two hundred settlements established between 1847 and 1869; more variations developed as an additional three hundred settlements found footholds during the last thirty years of the nineteenth century.[25] The spine of the Mormon Corridor stretched southward from Salt Lake City through southeastern Utah to Las Vegas, Nevada, then west to San Bernardino, California, with the original expectation of access to the sea at San Diego. Northward, the corridor ran through Utah's valleys into what would later be southeastern Idaho.

Typically, Brigham Young sent out exploring parties to find sites for successful communities, then called a leader, usually a bishop but sometimes an apostle, who combined both ecclesiastical and temporal responsibilities. Frequently, church authorities also named other settlers, hand-picking some for essential crafts and skills. The expedition's leader often recruited colonists as well, and people looking for new opportunities were free to join a new pioneering company. They met together, usually in Salt Lake Valley or Utah Valley, checked on necessary supplies and equipment, then journeyed together to their destination. Borrowing the organization of the exodus, captains of tens, fifties, and, if necessary, hundreds supervised individual settlers en route. Being called to colonize was considered equivalent to a proselyting mission, especially for some of the more difficult zones; and relatively few refused this test of faith.

Upon arrival, the company dedicated the land to the Lord and immediately set to work. Each male settler was assigned particular tasks, according to his skills and family and group needs. Constructing a protective palisade or fort often provided temporary group shelter, as well as protection from Indians. Individual families often lived in wagon boxes lifted off their running gears and in dugouts until more permanent dwellings were possible. All of the able-bodied men cooperatively dammed the streams, dug irrigation canals and ditches, plowed, planned, built roads, cut timber, and hauled it from the nearest canyon. Building individual houses was often the last assignment. The earlier settlements tended to follow the composite plat of Zion model, as established in Salt Lake City, with farmers living in the village and traveling out each day to their farms. Other villages, depending on the time period and terrain, were more dispersed.[26]

Next developed blacksmith shops, tanneries, sawmills, and gristmills; those who worked in these specialties were expected to serve the settlers at reasonable rates. This settlement pattern, atypical in rural America, at least in theory provided for the basic economic needs of all and permitted the Saints to live in relatively close proximity. In addition to providing protection from the rare difficulties with Indians,[27] this arrangement permitted all Mormons to work, worship, and play together as a community. Generally, the bishop informally mediated disputes. It was comparatively rare to convene even an ecclesiastical court, and to seek redress against a fellow Saint in a secular court had long been considered a sin.[28]

The Mormon settlement plan thus let an arid or semi-arid environ-ment absorb thousands of people, thriftily capturing water from mountain canyons in small reservoirs and efficiently distributing it through cooperatively owned canals. To provide a living for the max-imum number the land and water would support, individuals were not allowed to monopolize resources or amass land for speculative purposes. The Mormon system valued group welfare, even while it recognized individual achievement.

A secondary objective of settlement was staking a Mormon claim to the habitable portions of the region. Some settlements were estab-lished as way stations to California, at ferry points in Wyoming, as production centers for iron, cotton, and lead, to anchor Indian mis-sions (Fort Limhi in Idaho and Santa Clara in southwestern Utah), and also as buffers between troublesome Indian bands or gentile min-ing establishments.[29] As overpopulation threatened the core area in the 1870s and early 1880s, settlements spread to more marginal lands in Arizona, Colorado, and New Mexico, farther afield in Nevada, Idaho, and Wyoming, and into the remoter areas of Utah. Despite increasingly harsh circumstances, the assumption remained that de-voted Saints would go when called and stay until released. Ecclesiasti-cally directed colonization had largely ceased by the mid-1880s, only to make a last return during the 1890s depression. Anti-polygamy prosecution and land hunger combined to propel individual Saints into northern Mexico and southern Alberta during the late 1880s and 1890s.[30]

Every Saint bore dual expectations: individual self-reliance and contribution to the community. Church leaders publicly frowned on the individual pursuit of wealth, though the successful were honored as long as they maintained their church allegiance as a first priority. Although mining precious metals was considered spiritually danger-ous for ordinary members, a number of Mormon mining entrepre-neurs remained both influential and welcome in Mormon circles.[31]

Mining base metals as raw materials for manufacturing was an-other matter. Coal was readily available, first at Coalville, less than fifty miles from Salt Lake City, and, by the 1880s, from Carbon and Emery counties in east-central Utah. Despite dedicated efforts by the colonists, attempts during the 1850s to mine lead in southern Nevada, establish an iron industry at Cedar City in southern Utah, manufac-ture sugar at Sugarhouse (now a Salt Lake City neighborhood), and to establish a silk industry by the women throughout the territory dur-ing the 1860s-80s were all unsuccessful.[32] But the calls and responses continued just the same. The goal was group self-sufficiency—manu-factures to replace the costly imports from the eastern states and to create low-weight/high-value exports to overcome the transportation difficulties.

Meeting Natural Disaster in 1856

After the difficulties of 1848 and 1849, harvests were generally good until 1855 and 1856 when natural disasters brought on a near-famine. During 1855 the periodic plague of grasshoppers, or Rocky Mountain locusts, was much more destructive than in any previous year. One Salt Lake resident described their infestation "like snow flakes in a storm," which filled the valley "as far as the eye can reach."[33] In addition, 1855 was a very hot, dry year, reducing the avail-able irrigation water and causing late-season drought. Estimates of crop destruction from these causes ranged from one-third to two-thirds, depending upon the area. Furthermore, about 4,225 immi-grants swelled the population of 35,000 in 1855, more than in any year since 1852. Then, as a fourth blow, the winter of 1855–56 was the most severe since the Mormon arrival in 1847, killing possibly half of the cattle in the territory. During the summer of 1856, grasshoppers invaded again, decimating the harvest for a second time. Thanks to a substantial harvest in 1857, actual starvation was averted; but begin-ning in the spring of 1856, church leaders asked the Saints to plant every possible acre and tend the crop carefully, then asked bishops to organize gleaners to assure maximum harvest.[34]

During these two catastrophic years, almost everyone suffered. But people did not starve, primarily because of two programs insti-tuted or emphasized by the church leaders. Giving donations for the poor, combined with fasting, though practiced occasionally earlier, became, during the winter of 1855–56, an institutionalized monthly practice which has continued to the present.[35] The First Presidency also instituted voluntary rationing throughout the settlements, asking households to limit their consumption of breadstuffs to half a pound per person per day and to donate the surplus for the needy. Brigham Young threatened, "If necessary we will take your grain from your bin and distribute it among the poor and needy, and they shall be fed and supplied with work, and you shall receive what your grain is worth."[36] While there are no documented examples of forcible expro-priation, the threat itself illustrated the gravity of the situation. Sim-ilar pressures were exerted to prevent exploiting those in need, either in prices or wages. Public works were expanded, and surplus or idle men in Salt Lake City were sent on missions or to outlying settlements.[37] Though all suffered, the settlements survived.

Welfare and the Bishops

The bishops continued to shoulder the main burden of seeing that the people had the necessities of life.[38] Beginning in 1849 the nineteen bishops in the Salt Lake Valley met monthly with the newly established Presiding Bishopric, a practice which continued into the 1880s. This meeting served as a forum to discuss the secular affairs of the kingdom, and caring for the poor had first priority on the agenda. Wards with surpluses agreed to share with needier wards. Non-Mormon traveler William Dixon left an 1866 account of one of these meetings:

> The unpaid functions of a bishop are extremely numerous; for a Mormon prelate has to look not merely to the spiritual welfare of his flock, but to their worldly interest and wellbeing; to see that their farms are cultivated, their houses clean, their children taught, their cattle lodged. Last Sunday, after service at the Tabernacle, Brigham Young sent for us to the raised dias on which he and the dignitaries had been seated, to see a private meeting of the bishops, and to hear what kind of work these reverend fathers had met to do. . . . The old men met in a ring; and Edward Hunter, their presiding bishop, questioned them each and all, as to the work going on in his ward, the building, painting, draining, gardening; also as to what this man needed, and that man needed, in the way of help. An emigrant train had just come in, and the bishops had to put six hundred persons in the way of growing their cabbages and building their homes. One bishop said he could take five bricklayers, another two carpenters, and a third a tinman, a fourth seven or eight farm-servants, and so on through the whole bench. In a few minutes, I saw that two hundred of these poor emigrants had been placed in the way of earning their daily bread. "This," said Young with a little smile, "is one of the labors of our bishops."[39]

During the intensive immigration of the 1850s, the bishops were responsible for meeting the arriving wagon trains at the campgrounds on what is now the block of the City-County Building and taking the number of families for whom they could provide shelter and employment. Dixon gave a sympathetic account of this process:

> I went with Bishop Hunter, a good and merry old man, full of work and humor, to the emigrant's corral, to see the rank and file

of the new English arrivals; six hundred people from the Welsh hills and from the Midland shires; men, women, and children; all poor and uncomely, weary, dirty, freckled with the sun, scorbutic from privation; when I was struck by the tender tones of his voice, the wisdom of his counsel, the fatherly solicitude of his manner in dealing with these poor people. Some of the women were ill and querulous; they wanted butter, they wanted tea; they wanted many things not to be got in the corral. Hunter sent for a doctor from the city, and gave orders for tea and butter on the tithing of-fice. Never shall I forget the yearning thankfulness of expression which beamed from some of those sufferers' eyes. The poor crea-tures felt that in this aged bishop they had found a wise and watch-ful friend.[40]

Certainly, the bishop did not carry the burden alone. As Dixon re-corded, perhaps exaggerating the efficiency of the system:

Care of the poor is written down strongly in the Mormon code of sacred duties. A bishop's main function is to see that no man in his ward, in his county, is in want of food and raiment; when he finds that a poor family is in need, he goes to his more prosperous neigh-bor, and in the Lord's name demands from him a sack of wheat, a can of tea, a loaf of sugar, a blanket, a bed; knowing that his requi-sition will be promptly met. The whole earth is the Lord's, and must be rendered up to him. Elder Jennings, the richest merchant in Salt Lake City, told me of many such requisitions being made upon himself; in bad times, they may come to him twice or thrice a day. In case of need, the bishop goes up to the Tithing Office and obtains the succor of which his parishioner stands in need; for the wants of the poor take precedence of the wants of the Church; but the appeal from personal benevolence to the public fund has sel-dom to be made. For if a Saint has any kind of store, he must share it with his fellow; if he has bread, he must feed the hungry; if he has raiment, he must clothe the naked. No excuse avails him for neglect of this great duty.[41]

Although this view is undoubtedly over-optimistic, within a few pages, Dixion had captured a fairly comprehensive account of expec-tations for both bishop and member.

Brigham Young's Welfare Philosophy

Welfare in Brigham Young's day was not simply providing goods or land to those in need; it also included motivating, showing, and instructing people how to take care of themselves. In August of

1860 Young preached: "The reason we have no poor who are able to work is because we plan to set every person to work at some profitable employment, and teach them to maintain themselves. If a person is not able to take care of himself, we will take care of him." He added that "if a Bishop will act to the extent of his calling and office, and magnify it, there will not be an individual in his Ward that is not employed to the best advantage." He also explained that a family should take care of its own, including the relatives. But he recognized this would not happen in many cases; then the church assumed the responsibility.[42]

Young believed some people were destitute through simple mismanagement. An intensely practical man, he often preached specifics of how people could improve their material as well as their spiritual lives. In one classic sermon in April 1857, he encouraged people to maintain milk cows, laying hens, vegetable gardens, meat animals, and fruit trees. He encouraged the women to knit and sew. He even told them how to cook so as not to waste any food. He inveighed against waste and, as an example, pointed out that the life of boots could be prolonged by oiling.[43] William Dixon recorded Young's instructions to a new group of immigrants in 1866:

> You are faint and weary from your march. Rest then for a day, for a second day should you need it; then rise up and see how you will live. . . . Be of good cheer. Look about this valley into which you have been called. Your first duty is to grow a cabbage, and along with this cabbage an onion, a tomato, a sweet potato; then how to feed a pig, to build a house, to plant a garden, to rear cattle, and to bake bread.[44]

Throughout the 1860s, Young and other leaders criticized the practice of selling grain to non-Mormons for cash and pleaded with the Latter-day Saints to store food, particularly grain, against times of personal difficulty or famine in their own storehouses—a foreshadowing of modern counsel to store food and water. Simultaneously, however, they warned members against hoarding when others were in need. Because the Saints generally ignored his advice to store grain, in 1876 Brigham Young asked Emmeline B. Wells, a plural wife of his counselor Daniel H. Wells, to spearhead an effort by the women; grain storage eventually became an enormously successful long-term Relief Society project.[45]

Brigham Young and his colleagues did not limit welfare concerns to food and shelter. Health was also a priority. During the Reformation of 1856–57, Jedediah Grant, then a member of the First Presidency, preached vigorously on cleanliness of both person and premises. Brigham Young publicly charged that some children died, not because God willed it, but through "the inattention and ignorance of parents" who "let them run out in the cold and wet," then sent them to bed "to lie all night with a burning fever." When the finally alarmed parents sent for the doctor, the medico, charged Young, was "just as apt to destroy the life of the child as to restore it."[46]

Young's low estimate of the medical profession was widely held among the Saints. When illness struck, they usually relied on faith and the ordinance of laying on hands. During this period, women as well as men administered blessings of healing; and pregnant women customarily received a special ordinance of blessing shortly before delivery.[47] Midwives provided a great deal of the medical assistance. In 1852, Willard Richards, an apostle and Thomsonian practitioner (a school which held that natural remedies existed for most ailments), organized his like-minded colleagues into a Council of Health to improve medical care.

There were periodic proposals, at times even from Presiding Bishop Hunter, to institutionalize care of the chronically needy at a poor farm, apparently to equalize the burden among wards. Brigham Young rejected this method of caring for the destitute, common among local governments across the nation. He insisted that the poor be taken care of in their own wards by their own bishops. Bishops who were overwhelmed could send their poor to the general tithing office for help. Instead of special institutions for the poor, Young proposed scattering them throughout the settlements where they could be taken care of while learning how to sustain themselves. His theory seemed to be that congregating the poor would tend to create a special class who could perpetuate themselves by seeing each other's bad examples. Isolating them in areas where there was plenty of work to do and where they could observe industrious habits all about them would teach them to be self-sustaining.[48]

Brigham Young's optimistic philosophy held that, in the proper social and physical environment, all people could succeed. This followed quite naturally from such basic LDS concepts as eternal progression, the possibility of universal salvation, and the 1831 law of consecration and stewardship, which encouraged individual initiative and development but equalized consumption. Thus, Young's philosophy stood at odds with Social Darwinism which, achieving its greatest popularity in America during the last third of the nineteenth century, emphasized competitive economic struggle. It prescribed only the meagerest of assistance for the inevitable losers lest benevolence perpetuate the weak and upset the natural system of selection.[49]

Centralization and Dispersion of Welfare

The problems of poverty were apparently more manifest in Salt Lake City than elsewhere, whether because of the greater concentration of population, the more formal requirements for urban employment, or the greater resources of the central tithing office. Despite encouragement from the bishops, some poor Mormons were reluctant to move to rural settlements where land for subsistence farming was still available. Some of these needy, according to Hunter, lived in despicable housing. Others were assigned to successive families, who provided for them temporarily. Ward bishops sent people needing special medical attention to Salt Lake City where the Presiding Bishopric usually paid the cost. They also assisted needy nonmembers, of whom there was a greater concentration in Salt Lake City than in other settlements.

Some of these demands may have underlain a Presiding Bishopric decision on 28 November 1878 to require a local bishop's recommend for applicants at the central tithing office. In August 1883, President John Taylor systematized the process further by asking each bishop to report periodically the number needing assistance, the amount of fast offerings being donated monthly and, in case of a projected shortfall, the amount of assistance which would be needed from the tithing office for the next six months.[50]

The Return of the Relief Society

The central organization of the Women's Relief Society had been largely dormant since the Nauvoo period, though Relief Societies had emerged sporadically in individual wards. When Brigham Young authorized the reestablishment of ward Relief Societies in 1867, one of his reasons was that the women of the church could solicit donations for the poor more effectively than the men.[51]

> Sisters, [he exhorted,] do you see any children around your neighborhoods poorly clad and without shoes? If you do, I say to you Female Relief Societies, pick up those children and relieve their necessities, and send them to school. And if you see any young, middle-aged or old ladies in need, find them something to

do that will enable them to sustain themselves; Relieve the wants of every individual in need in your neighborhoods. This is in the capacity and in the power of the Female Relief Societies when it is not in the power of the bishops. Do you know it? I do whether you do or not; and you are learning it.[52]

The minutes of various ward Relief Societies show that they regularly solicited donations and worked in a variety of ways to help the needy. From time to time in the Presiding Bishopric meetings, bishops expressed appreciation for the help of their Relief Societies in caring for the poor. By the fiftieth anniversary of the church in 1880, the Relief Society had helped the bishops to distribute 1,000 cattle and 5,000 sheep to poor families and loaned 35,000 bushels of seed wheat without interest to farmers in need.[53]

Cooperatives and the United Order

Though the law of consecration and stewardship in its Ohio and Missouri form was never reintroduced, it was also never forgotten and retained its status as the eternal model which would ultimately be restored. During the mid-1850s, tithing receipts could not meet the demands for community-building and immigration. Some were manifesting symptoms of "worldliness"—succumbing to the temptations of California and the lure of goods offered by gentile merchants. In consequence, during the agricultural crisis of 1856, the First Presidency again asked members to consecrate their all to the church, for which they would be assigned "inheritances" according to their needs.[54] Forty percent of the heads of Utah's seven thousand families filled out and signed formal deeds of transfer, including personal and real property. However sincere the intention, the result was purely symbolic. The church never acted upon the deeds, perhaps because, at that point, Utah lacked a legal system by which land titles could be transferred. Other reasons may have been disappointment at the member response and distrust of the managerial capacities of local bishops.[55] Probably decisive, however, was a looming conflict with the federal government that led to an armed invasion.

Acting on the uninvestigated reports of disgruntled federal officials, President James Buchanan sent an expeditionary force to escort Utah's new territorial governor. Intensive guerilla activity during the winter of 1857–58 stalled the army in Wyoming for the winter; and after a negotiated compromise, the army peacefully installed itself at some distance from the city in 1858. However, the soldiers, their mining activities, and their camp followers broke the Saints' much-desired isolation. The final blow was the arrival of the railroad in 1869, which the church welcomed because it would ease immigration and make essential goods more available. However, it was also a threat. Immigration now had to be paid for in cash instead of labor, Mormon freighters were put out of business, cheaper manufactured goods competed with expensive home manufactures, both luxuries and necessities absorbed Mormon purchasing power, and non-Mormons arrived with the immigrants. Marked inequality of income and wealth can be traced to this period.[56]

Brigham Young countered in several ways. In 1869, the very year of the railroad's arrival, he instructed his wives and daughters to "re-trench" from "extravagance and vanity" in dress and behavior. By 1880, this movement had become the Young Ladies Mutual Improvement Association.[57] He also dealt sternly during the 1870s with the "Godbeites," a group of bright and ambitious young Mormons who rejected the traditional LDS cooperative model in favor of competitive individualism.[58]

A broader economic response was the launching of a cooperative movement to let Mormons compete more effectively with imported goods and non-Mormon merchants. The wholesale and retail activities of Zion's Cooperative Mercantile Institution (ZCMI), founded in October 1868 with branch cooperatives throughout the territory, was the major but not the sole example. It also included as many as two hundred projects—cooperative iron works, textile mills, cotton factories, woolen mills, farming, and agricultural processing.[59] A particularly successful venture was the Brigham City Cooperative, established and led by stake president Lorenzo Snow, an apostle and future church president.

Brigham Young saw within this cooperative movement aspects of the Order of Enoch, another name for the law of consecration and stewardship. With the goal that the people could become "of one heart and one mind" with "no poor among them" (Moses 7:18), he launched the United Order movement of the 1870s.

Although Joseph Smith had called the leadership of his Ohio and Missouri economic experiments the "United Order" or "United Firm," the United Orders of the 1870s were quite different in both structure and practice. They were essentially of four kinds. In some, such as that in St. George, individuals contributed their productive property but not personal effects to the order and received different levels of wages and dividends depending upon their labor and the property contributed. The Brigham City model was a community cooperative. Individuals did not consecrate property or labor, but the community itself owned and operated a significant number of cooperative enterprises. In the third model, typical of Salt Lake City, an individual ward would finance a single enterprise such as a dairy or soap factory, which provided employment to needy ward members. The fourth, typified by Orderville, Utah, was fully communal. Settlers contributed all of their property to the order, worked together at communal enterprises, ate at a common table, shared equally in the common products, and rose, prayed, ate, and worked to a common signal.[60]

The cosmopolitan Salt Lake City Saints gave little more than lip service to the movement; in fact, Young himself did not join.[61] Most of these United Orders were hard hit by the national Panic of 1873 and its subsequent depression, which closed banks, shut down mines, and dampened economic activity generally throughout the Utah Territory. Only a handful survived Brigham Young's death in 1877. Others suffered from poor and discontinuous leadership, particularly during the federal "raid" against polygamy during the 1880s. Most of the survivors drifted into private ownership.

John Taylor, president of the Quorum of the Twelve and Young's successor, had not been in favor of United Orders and did not encourage them during his presidency.[62] By the late 1880s with the church in the throes of its struggle with the federal government, private enterprise had become almost universal. Yet in retrospect, church leaders credited the movement with speeding the construction of several temples and with tempering the growing spirit of acquisitiveness and individualism. In 1877, the year of his death, Brigham Young concluded, "It was not a part of this Order to take away the property of one man and give it to another, neither to equally divide what we possessed [but] to afford all the opportunity of enriching themselves through their diligence [and devote the output to] carrying on the work of God generally."[63] Another experimental stretching toward Zion had ended.

The End of Self-Sufficiency

John Taylor, who headed the church from 1877 until he died in hiding from federal marshals in 1887, attacked the economic problem in a different way in 1879. His Zion's Central Board of Trade, with subordinate local boards throughout the territory, sought to plan economic development, organize home industries, develop markets for local production, control output, regulate competition, maintain prices, promote quality, disseminate information, and generally foster a self-sufficient but private-enterprise Mormon economy to compete with the growing external pressures.[64] It had many of the aspects of the ill-fated National Industrial Recovery Act, inaugurated by Franklin D. Roosevelt, early in the Great Depression of the 1930s. The anti-polygamy "raid" of 1884 destroyed any effective structure in the Zion's Central Board of Trade by chasing the principals underground, so it is impossible to know how it might have fared in better times.

Taylor's efforts were the last gasp of Mormonism's self-sufficient economy. Defending the kingdom against anti-polygamy legislation consumed the energies of local and general leaders, most of whom were either in hiding or in jail; and the escheatment of church property by the federal government under the provisions of the Edmunds-Tucker Act (1887) destroyed most Mormon economic institutions.

Wilford Woodruff, fourth church president, succeeded John Taylor in 1887. He realized that the church faced two choices, accommodation or destruction, and led it into the long passage of abandoning plural marriage, which only began with the Manifesto of 1890. Equally important signs of integration into the broader American society consisted of dismantling the church's political party and entering the national economy. The church abandoned its opposition to non-Mormon enterprises, sold some church business, secularized the management of others, and encouraged private enterprise among the Saints.[65]

The national economy, however, was struggling with the long "Cleveland depression" of the 1890s. The church did not abandon its poor nor stop trying to promote economic and employment opportunities, but it now looked to outside sources for jobs. The First Presidency, Presiding Bishopric, and the Relief Society general presidency developed a comprehensive program of economic stimulation and relief for the unemployed and needy. Members were encouraged to avoid urban areas, particularly Salt Lake City, and to remain or relocate in the rural settlements where living was cheaper and where there was more opportunity to support themselves. Wards in Salt Lake City encouraged property owners to lend unused land to the poor for gardens and organized post-harvest gleaning parties at nearby farms.[66] In March 1894, Salt Lake Stake, which included all of the city, reported that 1,637 people were being helped by the church, one-third of the needed supplies coming from fast offerings and the remainder from tithing. Since cash was in short supply, the church printed tithing scrip, in essence, a local currency backed by produce in the tithing storehouse. In November 1896, the General Authorities officially changed the monthly fast day from the first Thursday to the first Sunday of the month to increase meeting attendance and participation.

During the winter of 1896–97, the Presiding Bishopric's Office established an employment bureau with branches in each of the stakes and wards. On printed forms bishops listed those in need and opportunities for employment. These reports were regularly published in the *Deseret News*. A bulletin published on 4 September 1897, for instance, listed opportunities for nineteen schoolteachers, seven shoemakers, eleven blacksmiths, four carpenters, two masons, one dressmaker, and one tinner, plus four farms available for half the crop, and opportunities to purchase farms in seventeen places for five dollars an acre and up. The bulletin was last published on 28 October 1899, when the depression was coming to an end and the employment situation had stabilized.

Since jobs were so scarce during the 1890s, church leaders officially discouraged new converts from gathering to Utah. From 1896, the year Utah finally achieved statehood, until 1904, two members of the Quorum of the Twelve acted as a Colonization Committee, seeking arable lands away from the Utah core. New settlements were established in southern Alberta, in Sonora and Chihuahua in Mexico, and in Nevada, Oregon, Idaho, Wyoming, and Colorado. Some of the colonists were officially called by ecclesiastical authorities in the pattern of the earlier colonization efforts. Others went on their own but with church approval and encouragement, making this decade one of the most intensive colonization periods in church history.[67] At the same time, church leaders tried to rebuild the economy by promoting and providing financial assistance to such industries as sugar, salt, hydroelectric power, recreation, coal mining, railroading, and even gold- and silver-mining.[68] However, it concentrated on encouraging and promoting—investing only to the degree necessary to attract private capital[69]—and promoted these enterprises as components of the regional economy, not as Mormon businesses.

Ward records of the 1890s show that the Relief Society continued to supply food, clothing, bedding, and funds for the needy; and care for the sick, bury the dead, and comfort the bereaved. Ward societies also organized special projects to raise needed goods for the poor, even held surprise parties for them, and assisted the families of men called on proselyting missions. During the depression of the 1890s, the Relief Society loaned seed grain to needy farmers and gave wheat to the drought-stricken.[70] Per capita ward expenditures for welfare from fast offering, tithing, and Relief Society sources fluctuated between $.33 and $.47 per year between 1890 and 1915; the First Presidency and Presiding Bishopric also disbursed large amounts.[71]

As the nineteenth century became the twentieth, three elements of Mormon welfare remained firmly in place: a commitment to care for the poor in local units, the responsibility of the bishop, and the assistance of the Relief Society. The church still made member self-reliance a high priority; but it now encouraged its members to seek success within the secular economy and abandoned the goal of group self-sufficiency. The isolated and insulated Mormon economy became a pursuit of the past, while the Zion society receded into a millennial future.[72]

CHAPTER 5

Twentieth-Century Welfare

1900–1930

BY THE DAWN of the twentieth century, all of the arable land in traditional Mormon country had been settled and even overpopulated. After Brigham Young's death in 1877, church leaders had encouraged further expansion, although not supporting it financially; and by 1910, a Mormon corridor extended from southern Alberta to northern Mexico. Simultaneously, the gathering ended; and official policy encouraged building Zion in one's own locale.

Economically, self-reliance became primarily individual, while the law of consecration and the United Order gradually became esoteric concepts to be lived in a millennial future. Most Mormons continued to farm or find individual employment. However, concern for those in poverty had not lessened. Contrary to a common misconception, the Church of Jesus Christ of Latter-day Saints operated a systematic welfare program during the first thirty years of this century. During the 1920s the program became more complex; and from that foundation rose the edifice of the Church Welfare Plan of 1936.

Between 1900 and 1930, local leaders—both the bishopric and the Relief Society—continued to care for routine needs. Essentially in response to special needs, the Presiding Bishopric directed and coordinated the welfare program at the general level, with the Relief Society taking considerable independent action, as well as supporting the bishopric's efforts. This central program supplemented the ward activities conducted by bishops and Relief Society presidents. Because of the combination of central and local effort accompanying the emergence of urban-centered economic challenges, welfare was more comprehensive in the Salt Lake City area than elsewhere. Also the Relief Society developed a social services program restricted geographically but analogous to the much later professional church programs.

The standards of care in this pre-1930 welfare program may appear meager in comparison with present expectations, but they were more elaborate and comprehensive than those of any of the contemporary private or public agencies.[1]

The National Economic Setting

Nationally, the hallmarks of the period were industrialization and urbanization. Railroading had reached its apogee and the era of motor transportation was dawning. The rapid spread of electric power generation was changing both home and industry, at least in the urban setting. Industrial firms were growing still larger, but the impetus was shifting from the transformation of raw materials into intermediate products, such as steel, to consumer production, such as the automobile and the radio.

European immigration reached its peak with over 8 million new entrants between 1900 and 1910, dropping back to 5 million during the next decade. Mechanized agriculture displaced rural Americans. Mass production and the assembly line drew both populations into the burgeoning cities, where slums and ghettoes housed an increasing number of these newly urbanized citizens. Industrial employees struggled to unionize against great opposition. A central bank and currency system was created to shield the country against the recurrent money panics of the previous century, but the lack of contiguity between production and consumption created the business cycle as a new form of economic instability. Government regulations began to limit the extremes of *laissez faire* capitalism, and a new "conservation" movement began to protect natural resources, heretofore deemed inexhaustible.

After recovering from the decade-long 1890s depression, manufacturing, transportation, and communications industries generally flourished throughout the period, except for a serious but brief depression following World War I. Agriculture prospered and expanded from 1900 through World War I, mostly by taking over world markets from a war-devastated Europe. Sharp legislative reduction in immigration after World War I slowed the growth of the u.s. population and, hence, the potential demand for agricultural products. Farm prices were low, while the prices of the products required by farmers were high.[2] As a result, the agricultural depression continued throughout the 1920s.

The formation of the Utah Copper Company in 1902 coincided with the nation's new need for copper-cored electrical wire, and

Utah's open-pit copper mine at Bingham became the state's largest employer. Lead, zinc, and coal mines had also become more important in Utah's economy, providing more jobs in good times but tying the state's economic well-being to the fortunes of those cyclical industries and the vagaries of absentee ownership. The demands of World War I had increased mining capacity beyond post-war demands, leading to stagnation during the 1920s.[3]

Mormon missionary effort was at a low ebb during the long European war; and thereafter new immigration laws restricted the trickle of converts who, without official encouragement, still wished to "gather." "Mormon country" was still a solid core in Utah, southeastern Idaho, and northern Arizona; but the Great Basin kingdom of Brigham Young had become an economic colony with little control over its economic destiny and little possibility of self-sufficiency.

The Presiding Bishopric's Welfare Role, 1900–1914

Poverty became less severe as the 1890s depression ended, but it did not disappear. Even in prosperous times, residual unemployment, old age, chronic illness, family crises, divorce, abandonment, and social maladjustment continued to produce a steady need. LDS areas were subject to the same problems as elsewhere.

For the most part, the general prosperity in agriculture between 1900 and the close of World War I stemmed from such export crops as wheat and corn, neither of them a crop in which Utah had comparative advantage. Rural overpopulation remained a significant problem in Mormon country, given the low carrying capacity of the mountainous and arid terrain. Those who remained on the land lived in grueling subsistence, never affluence.

And in urban areas, especially Salt Lake City, welfare needs steadily increased for three reasons. The Mountain West was following the national drift of population from rural areas to the cities in search of a more attractive life-style and greater economic opportunities. New Mormon immigrants to Utah, mainly city dwellers, also tended to remain in the Salt Lake vicinity. In addition, LDS unemployed, wherever their residence, gravitated toward church headquarters. Consequently, from 1900 to 1914, welfare problems were much greater in Salt Lake City—per capita as well as in total numbers—than elsewhere in the church.[4]

During the transition from the 1880s to the early twentieth century, agriculture in Mormon areas followed the national trend and became increasingly commercialized. Farmers paid more tithing in cash and less in kind. By 1900, 60 percent of all tithing was paid in cash; by 1908, this figure had risen to more than 83 percent.[5] During that year the Presiding Bishopric, deciding to discontinue the operation of the Bishop's General Storehouse in Salt Lake City, requested that ward bishops dispose of tithing in kind locally. During the transition of the next few years, local tithing offices and granaries also fell into disuse.

The basic system of Mormon relief during the early twentieth century remained primarily in the local bishops' hands. Joseph F. Smith, president of the church between 1901 and 1918, made one of the most direct and forceful public statements of this policy in October 1916:

> When a man is ordained a bishop . . . he becomes a father to the people. . . . It is his duty to be acquainted with every member of the church in his ward. It is his duty to minister to every member. . . . It is his duty to look after the poor, the needy, the sick and the afflicted, not that he himself is expected to do everything that is to be done in his ward, not at all; but through the agencies that he may call to his support to perform the duties that are requisite to be performed in the ward.[6]

Seventeen years earlier, in 1899, the Presiding Bishopric had issued the first handbook of instructions to stake presidents and bishops describing their responsibilities, a practice which has continued to the present. A substantial section of each handbook gave the bishops detailed instructions on collecting and handling tithing and fast offering funds. Additions and minor changes appeared in the fourteen editions issued between 1899 and 1928. The 1928 handbook, unchanged until 1934, provides a useful summary of local policies related to relief. The bishop was to be "personally acquainted with the conditions of the poor" in his ward, with the Relief Society "operat[ing] under the direction of the bishopric [as] their chief aid in caring for the poor and unfortunate." Ward teachers were to alert the bishop, and Relief Society visiting teachers the Relief Society president, about any illness, poverty, or distress noted in their at-least monthly visits to assigned homes. The bishopric and Relief Society presidency met at least monthly to plan for relief. Local church officials should help the poor help themselves, then persuade families and county relief officials, in that order, to accept next responsibility before the church took action; but the final charge was to "see in every instance that no Church member suffers for lack of the necessities of life."

The church's obligation was to the "worthy poor," whose poverty was caused by such "unfavorable conditions" as "sickness, injury, infirmity, unemployment, lack of education, poor management, or mental or physical deficiency." Therefore, after necessary emergency help, "persons trained in social service work, and possessed of sympathy and good judgement" (the Relief Society's professionally trained caseworkers) investigated the recipient's religious activity and causes of poverty. After this investigation, the bishopric, in consultation with the Relief Society presidency, developed "a well-defined plan" relating assistance directly to the roots of the family's poverty and leading to permanent self-sufficiency, when possible.

In the early part of the twentieth century, the Presiding Bishopric tried to increase and regularize the payment of fast offerings, which then began to fill a greater percentage of charitable expenditures. Early handbooks reminded ward bishops to ask members for donations at least equal to what they saved by fasting, to collect fast offerings monthly, and to send the surplus to headquarters for use in wards where local sources were inadequate. However, rarely did any ward use less than its members contributed.[7]

Funds for charity came "from the fast offering, the Relief Society Poor Fund, private benevolences, and, when conditions render it necessary, from the tithing funds." The bishop directed all disbursements, although "funds collected by the Relief Society may be disbursed by the Relief Society officers for emergency and other purposes, and reported to the Bishops." The handbook encouraged cooperation with local charities to prevent duplication, but organized affiliation required approval from the Presiding Bishop. Details of relief cases were considered confidential.[8]

The 1901 handbook began instructing bishops to provide employment, however minor, to any aid recipient capable of working. If jobs were not available, bishops should assign them work on church properties. In 1903 the Presiding Bishopric announced the revival of the Church Employment Bureau, previously active from 1896 to 1899, to help people find jobs. The Presiding Bishopric also provided special forms for bishops and other ward and stake officers for employment information.[9]

During these early years of the century, President Joseph F. Smith fostered priesthood reform.[10] Part of that reform was to assign young men ordained to the Aaronic Priesthood the responsibility for collecting fast offerings monthly. This system produced a much more consistent level of contributions than before. As another innovation, some bishops sent out self-addressed envelopes for member contributions. The Presiding Bishopric recommended the practice to all bishops in 1908, and it eventually became standard procedure.[11]

Specific ward reports illustrate some aspects of the system. In

1907, for example, the Preston First Ward of the Oneida Stake in Idaho disbursed $148.90 during the year to several people in the ward, mainly because of poverty or sickness. This money was paid from $103 received in fast offerings and $45.90 in donations to the Relief Society. The Ephraim Second Ward of South Sanpete Stake used $574.50 for relief, of which $215.95 came from fast offerings, $146.55 from Relief Society donations, $200 from tithing, and $12 from other sources. Most of the funds went to widows. The Twenty-second Ward in Salt Lake Stake spent $961.47, which came from fast offerings, tithing, and Relief Society donations. Eighteenth Ward, also in Salt Lake Stake, used $1,672.22 for poor relief from the same sources to help 152 families in 1907; problems included being out of work, sickness, old age, and blindness. In 1910 the bishop of Salt Lake City's Second Ward reported that the ward paid the hospital and funeral expenses of a nonmember, supported his wife and five small children with money, food, coal, and clothing, and provided them "with Christmas." The bishop explained that all needy families in his area were looked after systematically and that suffering could not long continue because the Relief Society visited every family monthly and reported to him all needy cases. [12]

The Presiding Bishopric kept careful note of the ward bishops' expenditures but, except in selected years, did not make systematic records of central spending. Similar gaps mar the account of charity disbursed from the trustee-in-trust account, provided directly from the church president, presumably to individual cases. However, most central expenditures came from tithing. After 1915 the First Presidency usually included the total of funds disbursed for charitable purposes in semi-annual general conference reports. In some years, this figure was much greater than the amount accounted for in Presiding Bishopric records. The accounting report may thus have included as charity some forms of church employment, certain building expenses, or part of mission office upkeep. Church pensions, for which there are only scattered references, may also have been included.

For example, in April conference 1916, Joseph F. Smith reported that $3,279,900 had been paid to the poor during the previous fifteen years through all church channels, an average of $218,660 per year. Four years earlier, in April conference 1911, he announced that "over $200,000" had been used for this purpose during 1910. Presiding Bishopric Office records show that $135,153 was spent directly in the wards during 1910. An additional $28,787 had been spent in missions or by the Presiding Bishopric. These figures of Presiding Bishopric-supervised charity totaled $163,951, leaving over $36,000 unaccounted for, unless it was disbursed through the trustee-in-trust account.

Although the number assisted before 1915 cannot always be ascertained, generally around 5 or 6 percent of the members received help in any given year. In 1907, for example, 14,230 people were assisted in wards out of a population of 288,970, or 4.9 percent. During 1908 a total of 17,734 were aided out of 301,693 members in wards, which equals 5.9 percent. In 1915, 19,547 members, or 5.2 percent, received charitable assistance—4,497 or 23 percent of these permanently enrolled throughout the year.

The per capita welfare expenditure in wards from fast offerings, Relief Society collections, and tithing was about 47 cents in 1891 and a penny less in 1895, probably reflecting the severity of the 1890s depression. Then it dropped to 33 cents for 1900, climbed to 38 cents for 1905 and 39 cents in 1910, before rising to 45 cents in 1915, which approximated that expended during the depression years of the 1890s. These proportions, of course, did not include other donations nor the central accounts of the Presiding Bishopric and trustee-in-trust. From the early 1890s to 1901, the fast offering per capita alone varied between 12 and 16 cents. From 1901 to 1909, following steady emphasis in the handbooks and more prosperous times, it rose from 12 to 20 cents, where it remained until it began to rise again after World War I.

Because of the higher welfare expenses in Salt Lake City, a greater percentage of welfare funds came from tithing. For example, during 1906 Salt Lake City wards used about 40 percent of the tithing, fast offerings, and Relief Society collections spent by all wards. In 1915 this figure had dropped to 34 percent. In addition, most of the Presiding Bishopric and trustee-in-trust sums were disbursed for relief assistance in the city. Yet Salt Lake City membership was only about 13 to 14 percent of the total membership, excluding missions.

In addition to its support of its own members, the church also participated in humanitarian relief. Coal-mining disasters at Scofield in 1900 and Castle Gate in 1924, both in Utah, brought prompt church response even though few members were involved. Nearly $100,000 in cash and several dozen carloads of food and supplies went to the victims of the San Francisco earthquake in 1906. Besides assistance sent to Europe for church members during and after World War I, the church also sent $110,000 to the European Relief Council and the Near East Relief Committee during 1914–21.[13] Significantly, church leaders announced a special fast day 23 January 1921, with the funds earmarked for Near East relief.[14] Church leaders were also generally supportive of progressive and reformist legislation, including work-

place health and safety, resource conservation, economic development, and social welfare; however, they were not favorable to organized labor and had no sympathy for socialism.[15]

The Relief Society and Social Welfare, 1914–1930

Compassionate service was the core purpose of the Relief Society, both at its inauguration in Nauvoo and its reemergence in the
Great Basin. Training women to perform such service in homes and
communities was a natural outgrowth of its mission. In the early
years of the twentieth century, the Relief Society continued to collect
and store grain and encouraged women to enter the health-care professions.[16] Beginning in 1902, it sponsored a church-wide curriculum
to replace lessons created strictly on the local level, with instruction
ranging from civics to mother education. In 1905 the Relief Society
also established an employment service for women parallel to that established primarily for men by the Presiding Bishopric two years earlier. To ensure suitable employment for young rural women moving
to the city, it investigated working conditions, monitored wage rates,
and operated a boardinghouse.[17] On the health front, the Relief Society
maintained a school for practical nurses and midwives between 1898
and 1924, administered through its Deseret Hospital in Salt Lake City.
The LDS Hospital, completed in 1905, cared for the poor free and
sponsored a three-year nursing program in which the church defrayed
most of the personal expenses.[18]

During World War I, American ward Relief Societies became units
of the national Red Cross and intensified their concern for social welfare. This new emphasis, a logical outgrowth of the prewar concern
for civic betterment, carried over well into the 1920s and found a natural expression in urban social work. Urbanization trends not only increased social problems but made them more visible, decreased the
availability of the extended family, and decreased neighbor-to-
neighbor help. According to the 1920 federal census, for the first time
more Americans lived in urban areas than on farms. Private social
welfare agencies all across the country multiplied during the 1920s.
Local and state public relief and health and welfare institutions were
expanding at the same time, but their role was still minor. The national political climate of the 1920s, unfavorable to government
expansion of social services, encouraged the movement of private institutions into these areas. The Relief Society was a vigorous part of
this national process.

The Relief Society's involvement in trained, as contrasted to neighborly, relief work began when the federal government assigned the Red Cross responsibility in 1917 for needy families of American military personnel. The Relief Society volunteered to do this work for LDS families, and the Red Cross accepted the offer, provided that the Relief Society would train its workers to Red Cross standards. Consequently, four LDS women attended the first Home Service course given by the Western Division of the Red Cross in Denver during the autumn of 1917. They then helped direct the Home Service work in Salt Lake City, Ogden, Cache Valley, and Utah Valley.[19]

Because of this experience, Relief Society leadership and several General Authorities became more aware of social welfare philosophy, methods, and problems. Amy Brown Lyman, one of the original four Denver trainees, served as Relief Society general secretary, later became a counselor in its general presidency and, from 1940 to 1945, served as its general president. She read widely in social work, attended many national social welfare conferences, and served on numerous state and local welfare boards, both public and private.[20]

The Social Advisory Committee, made up of the heads of the five church auxiliary organizations and Apostle Stephen L Richards, encouraged the church to study and adopt current social welfare practices. Created in November of 1916 by the First Presidency to study and make recommendations on such things as church dress and dance standards, the committee soon began studying social problems and their solutions. After attending the National Conference of Social Work in Kansas City during May 1918, Richards urged LDS organizations to be current on social welfare. "If we are not the leaders in the social work in our communities," he explained, "strangers come in and take up the work."[21]

Joseph F. Smith, concerned about outside social welfare agencies handling LDS cases, showed a deep interest in Amy Brown Lyman's reports of the Denver Red Cross institute and he encouraged her to further her education in social welfare.[22] At the close of the war, upon the recommendation of Stephen L Richards, needy families of LDS military personnel under the Red Cross were assigned to the Relief Society rather than to the Charity Organization Society, the major private Salt Lake City non-Mormon social service organization. With this added responsibility, with increasing demands on church assistance, especially in Salt Lake City, and with the growing need to cooperate effectively with other welfare agencies, Relief Society leaders established a Social Service Department in January 1919, with Amy Brown Lyman as director. A similar department was organized for Utah Stake in Provo four months later.[23]

For the next decade, the Relief Society Social Service Department served as a relief and coordinating center to cooperate with other private and public welfare agencies in caring for needy LDS families. Inevitably, the society became deeply involved in community welfare developments. Almost all of this work was centered in Salt Lake City, but it occasionally cooperated with other urban agencies even outside of Utah.

These innovations were undertaken without diminishing the society's emphasis on health care. It continued to encourage nurses' training even after the accreditation movement kept the Relief Society from operating its own instructional program. Concerned for children's health, the Relief Society in 1916 introduced stations to supply milk, particularly to the children of immigrant families, lobbied for sanitation and pasteurization, operated maternity-care facilities, and encouraged dental clinics.

The Relief Society's forty-year tradition of wheat storage was climaxed in the spring of 1918, when the federal government purchased two hundred thousand bushels for the war effort. The Relief Society presidency hesitated, but the Presiding Bishopric concluded the sale on its own authority, later apologizing while the Relief Society reciprocated by approving the sale. The church received some positive national publicity, and the participating Relief Society units banked the cash.[24]

Four years later at the Relief Society semi-annual conference in April 1922, President Clarissa S. Williams recommended that the wheat fund, now totaling $412,000 with interest, be centralized under the Presiding Bishopric's funds with the yearly interest available for maternity, health, and child welfare projects on the local level. This plan was subsequently carried out. The Relief Society General Board added child welfare study to the curriculum and continued to support practical nursing classes. The Primary Association, responsible for the instruction and activities of children, enthusiastically undertook to finance and build a Primary Children's Hospital in Salt Lake City, completed in 1922, that provided health care free for poor children.[25]

The many-faceted Relief Society social welfare activities, concentrated in Salt Lake City but encouraged throughout the church, reflected national trends. Social work was characterized during the twenties by a shift from remediation to prevention. Controlling epidemics, for example, gave way to well-baby clinics, regular examinations, health education, and instruction in cleanliness and diet.[26] The Relief Society provided these services either directly or in cooperation with other private or public organizations, a mark of rapidly decreasing xenophobia.

After World War I, the Relief Society continued doing the case work on LDS families who applied at the Red Cross for assistance or who had lingering war-related claims. During the great influenza epidemic after the war, the Relief Society assisted whenever LDS families were involved, taking over some Red Cross cases completely.[27]

In August 1919, a Community Clinic was established in Salt Lake City, where doctors donated free medical service to the indigent. At the request of community leaders, the Relief Society Social Service Department investigated and supervised LDS cases, working closely with the patient's bishop in virtually all cases. By January 1929 the Relief Society had assisted with about 7,300 of the 8,600 patients who received treatment from the clinic.[28]

After the Relief Society Social Service Department began doing case work for the Red Cross and Community Clinic, the Charity Organization Society began referring its LDS cases to the Relief Society as well. The Relief Society Social Service Department either transferred responsibility for applicants to their respective wards or helped them directly, especially if they were transients. Soon other private and public agencies were calling upon the Relief Society Social Service Department for assistance when LDS people were involved.

In September 1921, the Presiding Bishopric, which presided over the Relief Society in welfare matters, allowed the society to register certain classes of clients with the community Social Service Exchange: transients, all unemployed, and "unstable families." The society had created its own church exchange at least three years earlier. The purpose of such "exchanges" across the nation was to help coordinate social agencies and reduce duplication of services. The Presiding Bishopric also authorized the Relief Society to meet with other social agencies in monthly conferences, which in 1924 led to the formation of the Central Council of Social Agencies in Salt Lake. In the 1921 bishops' handbook, the Presiding Bishopric encouraged similar cooperation in other cities. In November 1926, when the cooperating Salt Lake agencies decided to formalize their unofficial policy for sharing the case load, the Relief Society assumed responsibility for all LDS-headed families. The next year, it included Mormon families with non-LDS fathers. In the course of its work, the Relief Society cooperated and worked with over a dozen private social service agencies.[29]

This pattern was not markedly different from that existing elsewhere; for prior to the development of public welfare systems during the mid-1930s, much official and informal cooperation existed between public and private agencies. In the fall of 1919, the juvenile court judge in Salt Lake City requested that the Relief Society Social Service Department help with LDS offenders, and the department was soon working with other courts and penal institutions.

Across the nation, each county had some responsibility, however minor, for assisting the poor. Some of the larger counties maintained infirmaries for the elderly and hospitals for both the indigent and the paying public. During the early twentieth century, most states passed laws requiring either the state or the counties to provide small pensions to poor mothers (usually widows or abandoned wives) of minor children. Utah provided for mothers' pensions in 1919.[30] In the late fall of that year, the Salt Lake County Charity Office asked the Relief Society Social Service Department to investigate and supervise LDS mothers' pension applicants. After September 1921 it also helped the county investigate and supervise LDS families applying for general county assistance. In 1928 and 1929, approximately 330 cases, slightly more than a third of LDS applicants receiving county aid, were processed by the Relief Society Social Service Department. During the depths of the postwar depression in the early 1920s, the department also interviewed unemployed LDS applicants seeking work in the temporary county wood yard.[31]

Often the Relief Society worked with relatives of the needy or with local bishops to supplement the usually inadequate mothers' pensions and general county relief. It helped needy LDS elderly people enter the county infirmary and arranged for county hospitalizations, relieving overcrowded conditions at LDS Hospital. Additionally the Relief Society Social Service Department worked jointly with other public agencies like the Utah State Department of Health, to help needy Saints. The church policy on public assistance for Latter-day Saints was that, as citizens, they paid their fair share of taxes and hence had legitimate claims on relief available to the public. However, both the Relief Society general presidency and the Presiding Bishopric felt the Relief Society Social Welfare Department should interview, counsel, and supervise assistance to LDS families. This desire coincided with that of the understaffed public agencies requesting the administrative help.[32]

The Relief Society also worked for favorable welfare legislation. In 1923, as a member of Utah's House of Representatives, Amy Brown Lyman introduced the bill that accepted the provisions of the federal Maternity and Infancy Act, passed in 1922. Ward Relief Societies all over Utah and, to a limited extent, in several other western states

worked hard to implement this act. In 1925, Lyman helped organize
the Utah State Conference of Social Work; and representatives of the
Relief Society Social Service Department regularly held important
positions in this body, the Community Chest board, and other social
service organizations. After adding mental health to its educational
curriculum in 1926, the Relief Society also lobbied hard for a mental
institution—writing letters, visiting legislators, and submitting peti-
tions containing over twenty-five thousand signatures. In 1929,
Utah's legislature passed the necessary legislation. [33]

Funds for the Relief Society Social Service Department came
jointly from the General Board of the Relief Society and the Presiding
Bishopric. In 1929 its budget was almost $17,000. The salaries of a
ten-to-twelve-person staff, plus minor administrative expenses, accounted for about $12,500 of that sum. (Twelve hundred dollars per
annum in these years was a substantial salary.) The remainder went to
emergency relief.

The Relief Society Social Service Department was not a general
relief disbursing organization, as may be surmised from its limited
emergency funds. Instead, it provided service or relief only to nonres-
idents or transients, who seemed to gravitate to Salt Lake City in increasing numbers. The Relief Society helped place boys in the Lund
Home, a foster facility for LDS juveniles administered by Zion's Aid
Society and financed by the First Presidency. The Relief Society also,
at the Presiding Bishopric's request, inspected various public and
private institutions serving Latter-day Saints. In 1922 the First Presidency assigned the Relief Society Social Service Department responsibility for placing LDS children for adoption. When the state later
required licensing for adoption agencies, the Relief Society applied for
and was granted certification in 1927. In 1922 the Relief Society Social
Service Department reinaugurated its female employment bureau,
suspended during World War I; and by the end of 1929, it had placed
nearly 12,000 women in jobs. [34]

The Relief Society Social Service Department cooperated closely
with wards in Salt Lake City and, to a lesser extent, with wards elsewhere. From 1920 through 1929 it registered 8,409 cases, which included direct applicants plus referrals from the Presiding Bishopric,
other private and public agencies, and ward bishops or Relief Society
presidents. In virtually every case, the Relief Society Social Service
Department tried to plan assistance with the applicant's bishop. As the
decade progressed, it became more common for wards to refer only
their serious or aggravated cases to the department. Thus, the trained
and specialized Relief Society Social Service Department became a

precursor to the modern professional LDS Social Services, incorporated in 1974, which helps with or takes over completely difficult and serious social welfare cases referred to it by bishops, wherever it has regional offices.[35]

Although local bishops and Relief Society presidents disbursed most of the direct assistance in the wards under local officers, in some cases the Social Service Department provided direct relief. To supplement its emergency relief fund, the Relief Society General Board maintained a storehouse which it took over from the Salt Lake stakes in 1925, just four years after it had been established, where they received, renovated, and distributed clothing and furniture.[36] This storehouse resembled the Deseret Industries thrift shops that the church would establish in 1938.

Educational Functions

The Presiding Bishopric counseled the Relief Society leadership to avoid a program made top-heavy by too many trained professionals but rather to focus on local assistance administered by volunteers. Thus, it frequently encouraged the Relief Society to educate local leaders—bishoprics and Relief Society presidencies—in social welfare methods, at the same time preserving the basic Mormon institutional patterns of providing for the poor.[37]

Soon after its founding, the Relief Society Social Service Department began training social work paraprofessionals throughout the church. Amy Brown Lyman compared the department to "a laboratory for experimental work and training purposes." Just as training for nurses must include experience with a variety of patients, she argued, the Relief Society Social Service Department needed a varied case load. A crucial core of Mormon women, with her encouragement, graduated from eastern schools of social work. In 1923 caseworkers began lecturing public health nurse trainees at LDS Hospital and, in 1927, at the University of Utah medical school, clear illustrations of the department's professional status.[38]

Throughout the twenties, the Relief Society Social Service Department became deeply involved in educating local leaders and members in social service ideas and methods. In 1920 the Relief Society conducted an intensive six-week summer school course in family welfare at BYU. Sixty-five of the church's eighty-three stakes sent representatives. By the end of 1930, sixty-three training institutes averaging four weeks each had been conducted in thirty-six localities for 2,985 Relief Society officers and members. Some of these local officers also received additional training and experience by serving as caseworkers in the Relief Society Social Service Department. Social service topics were sermon subjects in stake and general conferences where Relief Society general board members spoke. From 1920 on, one lesson per month in ward Relief Society meetings was devoted to a social welfare topic outlined in the *Relief Society Magazine*.[39]

The Church Charity System during the 1920s

Throughout the 1920s, charity work in the wards continued to be the responsibility of bishops and Relief Societies. Many of the instructions of the Presiding Bishopric continued unchanged. However, the handbooks periodically added clarifications and new instructions. In 1921 it stressed helping needy members find employment through an employment representative and priesthood quorums. In addition to the Relief Society's employment service for women, the Deseret Employment Bureau (as the Presiding Bishopric's facility for men, first established in 1896, was called) was periodically functional, although the records are vague about its activities. (There was no public employment service at the time.) The 1921 handbook also instructed bishops to have ward teachers report cases of want observed during their monthly home visits and reminded the Relief Society president to have her visiting teachers do the same.

Probably more significant were the instructions to tighten organizational links locally. In the past the bishops and Relief Society officers had worked rather independently of each other; now, under the bishop's authority, they were to meet monthly or oftener to define detailed plans for working with the poor and distressed. In late 1921, after the appearance of the handbook, the Relief Society General Board sent a questionnaire to all stakes; the results indicated only limited bishop/president cooperation, indicating a need for the new instructions.[40]

On Lyman's recommendation, visiting teachers took on more social welfare responsibilities. Until early 1921, they reported specific needs in open meetings, decided how much assistance each poor family needed, and delivered the cash or commodities themselves. Under the new system, the visiting teachers reported privately to the ward Relief Society president. The president and the bishop, after an investigation, then decided what kind of and how much assistance to give; either the bishop or the president personally delivered the commodities or cash. In wards with many needy, the Relief Society president could appoint an assistant, later designated as a social service aide.[41]

As the economically stagnant decade dragged on, by circular letter and in bulletins to all bishops during June 1927, the Presiding Bishopric explained that they had to turn away many people seeking employment every day. They reiterated their request that bishops keep members in their own communities, appoint an employment agent, and report any surplus opportunities to the Presiding Bishopric.[42]

In 1928 the Presiding Bishopric sent a new handbook to ward bishops, repeating the previous year's employment instructions, pointing out that worthy needy members could be sent to non-LDS institutions if the latter would accept payment from the ward after services had been rendered, and gave the most extensive outline to date of how "charity work" should proceed in the ward. While affirming the traditional responsibility of the bishop and the Relief Society president, the handbook emphasized the important role of trained though unpaid Relief Society social service workers and their obligation to investigate each case carefully to assure that the recipients were truly needy.[43]

Predictive of future policies was the handbook instruction that the immediate family and close relatives had the primary obligation to meet an individual's needs, also a requirement of public assistance law. Then the county government was responsible, followed by the church. Presiding Bishopric instructions in 1921 had mentioned the responsibility of relatives in conjunction with hospital care and had advised the bishops to use mothers' pension laws in states where they existed. These instructions had coincided with the 1921 Relief Society/county charity organization cooperation in Salt Lake County to aid some LDS families. However, most needy Latter-day Saints continued to receive assistance from the church. Even after 1928 public assistance remained minimal and made no difference in church welfare spending trends until federal relief programs began in 1933.[44]

The percentage of the church population in wards who received some church assistance during the 1920s varied from approximately 4.5 percent in 1920 to about 5.5 percent for most of the decade, approximating the percentage assisted earlier in the century. The percentage rose to 6.5 percent in 1930 as the Great Depression began to be felt. However, the per capita expenditures for ward relief during the twenties climbed by approximately a third over the 1890s and mid-teens and was roughly 60 percent higher during the 1920s than the 1910s. Fast offerings rose from approximately 20 cents per capita during 1910–18 to 33 cents by 1924, which helped meet the increase, but declined to 22 cents toward the end of the decade. Relief Society collections remained fairly stable. Thus, bishops had to use a greater percentage of tithing.

The statistics for the 1920s also illustrate that the Salt Lake stakes consistently spent much more per capita for welfare than other areas of the church. The wards in the six Salt Lake City stakes, with between 13 and 14 percent of the church population, spent about 38 percent of the total church welfare budget from fast offering, tithing, and Relief Society funds during 1925, or $1.77 per capita compared with about 46 cents per capita for wards outside of Salt Lake City. In 1930 the comparative figures were virtually identical. In addition the Presiding Bishopric and Relief Society Social Service Department in both 1929 and 1930 spent nearly an extra $100,000 for charity in the city, or a total of $225,000 for 1929 and $240,000 for 1930, including the ward bishops' expenditures.[45] These sums did not include trustee-in-trust charitable disbursements. President Heber J. Grant (1918–45) stated in April 1931 general conference that total church charity during 1930 amounted to $667,496, suggesting that First Presidency relief expenditures were large.[46]

During this entire period, the church charity system operated in the missions under the direction of mission and branch presidents, but the figures are less complete than those of stakes and wards. In 1920 missions spent $44,499; by 1929 this figure had risen to $68,301, and then the amount for mission charity dropped off in 1930 to $56,574. Per capita welfare spending in the missions was lower than that for the Salt Lake wards but higher than the averages for wards outside the city. But then, rural members could at least grow their own food and had a stronger tradition of neighbor-to-neighbor assistance.[47]

A Welfare Program Preamble

Before the introduction of federal relief spending during the 1930s, the church spent much more on charity and assisted many more people in Utah than either the Community Chest or public charity. Even though the LDS population was not more than 50 percent of Salt Lake County, during 1929 Salt Lake County aided 1,188, while LDS wards in the same area aided more than 7,700, a figure which does not include those assisted by the Presiding Bishopric, general Relief Society, and trustee-in-trust. Relief Society leaders believed—and the statistics agree—that Latter-day Saints, having an organization to which to appeal and to which they might have contributed in the past, generally asked for help more freely than non-

Mormons. Similarly, bishops and Relief Society ward presidents felt more personal responsibility and were more likely to offer assistance than other relief officials. In comparison with the rest of the states during the twenties, Utah was one of the lowest in public spending for charitable purposes but much higher than average in expenditures for education and road maintenance.[48] Thus, public funds were available for welfare but, in terms of the standards of the time, could be spent on education and roads because the church was shouldering the charity burden.

In the summer of 1925, a national Red Cross representative visiting Salt Lake City commented to Presiding Bishop Sylvester Q. Cannon, "We realize today that one of the greatest problems in the matter of welfare is in the rural districts. I believe the Relief Society of the Mormon Church is in a position to do and is doing more good in that respect than any other organization that I know of."[49] After personally inspecting the church's welfare works during the winter of 1929, the field secretary of a national social welfare organization wrote to John Wells, a counselor in the Presiding Bishopric: "The church is certainly doing a great deal for its people and I would like to say to you something that I have said ever since my return to New York—I believe that your church group as a whole has the most socialized outlook on welfare matters [of] any other group that I have come in contact with."[50]

The vacuum in church care of the needy that presumably existed from the late nineteenth century to the inauguration of the more formalized welfare program in the 1930s, was in fact no vacuum at all. The LDS Church was engaged in providing an impressive array of welfare services, services that were, for their time, markedly progressive and, in the case of the professional Relief Society Social Service Department, on the cutting edge of the new field of social work.

CHAPTER 6

Response
to the Great Depression
1929–1935

ONE HISTORIAN, writing forty years later, would see in the 1936 announcement of the LDS Church Welfare Program "the abrupt end of a comparatively passive chapter in the history of social welfare activity among the Latter-day Saints."[1] Even an on-the-scene official could report to the federal government that it was "clear that the Church proposal came after six years of inaction during the depression."[2] Few, if any, histories of the Mormon experience have sought to refute that charge.[3]

Nevertheless, even in the earliest phases of the depression, local stake and ward leaders went beyond the general program in providing sustenance for needy members, in effect recreating local storehouses after the model of the pioneers. The Presiding Bishopric and the First Presidency gave added counsel, specific directions, and at times special grants which expanded, invigorated, and upgraded the system of church assistance. As early as 1932 the six Salt Lake area stakes (Salt Lake, Granite, Liberty, Pioneer, Ensign, and Cottonwood) were operating as a welfare region—basically using the elements of the same program which would be introduced church-wide in 1936. Other stakes also innovated programs similar to the Salt Lake City system. Rather than being a sudden departure, the 1936 Welfare Program evolved directly out of the experience and practices of the immediate past.

At least as early as 1933, the First Presidency considered creating a new program of church welfare but chose to rely instead on the already strong cooperation between church and public relief officials. However, these ad hoc arrangements became increasingly difficult as public assistance administration became more permanently established and professionalized. The first response of both local and

national government—direct relief—aroused fears among the First
Presidency and Council of the Twelve that "the dole" would sap the
self-reliance of recipients. Simultaneously, frequent statements by the
federal government warned that even its limited assistance would
soon cease, leaving the total burden to local government and private
charity. These factors reinforced a slowly growing awareness that the
church's existing welfare program would collapse under the demands. Between 1930 and 1935, church officials on both a general and
local level first recognized that the depression would not soon recede
and then experimented with longer-lasting solutions. Those efforts
were a necessary prelude to the 1936 announcement of a church-wide
program of relief with the goal of freeing Latter-day Saints from the
perceived dangers of public assistance.

Economic Problems of the Depression

From our perspective sixty years afterward, the Great Depression of the 1930s still ranks as the most serious economic disaster in
American history. The status of the economy had been viewed eu-
phorically almost to the moment of the stock market crash in October
1929. Thereafter, calculated in 1929 dollars, the gross national product fell from $104 billion in 1929 to $74 billion in 1933. National
income declined from $88 billion in 1929 to $40 billion in 1933. Of
particular significance to Utah, farm prices, which had already been
declining steadily after World War I, dropped a catastrophic 61 percent between 1929 and 1933. From 1929 to 1932, national farm income fell from about $13 billion to less than $6 billion. In just four
years' time, net incomes of farm proprietors fell by 68 percent. Net
revenues in the mining industry fell 89 percent, contract construction
83 percent, and manufacturing 65 percent.[4]

Unemployment statistics during the period vary according to the
reporting organization, but they all show a rapid rise in the numbers
out of work. The percentage of the work force unemployed went
from 3 or 4 percent in 1929 to 25 to 30 percent in 1933. This figure
does not include the many who were partly employed, underemployed, or had given up looking for work. And having reached that
low point, the economy mired with only minor fluctuations until
World War II.

State and local governments quickly exhausted their relief resources. The federal government seemed paralyzed before the enor-
mity of the task until gradually, beginning in 1933, a series of direct
relief, work relief, farm and home credit, and farm price support pro-

grams emerged, characterized collectively by Franklin D. Roosevelt's political slogan, the New Deal. The package included such long-term reforms as the Social Security Act, the National Labor Relations Act, and the Fair Labor Standards Act; but they could have no significant effect until private employment was available. Hence, only the direct and work relief programs substantially helped hungry Americans. The series of job-creating programs enumerated later in this chapter employed numbers fluctuating between 2 and 4 million between 1933 and 1941, primarily in significant public works construction.[5] If both direct relief and work relief are included, 20 percent of the u.s. population in 1934 was in families receiving some type of government assistance.

Utah, the center of Mormon population, along with the rest of the intermountain states, was one of the hardest-hit areas of the nation. The regional economy was based on mining, stock raising, farm products, and transportation, industries which had expanded greatly during World War I but which, during the postwar collapse in demand, had slid into a regional depression that lasted throughout the 1920s and then worsened significantly during the 1930s.[6]

There were exacerbating reasons for Utah's poverty. In 1930, well before the full effects of the depression had spread across the nation, only 33.5 percent of the population in Utah was gainfully employed, a smaller proportion than in any other state except for Mississippi's 33 percent. Mississippi had the highest percentage of blacks in the nation, while Utah had the highest proportion of children.[7] The actual employment rate for heads of families may have been no worse or no better than was common throughout the nation, but the per capita income—again influenced by large family size—was decidedly low.

Because of the high birth rate and the scarcity of arable soil, the population pressure on the land was intense. During the previous three or four generations, parents had divided and redivided their land among heirs until many farms were too small to support families, especially during the agricultural depression of the 1920s and 1930s. Though no contemporary figures now seem available, an official in the Federal Farm Credit Administration claimed in 1938 that population pressure on Utah farms was greater than in any other place in the United States, with the exception of one Pennsylvania county.[8] The 1920s saw some outmigration to urban areas in the West, particularly to California; however, during the 1930s, as economic prospects dried up everywhere, the number of Utah farms seems to have actually increased. Families were subdividing existing farms or reoccupying abandoned ones. Attempting to wring a living from the land despite low prices, farmers often overstocked their range and overplanted the soil, depleting both and leaving them vulnerable to wind and water erosion. While these practices were not uncommon elsewhere, Utah's population pressures almost certainly intensified the trend. Statistics from the Farm Credit Administration, though inconclusive, suggest that Utah's farm mortgage delinquency rate was even higher than the intermountain area's 1933 rate of 50 percent.[9]

Other statistics reinforce this grim Utah image. The National Industrial Conference Board (NICB) estimated that Utah manufacturing wages, which stood at $23 million in 1929, had dropped to $10 million by 1935. Bureau of Census estimates for the same years were $26 million and $15 million, respectively. With a 1929 index equal to 100, the NICB estimated that the agricultural income in the state, already depressed, dropped to 49 in 1932 and then rose to 72 in 1935. The corresponding Department of Agriculture estimates were 44 and 63, respectively.[10]

Despite the decades of acute poverty and deprivation for Utah farmers, subsistence was still less of a problem for Utah's rural population with their cows, chickens, and gardens than it was for city dwellers with their dependence on employment and wages. In November 1932, the presidency of the Grant Stake on the east side of Salt Lake City reported that Southgate Ward was desperate: 110 out of the ward's 173 heads of household were unemployed—a staggering 63.5 percent. Since fast offerings in the stake averaged only $8 per month per ward, the stake presidency appealed to the Presiding Bishopric for relief funds. In Pioneer Stake on the west side of Salt Lake City, over half of the workers were unemployed early in the decade; three bishops and four high councilors were among those who had lost their jobs. Harold B. Lee, then stake president, speaking as an apostle a quarter century later, remembered poignantly the number of families who were deprived of any Christmas celebration.[11] In the northern Utah community of Smithfield, 340 families, comprising 1,200–1,500 individuals out of a total population of 2,400, were either entirely or partly dependent upon some form of assistance by mid-1932.[12]

The statistics represented physical hardship intensified by emotional suffering. Joblessness blighted a father's hopes for himself and his family and damaged his personal esteem. In a nation and state brought up, not only on the work ethic, but also on the more recent philosophy that the poor had nothing to blame for their condition but their own sloth, unemployment spelled shame. Since the LDS scriptures and the sermons of LDS leaders glorified the value of work to an extraordinary degree, loss of self-reliance, even in the presence of a supportive social system, may have inflicted an even greater humiliation on the unemployed Mormon male.[13]

Probably because Salt Lake City was the only major concentration of urban Mormons, and perhaps because the problems were more visible to them there, church leaders focused their major relief efforts in that city. During the latter 1920s and into the 1930s, they had counseled church members to remain in their rural communities, rather than move to urban centers in search of work. Agricultural depression had frequently made this counsel difficult to follow. In addition, numerous anecdotes circulated about the relative ease of obtaining assistance closer to church headquarters; some converts of convenience and even some nonmembers claiming church membership swelled the relief rolls. While there are no statistics to document the magnitude of these reported problems, the repeated requests for assistance made to Salt Lake City bishops by both members and local public officials during this period made relief needs a more visible issue than in the rural areas where, reportedly, neighbors quietly helped neighbors and most raised at least some foodstuffs.[14]

As noted earlier, both before and during the depression, available statistics for Utah and Salt Lake City indicate that a higher proportion of the LDS population received relief than non-LDS people.[15] In addition to the genuine needs described above, the higher levels of aid may have been a function of the church's availability and delivery organization, while its long tradition of responsibility no doubt motivated leaders to supply help and members to seek it. The general presidency of the Relief Society believed that the Latter-day Saints would more readily ask for assistance while bishops and Relief Society presidents were more likely to seek out and assist the needy than were other denominations and public officials. Both local leaders and members believed that, through their own or their ancestors' payment of tithes and fast offerings, those in need had a right to church assistance. Furthermore, adding to the imbalance, nonmembers in Salt Lake City were more likely to be office employees of large businesses like Kennecott Copper Corporation and less likely to become unemployed—though working miners in mining towns like Bingham and Price certainly had no such cushion.

Early Responses to the Depression, 1930–1933

Early in 1930, long before any level of government attempted to meet the obvious problems, LDS Church leadership began responding to the deepening crisis. In February, the Presiding Bishopric met with the presidents of the six stakes in the Salt Lake Valley and with the executive committee of the Deseret Employment Bureau, which had again been reactivated in 1929.[16] This bureau had been founded by the church in 1896 and operated sporadically according to need thereafter; its first public counterpart in Utah would not be organized until 1934.

Under the chairmanship of Henry D. Moyle, businessman/lawyer and Cottonwood Stake president, this group of men began treating their stakes as a regional unit, organizing themselves into a joint committee on employment. The long-lasting welfare orientation of the church from the 1930s through the 1970s undoubtedly stems from the fact that four of the six stake presidents—Hugh B. Brown, Harold B. Lee, Henry D. Moyle, and Marion G. Romney—later became members of the Quorum of the Twelve *and* members of the First Presidency; Lee, Moyle, and Romney successively served as chairman of the Church Welfare Committee, and Harold B. Lee also became church president.

The group agreed to meet periodically at Moyle's call. One of their first initiatives was to enlist ward organizations in both searching for and creating new employment sources. These stake presidents, working through their bishops, organized employment committees in each ward under the direction of the bishopric, consisting of the chairmen of the respective Melchizedek Priesthood welfare committees plus the social service aide of the ward Relief Society.

To increase coordination, the Deseret Employment Bureau, formerly under the direction of the Presiding Bishopric, was assigned to the six-stake executive committee, where it remained until 1932 when it was returned to the Presiding Bishopric's direction. As in the past, it continued to operate almost entirely in the Salt Lake area. During that spring of 1930, it began requiring applicants to bring signed recommendations from their respective bishops, the beginning of efforts to give active church members priority in services.

The Presiding Bishopric envisioned similar arrangements elsewhere throughout the church. On 11 February 1930, they printed a pamphlet, *Ward Charity: Details of Administration,* as a supplement to the 1928 handbook.[17] The supplement was written primarily for cities or larger towns, not for rural areas. As in Salt Lake City, wards and stakes were to organize employment committees. The Presiding Bishopric advised counties or communities with more than one stake to organize joint stake committees. Not only should these committees seek employment for members, but they were also to negotiate public assistance for needy Mormons from county officials. Direct church

relief was a supplement for those who could not obtain aid from relatives or from the county. How widely these guidelines were followed
or how useful they were outside Salt Lake City is unknown, a possible
subject for local research.

In April 1930, the Presiding Bishopric and Relief Society presidency expressed pessimism about the effectiveness of the employment committees and the rising charity costs of the Salt Lake stakes.
However, by the October 1930 general conference, Presiding Bishop
Sylvester Q. Cannon praised the Deseret Employment Bureau for
registering 1,800 men and placing 1,200 of them during the first nine
months of the year; he cited the Relief Society's employment service
for doing "at least as much in the way of getting employment for
women and girls during the same period." He encouraged all bishops
to organize employment committees composed of one high priest,
one seventy, one elder, and one Relief Society representative to identify the unemployed and potential job openings, referring those
unplaced by ward efforts to a corresponding stake committee. He described as a model the "splendid results" of Mar Vista Ward's employment committee in Los Angeles. "I am sure," he said, "that if the
priesthood quorums throughout the various wards of the church will
carry out this plan wherever unsatisfactory conditions prevail, a great
improvement will be manifest."[18] At the same time, Cannon opposed
church public works efforts of the nineteenth-century variety or placing nonmembers through church employment services; government
was the appropriate arm for those efforts. He spelled out what he saw
as the church's role:

> The Church is carrying a heavy responsibility to see to it that none
> of the active members of the Church suffers for the necessities of
> life. But in all of this, the effort of the Church authorities, the bish-
> ops, presidents of stakes, and Relief Societies, is to help people to
> help themselves. The policy is to aid them to become independent,
> in order to be able to serve and to help build up the Church, as well
> as the community, rather than to have to depend upon the Church
> for assistance. Yet in times of need,—and there are such times that
> come to many people—the Church properly steps in and under-
> takes to help them, and to bring into action other agencies which
> can help to promote better conditions and the avoidance of suffer-
> ing.[19]

Concerned with rising costs, the Presiding Bishopric had suggested to the Relief Society during the spring of 1930 that it cut its
staff of paid social workers, urging that the salaried staff be used pri-

marily to train workers at the ward level. In response, the Relief Society returned to the social service institutes it had sponsored between 1920 and 1928. One delegate from each of twenty-five stakes in Utah and nearby states came to Salt Lake City for six weeks of intensive training, 18 August–27 September 1930, including fieldwork with non-church public and private agencies in the city. Two more training sessions were held for new delegates during 1931. Stake presidents were instructed to use the graduates as "social service aides," releasing them from all other church duties so that they could do local social work full-time—helping ward leaders with investigations, training parents to make frugal budgets, and participating generally in plans for restoring the needy to self-sufficiency.[20] In another effort to reduce costs, the stake Relief Society presidencies in Salt Lake City organized employment committees to act under the direction of the general Relief Society employment agency, reducing the need for paid staff.

As part of this extended consideration of charity, the Presiding Bishopric with approval from the First Presidency requested that all stake presidencies and bishoprics during April 1930 stress tithing in all church meetings and through the ward teachers, a practice which was repeated periodically throughout the decade.[21]

Throughout these discussions, both the Presiding Bishopric and the Relief Society presidency intensively considered how to solve the unemployment problems besetting church members, but their repeated hope that special employment committees or rehabilitative counseling by fieldworkers would have a major impact betrays that they had not fully grasped the magnitude of the national economic disaster. Such statements reflected the Hoover administration's assurances of early recovery. However, the church was already laying the foundation for a full-fledged program that would come nationally only in Franklin D. Roosevelt's third year.

Several church leaders spoke on unemployment in October 1930 general conference, urging neighbors to help each other and requesting bishops to see that no one suffered for physical necessities. They stressed the value and morality of work, reminded the Saints to pay their tithes and fast offerings, asked local leaders to try to find jobs for the unemployed, and relieved the shame of unemployment by assuring the jobless that they were not "idlers."[22]

Out of a church population in wards and stakes of about 533,000 in 1930, church welfare efforts assisted 34,670 at least for a short time, nor were more than a fraction of that number dependent upon such help for the entire year. Still, this figure represented a 17 percent increase over the approximately 29,000 assisted in 1929. The total 1930 relief disbursements in wards came to $349,065. The Relief Society contributed $24,345 in interest from its wheat fund, more than doubling its 1929 contribution of a little over $12,000. The annual average of relief costs for the 1920s, minus the wheat fund, had been approximately $302,000.[23] In other words, the church had already been spending near its maximum during the long agricultural depression of the 1920s. Even with good will and increased efforts, there was little additional money available for the intensifying needs of 1930. Most of the welfare expenditures of the 1920s had come from fast offerings; tithing was the chief 1930–32 source.

Besides direct disbursements in the wards, the general church spent approximately another $100,000 on charity in Salt Lake City, while mission offices, branches, and districts paid out nearly $40,000 for welfare in 1930, an increase from 1929, but a drop from the previous two years. Again, escalating needs simply outpaced resources. Another $22,000 paid missionary medical bills and other assistance. Thus, welfare in 1930 took about $535,000 altogether, virtually none of it for administrative expenses. Heber J. Grant, church president from 1918 to 1945, reported in the April 1931 general conference that the church had spent $667,496 for welfare during 1930, but this larger sum probably included some salaries of church employees, direct charitable expenditures by the First Presidency, and other related costs.[24]

The high relief spending in the Salt Lake area may reflect either greater need or readier access. In 1930, membership in the Salt Lake area stakes stood at almost 71,000, or 13.3 percent of church members in stakes. Bishops in these stakes disbursed about $132,500 in 1930, nearly 38 percent of expenditures by bishops for relief throughout the church. Yet in addition, the Presiding Bishopric and Relief Society presidency spent an additional $100,000 in the city. Thus, more than 46 percent of the church welfare budget went to 13 percent of the members.[25]

The historical cooperation between state and local civic officials which had begun after statehood in 1896 intensified during the early 1930s. The Relief Society had pioneered this community-based cooperation during the late teens and 1920s (see Chapter 5), its Social Service Department holding joint staff meetings with the County Department of Charities and the private Family Service Society. To prevent duplication, most relief institutions of Salt Lake City and County, public and private, used the Social Service Exchange as a case clearing house. Most of the private agencies, including the LDS Relief Society, worked together in the Community Chest which had been organized in 1926. During 1930 Community Chest agencies spent $150,000 in Salt Lake City (the church contributed $5,000) compared with church relief expenditures of about $250,000.[26]

In the fall of 1930, President Herbert Hoover suggested that the nation's mayors organize broad-based unemployment committees. Salt Lake Mayor John F. Bowman convened such a committee in October. Remembering that during the war the church had, at the request of the federal government, inventoried the food and fuel in Utah, Bowman requested church cooperation in making a citywide, house-by-house unemployment survey. This unemployment census was completed in early November under the direction of John Whitaker, the Deseret Employment Bureau manager. In addition to its regular relief program, the church then contributed over $12,000 and almost 420,000 pounds of fruits and vegetables to the mayor's committee. Other civic organizations contributed food, coal, and clothing. All three—the church, the Community Chest, and the county welfare department—delivered these supplies to the needy throughout the winter.[27] This winter's shared effort was the beginning of even greater welfare cooperation between the church and the other public and private organizations during the next several winters.

There was little change in church welfare during 1931. Ward welfare funds were mainly fast offerings, Relief Society donations, and, with permission from the Presiding Bishopric, tithing. In addition to the central Relief Society storehouse, many ward Relief Societies began to stockpile food and clothing in storage rooms.[28] Heber J. Grant, the Presiding Bishopric, and the Relief Society presidency were receiving letters from throughout the church asking for assistance. In most cases, they advised writers to contact their bishops. Fast offerings had increased from $113,827 in 1930 to $127,945 in 1931, a remarkable achievement considering how hard-pressed the Saints were themselves. Still, it was inadequate, and the Presiding Bishopric received numerous letters from bishops asking permission to use tithing for welfare funding. Charitable expenditures from tithing increased from $130,836 in 1930 to $151,198 in 1931; and Relief Society assistance also moved upward from $86,618 to $93,883. The number of members given some help in the wards increased from 34,670 to 45,718 between the two years. Wards spent $385,465 for charity during 1931, an increase of approximately $36,400 or about 9.5 percent. Of the total, $172,949 or 45 percent was used in the six Salt Lake stakes, while the four stakes in Salt Lake Valley outside the city used only $13,279. Mission field expenditures increased from $16,000 to $56,000.[29]

During the October 1931 general conference, several General Authorities stressed the continuing significance of Mormonism's heritage and values, especially during troubled times. For example, Charles W. Nibley, second counselor in the First Presidency, explained that the United Order (by which he clearly meant the Ohio/Missouri law of consecration and stewardship) was the Lord's plan for overcoming such economic problems as the depression. The Saints, through tithing and fast offerings, he said, were "only ten percent in the United Order. Why could we not be twenty percent or forty percent or all?" Members must overcome selfishness and seek equality because "'if ye are not one, ye are not mine.'"[30]

Apostle Melvin J. Ballard concurred, predicting recurring depressions until the Lord's plan became established. Ballard added that modern society had succeeded marvelously in mass production but had failed to create equally effective means of mass distribution. That assessment encapsulated what ultimately became the prevailing view of economists about the causes of the Great Depression; it predicted the consequent policies of income redistribution and purchasing power maintenance, two devices used to prevent a recurrence of catastrophic depression. Ballard also chastised the "stingy" rich for finding it so hard to "pay an honest tithe when they made so much money" and warned the poor "not to be possessed of the spirit of Bolshevism that would unlawfully take possession of that which does not belong to them."[31]

In similar vein, Presiding Bishop Sylvester Q. Cannon preached that the "teachings of Mormonism . . . stimulate in those who accept them the spirit of consecration of their time, means and efforts to the welfare of others as well as themselves." Payment of tithing and fast offerings was "a most effective test of our faith in God and his work," a test that church members met heroically. In ward areas where the majority of the people were LDS, he declared, the bishops should ensure that none lacked food and shelter, whether LDS or not. Cannon also summarized the classic advice: "Live within your income, cultivate thrift, get out of debt, avoid speculation, pay as you go, patronize home industry and overcome selfishness." He told agriculturists to "watch the markets and avoid overproduction," to diversify, and to produce their own food.[32]

Funds controlled at the general level continued to be concentrated on relief in Salt Lake City. The Relief Society, for example, was responsible for transients; and Salt Lake City, with its crossroads location, appeared to become a kind of Mecca for them during the depression. Funds could also be solicited from wealthier neighborhoods for special cases. When a bishop and his family of ten children in Tintic Stake lost their home and all household effects in a fire, the Presiding Bishopric approved the Relief Society General Board's request to canvass well-to-do stakes for assistance. The Presiding Bishopric also made selective loans. For example, in December 1931, it loaned funds to two wards in Young Stake, New Mexico, so the members could buy feed for their animals. At the April 1932 general conference, President Grant reported that the church had spent $679,980 for charity during 1931—$224,556 from tithing and $455,423 from fast offering and Relief Society sources.[33]

The cooperation between church and public officials, especially in Salt Lake County, is wholly natural given historical conditions. Public welfare was a local responsibility at the time, and non-Mormons were relatively few except in mining towns; thus, any separation of church and government in welfare matters would have been artificial. In an expression of appreciation for the Relief Society-trained workers, the Salt Lake County Commissioner of Health and Charities stated, "If we did not cooperate with the Relief Society, it would mean that within Salt Lake City, Salt Lake County would have to maintain five or six additional workers."[34] During August 1931, Governor George H. Dern, a non-Mormon, appointed Sylvester Q. Cannon chairman of his state-wide unemployment committee, composed of a hundred men, to advise on and implement ways to increase employment. Cannon was also appointed vice-chairman of the Salt Lake City and County advisory committee on unemployment.[35] Local and state governments in Utah did not develop professionally organized welfare programs until required to do so by federal disbursement policies. By sheer continuity in social services for the previous two decades, the Relief Society's professionalism was much greater, the Relief Society and the Presiding Bishoric's employment bureaus were smoothly functioning entities (though overwhelmed by demands), delivery systems for goods and services within wards and stakes were tried and tested, and public and private cooperation to meet civic crises was a traditional virtue.

During the fall of 1931, this cooperative effort organized and stocked a food warehouse in Salt Lake County, which included some clothing and shoes. It was jointly funded by the county, the LDS Church, and the Community Chest. The Utah Coal Producers' Association contributed a thousand tons, greatly alleviating concern about winter fuel needs. To prevent duplication, all welfare orders had to be issued through the Council of Social Agencies, consisting of representatives of the Community Chest, the Relief Society Social Service Department, and the County Charity Department. The assumption was that each agency would issue about one-third of the orders; but because Mormons were the majority and more likely to seek help from the church than from other agencies, almost half of the outgoing goods were distributed by Relief Society orders.

Initially Latter-day Saints applicants brought a referral from their bishop or ward Relief Society president to the Relief Society Social Service Department for verification, then went to the warehouse for the authorized supplies. This cumbersome and time-consuming method was modified in January 1932 so that stake social service workers took the relief slips to the general Relief Society office, and officials there delivered the orders to the county warehouse where the orders were grouped by ward to which deliveries were made by truck about every other week. These supplies were not intended for all of the poor, only for the able-bodied unemployed; the Presiding Bishopric instructed bishops to follow the traditional procedures in directly assisting unemployables like widows, the handicapped, and the aged.

By February of 1932, the warehouse was almost out of funds. The church made a further contribution from central funds which kept the warehouse functioning until April, when it closed in anticipation of greater employment opportunities in the spring. Instead, the sagging economy slumped further, and the relief coalition began planning another warehouse.

During that 1931–32 winter, in addition to the ongoing problems of production, distribution, and direct relief, a delicate social and political problem emerged which would remain a high-profile concern for church and public relief administrators throughout the depression. Because of the increasing demand for limited relief supplies, church officials became acutely aware of the relief burden represented by inactive Mormons and transients, not only in Salt Lake City, but also throughout the church. Taking the view that active and stable Latter-day Saints had first claim on the church's resources, the Presiding Bishopric with the approval of the First Presidency advised bishops to refer inactives to the county. This policy increased the demand on limited county resources and its harassed administrators, some of whom bucked the applicants back to their bishops.[36] It was a never-resolved dilemma: local government officials had legal responsibility for the poor but inadequate funding; the equally strapped church acknowledged a moral responsibility that conflicted with its own remorseless limitations on resources.

For many farmers at many times during the early 1930s, agricultural prices dropped below the costs of harvest labor. Crops rotted unharvested while city residents were unable to buy food. Individual families, then groups (including wards and stakes), made sharecropping arrangements; they provided the harvest labor in return for a share of the crop. As early as the summer of 1930, some bishops and stake presidents were taking the initiative on behalf of their members in organizing such exchanges.[37] Cashless, faithful farmers offered their tithing in kind, which both local bishops and the Presiding Bishopric accepted willingly, establishing makeshift storage facilities from which to distribute the foodstuffs to the needy. To further supplement food supplies, both local governments and the church encouraged people to plant gardens and arranged to irrigate vacant lots.[38]

As the national depression deepened toward its lowest point in 1933 without significant government initiatives, church leaders intensified their pleas for more tithing and fast offerings and for neighborly sharing. Though no reports of the results are available, the response was believed at the time to have been substantial.[39] And though painfully meager in view of the need, this steady course averted feelings of powerlessness and selfishness which might otherwise have overwhelmed the communities and upheld traditional ideals which provided powerful motivation to participate in the production projects that would be organized within the next few years.

In May 1932, the six-stake committee planned to conduct a September survey in each Salt Lake area ward to determine winter needs. However, on 13 June 1932, President Heber J. Grant instructed the Presiding Bishopric to broaden the survey's scope to the entire U.S. membership, cover probable needs of members, both active and inactive, who would require assistance, and predict the projected sum available from fast offerings, tithing, and Relief Society collections during the same period. This census letter was mailed in June with instructions to return the information immediately so that tabulation could be completed by July 10. The results projected a 50 percent increase in the number of families needing assistance during the second half of 1932 over those who had sought help during the first six months.[40] Could the church's existing welfare organization fill those needs by encouraging local leaders and members to greater efforts? It seemed doubtful.

Stake and Ward Initiatives

Many wards and stakes on their own initiative were going beyond the basic program. Granite Stake, a rural stake in the southeast part of Salt Lake Valley, under the presidency of Hugh B. Brown,

Marvin O. Ashton, and Stayner Richards, was probably the most innovative and aggressive in addressing welfare needs during 1929–32. As early as November 1929, it organized a stake welfare and employment committee, began planning work projects for the unemployed in 1930, and in 1931 began implementing them. The stake welfare committee encouraged all stake members with jobs to spread their salaries by hiring unemployed members part-time or for odd jobs. It solicited commodities from farmers, organized sharecropping, and created a wood yard where the unemployed could cut wood which the stake sold or gave to the needy.

The Granite Stake Relief Society under President Emmarretta G. Brown (no relation to Hugh B. Brown) energetically pursued its own stepped-up program. The stake board purchased a steam cooker for canning, which it loaned to its wards, continued its traditional work of making quilts and baby layettes for the needy, but also opened a sewing and clothes shop in October 1931 where the wards worked on rotation. Besides mending and cleaning used clothing, the women made new clothing, some of which the stake purchased for those in need.

In November 1931 the stake opened its own food shop stocked with solicited items, produce harvested on shares, and commodities contributed as in-kind tithing and fast offerings. During the same fall, the stake organized a coal committee, which delivered about 1,700 tons to the needy during the winter. Those who received any of these commodities either paid in immediate labor or signed promissory labor notes to be filled when the stake could provide work. Throughout 1931 stake relief efforts supported an average of about 125 people. By September of 1932 this number had risen to 345.[41]

During the fall of 1932, the County Relief Commission, still chaired by Sylvester Q. Cannon, recognized the Granite Stake Relief Committee as an auxiliary to its own relief organization; Cannon, as Presiding Bishop, formally gave Hugh B. Brown ecclesiastical permission to proceed while Amy Brown Lyman, who served as first counselor in the Relief Society general presidency from 1928 to 1939 and then as president from 1940 to 1945, authorized the stake Relief Society to continue its cooperative efforts under the new rubric. A stake Relief Society aide cleared all names of the needy through the general Relief Society office. The county warehouse filled and delivered bulk orders to the stake warehouse. However, the stake continued its own program to supplement the public relief. Cannon reported on these and other such efforts in other stakes at the October 1932 general conference.[42]

In 1932 Liberty Stake in central Salt Lake City under President Bryant S. Hinckley established the first bishop's storehouse in modern times by remodeling an empty store building. Here they stored and distributed produce and wood for fuel that stake members had sharecropped.[43] Cottonwood Stake, a suburban stake encompassing Murray, Utah, and headed by President Henry D. Moyle, purchased five acres of land in 1932, planted it with fruit trees, and established a cannery, thus providing both work opportunities and food for the needy.[44]

In Pioneer Stake, an urban stake on Salt Lake City's west side, unemployment and poverty were even more acute than in rural Granite Stake. As Paul C. Child, second counselor in the stake presidency, later remembered it, over half of the men had no work in 1932.[45] Harold B. Lee, stake president, school principal, businessman, and city commissioner, with his counselors, Charles S. Hyde and Child, led out in a series of innovative programs that became the pace-setters for the church. The wards had obediently appointed employment directors, but to little avail. By combining the ward fast offerings and, by the Presiding Bishopric's permission, retaining its tithing, Pioneer Stake amassed a small welfare fund which it used not only for direct assistance but for underwriting various projects.

Like other stakes, Pioneer Stake established sharecropping arrangements with farmers within a forty-mile range, storing the commodities in warehouses belonging to stake members that otherwise stood vacant. Unemployed members cleaned and refurbished these facilities. The stake leaders also obtained permission from the owners of idle lots within stake boundaries—a total of forty acres—to plant sugar beets and vegetables which they irrigated, with permission, from city fire hydrants. The farming and harvesting was done by unemployed stake members. Families bottled the vegetables, while the sugar beets were sold as a cash crop. Stake leaders canvassed for home bottling jars, used clothing, and furniture which unemployed members rehabilitated at the warehouses. The stake set up a coalyard on a vacant lot near the railroad tracks and purchased coal at carload prices to distribute to those in need or sell to those able to pay.

Since much of the sharecropped harvest was onions from farms in Davis County north of Salt Lake City, volunteer work teams sorted and bagged them, volunteer mechanics repaired loaned trucks, and volunteer drivers hauled the onions to California, selling them for cash and trading them for citrus fruit. The Relief Society purchased unsalable women's knit suits from surrounding woolen mills and remodeled them, also sewing other clothing from cheaply obtained yardage.[46]

Though Pioneer Stake came to have the most extensive program, similar efforts were under way among the neighboring five stakes, which shared ideas and efforts through their presidents' committee. With the advantage of adjacency, the Salt Lake stakes worked closely with the Presiding Bishopric, the Relief Society general presidency, and the Deseret Employment Bureau, which operated mostly to help members in these six stakes. As unemployment worsened, these general church and stake bodies jointly concluded by August 1932 that the bureau would no longer accept applications and place job seekers directly. Instead, it developed job orders from employers, apprised stake employment representatives of the openings, and allowed them to make the referrals, thereby broadening access and allowing bishops to allocate scarce employment opportunities to the neediest.[47]

By the fall of 1932, all six of the Salt Lake stakes were involved in storehouses and projects to fill them, either as individual stakes or jointly. Food was being gathered and processed, clothing donated and refurbished, and coal furnished free or at wholesale prices. Members planted, tended, and harvested community gardens. The Relief Societies preserved countless bottles of fruit and vegetables. Meat animals were purchased at depressed market prices and slaughtered, the meat being distributed on the same basis. Houses were rehabilitated and sometimes built for needy families by volunteer laborers who received food and clothing.[48]

In short, before the winter of 1932–33 settled over Utah, these six city stakes were acting like the multi-stake welfare regions created in 1936 and were operating a welfare program virtually identical to the 1936 general program. Innovation was certainly not limited to these stakes; documenting and describing other projects offer a fertile field for local historians.[49] But as the only sizeable urban concentration of church population, these Salt Lake stakes had the problems and responses most visible to general church officers.

The Emerging Role of Federal Government

Throughout the nation, as unemployment and relief conditions steadily worsened, pressure mounted for public relief. In January and February of 1932, President Herbert Hoover asked the Red Cross to distribute surplus government flour free to the needy. In areas of heavy Mormon concentration, at the Red Cross's request, the Relief

Society administered this distribution. Finally in July 1932, under strong pressure from Congress, Hoover reluctantly signed the Emergency Relief and Reconstruction Act, which authorized the Reconstruction Finance Corporation (RFC) to lend a limited amount of funds to the states for direct and work relief. Utah received its first loans during August, the summer that the six stakes were joining hands in concerted food production and distribution projects.[50]

The church welcomed the new government assistance. Two months before the signing of the bill, a *Deseret News* editorial called the government the "appropriate agency" to "meet the emergency."[51] At the April 1932 general conference, Anthony W. Ivins, one of the Seven Presidents of Seventy, commented that the cooperation of the government and its citizens was necessary to "overcome the clouds of financial depression."[52] There was no public response by church officials to either the signing or to the first disbursement of funds; but in October general conference, Apostle Joseph F. Merrill stated that "government in times like these ought to give help to the needful to keep people from suffering for the necessities of life." Apostle Stephen L Richards believed that both church and government "were obligated to assist the poor" but was concerned that the resources would be limited and the distribution very difficult.[53] In a bulletin also dated October, the Presiding Bishopric, with the approval of the First Presidency, recommended that the bishops, in addition to using fast offerings and tithing, secure employment and direct relief from federal funds for their needy, a policy they reiterated into the winter of 1932–33.[54]

In Salt Lake City during the winter of 1932–33, the county reopened its commodity storehouse. Unemployed Mormons contacted their bishops, who relayed the order to the Relief Society president or aide, who placed the ward orders with the stake representative. The stake representative took the orders to the Relief Society general office, which cleared and submitted them to the county office. The county, which was partly subsidized by RFC loan funds, either delivered the goods directly to the needy families or to the stake warehouse if the stake had one.[55]

At the April 1933 general conference, Heber J. Grant reported charitable expenditures for 1932 as $715,844—$272,164 from tithing and $443,680 from other sources.[56] The real value would have been substantially greater if there had been a way to estimate the value of sharecropped produce, bottled fruit and vegetables, other items in wards and stakes with supplementary welfare programs, and informal neighbor-to-neighbor aid. It is not clear how the reported figures were compiled, but they may have included LDS hospital expenses for the poor, the central Presiding Bishopric relief accounts, and the trustee-in-trust central accounts for welfare. Grant's 1932 figures represented a 5 percent increase from 1931, a small increase but the fourth straight year of climbing costs. It was also the highest level; not until 1936 with the new church-wide Welfare Program did the funds spent on welfare rise above the 1932 figures. Predictably, the numbers of church members assisted, either temporarily or permanently, in 1932 exceeded those of any previous year and set a high-water mark that also stood until 1936. Again predictably, the largest stake relief totals were for the six Salt Lake area stakes. Mormon expenditures were $715,844 in 1932, declined to $512,776 in 1933, rose slightly to $518,266 in 1934, and rose again to $586,749 in 1935.[57] The lower figures from 1933–35 may be attributed to stronger public programs, which began in 1933, or slight improvements in the national economy before it declined again in 1937 and 1938.

The Presiding Bishopric and the Relief Society presidency continued their cooperation with city and county welfare agencies during 1933. Amy Brown Lyman revived a movement to create a state department of public welfare for Utah to coordinate all public relief and social welfare efforts.[58] In general conference during October 1933, Sylvester Q. Cannon reminded the members once again that "first of all, relatives of those in need should extend all the help that they can possibly do, and next that the counties in the various states are responsible for the care of those in need," with the church "standing by . . . to see that the members of the church shall not suffer."[59] Even had that rule been strictly followed, which it was not, the church would have floundered under an enormous responsibility. Few families of the poor had any additional resources. Federal and state funds went, by priority, to the temporarily unemployed, not the unemployable. Cannon also reiterated that "especially does the church feel the responsibility for the faithful devoted members who may be in need." Those in need were not to be required to dispose of all they owned before being eligible for relief. He noted that the church was "endeavoring to cooperate with the various relief agencies" and urged "coordination of relief by all agencies engaged in caring for all of those who are in need, including federal, state, county and private agencies."[60]

Ward, stake, and inter-stake welfare activities continued, but official rhetoric about self-help masked the reality: the unemployment problem was simply beyond control. More telling are these statistics: From September 1932 through March 1933, Utah received $2,560,299 from the Reconstruction Finance Corporation for relief,

an average of $5 per capita, when the U.S. average for the same
months was $1.87. In Utah one family in four received help from RFC
funds; the U.S. average was one in seven. Only Illinois distributed
more RFC relief per capita than Utah. Salt Lake County alone in May
1933 received over $212,000. By May 1933 when RFC emergency relief
concluded, Utah had absorbed more than $4 million, a sum which
dwarfed church expenditures.[61] Nor can the discrepancy be explained
by church membership. By September 1933, over 70 percent of the
families receiving public assistance in Salt Lake County were LDS,
even though Latter-day Saints were only sightly more than 50 percent
of the total population.[62]

The Church and the New Deal, 1933–1935

Franklin Delano Roosevelt was inaugurated 4 March 1933 to
head a new Democratic administration supported by overwhelming
majorities in both houses of Congress. Nationally, at least 13 million
workers were totally unemployed, and millions more were only partially employed. Farmers had been dispossessed, tenant farmers displaced, and small businesses forced into bankruptcy. The capabilities
of state and local governments were near exhaustion; and the indigent
aged, the blind and disabled, and widows and dependent children,
previously dependent upon private or local government charity, were
in distress. The Hoover administration was not unsympathetic but
was constrained ideologically from infringing upon the traditional
state and local responsibility for public welfare to any greater degree
than making loans to such governments through the RFC. The new administration felt no such restraint.

For the first month, the failing banking system demanded priority,
but by April executive orders and legislation were flowing toward relief for the unemployed and poor. The preference from the beginning
was to solve the depression problems by putting the unemployed
back to work; but that would take time, while direct relief required
only putting more federal dollars in the hands of state and local administrators. The first New Deal program was the Civilian Conservation Corps (CCC), established by executive order on 5 April 1933 to
provide work for young men in national forests and parks. Over the
next eight years, their number varied between a quarter million and a
half million. On 12 May, Congress approved the Federal Emergency
Relief Administration (FERA) and gave it $250 million for matched
grants to the states for unemployment relief. Family payments averaged $15 per month per family in 1933 and $24 in 1934; the interstate

range was between $4 and $45, supplemented by distribution of surplus commodities. Another $250 million launched a Civil Works Administration (CWA), which employed over 4 million persons on work relief projects during the winter of 1933–34. An enhanced Public Works Administration (PWA) let contracts to private contractors, expanding the numbers of jobs available to skilled construction workers.[63]

When it became apparent during 1934 that the depression could not be solved by short-term efforts, the federal government decided to leave direct relief to state and local governments, concentrating instead on work relief. The FERA and CWA were phased out in 1934, leaving little federal support during the winter of 1934–35. PWA was concentrated narrowly on one segment of the unemployed; but the Works Progress Administration (WPA), initiated in the spring of 1935, put an average of 3 million, mostly male family heads, on the public payroll performing primarily construction work but with some white collar projects. A National Youth Administration (NYA) supplemented the CCC by employing youth in local community and school-related maintenance. Two programs of the Social Security Act of 1935, unemployment insurance and old-age and survivors insurance, required steady employment for eligibility and, hence, had little impact until after the depression was over. However, the new act offered old-age assistance, regardless of work history, aid to the blind and totally disabled, and aid to female-headed families with minor children.

Unquestionably, such federal spending sustained church members during 1933–35 and beyond. Utah spent about half of its FERA allocation on food for the needy and paid out a monthly average of $8.27 per family in cash assistance. The CWA provided jobs for 20,000 Utahns during the winter of 1933–34. The CCC spent $52 million in Utah during its 1933–41 history, but the young men enrolled to work on conservation projects in Utah came from all over the nation. The NYA enrolled an average of 2,200 young Utahns per year throughout the depression. Beginning in 1935, the WPA employed an average of 11,000 Utahns per year, peaking at 17,000 in 1936. Rural Utah counties saw from one-quarter to three-quarters of their population on federally sponsored relief at various times between 1933 and 1941. More than $55 million in work relief funds and $22 million in reclamation funds went into Utah roads, schools, airports, dams, and irrigation systems.[64] This mix of federal, state, and local relief efforts dwarfed the church's sharing and self-help activities until war-related economic recovery allowed its phasing out in 1941.

Welcoming the assistance, the Presiding Bishopric and Relief Society general presidency cooperated closely with public officials in administering RFC and FERA direct relief. They shared the national view of the time that the crisis was short-term—every state was administering relief through an "emergency" or "temporary emergency" agency—but most states began organizing permanent departments of public welfare during 1935.

Since FERA legislation required that states match federal relief grants, those funds were available only to the extent that state legislatures taxed their citizens to provide the matching funds. Utah, like most states, received less federal relief than the legally available amount because it did not or could not meet the full matching requirement. Since the federal government frequently reiterated the temporary nature of its relief intentions at this early stage, it was a common impression throughout the nation, including Utah, that the federal government might leave local governments to bear total responsibility again.[65]

Then a June 1933 ruling required FERA funds to be administered through paid employees of public agencies, rather than through private and volunteer organizations.[66] Perhaps because the church had been carrying much of the load, Utah counties did not have enough trained social workers to implement the directive. Salt Lake County faced an immediate problem because it was the largest Mormon urban area, nearly 40 percent of all church members on relief residing there, and cooperative efforts had been particularly close, especially under the RFC.

In this context the First Presidency sent a circular letter to all stake presidents under the date of 28 August 1933.[67] Their introduction reflected the national concern that federal relief funds might cease:

> Reported conditions in the state and nation suggest that a considerable burden may rest upon our church relief activities in the near future. While it seems our people may properly look, as heretofore, for relief assistance from governmental and perhaps other sources, it cannot now be certainly foretold either what or how fully sufficient this assistance will be, and we must therefore prepare ourselves to meet the necessities that may fall upon us.

Though cooperation with public programs was advised, the First Presidency insisted on the ultimate responsibility of the church for its active members:

> The Lord will not hold us guiltless if we shall permit any of our people to go hungry, or to be cold, unclad or unhoused during the approaching winter. Particularly, He will consider us gravely

blameful if those who have heretofore paid their tithes and offerings to the Church when they had employment, shall now be permitted to suffer when general adversity has robbed them of their means of livelihood. Whatever else happens, these faithful persons must not be permitted to come to want or distress now.

They described the existing church structure as adequate to the challenge, if members would pay their tithes and offerings, contribute to the needy, and practice thrift and industry:

The Church organizations set up by the Prophet Joseph in the very early days of the Church, if properly coordinated by the bishops and presidents of stakes, are qualified by purpose, jurisdiction, ability of membership, and experience, to carry on adequately, during the coming winter, the work of caring for Church members. Indigent non-Church persons will obviously look to other sources. But no one must be permitted to starve or freeze in our midst.

The "prime consideration" in relief, however, was work:

Relief, except to the sick, infirm, or disabled, should not be extended as charity. Our faithful members are independent, self-respecting, and self-reliant; they do not desire charity. Our able-bodied members must not, except as a last resort, be put under the embarrassment of accepting something for nothing.

Therefore, bishops were charged to devise ways for recipients to "make compensation for aid given them by rendering some sort of service." The primary responsibility rested upon the wards, but the central church stood ready to help the neediest wards, even though, they noted, all funds ultimately came from the membership and had to be shared with proselyting, education, and other church responsibilities.[68]

Accompanying this letter, also over the signatures of the First Presidency, were specific instructions about relief activities for the following year and a questionnaire of projected relief needs for July 1933 to July 1934. The instructions challenged bishops and presidents of stakes to new heights of thrift: to waste nothing, to preserve all available fruits and vegetables, to recycle used clothing, to secure coal and wood for the needy, to use tithing in kind properly, and to share with wards having greater needs. Needy members were not to be expected to divest themselves of essential personal property before receiving help. Although bishops should seek governmental aid where available, they should not assume that it would continue to be available.[69]

Although these principles simply reiterated long-held beliefs, the First Presidency added a final note to its survey instructions: "When this material now called for is received, such special measures and plans as may be necessary to meet the situation will be made," a possible hint that a new church welfare plan was under consideration.

By the end of September, the Presiding Bishopric, the Relief Society presidency, and county relief officials, responding to the new FERA regulation for professional caseworkers, had established a compromise arrangement which they followed through the end of 1934. The Relief Society Social Service Department divided into two sections, one for public and transient assistance and the other to train stake and ward Relief Society officers in welfare. The Relief Society Social Services Department was designated as District 7 of the Salt Lake County Department of Public Welfare. One qualified LDS social worker from each of the six stakes moved into Relief Society offices where they were paid by the county but supervised by a church-paid Relief Society social worker. Each bishop could choose between full direct care of a needy family or referral to public relief through the stake's representative. The latter cleared the family and made out relief orders for goods purchased directly from local merchants, reserving goods in stake storehouses only for families the bishop chose to assist directly. Mormons who applied to the stake Relief Society/county representative for help were supposed to be referred back to their bishops, although sympathetic social workers sometimes bypassed that step.[70] This arrangement simultaneously relieved the burden on the county and let the church handle relief for its own members, a psychologically important issue to church leaders and members alike.

Still, separating church and government responsibility was not as simple as the 1933 FERA directive assumed. The working policy of referring active Mormons to their bishops and inactive ones to public relief was reasonably well accepted by most local governmental officials and ecclesiastical leaders; but some active people had always applied for public assistance while the church assisted many inactives. In addition to these customary variations, the local public agencies were understaffed and needed Relief Society personnel; but these social service aides were more likely to respond to the church's priorities than to the government's.

There was also confusion within the public relief programs. Neither RFC nor FERA federal grants were intended for unemployables like the incapacitated, the elderly, or single mothers receiving assistance from local governments—at least until the 1935 Social Security Act provided direct federal funds for some of these individuals. The church, on the other hand, felt equal responsibility for the employable and the unemployable, making its differentiations by degree of church activity. Thus, treatment of individual cases varied widely even while the Presiding Bishopric, throughout 1933 and into 1934, repeatedly told bishops to refer all inactive members for public relief, to assist active members, employable and unemployable, to the degree possible, but to welcome work relief programs and refer employable members to them as they became available.

It was no secret that the new federal relief programs were, in fact, shifting a substantial burden from the church's shoulders. In November 1933, the bishops of Granite Stake voted to close down their supplementary welfare system including the storehouse and clothing and sewing shop, in operation since 1931, "as the people seemed to like federal relief better."[71] Such candor may have prompted sermons of concern at October 1933 and April 1934 general conferences that "the dole" would seduce members into idleness. The simple facts, according to the Presiding Bishopric, were that 1933–34 government relief in District 7 was three to four times the amount of church relief expenditures in the six Salt Lake stakes; even in the highly active Pioneer Stake, 470 members received public assistance while 243 received church relief.[72]

Newly appointed public relief officials, who had not been part of the long mutual relationships going back to the 1920s, began to complain that the quasi-public/private policy was not only contrary to the spirit and even the letter of the federal regulations but was also inconvenient. Some were concerned that the church might take credit for distributing government assistance. It is true that state-paid Relief Society social workers distributed FERA funds to needy members. Some recipients may have mistakenly thought they were receiving church, not public, relief, but the church made no such claim. Nor was this church-county arrangement unique. Similar arrangements with private organizations were patched together in many states when public agencies could not hire social workers fast enough to meet the needs of the destitute. Furthermore, many private agencies were "federalized" in many jurisdictions by the simple expedient of posting a notice that the office represented the federal government and followed FERA regulations.[73] Consequently, District 7 was dissolved in November and December 1934, and its six stake social workers were transferred to the county offices as regular employees.

The magnitude of the Relief Society's contributions to the public relief program cannot be fully measured because the voluntary organization—ward and stake Relief Society officers, stake presidents, and bishops—absorbed a large part of the cost of administering the program. But the case load was enormous. One Relief Society social worker reported that her case load of 78 in 1929 had risen to 775 by 1934.[74] In November 1933, the Presiding Bishopric reemphasized to the Relief Society presidency that the Relief Society Social Services Department must train local Relief Society officers in welfare; these local women, under the direction of bishoprics and stake presidencies, would then do the actual relief work. The general Relief Society would also act as a bureau of information for church relief workers, cooperate with other relief agencies, and work with transients, aggravated cases, emergencies, and special assignments like unwed mothers and child placing. But the Relief Society would no longer administer direct relief. Instead, applicants were to be referred to their respective wards. How the Relief Society presidency felt about these new instructions is unrecorded; but some of the caseworkers quietly resisted, making referrals to local bishops or to public relief agencies according to the expressed preference of the applicant. Some "did not want the bishop to know," while others "wanted funds from the church."[75]

At the same time, the Presiding Bishopric instructed bishops to continue to decide which members should be referred to the county and which—primarily the "faithful"—should receive direct ward assistance. If the bishops gave supplementary aid to persons receiving county relief, they should report it to the County Social Service Exchange. At that point a separate system was in the making, one which, furthermore, was organized along the value-laden lines of "faithful" and "inactive" and, hence, was only a step away from "the Lord's way" versus "the world's way."[76]

Meanwhile, Amy Brown Lyman concentrated on bolstering the educational portion of the Relief Society's mission. Beginning in June 1934, she sent out a monthly social welfare newsletter to stake and ward Relief Societies. That first month's topic was the problem of transients and federal provision for their care. In September she outlined community resources available in Utah.[77] Consistent with her position for the past two decades, she advocated progressive changes in public welfare practices and institutions. During Relief Society conference in October 1934 she urged the sisters to take "a leading part" in sponsoring social welfare legislation, singling out unemployment insurance as particularly important.[78]

To summarize, then, the church, both on a general and a local level, had greeted increased federal welfare with unmistakable relief and cooperation. Bishops and stake presidents, who were trying to combine welfare with other administrative duties and their own work and families, seem to have relinquished some of this heavy burden without regret. The Relief Society, with its professionalized arm, had welfare service as its major mission and continued to provide professional casework unabated. But even as the government lifted some of the most pressing burden from the church, a reappraisal of welfare was under way in the First Presidency's office. The orientation, though still focused on the church's responsibility to care for its members' physical needs, was becoming social and spiritual.

J. Reuben Clark and Expansion of Church Welfare

The role of J. Reuben Clark, Jr., in the instigation and design of the Church Welfare Plan announced in 1936 cannot be overemphasized. Former solicitor of the State Department and ambassador to Mexico,[79] he brought a complex new influence into church relief policy when he was sustained as second counselor to Heber J. Grant at the April 1933 general conference. He was undoubtedly involved in drafting the First Presidency message of 28 August 1933, which can be seen as predicting a new and augmented church welfare program. Nevertheless, he took a public position against two provisions in the letter, notably cooperation with government relief programs and ward-centered welfare activities.

Decidedly conservative in his attitude toward governmental involvement yet highly activist in his vision of church responsibility, he took it upon himself as his first major assignment to write a prospectus on church welfare. He began 30 June 1933 and, twenty days later, had drafted a comprehensive twenty-eight-page pamphlet titled "Suggestive Directions for Church Relief Activities."[80] The pamphlet outlined what was basically a new church welfare plan, including many aspects of the final version inaugurated nearly three years later on 7 April 1936. In his introduction to the pamphlet, Clark said that the relief plan in the pamphlet was "to meet the situation" reported by the survey, though he was obviously anticipating results, since the returns from the survey were apparently not compiled until October.[81] Noting the gravity of the general economic situation, he said that relief could supply "only the very essentials for the needy" and then only if able members fulfilled "the great law of giving." He quoted a number of scriptures affirming the divine challenge to assist those who wanted sustenance and formalized Sylvester Q. Cannon's policy that priority in relief must be given first to those who had supported the church in the past, when they were able, with tithes and offerings. He also strongly affirmed the long-standing church principle that those capable should be given work for the relief they received.

Clark declared that fast offerings should be the main source of relief funding, followed by other voluntary contributions, including various types of commodities, before drawing upon tithing. He challenged wards to look after their own poor and also to help neighboring and even distant units. However, he did not mention production projects other than what might be devised in each ward and defined wards and stakes as the basic relief unit, with bishoprics and stake presidencies serving as general administrators. He suggested the advantage of grouping stakes into regional units, all of which would operate under direction of a central church committee composed of the Presiding Bishopric and other appropriate advisors. He specified ward storehouses but saw no purpose for storehouses at stake levels or higher. Though he mentioned the Relief Society several times, he was not specific about its role except that it would help the bishop in his ministrations.

This pamphlet clearly anticipated the direction of the 1936 program in such elements as centralized direction and reduced dependence on government. On the other hand, both in principle and in practice, this proposal was not a great deal different from the system already in operation in the Salt Lake stakes—not as different as Clark would have preferred it be. For example, in his original draft he had stated that, after help from their families, needy members should look first and primarily to the church for assistance. But that was apparently an as-yet-unacceptable departure from the existing policy that government aid be sought before resort to the church. The draft was modified to reiterate that "members of the church are entitled, because they are taxpayers, to receive their fair proportion of all government aid...," but, he added, "it is to the church that church members may rightfully look in these times of stress for a guarantee against hunger and want when other sources fail."[82]

Reflecting his strongly held views about the corrupting influences of government programs, he declared that church officers and members must not let the attitude of "get all we can because everybody else is getting it" influence them. He also established a hierarchy of assistance. Members should not become a public charge when relatives could supply the need. Then came unspecified "other sources," apparently as near as he was prepared to go in legitimating government's role, and finally, church assistance, which was a guarantee against hunger should these other sources fail. He appeared to be pointing to his future advocacy of church independence when he added:

> The Lord has set up an organization in His Church for the very purpose of keeping want from the doors of Church members. It has heretofore been our boast that these organizations were not only efficient but sufficient for the purpose. They have so proved in the past; we are sure they are now ample if the people will obey the great law of giving.

Clearly, Clark assumed that the total resources of the church membership would be adequate to demands upon them, if members would freely share. He probably overestimated the wealth and income of the church membership, having been so long away from Utah and living among a wealthier population. But even the limited resources which did exist in the Mormon communities might have been sufficient had the Saints been as isolated, as subject to church control, and as accustomed to subsistence living as they had been during the previous century. Although it may have been a persuasive view to many in 1936, Clark's premises appear unrealistic in a pluralistic urban society now accustomed to the welfare state.

Clark came into the First Presidency as a strong believer in self-reliance and local control of civic activities. He immediately took a strong public position on both issues. In April 1933, his first general conference address, which was given before drafting his "Suggestive Directions," he forcefully preached:

> It is the eternal inescapable law that growth comes only from work and preparation. . . . Work has no substitute. . . . If people shall shun idleness, if they shall cast out from their hearts those twin usurpers ambition and greed and shall reenthrone brotherly love and return to the old-time virtues—industry, thrift, honesty, self-reliance, independence of spirit, self discipline and mutual helpfulness—we shall be on our way to returned prosperity and worldly happiness.

Except "in extremity," he emphasized, "no man may rightfully violate that law by living by the sweat from the brow of his brother."[83] In a 19 June speech to the Community Chest, he urged increased efforts to handle unemployment relief problems locally, criticizing Utah for making liberal use of federal funds for charity.[84] In October general conference he warned his listeners that government relief would "debauch us" if church members believed they should get all they could from the government because everyone else was getting it. Scandalized, he commented, "Report has reached us that a man having a hundred tons of hay, two hundred head of cattle, four milk cows, several pigs and a flock of chickens, last year accepted relief." He approached "the subject [of government relief] with a great deal of feeling and strong conviction," warning of dire consequences from "something-for-nothing" programs.[85] Whether because of his expertise in constitutional law or his thirty years out of the state, he seemed especially troubled by the mixing of church and state in charitable affairs. He later revealed a bias going back to the 1920s when he recounted having visited Utah and "heard one of the Presiding Bishopric exhort the brethren and sisters of the audience to make application and send their needy to the County," because the church members had paid for county services through taxes. "I never had a greater shock in my life. He just turned around everything I had been more or less bragging about to my acquaintances in the world. So when we began to consider this thing in 1933, it seemed to us it would be better to get back to the old way."[86] These strong personal beliefs about work, his possibly inflated estimates of the resources of church members, and his mistrust of government relief programs would significantly affect church welfare for the next three decades, even though they were not uniformly endorsed by all church leaders at the time.

Opposition was especially strong from Presiding Bishop Cannon (who may have been the source of Clark's 1920s quote), and possibly from the Relief Society general presidency, who had shared primary responsibility for welfare activities and had cooperated closely with government agencies in the process. At this point, the Relief Society was in the process of making a successful adaptation to the FERA guidelines, announced that summer, by becoming District 7, an agreement primarily negotiated by Cannon and Amy Brown Lyman. Cannon had endorsed and maintained such cooperation with local government throughout his tenure since 1925 and in July 1933 had been appointed by Roosevelt to Utah's three-man advisory committee to the new Public Works Administration (PWA). Nor was the issue limited to church/government cooperation. The church's long-standing policy was for stake and ward initiatives, a policy reinforced in the Relief Society's recent changes in social service activities and the emergence of the six-stake Salt Lake area committee. Clark advocated a more centralized approach.

In a meeting between the First Presidency and the Presiding Bishopric on 30 October 1933, Cannon bluntly asked whether the First Presidency was dissatisfied with the relief activities of the bishopric.[87] He questioned the advisability of altering the church's relief system and expressed concern that the Clark pamphlet would demoralize those currently working in the church relief effort. Clark defended himself and his pamphlet vigorously in a lengthy letter to Cannon on 9 November 1933, responding in part:

> Your observations and arguments...seem based on the assumption that our existing church arrangements are operating satisfactorily and adequately....
>
> The reports which have come to me regarding the operation of our church relief organizations indicate without exception the opposite....
>
> I am unalterably opposed to the continuance of the greed, graft, and corruption which has characterized the use of relief funds during the past two years. It is destroying the morale of our people and is seriously undermining our moral and spiritual stamina. If continued, it will make professional paupers of very many of us and our spiritual welfare will be equally threatened....
>
> Our course during the last two years has given the lie to our talk about taking care of our own, which was one of our most glorious material achievements and principles.[88]

He pointed out that he was advocating no new church agencies. "All that is contemplated and provided for is a giving of centralized direction to organizations that now operate in a loose, uncoordinated, and largely undirected way."

Defenders of the status quo held their ground. Minutes of the next meeting between the First Presidency and Presiding Bishopric 27 November 1933 conclude: "After considerable discussion it was felt not necessary to issue [the Clark pamphlet] for reasons that the relief work throughout the church is being carried out effectively, and the instructions in the pamphlet might cause some confusion and misunderstanding."[89] Instead, the church published the Presiding Bishopric's pamphlet, *Care of the Poor,* which reiterated the priorities of resources: first the family, then county relief agencies, with the church rendering assistance "only in a supplementary way, and chiefly in emergency cases."[90]

But Clark did not abandon the campaign. He had already informed numerous groups, including Roosevelt and the six Salt Lake stake presidents, that the church was on the verge of setting up a new organization to govern its relief efforts.[91] In October 1934, he reminded his general conference listeners of his address the previous year when "I urged you and pleaded with you that...we do not soil our hands with the bounteous outpouring of funds which the government was giving unto us.... This people would have been better off materially and spiritually if we had relied on the Lord's plan and had not used one dollar of government funds."[92] Quite clearly, "the Lord's plan" was that proposed in his pamphlet—a more vigorous and centralized system independent of government aid, rather than cooperating with it.

Portents for 1936

Clark's proposal of regional welfare units simply extended church-wide the system already used by the six Salt Lake stakes. A more important structural proposal was the creation of a general church welfare committee including the Presiding Bishopric, but with a managing director reporting directly to the First Presidency. The Clark-Cannon clash, more than a difference of opinion between two individuals, can be perceived as a parallel to the transition in government—from a localized system of cooperating private and public charity agencies to a nationalized welfare state. Social welfare leadership was inevitably shifting to the federal government, and separation of church and state in welfare matters would become essential. The intensive cooperation between church and county was largely an artifact of Salt Lake City's history. It could not be duplicated elsewhere as the LDS Church membership spread across the land and abroad in years to come. Both systems would require more centralized direction and specialized functions; the church eventually focused on emergency help and the restoration of self-reliance while the federal government maintained the incomes of the long-term needy.

Clark had considerable support in his mistrust of government aid. Even church leaders who perceived an appropriate role for government aid were disturbed by direct assistance, the dominant method in 1933 and 1934. Many worried that direct relief payments would demoralize people if they did not work for them; Clark became the primary spokesman for that view, but others frequently reiterated the church's long-standing counsel on work and self-reliance.

Even though President Heber J. Grant and First Counselor Anthony W. Ivins were not willing to support Clark's plan over Cannon's resistance, they shared much of Clark's ideology. Grant, though a Democrat, later became an outspoken opponent of the Roosevelt administration, famous for his frequent criticism of the demoralizing effects of "the dole." As early as October 1933 general conference, he preached against idleness at some length, denouncing Saints who justified getting something from the government with the attitude "Well, others are getting some, why should not I get some of it." Referring to the 1890s depression, he doubted whether there was the "same moral sense among the people today that there was forty-five years ago."[93] A body of welfare rhetoric was emerging which would swell in subsequent years, often carrying well-meaning local authorities toward decisions in individual cases nöt justified by central policy.

Apostle Stephen L Richards, also speaking at the October 1933 general conference, was initially more sanguine. He counseled the Saints to exercise patience in awaiting "the outcomes of these experimental programs," warning, "unless we give our government our united support, we are going to be thrown into the throes of more confusion than that which we now suffer."[94] However, a year later in 1934's fall conference he expressed "grave concern" about the enormous expenditures for relief and the "regrettable tendency to 'sponge' on the government." He proposed no alternatives but pled with church members to be as self-reliant as possible and honest about their needs before accepting relief. "We have been taught all during our history the gospel of work, of self-support and freedom from debt," he exhorted.[95]

Thus, both Clark's personal mistrust of federal involvement and two years' experience with the RFC and FERA cooperated to distance the church from federal relief efforts. During the late summer or early fall of 1934, the First Presidency again seriously considered establishing a church relief program which would make Latter-day Saints independent of government agencies. They directed the Presiding Bishopric to gather statistics on government relief expenditures for church members compared with church expenditures, specifically asking them to determine whether a number of people on relief did not need it, a particular lament of Clark. Amy Evans, in charge of the section of the Relief Society Social Service Department which worked with the Salt Lake County Relief Administration, supplied the figures for the county to Cannon. In Salt Lake County alone during 1933, public expenditures were almost $1,750,000 for direct relief, exclusive of administrative costs. The first nine months of 1934 had almost reached the 1933 totals. When 1934 closed, expenses in the county for work and direct relief from federal, state, and county funds topped $3.7 million. It was estimated that between 60 and 75 percent of this sum went to LDS families. The public funds spent through the Relief Society Social Service Department in the six Salt Lake area stakes, which could be considered as going mainly to active church members, were between three and four times as much as church funds spent in the same stakes during 1933 and 1934. As noted earlier, even in Pioneer Stake which was making the most intense efforts of any of the Salt Lake City stakes, 470 members received public assistance while 243 received church relief.[96]

Reviewing the data, Cannon commented: "If the Church were to undertake to take care of this amount, it would bankrupt us."[97] Meeting with the First Presidency on 15 October, Cannon pointed out an inescapable fact: Welfare independence was beyond the means of the church at a time when 17.9 percent of the entire church membership was receiving relief, 16.3 percent from the county and only 1.6 percent from the church.[98] Cannon also relayed the Relief Society Social Service Department appraisal that "not more than 5% are undeserving—95% are in every way deserving."[99] The situation was familiar to social service administrators. Those closest to the front line identified with the clients while those without direct contact dealt in abstracts and viewed the system with suspicion. Nevertheless, the First Presidency advised the Presiding Bishopric that they still desired "to develop some system by which the deserving poor of the church now drawing federal relief [may] be taken over by the church" because the prolonged relief "was destroying the morale of the Latter-day Saints and developing humiliating situations."[100]

Certainly they were not alone in this assumption. The fear was widespread throughout the nation that direct relief to employables, "the dole," would destroy morale and character.[101] Even Roosevelt shared this feeling, proposing to Congress in early January of 1935 that the federal government organize a massive, nationwide work relief program and let states care for the unemployable. In words reminiscent of Grant and Clark, Roosevelt declared:

> The lessons of history, confirmed by the evidence immediately before me, show conclusively that continued dependence upon relief induces a spiritual and moral disintegration fundamentally destructive to the national fibre. To dole out relief in this way is to administer a narcotic, a subtle destroyer of the human spirit. It is inimical to the dictates of sound policy. It is in violation of the traditions of America. Work must be found for able-bodied but destitute workers. The Federal Government must and shall quit this business of relief.[102]

Since the commencement of the early New Deal relief programs, federal officials had constantly threatened to cut back relief grants in an effort to produce greater relief spending in states and their local political subdivisions. Apparently Stephen L Richards was responding to such statements in October conference 1934 when he noted that

Washington had indicated local communities might have to "shoulder more of the relief burdens." Reflecting the continued concern, Melvin J. Ballard warned during October conference 1935 that people would "be thrown off" public relief.[103]

By the latter date, the nation had experienced three years of federal relief measures. The RFC loans of the Hoover administration had gone almost totally to the support of direct relief. FERA grants had been limited by the states' abilities to come up with matching funds. The moneys could have been used for either direct or work relief at state discretion, but more people could be helped faster through direct relief and that was where most of the money went. The Civil Works Administration was a work program but it existed only briefly during the winter of 1933–34. Since the Public Works Administration contracted with private construction contractors, it was not recognized as a work relief program. The CCC was a parks and forest project and, hence, almost invisible except to those whose sons were employed by it. The Works Progress Administration (WPA) and the National Youth Administration (NYA) began in late 1935 and had not entered the public consciousness while the church was considering launching its welfare program. Hence, direct relief—the dreaded dole—was a justifiable perception of federal policy to that date. Furthermore, the 1935 social security legislation provided immediate support only for the aged, blind, disabled, widows, and orphans. States still had a great many needy: the unemployed who were not accepted for the few federal work projects and the unemployable who did not fit the five social security categories.

After considerable vacillation, the Roosevelt administration by 1935 was solidly committeed to major work relief but had shunned any direct relief but social security. Yet Roosevelt may have contributed to fears of a federal pull-out when he said, asking Congress for support of a 3-to-4-million-person work relief program, "The Federal Government must and shall quit this business of relief."[104] The FERA was a familiar reality, and it was ending. As LDS leaders prepared for their October 1935 general conference, the Social Security Act and the Works Progress Administration were only words in newly printed legislation. Work relief, except for youth through the NYA and CCC, was yet to appear in substantial reality. With an election coming up in 1936 and the newspapers of the country largely anti-administration, those not in close daily contact with the frightened lower-income citizens were unlikely to foresee the landslide that would continue Roosevelt in office. The speculations about the end of federal assistance may have reflected either memories of past public policy

debates, fear at the demise of FERA, or predictions of the election outcome. In either case, the threat of becoming responsible for those currently receiving federal aid alarmed state, local, and private relief
agencies, as well as church leaders.

It was not yet apparent that both church and government were on
a parallel track, developing an ever-stronger preference for work relief. Instead, the only alternative to the federal "dole" seemed to be an
independent church works program.[105] In April 1935, J. Reuben Clark
drafted a First Presidency statement announcing just such a plan, and
Harold B. Lee was brought in full-time at that point to prepare for the
program.[106] Yet Presiding Bishop Cannon, at least, remained a hold-
out; and his opposition was probably a factor in the decision not to issue the statement in April. In October 1935, he again questioned
whether the church had the resources to care for all its needy members
and foresaw danger in promising what it could not perform. He
feared that people would join the church and move to Utah just for
church welfare and also worried that active members would become
discouraged if they saw "the indifferent" receiving assistance from
tithes and fast offerings.[107] But events were now rolling toward the inevitable introduction of an independent churchwide program. Grant,
Clark, new Second Counselor David O. McKay, and Cannon all addressed a 7 October 1935 special priesthood meeting in which it was
announced that another survey of economic conditions was to be
made, precedent to the formulation of a program.[108]

The First Presidency, in a meeting 8 October 1935 with the Presiding Bishpric, insisted, "We must not be forced to shape our course by
false or inaccurate data. If any attempted relief work is to be successful, it must be founded upon actual facts."[109] With that, it ordered another survey of members' economic status as of September. That
survey—reporting that 88,460 Latter-day Saints (17.9 percent of the
entire membership) were receiving some kind of relief, 16.3 percent
from public sources and 1.6 percent from the church—apparently ce-
mented the First Presidency's decision to undertake the churchwide
welfare program announced the following April.[110]

Decision Point

Thus matters stood during the winter of 1935–36. The competing philosophies must have seemed abstract and theoretical to
needy church members and their children. For those who were both
landless and jobless, the alternatives were meager and the prospects
frightening. Members of the church heard the confusing messages

that they had a right, as taxpayers, to public assistance wherever it was available but that "the dole" was evil because it gave something for nothing; simultaneously, they heard that they should give more to others and that church members could be independent of government relief if they would. Where ward and stake projects existed, members must have seen some hope of reconciling these conflicting instructions. Their bishops heard the same conflicting messages: Save church resources for active members, but use public assistance wherever possible. These double messages led to inconsistent referrals, as some active members continued to receive public assistance while the church continued to assist some of the inactives. The Presiding Bishopric's 1934 instructions to direct active LDS employables toward public assistance were another complication.

Meanwhile, as a result of the 1933 FERA regulation that federal funds be administered by public officials and agencies, cooperation between the church and public relief officials was becoming increasingly complex, despite the initial accommodation. Clark's ever more persuasive voice pointed out the moral dangers of direct relief with no work requirement, even though the church had no viable substitute as yet. It was clearly a situation where current resources could not stretch far enough to fulfill what Mormon leaders perceived as their divinely imposed responsibility. But as they sought inspiration "to turn the tide from government relief, direct relief, and help to put the church in a position where it would take care of its own needy,"[111] the federal government also turned from direct relief to work projects—and it could offer cash rather than commodities.

CHAPTER 7

The Church Welfare Plan
1935–1960

IT WAS PERHAPS INEVITABLE, given the doctrinal and historical values of the LDS Church, that it would eventually seek a way of caring for its poor that was independent of federal or state relief efforts. But certainly J. Reuben Clark, Jr., played a key role in how and when that effort toward independence was forged. Although the popular image of the Church Welfare Plan announced in 1936 stresses its innovativeness, the plan in its first generation primarily endorsed and centralized activities that were already being conducted, with church approval, on a decentralized basis. The first generation of the Welfare Program would build and expand from that beginning, but with little change of direction, throughout the remaining years of the depression and through the Second World War and beyond, until events culminating in the 1960s brought significant broadening of church welfare services.

Announcing the Program

On Monday, 6 April 1936, the tall, bearded, seventy-nine-year-old president of the church, Heber J. Grant, called a special priesthood meeting at the conclusion of the 106th general conference to read a long document signed by the three members of the first Presidency. According to Henry D. Taylor, managing director of the program from 1959 to 1972, this charter of the new Welfare Program, entitled "An Important Message on Relief," was a revision of Clark's "Suggestive Directions for Church Relief Activities," written and printed but withheld in 1933.[1]

The message began by combining the numbers aided and the

amounts spent by county and church in 1935 with the projected needs developed from the survey data of the previous September to predict the funds required for welfare purposes in 1936.[2] Of the total of 88,460 church members receiving relief, 80,247 were receiving it from governmental sources and only 8,213 from the church. Of those, 13,445 were on relief because of unemployment; the rest, by implication, were either unemployable (including women and children in the families of unemployed male heads of household) or receiving supplemental assistance while employed to some extent. The message concluded, without stating the source or basis of the conclusion, that "11,500 to 16,500 persons received relief, who either did not need it, or who had farms that might, if farmed, have kept them off relief."

With church relief costing an average of $2.48 per person per month compared with $5.41 for county relief and the non-needy eliminated, the church could, it was estimated, meet projected welfare needs for $842,000 during 1936, a figure 25 percent above the expenditures of 1935. The federal government, the presidency continued, would probably curtail aid to states and counties,[3] making it "imperative that the church shall, so far as it is able, meet this emergency."

Consequently, fast offerings must be increased to an average of one dollar per church member per year, tithing should be fully paid, preferably in cash but, if not, in kind, the ward teachers and Relief Society should continue to discover and appraise the wants of the needy in each ward, and bishops should make every effort to accumulate enough food and clothing to provide for every needy family during the coming winter. Wards in less need were to collect the full sum of fast offerings to pass on to those in greater need. The Relief Society was to "assist the needy sisters of the ward in drying and preserving fruits and vegetables, providing clothing and bedding, etc." Relief was not to be given away, the document emphasized. "It is to be distributed for work or service rendered."

None of these instructions portended any change from past policies nor justified the drama of the presentation. What *had* changed— the locus of decisionmaking—can be recognized only in retrospect. Relief was to continue to "be accomplished through local organizations and operations" as "the responsibility of the bishop and his ward organizations—priesthood quorum, auxiliaries, Relief Society." But a significant change was the statement, "The Church itself will be prepared to assist to the utmost extent possible in providing work on its own properties for its unemployed members, as also in providing other work in wisely rehabilitating ranches, farms, gardens and orchards that may be used to furnish foodstuffs for those in need." And another major change lay in the structure. "The work of directing and coordinating all this work will be in the hands of the Presiding Bishopric"—a confirmation of existing arrangements—but the First Presidency would "appoint a Church Relief Committee to assist the Presiding Bishopric in their work." This change, as it turned out, had profound significance.

The only mention of governmental relief efforts was a short sentence: "All persons engaged in W.P.A projects should endeavor to retain their positions, being scrupulously careful to do an honest day's work for a day's pay." Apparently Saints should seek and accept work relief but, although the directions were vague, should forgo direct relief from public sources. Also unmentioned but not reversed was the existing policy that the church "interposed no objection to needy church members 65 years old and over receiving pensions from state and federal sources, or to members in need being assisted by the Old Age Assistance provisions of the new federal Social Security Act."[4] These two provisions together would take a substantial load off church welfare needs and make more realistic the $842,000 estimate.

Within the church, "no pains must be spared to wipe out all feelings of diffidence, embarrassment or shame on the part of those receiving relief; the ward must be one great family of equals. The spiritual welfare of those on relief must receive especial care and be earnestly and prayerfully fostered. A system which gives relief for work or service will go far to reaching those ends." Policy would now be more centralized, but the necessary resources had only one source:

> Whether we shall now take care of our own Church members in need and how fully, depends wholly and solely upon the faith and works of the individual Church members. If each Church member meets fully his duty and grasps his full opportunity for blessing, full necessary relief will be extended to all needy Church members; insofar as individual members fail in their duty and opportunity, by that much will the relief fall short.[5]

The details which would unfold in months to come could not even be foreseen at the time. Schooled in group self-sufficiency and self-reliance, taught that idleness was an evil and that work was the basis of progress in this world and the next, the church was on the threshold of adopting a plan of independent action. But the preceding six or seven years had changed conditions; the church could not longer act without interaction and some inherent competition with government efforts.

Initiating the Church Welfare Program

On 20 April 1936, two weeks after Grant read his "Important Message" to priesthood leaders, the First Presidency met with the Presiding Bishopric and presented the outlines of the new plan, apparently as a *fait accompli*. A General Church Relief Committee had been appointed, they announced, chaired by Apostle Melvin J. Ballard with Harold B. Lee, president of Pioneer Stake, and Mark Austin, former president of the Fremont Stake in Rexburg, Idaho, as the initial members. Campbell M. Brown, Stringham A. Stevens, and William E. Ryberg were added shortly thereafter. Harold B. Lee was its managing director. Sylvester Q. Cannon, the Presiding Bishop, was asked to familiarize himself with the the new plan so that he could begin traveling with the General Relief Committee to explain the new program region by region as the new regional structure was inaugurated.[6] Despite his earlier staunch resistance, he apparently followed the Mormon priesthood tradition of sustaining his leaders, accepting and obeying these instructions with good grace until ordained an apostle in 1938.[7] That he was not totally persuaded would occasionally become apparent during the intervening two years.

The new Church Welfare Program used existing church officers and organizations, modifying a few functions. In his 1933 pamphlet of relief proposals, Clark had indicated that the basic church organization was sufficient for administering the needed relief to church members, even though he recognized the need for new coordinating units.[8] Harold B. Lee not only had had invaluable experience as president of a stake with desperate welfare needs but had been called to full-time service by the First Presidency on 20 April 1935; thus, he was instrumental in developing the plan Grant announced a year later.[9] He later recounted that, the morning after his "call," he went to Rotary Park in City Creek Canyon just north of Salt Lake City to contemplate this "staggering responsibility." In kneeling prayer, he besought the Lord, "What kind of an organization should be set up in order to accomplish what the Presidency has assigned?" He then added, "There came to me on that glorious morning one of the most heavenly realizations of the power of the priesthood of God. It was as though something were saying to me, 'There is no new organization necessary to take care of the needs of this people. All that is necessary is to put the priesthood of God to work. There is nothing else that you need as a substitute.'"[10]

How much of the structure which emerged was decided upon in collaboration between Lee and Clark over the next year and how

much developed after the April 1936 announcement is unknown, but
the new organization was made known piecemeal between the latter
date and the October 1936 general conference. A newly created administrative level above wards and stakes was the welfare region,
composed of four to sixteen stakes each, determined primarily by the
geographical concentration of membership. This region was directed
by an executive council composed of the stake presidents in that region and chaired by one of them. Of the thirteen regions designated in
the original announcement, nine were in Utah and Idaho. There was
one each in Los Angeles and Oakland, California, and Mesa, Arizona.
Each region was to develop work projects that would both provide
employment and raise or manufacture commodities (furniture, foodstuffs, clothing, cattle feed, etc.) for the regional storehouse. Regions
could trade commodities with other regions or possibly even trade labor for commodities. Surpluses should go to church headquarters or
directly to regions in need. The regional storehouse would accept surpluses from stake and ward welfare projects and assist stakes within
the region.

Each stake had its own relief organization, consisting of the stake
presidency, the presidency of the stake Relief Society, the chairman of
the Bishops' Executive Council, and an appointed stake work director. The Bishops' Executive Council consisted of all ward bishops and
the manager of the stake storehouse. The ward relief organization
consisted of the bishop, the president of the ward Relief Society, and
ward Relief Society Social Service aides. Each ward also had an
employment committee consisting of the bishop or a counselor, representatives of each of the Melchizedek Priesthood quorums, the
president of the Relief Society, and the ward work director. The employment committee would not only help find jobs, as before, but
also suggest and help organize work projects at both the ward and
stake level. The work projects would provide employment and also
produce goods for the needy. The ward committee, in regular contact
with the stake work directors and regional executive committee,
would supply the numbers of workers which the stake and region requested. Recipients received commodities according to need, not according to the value of the labor rendered.

Although for the time being members could accept government
assistance, a description of the new program published in the June
1936 issue of the official church organ, the *Improvement Era,* declared,
"The ultimate objective is to set up within the church an organization
to make it possible for the church eventually to take care of all of its

people exclusive of government relief and to assist them in placing themselves on a financially independent basis."[11]

In substance, the newly announced plan contained no element not already functioning among at least some of the participating Salt Lake stakes. Perhaps its most significant structural aspect was the reemphasis on the bishops' storehouses, obviously a transformation of the nineteenth-century storehouse for tithing in kind, now a facility to store commodities produced by welfare projects. But the Salt Lake stakes had been warehousing and distributing commodities for several years. Pioneer Stake had built its programs around job-creation and commodity-production projects. The Salt Lake City stakes had been acting as a welfare region since 1932, with regional coordinating officers and the approval and cooperation of the Presiding Bishopric. Thus, the program had only two major innovations: the announced ambition of removing church members from public relief, and top-down priesthood responsibility for carrying out the program. The first would never become a full reality, but the last did immediately, thanks to the directive.

The response of the members was positive. They readily accepted the program as it was presented—as a revelation and the will of the Lord. Its evolution had followed the peculiarly Mormon approach of working out a plan, then seeking divine confirmation for it. William E. Berrett, an LDS historian and educator, was present at a local meeting in April 1936 in which Heber J. Grant declared:

> We have been meeting morning after morning for months, and we have evolved a plan. After we had evolved a plan I went especially in prayer to the Lord and prayed with all earnestness to know whether or not this plan met with His approval. In response there came over me, from the crown of my head to the soles of my feet such a sweet spirit and a burning within, that I knew God approved.[12]

This method of confirmatory revelation was familiar to Latter-day Saints from Doctrine and Covenants 9:8–9.

> But behold, I say unto you, that you must study it out in your mind; then you must ask me if it be right, and if it is right I will cause that your bosom shall burn within you; therefore you shall feel that it is right.
>
> But if it be not right you shall have no such feelings, but you shall have a stupor of thought that will cause you to forget the thing which is wrong.

In the broad context of Mormon history it was almost predictable that the First Presidency would create a plan of relief separate and distinct from public assistance. The Latter-day Saints were a covenant people; the restored gospel was meant to encompass all of life's activities. The special concern of the church for its members assured that historic values would be given special emphasis in a time of national crisis. In the 1936 October general conference, about six months after the announcement of the Welfare Program, J. Reuben Clark, Jr., exclaimed, concerning the new plan:

> I repeat what I have said several times since this conference began: The eyes of the world are upon us. . . . We are the city set upon a hill. If we should fail in this, and the Lord will not let us fail, great would be our condemnation. We should have lost the opportunity that has again come to the church now after its early coming at the beginning of our church life.[13]

That image of independence was important to church leaders. How the membership at large responded is impossible to reconstruct. Leonard J. Arrington, Feramorz Y. Fox, and Dean L. May in their history of cooperative movements in the church, agree that the Church Welfare Program, rather than conflicting with or replacing the government programs then emerging, "in many ways . . . supplemented parts of the New Deal."[14] One suspects that needy church members were simply grateful for any help, whatever the source.

Unifying the Saints

Immediately upon their appointment, members of the General Church Welfare Committee (as it would soon be called) began touring the stakes to create the newly authorized welfare regions. Along with administrative organizations, the men preached inspiring sermons that created an appealing vision of security and unity through economic self-sufficiency. Ballard, the chair, promised that following the program would "bring into the Church a joy in its accomplishment, a pride in bringing about the purposes of the Gospel and attracting the attention of the world."[15] He believed that, just as united and diligent effort throughout church history had accomplished great tasks, so would marvelous accomplishments be achieved through the reinstitution of such values as sacrifice, work, and cooperation.

Meeting with Franklin D. Roosevelt on 22 May 1936, about a month into the committee's efforts, Ballard explained that the new program was motivated by the "pride of the Church in taking care of its own and a sympathy of the leaders with the unfortunate people."[16] At the same time, J. Reuben Clark was in New York City where, in a press conference, he reportedly said that to enable members to care for themselves, "the LDS Church will remove its 88,000 needy members from public relief rolls and launch coooperative work projects tending to make them self-supporting," adding "the President of our Church feels it is time to get back to first principles and take care of our own."[17]

Some newspapers and several national magazines picked up the story and, over the next two years, published articles as if this stated intention were an accomplished fact, apparently anxious to praise this alternative to the "liberal" New Deal.[18] On the other hand, critics of the church, including appointees of the Roosevelt administration, both in Utah and at the national level, read less positive political motivations into the Welfare Program.[19]

How accurate were these views? Separating spiritual and political motivations within oneself is difficult enough; and without first-person documents, the task is probably impossible for individuals long dead. It is not unlikely that Clark, an ideological conservative and staunch Republican, was partly motivated by his opposition to the New Deal in emphasizing Mormon economic independence. Grant, a lifelong Democrat turned Roosevelt critic, may have shared the same view. On the other hand, committed church members who were Roosevelt supporters such as Sylvester Q. Cannon, James Henry Moyle (father of Henry D. Moyle, who was a member of the Church Welfare Committee, and a future apostle and counselor in the First Presidency), and Hugh B. Brown, Granite Stake president and another future apostle and First Presidency counselor, saw the church plan as supporting the New Deal.[20]

There would have been no reason for Clark to divorce his political and religious convictions; but his 1933 outline for church welfare could not possibly have been a reaction against the New Deal, which did not yet exist. It clearly reflected his dismay with direct relief provided by local government, supported by the Hoover RFC, and reaffirmed by Roosevelt's just-introduced FERA provisions. Political views were doubtless secondary to human needs, the church's ongoing practices, and its commitment to care for LDS poor. Whatever the inflated rhetoric of its claims, the new program was simply a next logical step—not a spectacular leap—beyond its philosophical and practical foundations.[21] That its exalted goals were never fully accomplished will come as no surprise to observers of the human experience.

Grant's instructions for WPA recipients to remain involved in those

public projects was a tacit acknowledgment of accommodating the
emerging federal work relief program. He was obviously not think-
ing of the WPA when, six months into the new church effort, he pro-
nounced to the October general conference the justification which has
been repeated as the underlying philosophy of LDS welfare activities to
this day:

> Our primary purpose . . . was to set up, in so far as it might be pos-
> sible, a system under which the curse of idleness would be done
> away with, the evils of the dole abolished, and independence, in-
> dustry, thrift and self respect be once more established amongst
> our people. The aim of the church is to help the people to help
> themselves. Work is to be re-enthroned as the ruling principle of
> the lives of our Church membership.[22]

Obviously, work relief programs did not create the need for "re-
enthroning" work, and the "dole" which Grant decries must, on the
basis of consistency, also include church aid which had not uniformly
required work.

Implementation of the Welfare Plan, 1936–1938

The General Church Welfare Committee worked concertedly
to implement the new Church Welfare Program during the spring and
summer of 1936. Subdividing to increase their coverage, they set out
to organize the thirteen regions announced in April and to instruct
these local leaders in the goals and mechanics of the new program.
Only the three stakes in Canada plus those in Chicago, New York,
Oahu (Hawaii) and Juarez (Mexico) were omitted from this original
organizational effort, and they were added in subsequent years. Enthusiastic articles and notes of instruction appeared in the *Improvement
Era* and the Church Section of the *Deseret News*.[23] The committee, and
particularly Lee as managing director, answered procedural inquiries
from stake presidents and bishops, either personally or through circular letters and bulletins. Visiting General Authorities preached the
new welfare program at quarterly stake conferences. During the summer of 1936, the Church Welfare Committee instructed each ward to
carry out two surveys. One, conducted by the Relief Society and due
by October, projected the amount of food, clothing, fuel, bedding,
and furniture required by prospective welfare recipients for the coming winter. The second, conducted by the priesthood quorums,
counted the unemployed and, using a simplified index provided by
church headquarters, classified them according to occupational skills.

The ward employment committee was instructed to place as many of the unemployed as possible in private industry but to protect them from unscrupulous employers who might pay starvation wages, due to the glut of workers. Regional, stake, and ward committees should also use the survey in planning work projects that would use the capabilities of the needy.[24] Regional leaders, themselves challenged by the general committee, challenged every stake, ward, quorum, and Relief Society to develop a successful welfare project.

To facilitate that process, the General Church Welfare Committee also suggested types of projects local church units could undertake, most of them food production suitable to the rural or semi-rural intermountain region where church population was concentrated. As early as 1933, Grant had suggested sugar beets as an appropriate stake work-creating and money-earning project and, under date of 21 April 1936, requested each ward in western areas that could grow sugar beets to initiate a project that would involve the land and machinery of growers and the hand labor of the needy.[25] The Church Welfare Committee also suggested urban work projects, citing as an example the soap factory which Liberty Stake of Salt Lake City had been operating for several years. The stakes were to finance their own projects, but no-interest start-up loans were available for projects approved by a field representative employed for that purpose.

The response was gratifying. By about June, approximately six weeks after the announcement of the new plan, more than two hundred farming and other projects had been established; by fall another two hundred had been approved. At October 1936 general conference, Heber J. Grant reported with satisfaction that "98 stakes out of a total of 117 had reported on their organizations and achievements, and 83 answered that they are prepared to supply food, clothing, bedding, etc., to every person in need."[26] Over 15,000 persons (not all of them needy) had worked on production projects; and though the harvest was not yet completed, a long list of foodstuffs was cited along with 300,000 cans and bottles of fruits and vegetables, 23,000 articles of clothing, and 2,000 quilts. At this point, most projects involved idle land made available without cost rather than church-owned farms. By the end of 1936 approximately 17,000 people had worked on church welfare projects and 700 had been placed in private employment through church efforts. At the same time, the number paying tithing had increased 7.9 percent over 1935, the amount of tithing by 17.9 percent, the number paying fast offerings by 67.8 percent, and the amount of fast offerings by 107.3 percent.[27]

One of the immediate purposes of the work projects was to fill storehouses with basic commodities for the poor. Stakes with functioning storehouses refurbished and upgraded them with improved facilities for canning and other projects. Other local units began to build or rent space. During the summer of 1936, the Church Welfare Committee inaugurated a reporting system to facilitate the transfer and exchange of commodities between storehouses and regions. By April 1937, there were twenty-four stake and regional storehouses. Marion G. Romney, then a bishop in a suburban Salt Lake ward and later a counselor in the First Presidency, used part of his meetinghouse for a storehouse. By 1940, bishops were pointedly discouraged from maintaining ward storehouses except for one-month emergency stockpiles in wards far from a stake or regional storehouse. Instead, centralized stake and regional facilities were strongly encouraged, partly in an effort to reduce overhead costs.[28]

At least part of this new productivity stemmed from new leadership. Previous welfare efforts had been supervised directly by the Presiding Bishopric with the help of the Relief Society presidency and general board, who had to sandwich welfare duties into their other responsibilities. Harold B. Lee, as full-time welfare general manager, headed a seven-man advisory general welfare committee who, though volunteers, contributed an enormous amount of time and business experience as they worked directly with regional, stake, and ward leaders. Henry D. Moyle replaced Ballard as chairman in 1938, serving in that capacity beyond his appointment to the Quorum of the Twelve in 1947 and replaced by Marion G. Romney in 1959 when Moyle became a member of the First Presidency.[29] Together, they generated enthusiasm, suggested projects, offered practical advice, recommended loans, and approved purchases. Gradually as the new program grew and became institutionalized over the following two years, permanent personnel were added at headquarters. The general committee met regularly, separately or with the First Presidency, sometimes as often as weekly, to approve projects, allocate funds and loans, devise policy statements, and generally supervise the new program.

As the welfare program was set up, all able-bodied members of the church from older children on up, whether in need or not, were expected to provide voluntary labor. No wages were paid. Needy recipients, who were expected to work according to their ability, applied to the bishop who authorized provisions, funds, or both at his discretion. Home teachers, a pair of men representing the priesthood quorums, and visiting teachers, a pair of women representing the ward Relief Society, had been part of every ward structure since the nineteenth century. They became information links in the welfare system, inquiring about family welfare on their at-least monthly visits and observing signs of unreported need which they relayed to their respective supervisors. The bishop then interviewed the family and, ascertaining need, assigned the ward Relief Society president to interview the mother, inventory the existing supplies, and propose a list of necessary commodities. The bishop's confirming signature made the list an order on the storehouse which the family could either pick up or have delivered by other needy persons working as storehouse personnel. If the supplies came from a stake or regional storehouse, the bishop paid for them with fast offering funds or, if this fund was depleted, with tithing if the Presiding Bishopric approved. Tithing had multiple uses, but fast offerings were earmarked for direct assistance only.

Church leaders had, since the beginning of the depression, constantly urged greater faithfulness in paying tithes and offerings. The trends had been consistently upward even during the darkest hours of the depression; but now, with the enthusiasm generated by a visible program, 1936 contributions were double those of 1935. Nevertheless, according to Henry D. Taylor, that sum still consisted of only 22 cents per capita; it was 1950 before the goal of $1.00 per capita, set by the First Presidency in 1936, was achieved; but in that year, the per capita figure reached $1.19.[30] The cash total spent through church organizations to assist the poor was just over $800,000 during 1936, surprisingly close to the April estimate and an increase of approximately $225,000 over 1935. It still fell approximately $100,000 short of 1932's expenditures, the record-setting year for church relief.[31]

Six months after the new program was announced, Cannon pointed out to the First Presidency in a meeting 6 October 1936 that Ballard as chair and Lee as managing director were entering into leases and contracts for land and buildings connected with welfare projects, adding substantially to the load of the Presiding Bishop's office and to the legal liabilities of the church. The First Presidency therefore authorized the creation of the Cooperative Security Corporation to handle the legal and financial transactions of the Church Security Program in Utah. This entity came into being on 22 April 1937, followed by similar corporations in other states as necessary.[32]

Church beautification was an important program launched in the spring of 1937 to "provide employment, improve the environment, present a favorable image of the church, and foster a love of cleanliness, order, and beauty." Ward renovations, remodelings, and landscapings were an inevitable part of building maintenance in which all wards were engaged, and most bishops had used the labor of needy members on such jobs throughout the depression. Reinforcing the church-wide formal effort, members were also encouraged to beautify their own yards, homes, farms, and buildings. The First Presidency offered 60 percent in cash for any beautification project if the local church unit would raise the other 40 percent either in cash or material and labor. A Church Improvement and Beautification Committee also offered several cash prizes to the winners of two beautification contests, one to end 1 October 1937 and the other on 1 October 1938.[33]

During the winter of 1936–37, the Church Welfare Committee identified temple work as a welfare project and, during the spring of 1937, presented the plan to local church leaders. Members who wanted temple ordinances performed for their ancestors could contribute cash or goods to storehouses; these donations were earmarked for needy elderly people to act as proxies in the temple ceremonies. The plan also contemplated constructing living quarters for the elderly near temples, beginning at Mesa, Arizona, and St. George, Utah, to make such service easier.[34]

Also during 1937, the Church Welfare Committee established the Deseret Clothing Factory to manufacture knit goods, including the special underclothing worn by LDS temple-goers. Still another program was a loan fund to help returned missionaries pay college tuition.[35]

Tensions Surrounding the Program

It was too much to expect of any organization that such extensive shifts in administrative responsibility could be accomplished without some internal tension. First, the creation of the Church Welfare Committee with its broad authority and tendency to accrue more under Lee's energetic leadership, reduced the administrative responsibility and autonomy of both the Presiding Bishopric and Relief Society. The April 1936 "Important Message" confirmed the Presiding Bishopric in "directing and coordinating" the new program with the assistance of the committee.[36] But with an apostle chairing the committee and a full-time managing director, both energetic and persuasive men, while the Presiding Bishopric had a variety of other responsibilities, the outcome was predictable. Cannon's limited involvement was perhaps indicated by his October 1936 general conference address, six months after he was made a member of the committee. He discussed church growth, public relations and communications, the training of youth, increases in tithes and offering, and praise for the Relief Society; but he made no mention of the welfare program.[37] The following month, Cannon pointed out to the First Presidency that some of the new regional chairmen were putting so much time into the welfare program that they were neglecting their own affairs and consequently were in danger of needing relief themselves.

The Presiding Bishopric's responsibility for the temporal affairs of the Church, including the income and outgo of funds, was another issue. The impression was widespread, probably prevailing and shared by Cannon, that the welfare program was a temporary response to the depression's emergency and that it would not be needed afterward. The Presiding Bishopric therefore resisted investing in major equipment for welfare production projects, a position contrary to the promotional interests of the General Welfare Committee. It cannot now be determined whether Cannon's continued misgivings about the Welfare Program were a factor in the First Presidency's decision to release the Presiding Bishopric after thirteen years of service, at April 1938 general conference. Cannon was advanced to the Quorum of Twelve where he served until his death in 1943 at age sixty-five.[38] The new Presiding Bishopric, LeGrand Richards, Marvin O. Ashton, and Joseph L. Wirthlin, played no major policy role in the welfare program.[39]

The new plan also had major consequences for the Relief Society. Its ecclesiastically centered model in the wards and stakes eliminated the independence formerly exercised by the general Relief Society leadership, leaving it without a formal role or significant independent responsibilities.[40] President Louise Y. Robison and her counselors, including the highly committed and involved Amy Brown Lyman, had not been consulted in the formulation of the new program and were not represented on the General Church Welfare Committee. During that same year, Lyman left Utah to accompany her husband as president of the European Mission. Robison later confessed that she had originally perceived the new plan as a "priesthood activity" and therefore had told the October 1936 Relief Society conference that it would occasion "no real change in our work, we will just take care of our own in the same way we have done."[41] As Relief Society historian Jill Mulvay Derr records, "[Robison] admonished women to play a supportive role, though during 1936 the exact nature of that role was in process of definition, a frustrating process for Relief Society leaders at all levels."[42] To reduce uncertainty, Harold B. Lee wrote an article for the March 1937 *Relief Society Magazine* outlining a Relief Society role. Ballard and Robison jointly issued a bulletin stating that a member of the Relief Society presidency and the Presiding Bishopric would attend each Church Welfare Committee meeting to harmonize the new program "in all its phases [so] that the utmost of unity will result." The bulletin also announced that a special committee from the Relief Society general board would maintain relations with regional committees of stake Relief Society presidents and that the Relief Society retained its charity fund and emergency supplies.[43]

But still tensions persisted. During the 1936 rush to prepare needed supplies for the following winter, Relief Society women were called on so repeatedly that many felt they were neglecting their own families and complained that more of the unemployed and needy should have been put to work rather than relying primarily upon those whose husbands were able to support them adequately. Robison noted with concern at the October 1936 Relief Society conference that "we have had more resignations of ward presidents this fall than we have had at any other time." Still, during the following year Relief Society women gave 40,850 days of service, producing 4,097 quilts, 8,452 items of new clothing, 15,808 items of remodeled clothing, 102,585 quarts of fruit, and 134,585 quarts of vegetables. In 1938, the Relief Society general board decided to train "every woman who is able and strong enough to knit, sew, or use her hands in any useful way," thereby "lifting them up" while easing the load of those who had "worked beyond their strength."[44]

Meanwhile, the Church Welfare Committee, just before the Relief Society annual conference in October, composed a letter of complaint to the First Presidency: "The Committee are united in the belief that the failure of the Relief Society in their present three-day printed program to make any reference to the Church Security Program or to call to their assistance any member of our Committee is evidence of their lack of interest and cooperation," and urged the First Presidency to bring a closer relationship between "the General Relief Society Board and our Committee." Whether or not in direct response, Robison in 1938 appointed representatives to visit all stakes to acquaint the sisters with the welfare program "and to attempt to harmonize the work of the Relief Society with the Priesthood." The General Welfare Committee invited these Relief Society representatives to accompany them to regional welfare meetings; with the mutual exercise of good will, an accommodation was reached. The Relief Society found its role in training homemakers, continuing home production, and supplying women to work in production projects, a role that continues to the present.[45]

A third accommodation had to be worked out with government

welfare programs. The county welfare offices, with which such good relations had existed prior to the June 1933 divorce enforced by federal FERA officials, continued to provide public assistance with federal social security and state and local tax funds. The church continued to discourage Mormon reliance on public assistance but endorsed enrollment in work relief programs.[46] Access to WPA employment required certification by a public welfare agency, which was denied if the family received church assistance. Some Mormons felt more comfortable approaching an impersonal agency than their neighborhood bishop and preferred the cash assistance to the church's commodities. Many public officials sent Mormon applicants, especially those who claimed to be active members, back to their bishops for church relief, justifying it on the basis of church policy, while inactive Mormons occupied something of a gray area. The problem became so serious that Utah Governor Henry Blood intervened during the fall of 1936 to secure a meeting of minds. Nevertheless, some acrimony continued.[47]

Public welfare officials often claimed to provide a fuller complement of relief benefits than the church. Although the public agencies' cash was more flexible than Mormon commodities, the agencies offered fewer personal services. For example, throughout the 1930s, the Utah Department of Public Welfare had no provision for medical or hospital care for welfare recipients. Skimpy county funds, administered by county commissioners, were the only alternative, unless the recipient could also receive private aid. Bishops were therefore under the necessity of authorizing medical aid to ward members who were receiving public assistance.[48]

The Social Security Act of 1935, which gradually became better known during the late 1930s, created further tension since it combined the "earned benefits" of unemployment compensation and old age pensions (of which the church approved but for which few were yet eligible) and unearned public assistance for the aged, blind, disabled, and dependent children (toward which the church was ambivalent). It opposed direct relief for the employable but not for those unable to work, but where did those eligible under Social Security guidelines, including mothers of dependent children, fit? When asked if the church antipathy toward public assistance included "legal pensions," Ballard replied, "not at all," but the total issue was never clarified. Local bishops and members were left to make the final determination of what was appropriate.[49]

As a result of unclear or contradictory messages from General Authorities and from the Church Welfare Committee, the interpretations and political opinions of local leaders often became local policies;

and public officials quoted their understanding of the admittedly con-
fused church position on both sides of the issue. Coauthor Garth
Mangum, a teenager during the Great Depression and employed part-
time by the NYA, remembers painfully the implied rebuke of his father,
then working for the WPA, that he read into the frequent criticisms of
that program from the bishop and stake president. The family felt intense consternation when a public administrator visited the WPA project to threaten that all Mormons were to be laid off because that was
the way their church leaders wanted it. The regional storehouse manager, a member of the family's ward, confidently told Mangum's
aged and widowed grandmother that the church wanted her to forgo
her Society Security Old Age Assistance and manage instead with
church commodities and a much reduced amount of money. Such
confusions were to be expected of a new program but sometimes created long-lasting misunderstandings.

An additional tension resulted from excessively positive national
publicity. The Church Welfare Committee was careful not to make
extravagant claims or promises in its own materials, except for the announced goal of removing all LDS members from public relief rolls.
On the other hand, it did not correct the exaggerated claims of others
but took considerable satisfaction in the unusual praise for a Mormon
program.[50] Relief administrators, aware that Utah ranked fifth in 1937
and 1938 in the nation in receipt of direct relief and that it was 20 percent above the national average in WPA enrollment, double in CCC enrollment, and one-third higher for NYA, despite the church program,
were often irritated by this favorable press.[51] It must also be acknowledged that virtually every public structure built in Utah during the
1930s—some 250 buildings—plus thousands of miles of roads, side-
walks, curbs and gutters, sewers, concreted irrigation ditches, and
forest improvements were, in effect, gifts of the federal taxpayers to
create jobs in Utah.[52] Naturally, each organization tended to stress its
own accomplishments, but there was enough need in Utah and surrounding areas to exhaust the resources of both church and state.

In retrospect, what was the church's achievement during the first
two years of the Welfare Program? It could probably have been successful in encouraging and maintaining a subsistence barter economy
for its members in the Mormon core area, avoiding actual starvation.
It offered its poor cash only for rent, electricity, and transportation; all
else was commodities. It lacked the resources to provide the cash income, low as it was, provided from federal sources. Given the choice,
most members realistically preferred the greater range of discretion
provided by either the work relief paycheck or the social security

transfer payment, even as they also welcomed church-supplied commodities and services.

Modifications and Additions to the Welfare Program: 1939–1960

The Welfare Program was founded with an agricultural orientation for three reasons. First and most obviously, food was the most urgent necessity. Even poverty-stricken farm families could still raise their own food. Second, many of Utah's city dwellers had farm backgrounds, including a significant number of the General Authorities. Third, because of the sharecropping arrangements, the first expe rience many Latter-day Saints had with systematic and extended welfare projects was agricultural. Fourth, for these reasons but also reinforcing them, the Church Welfare Committee stressed ward, stake, and regional agricultural projects. Rural stakes responded quickly to the April 1936 call to establish welfare farms. Many urban stakes also acquired farms or orchards in the surrounding rural areas or specialized in processing, through canneries and other facilities. [53]

Many of these agricultural projects were economically feasible because idle land was plentiful, and farmers were frequently willing to loan it for ward and stake production projects. Individuals also donated livestock to be fed and slaughtered during these early years.

Although this agricultural emphasis was designed to ensure access to food production, it was not long before the General Welfare Committee turned its attention to the needs of the church's many farm families. In February 1938, the General Welfare Committee organized a general agricultural advisory committee to advise and help administer the Welfare Plan's agriculture programs and also to advise and set goals for Latter-day Saint farmers in general. [54] This advisory committee in turn encouraged rural regions and stakes to organize their own agriculture committees. [55] Even before that, during the spring of 1937, the General Welfare Committee had formulated a rural resettlement plan to move Latter-day Saint farmers and would-be farmers from unproductive to productive land. During 1939 the agricultural advisory committee identified and obtained over 100,000 acres of suitable land, loaning several thousand members money for its purchase, along with equipment and cattle. The committee gave continuing advice to these new settlers and, perhaps as important, dissuaded "some unsuited to agricultural pursuits . . . from what would seem to be unfruitful ventures." [56]

Specialized subcommittees, some of which, like the agricultural

committee, had their regional and stake counterparts, were formed
for finance, correlation, building, industries and projects, processing,
clothing, cooperatives, storage, and storehouses.[57] The food processing committee's assignment was to anticipate the food needs of each
region, help supervise the projects necessary to reach the production
goals, help establish welfare canning centers throughout the church,
and provide information about better methods of canning and food
conservation. The finance committee, operating through the Cooperative Security Corporation, provided and approved loans. Deseret
Clothing Factory and Deseret Industries had separate supervisory
committees. Two other committees had been created by 1939, one for
special projects and one for housing.[58]

With the number of stake welfare projects expanding, it was necessary to weld them together into a church-wide system and coordinate
production and distribution so that the surplus production of one
stake might meet the consumption needs of another. The General
Church Welfare Committee worked out budget allotments for the
various welfare subdivisions, based on a 1937 survey which numbered Saints receiving welfare assistance from the church and from the
government, the numbers unemployed, and the amounts spent for relief in each region and stake. Based on the locations of need and the
production capabilities of the various projects, the committee gave
out stake assignments at winter regional welfare meetings in preparation for spring 1938 planning. The stakes in turn divided up the assignments among the wards and priesthood quorums, which rarely
failed to make heroic efforts to fulfill them.[59]

A committee from the General Church Welfare Committee and
the Salt Lake Regional Committee went to Los Angeles in the spring
of 1938 where they were welcomed by the Protestant leaders who operated Goodwill Industries. The committee investigated the possibilities for employment in rehabilitating used household items and clothing, made a favorable report to the full committee, and, with the First
Presidency's approval, created Deseret Industries as part of the
Church Welfare Program. The project, which still operates in much
the same way today, solicited surplus clothing, furniture, and other
articles from people within the community, processed and repaired
them using the skills of members "who might find it difficult to qualify for employment in private industry," and resold the items inex-
pensively. Otherwise unemployable people could be trained in simple
manual skills and thereby become self-sufficient while aiding others
with low-cost goods. During the planning stages, the new program
was called Welfare Industries; but in early August 1938, just before the

first store opened in Salt Lake City, the name was changed to Deseret Industries.[60]

In October, the manager, Stewart Eccles, pointed out that bishops could also supply needy families with the finished products. By 1946, twelve Deseret Industries stores and workshops were functioning in Utah with one outlet in Los Angeles, and others were subsequently added.[61] (See Chapter 8.) When World War II absorbed the able-bodied, either in the military or civilian industries, Deseret Industries broadened its involvement with the aged, the physically and mentally handicapped, and new immigrants. After the war, as Social Security benefits became more pervasive and adequate and the immigration of church members declined, Deseret Industries shifted its focus to become almost exclusively a sheltered workshop, concentrating on employing the handicapped and, where possible, rehabilitating them for competitive employment.

Dwarfing both efforts was the most major project of the Welfare Plan's early years, the 1938–39 construction of Welfare Square at 7th West and 7th South in Salt Lake City where it still occupies a large city block. The Central Storehouse Building Project, as it was known initially, was a combined project of the Salt Lake region and General Welfare Committee. The church purchased the land in May 1938, and construction commenced the next month under the direction of contractor William E. Ryberg, who was also a member of the General Welfare Committee. Unemployed Latter-day Saints who had been receiving church assistance supplied the labor. Paid partly in cash and partly with commodities, they salvaged 1.5 million bricks, 250,000 feet of lumber, doors, glass, electrical wire, and plumbing fixtures for this project from a major demolition project in Salt Lake City. In less than a year, a thirty-car-capacity root cellar, canning center, administration building, and storehouse were completed. During the winter of 1939–40, construction began on a 318,000-bushel grain elevator, completed in August 1940 and paid for from the sale of Relief Society wheat. During 1941 a milk processing plant was completed, then construction virtually halted during World War II. In the meantime, a substantial number of other church buildings for worship, education, and recreation had been constructed on the same basis.[62]

During 1940, the first handbook of instructions devoted specifically to welfare was issued to bishops and stake presidents. It suggested welfare projects, encouraged ecclesiastical leaders to use welfare field representatives for guidance, and taught local leaders how to prepare and implement production budgets to meet the assignments from the general committee. The handbook stressed the responsibility of priesthood quorums for welfare production projects and for helping needy quorum members to become self-sustaining, outlined a suggested order of business for the weekly ward welfare committee, included standardized order blanks for relief items, and instructed bishops to keep a file of "green cards" containing information on the needs and skills of each ward family.[63]

In 1944, the church purchased Deseret Mill and Elevators in Kaysville, Utah, to mill flour and cereal for distribution through the storehouses and feeds for livestock on dairy and beef welfare projects.[64] With postwar prosperity, the church added additional concrete elevators at Welfare Square in 1950 which could contain 164,000 bushels of grain.[65]

As World War II solved the employment problem, welfare needs changed drastically; but those who expected the welfare program to disappear were mistaken. The church simply shifted its emphasis. The unemployables still needed welfare, and welfare projects still demanded staffing. Now, however, virtually all of the labor had to be performed by people already fully employed. The church began by emphasizing, not production, but finding gainful employment for the difficult to employ.

Next, it stressed family food storage. An uncompromising necessity in pioneer days, food storage had long endured as a tradition for economic reasons. For the first time, church leaders actively encouraged it as an official part of the Welfare Plan in 1941, perhaps foreseeing possible wartime shortages. In the April 1942 general conference, four months into World War II, Harold B. Lee, called as an apostle a year earlier on 10 April 1941, concentrated his sermon on food storage. Recalling the historic tradition of home storage, he urged families to build up a year's supply of essential foodstuffs, homegrown, as much as possible. Not only would it provide security for the family, but home production would release more food for the public, thus aiding the war effort.[66] The General Welfare Committee's subcommittee on food storage sent out instruction booklets on how to prepare and store food properly and also estimated the amounts of foodstuffs necessary per individual per unit of time to give concreteness to the concept of a year's supply. For those unable to fulfill the goal independently, the committee suggested that priesthood quorums or other organizations organize cooperative projects.[67]

Supplemental canning facilities at Welfare Square were one of the few construction projects completed during the war. Beginning in 1943, ward groups were encouraged to use them to help families increase their home storage.[68] In October 1943, reported J. Reuben Clark, the Welfare Program was operating sixty-five canneries; and during the summer of 1943, families and ward groups had preserved 1,253,000 cans of fruit and vegetables. In addition, Clark estimated that women had preserved an additional 50 million bottles of food in their own kitchens. This was, he praised, a "tremendous achievement, the greatest that has come from a united church effort in a generation," adding, "The most credit and gratitude is due to the sisters of the church who have done all the home canning as well as the bulk of the canning for the Welfare Program and the ward groups." He pointed out that most of the produce had come from gardens or was gleaned fruit that would have been wasted otherwise.[69]

In 1944 the General Church Welfare Committee published its second handbook, a volume almost double the size of the 1940 version. It represented the church's recommitment to the welfare program. New specialized subcommittees added since 1940 included the cooperative study committee, the storehouse planning and operating committee, the grain storage and milling committee, the budget committee, and the employment committee. The scope of many of the older committees had been enlarged since 1940.[70] Production and storage projects continued, even though their purpose was unclear for the moment.

Succoring the European Saints

The steady, focused concentration on welfare commodities, land in production, and storage facilities put the church in a position to respond quickly to natural disasters like floods and earthquakes, or to serious economic dislocations like World War II. The great quantities of aid sent primarily to Europe from late 1945 to 1949 exhibited the strength of the Welfare Plan and communicated the concern of the church for its needy in Europe. The church would have been unable to deliver such help before the inauguration of the Welfare Plan of 1936 and probably could not have done much for four or five years afterward. At the close of World War II, money was not scarce but goods were. If the Church Welfare Plan had been based solely upon money and not upon the production of commodities, the church would have had the will but not the way. Thus, although it is possible to see its commodity-based assistance to needy American Saints as a deliberate choice to make work primary and relief secondary, because of that emphasis, it could make a unique response to the European crisis.

Throughout war-torn Europe people were destitute of basic necessities. As soon as hostilities stopped during the summer of 1945, local members in various European countries organized relief programs of their own. Saints who had immigrated to America naturally sent a steady stream of food parcels to their families in Europe, as long as there was hope that the relatives were alive or that the parcels could be delivered. Church members, few of whom were of Japanese descent, sent nearly a thousand packages to needy people in Japan at war's end.

By October 1945 hundreds of cartons were being filled with clothing from the Salt Lake Regional Bishops' Storehouse on Welfare Square for mailing to Europe, despite the limitations. Only one eleven-pound package could be sent per week to any person in some parts of Europe, and mail service had not been restored to other locations. Food and clothing had to be shipped bulk, which could only occur with U.S. military permission. While individuals were encouraged to continue their parcel-post shipments then and for several years afterward, the church sought more effective means.[71]

George Albert Smith, president of the Church from April 1945 to 1951, met with President Harry Truman in November 1945 to ask permission to send large quantities of supplies to European Mormons. When Truman asked how long it would take to get the commodities ready, he was astonished when Smith said they were already prepared, waiting needed transportation. Truman pledged the cooperation of the government.[72] The First Presidency assigned Ezra Taft Benson, a junior apostle and an agricultural expert, to tour Europe in February 1946, reopen the missions, and organize and supervise the distribution of welfare supplies.[73] He was soon assisted by newly called mission presidents and by local church members. Church welfare goods continued to arrive in Europe until early 1950, by which time the greatest crisis had passed and national economies were recovering throughout western Europe with the assistance of the Marshall Plan. Even then, the wife of the first postwar mission president to Finland in 1951 found herself wrapping her children in quilts she herself had worked on in Chicago for shipment in those first postwar years.[74]

Altogether the total relief supplies sent to Saints in Great Britain, Germany, Austria, Holland, Belgium, France, Czechoslovakia, Denmark, Norway, and Finland amounted to forty-one freight carloads of clothing and some bedding and ninety-nine freight carloads of food. The value of the commodities was estimated to be approximately $1,232,000, plus $504,000 in transportation, insurance, and storage charges, for a total of $1,736,000.[75]

The Transformed Purpose of the Welfare Program

The economic crisis in the United States had ended with the advent of World War II. However, as the crisis in Europe ended about 1950, there was even less discussion of the "end" of the Welfare Program. The program was a permanent component of the church structure, and members and leaders alike saw it as essential to the image and mission of the church.

Considering the initial resource base and the church membership, which stood at 760,690 in 1936 and rose to 1,408,722 by 1960, the numbers of persons assisted and the extent of that help during the 1936–50 period is impressive. (See Table 1.)

Beginning in 1943, the General Welfare Committee published annual reports which provided a good deal of information about the workings of the program. In that year, the cash/commodity ratio was about 85/15; of that 15 percent commodities, about 80 percent was produced within the church program. This percentage increased steadily until, by 1949 and 1950, commodities represented about 24 percent of relief assistance provided, and close to 90 percent of these commodities were produced within the church program. The welfare report at April general conference in 1952 indicated that approximately 70 percent of the direct relief was in commodities—food and clothing—produced within the Welfare Plan. Obviously rent, medicines, and such needs had to be met in cash.

The solid base and potential of the Welfare Plan can be seen in the rapid growth of its fixed assets and total cash value. In 1943 its fixed assets were approximately $1,350,000, the value of commodities in stock was just over $600,000, and the total cash value of the Welfare Program was $2,276,000. By 1948 the value of the fixed assets had jumped to almost $5,000,000, the value of stored commodities to about $1,000,000, and the total cash value of the program to $7,600,000. In 1950 the fixed assets were calculated at about $8,300,000 and the total cash value of the Welfare Plan at about $12,000,000.

These financial valuations can be illustrated by the increase in acreage for commodity production. In 1943 there were 50 such pieces of property totaling 3,033 acres; in 1949 there were 406 separate properties totaling 32,224 acres. The inventories of commodities at the end of each year exceeded the distribution of commodities during the year except for 1946 when there were large shipments of goods to Europe. These figures also parallel the church's rapidly increasing budget dur-

TABLE 1—LDS Welfare Assistance, 1936–60

Year	Cash Welfare Expenditure	Number Aided
1936	$1,097,188	24,317
1937	1,502,454	44,440
1938	1,827,371	56,472
1939	1,490,982	155,460
1940	1,597,338	137,166
1941	1,682,762	124,599
1942	1,547,003	30,822
1943	921,384	17,913
1944	1,009,398	27,164
1945	1,181,239	30,937
1946	1,825,640	22,336
1947	2,928,812	49,458
1948	3,167,886	49,779
1949	3,407,890	45,280
1950	3,399,951	39,537
1951	3,395,193	35,128
1952	3,288,095	37,649
1953	2,974,723	not available
1954	4,645,684	56,566
1955	6,059,361	60,165
1956	4,863,513	65,130
1957	6,242,500	67,878
1958	6,881,667	87,419
1959	not available	89,997
1960	not available	98,411

Source: From the yearly statistical summaries given in *Conference Reports* each April. No church expenditures of any kind, including welfare, have been regularly reported since 1958. Definitions and methods of reporting were not identical in all years. No evaluation of the commodities produced and distributed from the several hundred welfare farms, factories, and other projects is available. The 1947, 1948, and 1949 numbers include 25,000, 17,000 and 7,000 European Saints, respectively. The reduced numbers needing assistance during the high demand periods of World War II (1942–45) and its immediate aftermath and the Korean conflict (1950–53) is notable.

ing those years. For example, in 1945 the total cash expenditures of the church amounted to $9,397,035, and in 1950 to $33,080,135.[76]

But perhaps the greatest contribution of the 1936–60 Welfare Plan was that it permanently shifted the church's image from that of a polygamous sect in the arid West to a solidly middle-class American church that exemplified hard work, family-centered values, and the frontier virtues of neighborliness and self-reliance. Certainly, the Saints saw themselves not only as doing a respectable and respected work but also as fulfilling deeper spiritual imperatives. The Welfare Plan was the distinctively Mormon way of caring for the poor who, as the scriptures reminded, "are always with us"; but it was also the chosen instrument to humble the well-to-do, maintain the self-respect of those in need, and teach crucial moral values to to all. This shift had come as early as 1941, when a pamphlet issued by the Church Welfare Committee stated persuasively:

> There will never be a time when what it [the Welfare Program] stands for is not needed. . . . The plan . . . is as valid in times of prosperity as it is in times of stress; in days of plenty it teaches thrift and industry; in days of scarcity it sets an example of self-help and brotherly kindness. The plan is having a chastening influence on the whole church, it gives every member something to think about, even [those] not immediately affected, budget more carefully, waste less; and as brother meets brother on the common ground of service to the Lord, a great deal of creative effort is being brought into the church. Fighting a common evil with a common will is giving a whole people a growing consciousness and appreciation of their own strength, their own resources, their own achievements and traditions.[77]

In less than a decade, the Welfare Program had become increasingly a means of teaching and reasserting traditional Mormon values. Numerous articles in church publications and countless sermons dwelt on welfare themes. The Melchizedek Priesthood lesson manual for 1939 was *Priesthood Church Welfare;* the adult Sunday School lesson manual for the latter half of 1946 was *The Church Welfare Plan.* The Welfare Plan became a tool for giving order and direction to the economic lives of Latter-day Saints; it was a means of teaching love, brotherly kindness, and charity; it was a program through which the Saints could gain a deeper understanding of their own collective identity—a greater sense of their uniqueness and special abilities as a people.[78]

The Welfare Plan's successes were substantial by 1950, so solidly based among its home stakes in the Intermountain West that it could reach out to the starving and struggling in both Asia and in Europe. It then continued to enlarge along essentially the same track for the next decade. If it did not live up to some of the ballyhoo in the national press, that was because the media claimed more for it than it claimed for itself. It never removed all of its members from the rolls of public relief programs; but after the first few months, it was clear that such goals should be considered rhetorical rather than objective.

Part of the impressiveness of the Welfare Plan story is its flexibility, its organic ability to adapt to circumstances. There is no indication that Grant, Clark, Lee, or Ballard perceived in advance the directions it would take nor the dimensions it would reach. It began in response to an emergency and unfolded piece by piece, more in apprehension that federal relief might stop than in opposition to it. Church leaders were anxious to replace direct relief payments with work projects but generally did not discourage or left carefully vague the status of public work projects.

Whether the originators thought of the program as temporary or permanent will probably never be known. But by the depression's end, the commitment to welfare as a unifying and identifying characteristic of the church was so intense that leaders identified new needs rather than let it die. That some would be in need of help, even in the most prosperous times, had been proven throughout the war. The European emergency demonstrated the value of a strategic reserve of commodities. The doctrinal commitment to care for the poor could, at least in times of plenty, be met in many ways. Commodity production and distribution was now perceived as the best way of doing so while teaching the values of hard work, serving others, and joining in a noble cause. It linked members with their historic past and the long-term assignment to establish Zion. With that identification came the promise of the millennial future. Whether the Welfare Plan could, ultimately, bring forth a Zion society, the spirit and commitment required were unquestionably appropriate preparation in the Mormon context. In that light, the faithful embraced the Welfare Plan and saw in it eternal significance.

CHAPTER 8

The Maturing of Welfare Services in the U.S. and Canada

1960–1990

DIVIDING AN ONGOING story is always arguable, yet 1960 is a reasonable date for marking an evolutionary stage in LDS Welfare Services for two reasons: (1) nationally the United States returned to social welfare considerations on a scale not seen since the Great Depression, and (2) responding to many of the same societal forces, the LDS Welfare Program broadened its services, undergoing significant reorganizations to accommodate them. The national impetus had died out and experienced some reversal after 1980. On the LDS scene, Welfare Services seemed to settle its agenda for the United States and Canada from 1960 to 1980, then grappled with a sharp series of international challenges during the decade of the 1980s. These challenges, dealt with separately in Chapter 9, certainly continue past 1990, the terminating date of this study.

This chapter describes the economic setting within which the Welfare Program functioned in the United States and, to a lesser degree, Canada during the 1960–90 period, the philosophy of welfare which emerged to undergird the LDS program in response to that changing economic and social environment, the organizational structure which supported that philosophy, the functional services which constitute its realities, the people who are its recipients, and the concerns with which the period closes.

The Economic Setting[1]

The United States enjoyed general prosperity and rapid economic growth, marred only by periodic mild recessions from World War II until the middle 1970s. The recessions deepened with rising energy costs during the 1970s and early 1980s, and a relatively mild but stubborn recession began in mid-1990 which continued at the end of 1991; but most Americans still lived in relative affluence.

During and following World War II, the u.s. economy became job-centered. Agriculture declined from 25 percent of the work force in 1930 to 3 percent in 1960. Three-quarters of all u.s. income stems from wages and salaries, most of it in the industrial sector. People's place in the system and the level of their earnings depend more on their skills and education than on owning property.

In the early 1960s, the nation rediscovered the chronic poverty among about one-fifth of its population. This poverty was not mass, but class-based, concentrated in rural depressed areas, on Indian reservations, and among minority racial and ethnic groups in big-city ghettos. The poor were those who lacked the prerequisites of employability, who were located where employment was unavailable, or who, for reasons of discrimination, had been denied the right either to become employable or to exercise their skills. The elderly, originally part of the chronically poor, soon organized politically to liberalize and inflation-proof their Social Security benefits. This action benefited millions, although it did nothing for those who had not worked long enough (or had a qualifying spouse) in covered employment.

The federal government's "war on poverty," declared by u.s. President Lyndon Baines Johnson in 1964, emphasized education and training for minority youth. A series of federal programs offered skill training and sometimes subsidized employment for low-income people unable to compete successfully in the private sector. The government also offered retraining and assistance programs during the 1970s and 1980s as international trade competition displaced American workers.

In 1962, eligibility for federal aid to dependent children in the relatively few women-headed households was broadened to include families headed by an unemployed but employable male and renamed Aid to Families with Dependent Children (AFDC). Half of the states chose to take advantage of the federal government's increased permissiveness. The other half did not. After 1981, with federal encouragement, most states withdrew AFDC support for two-parent families, though continuing to supply some lower-level assistance to two-parent households and childless single persons in extreme want.

Over 90 percent of the aged, regardless of income, were eligible for pensions under the Old Age and Survivors Health and Disability (OASHDI) component of the Social Security Act. A Supplementary Security Income program, introduced in 1972 to encompass the previous Old Age Assistance and Aid to the Blind and Totally Disabled programs, provided income maintenance to many unemployables omitted from other programs. Medicare and Medicaid paid for most of the health care of the aged and the indigent. Food stamps stretched the food budgets of the poor beginning in 1976; and a Women's, Infants', Children's Program (WIC) provided supplementary food, prenatal care, and well-baby checkups to relieve the suffering of dependent children and their single mothers; public housing and rent subsidies provided shelter.

Unemployment compensation was widely available to tide the temporarily unemployed over recessions but required qualifying periods of steady past employment, thus aiding only a third of the unemployed by 1990. A federally funded vocational rehabilitation program, continued since 1920, trained the physically and mentally handicapped for employment. All of these support programs were in place by 1980; over the next decade, most survived though resources and eligibility shrank, except for programs protected by entitlement status.

Programs provided under the Social Security Act—OASHDI, Medicare, Unemployment Insurance, AFDC, and SSI—are entitlement programs; that is, the federal government is required to provide sufficient funding to pay for all of those eligible and applying. However, the benefits are not lavish. OASHDI and Medicare are federally guaranteed and supported by a politically active constituency, the "senior citizen" population. Unemployment insurance is guaranteed to the eligible; but beyond an underlying federal standard, the states determine the levels and duration of benefits. AFDC, Medicaid, and SSI require state matching which limits the rules of eligibility and the level of benefits in accordance with the various states' willingness to appropriate. All of the other programs depend on the funds appropriated by Congress year by year; there is never enough money to enroll all of those eligible by the rules Congress itself has prescribed. Still, despite low funding thresholds, high eligibility requirements, and spotty coverage, a substantial body of resources was available by the 1980s to assist those who aggressively sought help.

Unlike the Great Depression, the main cause of poverty was not unemployment. The U.S. divorce rate climbed rapidly beginning in the 1960s; so did out-of-wedlock births. By 1990, one-quarter of all households in the United States were female-headed, an equal proportion of children were born out of wedlock, and 60 percent of children spent some part of their childhood in a single-parent household.[2] The resultant "femininization of poverty" was a new focus of public policy concern. One out of eight Americans was poor by federal government standards in 1990; the figures for children were one out of five and, in female-headed families, one out of three.

In the early 1980s after two decades of extensive public services, the federal government lowered taxes, boosted defense expenditures, and cut back sharply on the resources available to assist the poor. States, local governments, and private charities struggled unsuccessfully to maintain the accustomed range of assistance. With static real wages and rising housing costs, the number of homeless accelerated during the decade. Nevertheless, total government spending for income security and antipoverty programs was just under $300 billion in 1990. Although the problems are real and many needs remain unmet, it takes little comparison with countries other than the democratic West to appreciate the extensiveness of the social safety net that keeps most of the lower-income population in the United States from suffering real destitution.

The LDS Response

Latter-day Saints in the United States participated in all of these changes. Without the massive challenges of nineteenth-century gathering and colonization or the broad unemployment and poverty of the 1930s, the continuing church welfare plan required a new rationale for its existence. Like the design and development of the program itself, that rationale emerged pragmatically as new elements were added to the basic commodity production and distribution activities.

This new welfare system was family-based self-reliance, conceptualized in the mid-1970s as one of the first initiatives of the Welfare Services Department, established in 1973 to coordinate an increasing variety of welfare-related activities. In the welfare session of April 1975 general conference, H. Burke Peterson, counselor in the Presiding Bishopric, explained: "When we speak of family preparedness, we should speak of foreseen, anticipated, almost expected needs which can be met through wise preparation. Even true emergencies can be modified by good planning."[3] At the welfare session of October conference that same year, Presiding Bishop Victor L. Brown, Sr., described family preparedness as "the key to self-respect and self-reliance in personal welfare matters."[4]

The concept they were describing, then under development by Welfare Services Department staff, emerged as a six-part program: literacy and education, career development, financial and resource management, home production and storage, physical health, and social-emotional and spiritual strength. Though each of the six could be tracked back into early church philosophy, their structuring into a security formula was new; and welfare became, temporarily, a high-profile item. Although separate annual conferences for auxiliaries were terminated in 1975, a separate "welfare session" was added from 1974 until October 1982. In the welfare session of the October 1976 general conference, for instance, Vaughn J. Featherstone, a counselor in the Presiding Bishopric, challenged members to reach the goal of a year's supply of food and other essentials by April 1977 so energetically that many took it as a prophecy of impending disaster.[5] Although it is impossible to quantify compliance, commercial outlets specializing in food storage items mushroomed, particularly along the Wasatch Front in Utah. Since then, home storage of food, clothing, and fuel has been encouraged in more muted tones. However, there appears to be no evidence that H. Burke Peterson's 1975 estimate that, "on the average, 30 percent of the church had a two-months' supply of food; the remainder had little or none," has been exceeded since.[6]

In 1979, Nathan Eldon Tanner, first counselor in the First Presidency, introduced the concept of "economic constancy amid change" with five principles: pay an honest tithing, live on less than you earn, learn to distinguish between needs and wants, develop and live within a budget, and be honest in all of your financial affairs.[7] The speech was later made into a pamphlet delivered to every home in the church by home teachers.

Provident living is best articulated in the 1980 *Welfare Services Resource Handbook,* which spells out the principles and programs that may be considered the maturation of church welfare policy for the United States and Canada.[8] Significant changes during the 1980s were incorporated in a 1991 handbook (see "Reconsideration" below), but they almost all emerged from the challenges posed by international growth.[9]

Personal and Family Preparedness

The Welfare Program and the church's commitment to it remained unchanged by post–World War II prosperity and recession cycles and by expanded government anti-poverty programs. There have always been substantial numbers of aged, disabled, handicapped, or emotionally disturbed Saints who were ineligible for government assistance, who preferred church assistance, or who needed help from both. Strikes, recessions, natural disasters, accidents, and illness periodically impacted even the usually self-reliant.

Most Mormons lived in an agriculture-based economy until

World War II. Since that point, not only has Mormon country been industrialized but Latter-day Saints have also spread—both by migration and by conversion—across the entire United States and abroad. Most of them, like their mobile national counterparts, settled where career assignments or job opportunities took them, building vigorous wards and thriving stakes. Instead of individual self-reliance based on agriculture maintained through communally operated irrigation, self-reliance now stems from employment preparation, competence at jobs, and thrifty investments for the future.

Therefore, the church defines members' primary welfare responsibility as "provident living and prevention of problems through personal and family preparedness."[10] The 1980 *Welfare Services Resources Handbook,* designed for ecclesiastical leaders, describes this philosophy/program in words that remained substantially unchanged in the 1991 version. Bishops and other local leaders should teach individuals and families to live "providently," care for their own needs, and produce a surplus with which to help others. To make that possible, first, each individual should pursue the traditional goals of literacy and education for both spiritual and temporal reasons. Adults should continue to learn, read to their children, teach them to study the scriptures and other good literature, encourage them to write, and train them to speak well. Parents should teach work and self-reliance. Church instructions reinforce these values and teach family relations to help parents meet their acculturating obligations.

Second, parents should see each adolescent prepared for a career appropriate to his or her individual talents and interests, one that will provide a comfortable family income and allow leisure for church service. Adults should retrain professionally when appropriate. Third, LDS careerists should exercise wise financial and resource management, establish goals, save, avoid debt, and pay tithes and offerings. Fourth, a remnant of the traditional welfare program is embodied in instructions to engage in home production and storage, leading wherever possible to a year's supply of food and clothing. Fifth, Saints should proactively work for physical health through proper nutrition, sanitation, first-aid training, and exercise while maintaining prudent levels of health, medical, and life insurance.

Social-emotional and spiritual strength, the sixth of the categories, includes prayer and service. The manual does not even mention two of the most serious deterrents to economic self-sufficiency in the United States—substance abuse and teen pregnancy. The Mormon law of health, contained in the 1833 revelation called the Word of Wisdom, and the rigid requirement of premarital chastity are deemed to cover those situations.

The manual obviously assumes a u.s. context—that employment opportunities and community resources are reasonably available at most times. In such a setting, members who follow the rules for provident living will be self-supporting and generate surpluses to help others. Where assistance is needed, families should help needy members, first within nuclear families and then within the extended family. Community resources may be used; but the manual warns:

> No true Latter-day Saint, while physically or emotionally able, will voluntarily shift the burden of his own or his family's well-being to someone else. So long as he can, under the inspiration of the Lord and with his own labors, he will work to the extent of his ability to supply himself and his family with the spiritual and temporal necessities of life. As guided by the Spirit of the Lord and through applying these principles, each member of the church should make his own decisions as to what assistance he accepts, be it from governmental or other sources. In this way, independence, self-respect, dignity and self reliance will be fostered, and free agency maintained. [Consequently]...Latter-day Saints are encouraged not to accept unearned government assistance. If an individual accepts unearned government assistance, he may not accept Church commodity or financial assistance at the same time.[11]

Current Instructional Practices

This model of provident living shows that the church expects to keep its members economically and socially functional by teaching correct principles. The shortcoming is that the handbook was directed to ecclesiastical leaders without any specific instructional program to deliver concepts to members. Ecclesiastical leaders may theoretically use these concepts in counseling members, but most members who come to the bishop for welfare assistance are already in economic difficulties; and the program is one of prevention, rather than remediation.

A second way in which members could learn the concepts is through the lesson manuals prepared for classes in various auxiliaries and priesthood quorums; but fewer lessons are focused on these principles than one might expect, as a review of manuals used in the United States during 1991 illustrates. Most dealt in some way with personal characteristics important to self-reliance, but topics explicitly related to employment were infrequent.

The lds Primary Association, which is responsible for the instruction of three-through-eleven-year-olds, had numerous lessons in each manual about "helping," service to others, and self-sacrifice; but no lessons dealt directly with career choice or career preparation. The LDS Church is the largest sponsor of Boy Scout troops in the United States; its program, replete with employment skills and concepts, probably more than compensates for the limited career orientation not only for this age group but for teen boys as well.

The Young Women's and the Young Men's curriculum teaches weekly lessons to the twelve-to-eighteen-year-olds, almost always in gender-segregated groups that are further subdivided into age groups. All lesson manuals included lessons on self-mastery, honesty, emotional control, physical fitness, using time wisely, respecting property, valuing education, developing talents, making wise decisions, and serving others. The manual for twelve- and thirteen-year-old boys (deacons) contained no lessons on employment, but one lesson dealt with work values and another urged them to develop useful home skills.[12] The fourteen-to-sixteen-year-old boys (teachers) had one lesson out of thirty-six on "preparing for a career," while the seventeen-to-eighteen-year-old priests had one on "acquiring true manhood," which emphasized self-discipline and responsibility, and a second on consecration and sacrifice. None deals explicitly with careers.[13]

Manuals for the twelve-to-fifteen-year-old girls mentioned no career topics, but the sixteen-to-seventeen-year-old young women had lessons on vocational choice, money management, and leadership skills.[14] LDS girls were encouraged to be potentially self-reliant, but not career-oriented. Both Laurel manuals quoted Apostle Howard W. Hunter:

> There are compelling reasons for our sisters to plan toward employment also. We want them to obtain all the education and vocational training possible before marriage. If they become widowed or divorced and need to work, we want them to have dignified and rewarding employment. If a sister does not marry, she has every right to engage in a profession that allows her to magnify her talents and gifts.[15]

A reinforcing quotation came from Camilla Kimball, wife of church president Spencer W. Kimball:

> I would hope that every girl and woman here has the desire and ambition to qualify in two vocations—that of homemaking and that of preparing to earn a living outside the home if, and when, the occasion requires. An unmarried woman is always happier if she has a vocation in which she is socially of service and financially independent. In no case should she be urged to accept an unworthy companion as a means of support.[16]

Most Mormon men over eighteen are ordained to the Melchizedek Priesthood and have gender-segregated priesthood lessons while all women over eighteen are members of the Relief Society. Both have instructional meetings each Sunday. During 1991, welfare-related priesthood lessons included "Losing Your Life in Service to Others," "The Spiritual Nature of Welfare," and "Showing Compassion Through Obeying the Law of the Fast."[17] No lessons addressed career topics. Since the church's official position since the 1950s has been that all women, insofar as possible, should be full-time mothers, no lesson of the forty-eight in the 1991 Relief Society manual dealt with careers or employment. Doctrinally related to welfare principles, however, were "The Law of Consecration," "Continue in Fasting," "Teaching Compassionate Service in the Home," "Food Storage and Family Preparedness," "Planning Emergency Supplies," "Good Health Habits," and "Nutritionist in the Kitchen."[18] All manuals clearly make American assumptions: that other sources such as schools, families, and part-time early employment provide basic experiences in career development for Mormon youth, that most members belong to intact and economically viable families, and that these families function in a viable economy that offers a broad range of reasonably well-paying jobs. It also assumes that those with long-term needs are eligible for public assistance.

Remedial Resources

For those who fail to follow these principles or who suffer the random vicissitudes of life, the church offers temporary assistance and services. An integrated "storehouse resource system," accessible through the local bishop, includes cash from fast offerings, commodities provided through production projects and distributed through bishops' storehouses, job placement through church employment centers, handicapped employment at Deseret Industries, and personal counseling from LDS Social Services. Short-term emergency assistance is the domain of the bishop, closely assisted by the Relief Society. Longer-term economic rehabilitation, including education, retraining, and sometimes small business loans, are priesthood quorum responsibility, or, in the case of single women, the Relief Society.[19] In reality, emergency assistance is more available than rehabilitation.

Organizational Change

This restructured system of concepts and the newly developed "storehouse system" created a cycle of reorganizations during the

1960–90 period. Almost certainly, such internal changes will continue. Crucial to understanding the Church Welfare Program, however, are those reorganizations which explain relationships between directing authority, responding staff, and service delivery personnel at the member level.

Since production and distribution remained the primary welfare functions, the organization of the 1930s continued with strong continuity throughout the 1950s. Apostles Harold B. Lee, Henry D. Moyle, and Marion G. Romney, founding fathers of the 1936 program, directed it at the general level in turn, under continued guidance from J. Reuben Clark, Jr. The Presiding Bishopric were only indirectly involved in their role as custodians of church properties and temporal affairs. The General Church Welfare Committee, upon which the Presiding Bishopric was not represented, remained the primary policy-making body. In 1959, Romney became chairman of that committee; but Henry D. Taylor, an Assistant to the Twelve, became managing director.[20] He held that position until 1972 when he was replaced by professional church civil servants as part of a broad reorganization at church headquarters that removed General Authorities from most direct management positions.[21]

Despite the changes at the top, the field organization supervised by the General Welfare Committee remained essentially unchanged from the 1930s: regions, stakes, and wards were the structural and production units. Stake presidencies and bishoprics provided most of the local direction, assisted to some degree by the Relief Society presidents and priesthood quorum leaders. Stake presidents during the 1930s supervised the regional storehouses and chaired the regional welfare committees; but beginning in 1944, the chairmen of bishops' councils (consisting of all bishops in a region with rotating chairmanship) began supervising the regional storehouses.[22] Welfare handbooks describing the organization, functions, and operations of the welfare program were issued in 1948, 1952, 1966, and 1967, almost without change, except that by 1948, they omitted suggestions on general agricultural improvements for LDS farmers. This deletion reflected both the healthier national agricultural situation and the growing urbanization of the LDS population.

Until the early 1960s, the General Church Welfare Committee had a large but varying membership, consisting mostly of experienced businessmen called to this unpaid service. They traveled with General Authorities to quarterly stake conferences, where they encouraged and advised local bishops and stake presidents. At periodic meetings with the First Presidency, members of the General Welfare Committee presented for approval an agenda of proposed projects, land purchases or sales, loans and grants to local units, changes in local leadership, and themes and assignments for the quarterly stake conferences.

The Correlation Movement

In 1960, Harold B. Lee, then an apostle, chaired a far-reaching "correlation" program, designed to coordinate the church's extensive curriculum, activities, and programs, and to place the line priesthood leadership—First Presidency, Quorum of the Twelve, stake presidents, and bishops—in a more central role. Along with the worldwide expansion discussed in Chapter 9, each of the three Melchizedek Priesthood and three Aaronic Priesthood quorums, the Relief Society, the Sunday School, the Young Men's and Young Women's Mutual Improvement Associations, and the Primary organization for children had its own meetings, instructional programs, and sometimes recreational and service programs as well. Such functional departments as missionary, education, genealogy, temple, and welfare each had its own involved program and made separate demands on church members. The new correlation program had the assignment of coordinating, consolidating, and unifying procedures, programs, and curriculum throughout the entire church structure.[23] A result of correlation was an inevitable reduction in autonomy for every program, including welfare.

In that context in 1961, the Presiding Bishopric returned to a key welfare role for the first time since 1936. Each member of the Presiding Bishopric became responsible for a major function: Bishop John H. Vandenberg directed the Distribution Division, First Counselor Victor L. Brown, Sr., the Production Division, and Second Counselor Robert L. Simpson the Employment, Work Directors, and Rehabilitation Division. Each division employed a full-time staff administrator, who answered to Henry D. Taylor as managing director. The twelve subcommittees of the General Welfare Committee were divided among the three divisions, with the Presiding Bishopric, as an executive committee, meeting weekly with the First Presidency.[24]

The Presiding Bishopric's welfare role was further elevated in 1963 when Vandenberg replaced Romney as chair of the General Welfare Committee; Romney remained on the committee as an advisor from the Quorum of the Twelve, and Taylor continued as managing director.[25] Also in 1963, Lee announced an emphasis on four "priesthood programs": genealogy and temple work under the high priests, proselyting efforts under the quorums of Seventy, welfare under the elders' quorums, and home teaching under each quorum for its own members and their families.[26] Each program would have its own general committee, members of which would accompany General Authorities to quarterly stake conferences on a schedule that allowed each program to be represented in two conferences a year. All four programs were incorporated in a regional council chaired by a stake president just as welfare had been since 1936.

In 1967, the First Presidency and Quorum of the Twelve called a group of experienced former stake presidents to serve as Regional Representatives of the Twelve, each to be responsible for all four priesthood programs within his region. That change eliminated the need for large general committees and reduced the General Welfare Committee to the Presiding Bishopric, the managing director, a secretary, and an advisor from the Quorum of the Twelve. Semiannual regional meetings covering all programs were substituted for quarterly meetings of each.[27]

These changes inevitably reduced the attention given to welfare matters at each stake conference. Those whose primary concern had been the welfare program lamented that the teaching of welfare principles would suffer. The official response was that, if the regional representatives really understood welfare and believed fully in the program, it would not suffer at the local level where it counted. The purpose of the correlation program, after all, was to see that all programs were kept in balance and that no single program assumed a disproportionate share of the members' time and attention in the lay-operated church.

It was, however, precisely at the local level that inadequacies became apparent. Prior to the correlation changes, ward welfare meetings had been held weekly among the bishopric, Relief Society presidency, and priesthood quorum leaders. With the specialization of each priesthood quorum, joint planning was neglected. Hence, in 1972, new instructions reemphasized the need for the weekly ward welfare committee meeting in which each needy family could receive individualized attention. One counselor in each stake presidency, bishopric, and Relief Society presidency became responsible for commodity production and distribution and the other for personal welfare services. Each priesthood quorum became responsible for both the temporal and spiritual needs of its members. The four priesthood programs of 1963 had taken their shape from the 1962 three-part mission of "proclaiming the gospel, redeeming the dead, and perfecting the Saints." The last goal included welfare responsibilities, especially personal and family preparedness. Victor L. Brown, Sr., who succeeded Vandenberg and served as Presiding Bishop from 1972 to 1985, explained, "The welfare program in the past has been primarily concerned with the economic needs of the members. Welfare Services will not only deal with these needs, but also health, social and emotional needs. It provides for the total well-being of our members."[28] The reach of the goal exceeded the grasp of reality, but the direction of movement was clear.

Bureaucratization

General Authorities directly managed the welfare program from 1941 to 1972. After that, managing directorship passed to experienced church civil servants.[29] Succeeding Henry D. Taylor was Junior Wright Child (1972–76), followed for a few months in 1976 by Dr. James O. Mason, then by R. Quinn Gardner (1976–81), Glenn L. Pace (1981–85), and Keith B. McMullin (1985–present). All were men of substantial prior experience with private industry or government. Child and Gardner returned to the private sector, and Mason to public health, while Pace became a counselor in the Presiding Bishopric.

Such a major change was unlikely to occur without some organizational confusion. In April 1973, a new General Welfare Services Committee was formed, consisting of the Presiding Bishopric, the general Relief Society presidency, and the heads of three new divisions created within the Welfare Services Department: the Welfare Division, the Social Services Division, and the Health Services Division. In 1974, the functional divisions were renamed Production/Distribution, Personal Welfare, and Developing Welfare, the latter encompassing health activities but also undertaking the responsibility "to help priesthood and Relief Society leaders in developing areas of the world understand and prepare for the full Welfare Services Program of the Church."[30] Even though Child and Mason had ostensibly been, since 1972, managing directors of the total department, the heads of the functional divisions still reported directly to the Presiding Bishopric and had their budgets individually approved there as well. In 1976, these reporting functions were reassigned through the managing director, and all welfare functions were located on a single floor of the recently completed Church Office Building, 50 East North Temple, instead of being scattered among several locations throughout the city. The Welfare Services Department could now be considered a consolidated entity.

The shift to civil servant administrators did not indicate a declining General Authority interest in welfare matters. In fact, during the same year that the civil servant managing directors were gaining a clear line of supervision over their division head subordinates, the First Presidency and Quorum of the Twelve expressed concern about their lack of direct involvement in welfare decisions. The General Welfare Services Committee was reorganized, chaired by the church's president, Spencer W. Kimball. (He had succeeded Harold B. Lee in December 1973 when Lee died after only eighteen months in office). The members were selected apostles, the Presiding Bishopric, and the Relief Society Presidency. (After Ezra Taft Benson succeeded Kimball in 1985, Thomas S. Monson, second counselor in the First Presidency, has chaired the General Welfare Services Committee.)

One significant change remained. The initial post-1972 model was, in essence, a dual track of priesthood and civil service. Welfare policy was made by the General Welfare Services Committee but carried out by the Welfare Services Department, through its Welfare Services area directors in the United States and Canada and through directors of temporal affairs representing the Presiding Bishopric abroad. All of these men were and are church employees, constituting, in effect, part of the church civil service. The lack of direct priesthood line direction was not in accord with LDS tradition and soon came to be a matter of concern.

An area structure had first emerged within the welfare program in 1969 to facilitate joint projects among two or more regions. With the church's rapid overseas growth, it became necessary to add an area level of administration for all church functions. In 1975, area supervisors had been appointed from among the First Quorum of Seventy, but they were resident in Salt Lake City rather than in the areas they supervised. Finally, in June 1984, three-man area presidencies were created, resident in the areas they supervise and directly responsible for all church activities there including welfare. There were eighteen such areas worldwide in 1991.[31] At that point, welfare authority descended in a direct priesthood line from the General Welfare Services Committee to the area presidents, with welfare functions and functionaries in the field reporting directly to the area presidents rather than to the Welfare Services Department.

As of 1991, the competent but lean headquarters staff of the Welfare Services Department consisted of Managing Director Keith B. McMullin, Gary Winters (employment and Deseret Industries), Dennis Lifferth (production/distribution), Isaac Ferguson (humanitarian services), and Allen Litster (international welfare). (The latter two functions are described in Chapter 9.) They serve as advisory staff rather than as line officers, making recommendations to and counseling with the policy-making General Welfare Services Committee and offering their services to or responding to requests from the area presidents in carrying out those policies.

In descending order after the general level, area, multiregional, and regional councils train the next body below in the organizational hierarchy, determine needs, plan projects, and oversee production and services within the storehouse resource system to assure that resources are adequate and their use effective. A stake Welfare Services Committee consists of the stake presidency, the stake high council, the stake Relief Society president, and the president of the bishops' council. This committee is responsible for teaching welfare principles, coordinating relationships between the wards and the church employment, social service, and production facilities and projects, and overseeing and coordinating various work and service assignments.

It is at the ward level where the system focuses on needy individuals and families. Even at that level, the nuclear family is primarily responsible for its own self-reliance. According to the *Welfare Resource Handbook*, families should meet periodically as a council to discuss economic and financial issues, among other things. If outside help is needed, the first resort is the extended family and the second the bishop who brings the situation before the Ward Welfare Services Committee, which he chairs. This committee includes the Aaronic and Melchizedek Priesthood quorum leaders and the ward Relief Society president. The committee discusses the family's problems, decides what ward resources are available, and identifies additional sources of help in the stake or higher levels.[32] Assistance may include instruction; referral to LDS Social Services; physical help from neighbors, home teachers, visiting teachers, quorum/Relief Society members; positive social attention from peers; assistance from a ward or stake employment specialist or a church employment center; cash or commodities; or a combination.

The bishop's role is key. Despite the stress on individual responsibility and the assignments of priesthood quorums and the Relief Society, he is still institutionally responsible for the temporal welfare of the members of his ward. As in Nauvoo, the whole welfare system is a resource to assist him in that overwhelming task. Through him, a member in need may access the six components of the storehouse resource system: cash from fast offerings, production projects, bishops' storehouses, employment centers, LDS Social Services, and Deseret Industries.

Role of the Fast Offering

By the end of World War II, a firmly established tradition was
fasting for two meals on the first Sunday of each month, participating
in the "testimony meeting" of spiritual affirmation that took the place
of sacrament meeting that Sunday, and donating the cost of the two
meals to the church. Members understood that these funds were earmarked for the poor; and the church correspondingly channeled every
cent into relief, not into administrative costs or capital investments
within the welfare system. Shortfalls could be supplemented by tithing, but the fast offering could not be used to shore up other functions. In fact, tithing routinely supplemented fast offerings until the
early 1970s, when General Authorities, by repeated emphasis and new
goal-setting, increased the fast offering contributions.

During the 1950s and 1960s, church speakers frequently expressed
mock astonishment at how cheaply Mormons ate. Whether because
of the prodding or because of growing prosperity, the annual per capita contribution rose steadily: from 49 cents in 1936, to 85 cents in
1940, $1.17 in 1950, and $4.05 in 1970.[33] But an increasingly urban
membership required cash for an increasing percentage of items and
services. During the 1950s and early 1960s, the ratio of commodity to
cash welfare disbursements had been typically about 1 to 1.25; during
the 1970s, the ratio rose to approximately 1 to 1.75.

Concerned by the cash drain, church leaders appealed for more
generous offerings. For example, Apostle L. Tom Perry in 1971 suggested doubling fast offering contributions.[34] President Kimball set a
higher standard three years later at the April 1974 general conference,
appealing to members to "be very generous and give, instead of the
amount we saved by two meals...ten times more where we are in a
position to do it."[35] Other General Authorities and local leaders followed his lead; and within a year of his appeal, fast offerings increased
47 percent. Henry D. Taylor gives subsequent per capita fast offering
figures as $8.43 in 1979, $9.14 in 1981, $10.30 in 1982, and $12.61 in
1983.[36]

Total fast offering contributions and disbursements have not been
publicly released since 1958, and per capita contributions have not
been published since 1983. However, if one were to average the
returns of the two special fasts in January and November 1985, discussed below, and annualize them for the participating u.s. and Canadian membership, the resultant figure would be an annual per capita
contribution of approximately $20.[37] However, these special fasts were
in addition to the regular first-Sunday fasts of both months, were as-

signed to meet a cataclysmic and widely advertised need, and were drawn from U.S. and Canadian members only, who have higher incomes than the church-wide membership. Thus, it is difficult to judge how representative the results of these fasts were. Nevertheless, it is apparent that fast offerings have accelerated substantially since the 1974 Kimball sermon and the frequent emphasis on the subject since.

Another reason leaders stress generous cash contributions is relative convenience in international aid. With membership and leadership new, incomes low, and meal costs inconsequential in U.S. terms, it is unlikely that any nations except the United States and Canada, and perhaps a few in Western Europe, are self-sufficient in fast offerings. Even in the United States and Canada, self-sufficiency is most probable within traditional Mormon country; and even there, some stakes and wards would undoubtedly have to support other units of lesser income or greater need, either regularly or periodically. Outside the United States and Canada, exchanges must be in cash. Also, housing, health care, transportation, and other noncommodity needs form a rising proportion of living costs. Consequently, the importance of the fast offering will undoubtedly continue to grow.

Until 1988, bishops could overspend their fast offering income without prior consultation with their stake presidents, who would have to make up the deficiency. Since that date, advance consultation and monthly reporting are required; almost certainly the effect of such a policy has been to reduce per capita fund use.[38]

Production Projects and Bishops' Storehouses

Over half of all Latter-day Saints were employed in agriculture in 1930. By 1990, American Saints probably did not exceed the national average of 2.3 percent. Yet church welfare production projects remain almost entirely agricultural, either producing or processing farm products. One reason is almost certainly historical continuity and the need to maintain a "strategic reservoir" of commodities when cash is useless—as in Europe after World War II. Although it would probably be cheaper to purchase most agricultural products wholesale from commercial farms than to raise them on stake welfare farms despite volunteer labor, more important than economic efficiency are work opportunities for recipients and service opportunities for the well-to-do, both considered essential by the program's architects and current leaders. J. Reuben Clark's 1936 mission statement has never been philosophically replaced: "The real long term objective of the Welfare Plan is the building of character in members of the church, givers and receivers, rescuing all that is finest down deep inside of them, and bringing to flower and fruitage the latent richness of spirit, which after all is the mission and purpose and reason for being of this church."[39] Thus, while the church's welfare program adapted to an increasingly urban setting, the foundation of an agriculturally oriented production and distribution system did not diminish.

Potential conflicts between the church and public relief systems had been virtually eliminated by 1950 by the simple expedient of cutting off contact. In the 1940s, in an effort to prevent duplication, some county welfare departments had threatened to sue public assistance recipients to recover the equivalent of church aid they received. At the same time, some public welfare officials had asked bishops to pay the hospital expenses of Latter-day Saints receiving public assistance. This may be the reason for the 1980 instruction not to give assistance to those receiving "unearned government assistance."[40] (In this context, "earned" assistance is defined as unemployment compensation and social security pensions paid for by payroll taxes on earnings; needs-based assistance like AFDC, paid for out of general funds, is "unearned" by the recipient.)[41]

Welfare Farms and Processing Facilities

Throughout the 1950s, the commodity-based production and distribution component of the program spread across the nation and into Canada. There were 50 church-owned welfare farms in 1943, 41 by 1945, but 400 in 1950 and 541 in 1955, when there were only 180 and 224 stakes, respectively.[42] Many were small projects operated at the ward level on donated, rented, and even ward-owned land. As late as 1967, such ward projects reportedly represented two-thirds of the total system. However, during the 1970s, following national trends, welfare farms became larger, more mechanized, and more economically efficient units operated on a stake and, increasingly, multi-stake basis.

Such units required at least a farm manager, who customarily lived on the farm. Larger staffs grew out of the increased size of multi-stake farms, mechanization, and labor-intensive scientific agricultural practices. Dairy farms, for example, could not function with volunteer labor. Day-to-day management became the domain of full-time employees during the 1960s and 1970s, while stake and ward members provided volunteer labor for weeding, harvesting, and special projects which either required fluctuating amounts of labor, did not require specialized skills, or did not have to be performed to a specified schedule. These technological realities were recognized by the 1980 guidelines that farms under twenty acres should use 50 to 100 percent donated labor, those up to 300 acres 10 to 50 percent, while larger ones were expected to use only 5 to 10 percent donated labor.[43]

The expanded number of farms and the resulting increase in output required a parallel expansion of processing, storage, and distribution capability. Dating from the 1930s, a welfare fleet that hauled coal from a mine in Emery County (sold during the 1970s) and produce between farms and storehouses became a full-fledged transportation department with professional management and staffing.

Tilled acreage rose from approximately 3,000 acres in 1943 to 40,000 in 1950, 90,000 in 1960, 100,000 in 1970, 143,000 in 1975, and 145,700 in 1977, producing every major food crop grown in the United States.[44] Over those same years, canneries were established at each regional storehouse. Deseret Mills and Elevators at Kaysville, Utah, expanded and updated during the 1970s, stored and milled grain into a variety of products. During the late 1970s, grain storage silos were built at strategic locations around the nation. In addition, grain storage bins of five to ten thousand bushels were constructed in each regional storehouse during the same period, the objective being to have 50 pounds of grain per capita stored within 50 miles of every church population center. That policy has continued to the present, with an estimated 5 million bushels available within the entire system.

Since 1936 it had been official policy for every ward and stake to be involved in a welfare production project. Pre-1960 data is apparently not available about the level of compliance, and the proportion naturally declined as stakes were established more diffusely in the post-1960 expansion in the United States and abroad. Nevertheless, 73 percent of all stakes and wards in the United States and Canada reportedly had production projects in 1975, comprising 54 percent of all wards in the church.[45]

To facilitate nationwide distribution, a central storehouse was established in Indianapolis, Indiana, in 1977, serving smaller storehouses in the Midwest, eastern United States, and adjacent areas of Canada. In addition to the Indianapolis facility, the church owned two central storehouses at Welfare Square in Salt Lake City, eleven bishops' central storehouses, and at least seventy-eight subordinate area or regional bishops' storehouses.[46]

Each bishops' central storehouse, like that at Welfare Square in Salt Lake City, supplies its subordinate storehouses and coordinates production planning for its area. For example, one unit might raise cattle while another produces feed for them and a third operates a cannery that preserves the meat as stew. Taken as a national whole, this central storehouse system amounted to a self-sufficient agricultural economy. Mormons, through this system, could grow their own vegetables and fruits and can them, produce their own meat, milk and milk products, and mill from their own grains flour, cereals, and cattle feed. Its factories also produced soap and pasta while Relief Societies produced some clothing, both as service projects for the general membership and work opportunities for welfare recipients.[47]

In 1978, for the first time, the General Welfare Services Committee authorized the bishops' central storehouses to purchase commercially produced personal and household necessities to assure maximum availability of necessary commodities. To increase self-sufficiency, each welfare farm was encouraged to store a year's supply of seed, herbicide, pesticide, and diesel fuel. Storehouses were also encouraged to have on hand within the total system a "year's supply" of the goods projected for distribution within that period.

The number of producing units in the commodity production and distribution system went through a dramatic but short-lived expansion in the late 1970s. Many factors were involved, though simple growth in the number of stakes and wards is probably the most important. The number of persons assisted by the Church Welfare Program had increased from 39,537 in 1950 to 98,411 in 1960 (246 percent), while church membership had grown from 898,478 to 1,408,722 (57 percent), for the most part in the United States. Between 1950 and 1977, numbers of recipients had fluctuated with no discernible pattern between 96,429 (1969) and 113,138 (1968) except for extraordinarily low numbers in 1964 (82,315) and 1970 (84,507). During those same years, church membership grew by 257 percent to 3,618,331, but most of that growth was outside the United States and, hence, in areas without established welfare programs.[48] The 1950–77 church population in the United States had been growing at 4.5 percent per year, while welfare aid fluctuated between 3.5 and 7 percent of church membership; the trend, however, was stable.[49]

During the middle 1970s, the Presiding Bishopric had commissioned an "agronometric study," produced by a group of LDS scholars who reported with twenty-five volumes in October 1977. The report was apocalyptic in tone, recommending that the church be prepared to survive without viable organized government in any country where it had substantial membership. Welfare Services should move consciously toward a return to the law of consecration and stewardship and maintain a widespread and permanent disaster response capability. More production projects, processing plants, distribution centers, and transportation facilities were recommended, as well as greater emphasis on home storage. Contingency plans should include evacuation possibilities and a refugee influx. Areas should plan self-sufficiency in case system-wide transportation and communication became impossible. A computerized population and demand forecasting model should drive welfare planning.[50]

The General Welfare Services Committee apparently did not take this worst-case scenario seriously, but the findings reinforced the views of welfare-conscious leaders like Romney, who were committed to having a production project in every stake. Production projects had already started to expand in 1976, coinciding with the commissioning of the study, because of the expanding number of local units. Without advertising a doomsday rationale, expansion continued.

During the mid-fifties welfare farms had outnumbered stakes one to two. But the number of farms remained relatively stable at about 500 as the number of stakes continued to climb: from 319 stakes in 1960 to 537 in 1970, and more than 1,000 in 1979, 800 of them in the United States and Canada. The United States was now totally blanketed by stakes, yet there were no welfare production projects east of Denver. Since an assumed characteristic of stakehood had, since the late 1930s, been welfare production, the General Welfare Services Committee reemphasized production projects.[51]

Expanding the capacity seems to have been secondary in cause, though inevitable in result. The committee estimated that the existing capacity would meet the basic needs of 5 percent of the church membership temporarily or 1 percent on a continuing basis and initially decided to expand production to a threshold of emergency sustenance for 30 percent of the total membership living within welfare distribution areas.[52] The number of welfare farms jumped to over 900 by 1981, most of the additions coming in the Midwest, Northeast, and South. Many were very small, often less than thirty acres.

At first, this increased supply potential matched increases in demand. The 1979 national recession, followed by incomplete recovery and a deeper recession beginning in 1981, drained commodity use and cash resources at an accelerating pace. Expenditures increased from $4.2 million in 1951 to $6.2 million in 1957, when public reports ceased. However, total church welfare expenditures apparently increased more rapidly than could be explained by membership growth, economic conditions, or the number of recipients; by the late 1970s, it was into the $20 million range, part of which is explainable by inflation. In 1977, the number of persons assisted was 99,600; in 1978, it unaccountably jumped to 139,300, an increase of 28.5 percent, and again by 13.3 percent in 1979 to 160,600.[53]

The reasons for the increases remain obscure. Possibly they are related to the energy "bust" experienced by the Mountain West at the end of the 1970s. Speculation, based on oil at $45 a barrel, had pushed up prices for coal, uranium, and oil shale. However, faulty public policy adaptation to the rising energy costs resulted in unprecedented peacetime inflation; the Federal Reserve Board's reaction in 1979, among other forces, precipitated a recession. At the same time, energy conservation motivated by the rising costs cut demand, bringing the world oil price down to $15 a barrel by the 1980s, with similar impact on coal and other alternate fuels. Exactly how these economic developments impacted on Mormons is unclear, but anecdotes reported many bishops being asked to "bail out" overextended members and being advised by the General Welfare Services Committee only to "maintain life, not life-style."

Such increased demands proved temporary. Commodities distributed increased from 17,750,000 pounds in 1977 when 99,600 people were assisted to 35,441,230 pounds when 160,600 were assisted in 1979. That figure dropped 41 percent to 21 million pounds by 1982. Beginning in 1983, the number of bishops' commodity orders, rather than number of persons assisted or the pounds of commodities distributed, had become the measure of welfare volume; that figure settled at approximately 350,000 per year in 1984 where it remained throughout most of the decade.[54] One result was that the "boom" in production capability exceeded the needs of recipients, processing capacity, and storage.

Funding

Funds for welfare production and distribution between 1936 and 1980 had come from a combination of central church funds and assessments on the wards and stakes, calculated primarily on a per capita basis. The capital needed for expansion or improvements came from assessments for cash contributions on top of tithing and fast offerings. Local units paid 50 percent of costs for farms and other production projects and 30 percent of the construction costs for storehouses, canneries, and other processing units, their share being financible with no-interest loans from the general church.[55] Stakes and wards also received annual assessments for the projected value of distribution needs which they could fill either in cash or through commodity production. To relieve wards and stakes of some of the financial burden of the 1979–81 expansion, welfare farms were encouraged to overproduce and sell the surplus on the open market. This policy was short lived; it drew criticism from competing farmers and threatened the charitable tax exemption status of the entire system.

A cutback in the number of church welfare farms followed in 1981, but the acreage under cultivation did not shrink by the same proportion. Because many of the smaller farms were not viable, some were sold; others were turned over to a newly created Farm Management Corporation to be leased to private farmers yet remain available as a strategic reserve.[56] The General Welfare Services Committee then decided to fund commodity production from fast offerings and the church general fund.[57] At the same time (1983), it cancelled all outstanding debts of stakes to the welfare capital fund for past assessments.

By 1985, the production and distribution system had stabilized: 199 agricultural production units, 51 canneries, 27 large and 36 small grain-storage facilities, 12 bishops' central storehouses, 69 regional storehouses, and 32 branch (stake or other subregion) storehouses scattered about the United States with a few in Canada. These storehouses distributed commodities conservatively estimated at a value of $30 million per year by 1990. In 1990, 51,000 acres were planted to crops; 71,000 acres were used for grazing, and some 50,000 acres were leased but reclaimable. Along the Wasatch Front in Utah were a meat-packing plant, a milk-processing facility, a bakery, a soap factory, and a pasta factory.[58]

Since 1981, the formula for determining production efficiency is assigning a market price to the commodities delivered to the storehouse and eliminating any farm project which cannot show a 2 or 3 percent accounting return above costs or processing project which cannot return a simulated 4 to 5 percent. The surpluses, which are often greater, are plowed back into capital improvements.[59] The combined production projects and storage facilities by 1991 provide the total current commodity welfare needs of Saints in the areas served by the storehouse system, as indicated by bishops' orders, and leave a surplus sometimes donated to other charities, as described later in the chapter. Stockpiling more supplies for some overwhelming catastrophe is not part of the current plan.

Enthroning "Work"

The person-days of donated labor are impressive. The numbers reported each year from 1950 to 1985 fluctuated widely but, for the quarter-century of 1950–75, were between 100,000 and 200,000. With the mid-seventies growth spurt, time commitments also shot up—between 400,000 and 550,000 from 1975 to 1983. During 1984 and 1985, the figures were down to 277,000 and 245,000 person-days respectively.[60] No data have been published since 1985.

Despite persistent instructions to bishops that recipients should work, as able, in return for assistance, the proportion of recipients working in the program and the proportion of all donated hours contributed by recipients has declined steadily due to the urbanization of church membership, the consolidation of production units, and the concentration of need among those least able and least qualified to work. Marion G. Romney complained in 1975 that only one-fourth of welfare recipients were working, a fact he termed "an uncomplimentary reflection upon us, the priesthood leaders," though H. Burke Peterson estimated that another "25 percent of those receiving help are not in a position to work."[61]

That challenge remains unmet. Bishops recruit volunteer labor according to an assignment roster by making direct requests to priesthood quorums and Relief Societies. They generally fill their assignments with only a small amount of slippage. But there is little direct correlation between the availability of recipients, the type of work required, and the capabilities of those currently receiving assistance.

Paid hours probably exceed donated hours two to one on welfare farms and in milling and meat-packing plants; the work is continuous rather than episodic, requires skilled labor, and may have safety and health inspection concerns. Recipients probably supply no more than 10 percent of that donated labor. On the other hand, donated hours probably exceed paid hours four to one in storehouses. Since stocking shelves, cleaning, and warehousing can be scheduled predictably and since the elderly, the disabled, and women can participate, as much as half of donated storehouse labor may come from recipients. The amount varies by location depending upon accessibility, skill mix, and leadership effort. A few long-term recipients gain some experience at clerical work, forklift operations, and other potentially marketable skills. Most welfare canneries are operated only a few days per year with volunteers recruited through bishops. Limited supervision is required, with donated hours probably exceeding paid hours by a multiple of four. Recipient involvement, depending on the happenstance of availability, probably does not exceed 10 percent of the donated cannery labor.

No attempt is made to relate the hours worked to commodities or assistance. No record is available of the number of hours bishops may require recipients to work in the wards, maintaining chapels and assisting other needy ward members. But clearly the production system offers more opportunity for the financially independent to serve the needy than for the needy to contribute to their own assistance.

Delivering the Goods: Response to the Teton Flood

This extensive production and distribution system justifies itself by its ability to deliver the goods to the needy. Typically, the bishop becomes aware of needs, either when the individual asks for help or when home teachers or visiting teachers pass messages to their supervisors who alert the Relief Society president or bishop. Sometimes the bishop (but more often the Relief Society president on assignment from the bishop) visits the home to determine need and prepares an order for the bishop's signature. The order may be taken to the distribution center by the recipient or by a Relief Society representative or the commodities may be delivered to the home.

However, a continuing justification of the extensive production and distribution system has been its standby capacity in times of widespread disaster, particularly hurricanes, floods, and earthquakes. Usually manpower for preventative sandbagging and cleanup has been more important than commodities.[62] Probably the best test of the Welfare Plan in recent years was its response when the Teton Dam in eastern Idaho collapsed on 5 June 1976, sending a surging flood on an eighty-five-mile rampage through an area whose population was over 80 percent LDS.[63] This case involved the greatest concentration of Latter-day Saints at this magnitude of disaster, testing not only the program's ability to provide direct assistance but also the ability of Latter-day Saints to act within their local church structure, implement and follow authority, and cooperate with each other and federal authorities.

While only six people were drowned, this deluge wrecked machinery, killed 11,000 head of livestock, damaged or ruined approximately 90,000 acres of crops, destroyed possibly five to ten thousand acres of arable land, and damaged or destroyed approximately 360 businesses, slightly more than 4,000 homes, and a similar number of farm structures. The total property loss was estimated at close to $1.5 billion. Rexburg, Idaho, served as the major hub of relief efforts because almost 80 percent of the flood victims resided there or in nearby communities.

The organizational response of the LDS people was remarkably effective. LDS leaders, primarily stake presidents and ward bishops, knew without question that their responsibility was to provide material and psychological assistance and to begin cleanup and reconstruction. People within their units almost instinctively sought and followed that leadership. The disaster response suggests that the combination of internal authority, organizational training, cooperation, and sacrifice were redeeming virtues of tremendous consequence in alleviating the effects of the flood. Such organized activity, according to federal disaster officials, was unlike the stunned passivity normally found among disaster victims. Recognizing the effectiveness of the existing Mormon structure, government agents organized and funneled some of their assistance through those channels.

The Church Welfare Services Department provided great quantities of food and some clothing over the next ten weeks, at a total cost of $1,033,250. Church-owned Ricks College in Rexburg, fortunately above the flood line, provided meals and lodging for thousands during the same period. During the first week, up to 10,000 meals a day were served, and the total amounted to 386,690 by the time direct service ended in August. Many neighbors and extended family members contributed funds, food, personal items, and help with the cleanup. Through a specially organized church program, hundreds brought heavy farm or construction equipment to work in the cleanup; thousands of individuals responded to calls for hand-laborers organized through stakes and wards. On 19 June 1976, the number of volunteers bused in from outside the area peaked at 5,000. By the end of July when this program wound down, a minimum estimate of 1 million volunteer hours had been contributed.

It is natural for people, whatever their background, to respond altruistically in sudden, highly visible, severe, and widespread natural disasters. Characteristically, however, this spontaneous response lasts for only a few days. During the Teton flood, feelings of collective responsibility were intense for several weeks, then lingered, though at a diminishing rate, for a total of two and a half months. The institutional commitment of many LDS members appears significant, especially coupled with the experienced hierarchical structure which organized, directed, and channeled these impulses.

The disaster also provided several recommendations for future action. For example, local priesthood leaders were handicapped by lack of communication once the waters destroyed telephone lines and cut roads. Citizen-band radios helped, but not all leaders had access to them and no schedule of emergency channels had been worked out. On the recommendation of a stake president, the General Welfare Services Committee studied the possibilities of a churchwide emergency shortwave/CB system. It was instituted early in 1979 and was still expanding with volunteer operators in 1991.

Second, to respond even more quickly to disasters, the committee also authorized the Welfare Services Department to create two self-contained emergency response units which could be transported either by a single truck or airplane. They contain tents, medical supplies, a system for distilling water, and other emergency supplies for the first several days of a disaster. One unit is kept in Salt Lake City and the other on the West Coast.

As a third lesson, the stake president who was also the regional and area welfare chairman in Rexburg obviously had more than one man could do. At that time, welfare councils existed at the ward, stake, and general levels, consisting of the respective leaders at each level. The bishop was chairman of the ward welfare council, and the stake president chaired the stake welfare council. However, the two supra-stake levels, the region and the area, had no councils. In 1979, these missing steps were completed, with a General Authority presiding at the area level and the regional representative at the region.[64]

Deseret Industries

At its tenth anniversary in 1948, Deseret Industries had six stores, two in Salt Lake City, and one each in Los Angeles and the Utah cities of Ogden, Logan, and Tooele. Each refurbished donated items on site and sold the used products at retail. Employees were primarily the aged, the handicapped, and the otherwise unemployable.

Additional stores were added in 1950, including a new plant for the Los Angeles store in 1951. That year, the Los Angeles store introduced a work-at-home approach to avoid the difficult travel required, and the innovation spread throughout the system as "Homecraft." Thereafter, the General Welfare Committee directed Deseret Industries to produce new items, both for retail sale and for storehouse distribution. Rug-making began in 1954, and a woolen mill started making blankets in 1957. In 1978, a substantial furniture and mattress factory was added.[65] By its twenty-fifth anniversary in 1963, Deseret Industries announced that, except for the church's capital investments in buildings and equipment, the operation was self-sustaining.[66]

By the 1960s, rising social security benefits made work unnecessary for most elderly American Saints, although some continued at Deseret Industries to have something to do. As legislative and social changes encouraged the employment of the handicapped and disabled, Deseret Industries increased its focus on that population. Its stores were licensed as sheltered workshops for purposes of wage and hour regulation, and its goals became rehabilitation, followed by placement in competitive employment; supervisors' duties included on-the-job training. Nevertheless, it continued to supply long-term employment to the otherwise unemployable, with priority going to those referred by bishops.

To provide additional work opportunities and cash flow, beginning in the 1980s, usable clothing and reusable cloth was gathered and both sold and donated to international agencies operating in third world countries. Such gifts were welcomed; and as a result, in 1990 the General Welfare Services Committee decided to stop selling clothing or cloth in bulk quantities but to donate surpluses to domestic and international causes.[67] These surpluses constituted an estimated 6 million pounds per year consisting of an estimated 12 million individual items of clothing. A church-owned building in Salt Lake City was remodeled to provide a 75,000-square-foot facility where Deseret Industries employees prepare, bale, and store these fabric surpluses.

Church welfare leaders have considered church membership too sparse to support Deseret Industries beyond the Mountain West and the West Coast. But in the 1980s, volunteer "rehabilitation service workers" were called under Deseret Industries auspices in a few pilot areas to coordinate community rehabilitation services for members in need. This experimental program was successful but not widely replicated. (See discussion under "The Church Employment System" below.)

In 1989, Deseret Industries employed over 2,000 and placed more than 700 in competitive employment through 21 parent and 27 branch Deseret Industries installations.[68] Challenges of the 1990s again involve clientele. Increasing numbers of bishops' referrals are culturally disadvantaged or language-deficient immigrants. Deseret Industries must remain self-sustaining, which places a brake on its ability to assist more of the handicapped and difficult to employ; still, in relation to its capacity, its contribution to self-reliance is substantial.[69]

The Church Employment System

Post-World War II Facilities

Some stakes and wards may have continued their work directors throughout World War II; but with full employment and public employment services, these assignments gradually lapsed. The Deseret Employment Bureau also ceased to function during the period. However, the General Church Welfare Committee continued to monitor the need through ad hoc committees appointed in 1942, 1944, and 1945.

In early 1945, with the war in Europe over and victory in the

Pacific assumed, a study committee, mindful of the readjustment problems for returning veterans, advised establishing a permanent, professionally staffed church employment center in Salt Lake City to serve as both the central employment office for the church and as the Salt Lake regional employment office. Its executive officer would supervise and coordinate all employment-related activities of the regions, stakes, and wards throughout the church and supervise and train regional, stake, and ward work directors who should be called throughout the church. Each regional work director would assemble and distribute information on employment needs and possibilities. The stake and ward directors were to act as clearing houses for such information, counsel returning veterans, and provide job counseling for other unemployed Mormons. The Relief Society would staff and manage a women's division. Bishops were to administer a questionnaire among veterans in their wards, determining their work experience, work and school plans, service-learned occupational skills, and perceived needs.

Not all of the committee's recommendations were inaugurated at the time; but a Salt Lake Region Employment Office opened 1 March 1948, expanding into a four-region center serving the entire valley when the Salt Lake Region was split in 1950. The Relief Society established a separate women's employment center when it opened its own office building in August 1956; in February 1965, this center was recombined with what had become the men's center, perhaps reflecting a move toward a more intensive employment placement function within the welfare system. Even though the two centers were still separate in 1958, a memorandum that year records that both centers had interviewed 41,644 young women and placed 7,800 between 1950 and 1958.[70] The multi-region employment center also recruited and interviewed full-time employees for church headquarters, until the church Personnel Department was launched in 1968.

Church Employment Centers, 1960s and 1970s

During the 1960s, stake and ward employment centers fluctuating between fourteen and twenty were formed at local initiative, some of them functioning on a multi-stake basis. Then in 1967, the General Welfare Committee encouraged all stakes in the United States and Canada to establish employment centers, with the General Welfare Committee paying office expenses while the stakes provided the personnel.[71]

The General Welfare Committee provided little guidance to the directors of these centers at the time and it is not apparent how many stakes responded. Beginning in 1972, the employment centers were financed on the same basis as most other local church functions, 50 percent from general funds and 50 percent from stake funds. In 1975 LDS Social Services assumed responsibility for the employment system. It was transferred briefly to the Production-Distribution Department in 1976, then relocated in the Welfare Services Personnel Section when that entity was formed later in 1976. These relocations indicated the greater attention employment centers were receiving at the central level.

After considerable internal planning and discussion during 1976 and 1977, the Welfare Services Department introduced a centralized reporting system and periodic audits by field representatives from the headquarters employment division. Welfare Services staff prepared and introduced an operations manual, and training programs upgraded and professionalized the staffs of the twenty-four offices then in operation. Offices with unattractive locations and facilities were moved or refurbished. The number of persons placed in remunerative employment, which had fluctuated between 5,000 and 10,000 during most of the 1950s and 1960s, rose to the 25,000–35,000 range by 1978 where it has remained fairly stable since for U.S./Canadian operations.[72]

In 1981, employment became a full-fledged division of the Church Welfare Services Department, its thirty-one centers fully funded. Simultaneously, the Church Welfare Services Committee approved the department's proposal to establish satellite centers staffed by volunteers where competent persons were available. The Welfare Services session of the 1982 April general conference was dedicated to explaining the centralized employment system and career planning. Elder Thomas J. Fyans of the First Quorum of the Seventy identified the employment system as the "component of Church Welfare Services most capable of promoting member self-reliance" but both he and Elder Boyd K. Packer warned that the system must remain ward- and priesthood quorum-based, with the centers, whether staffed by professionals or volunteers in a supporting role.[73]

Reflecting that philosophy, the six-page 1982 *Church Employment System Guidebook* devoted only one-quarter page to church employment centers.[74] The remainder consisted of instruction for quorum, Relief Society, ward, and stake employment specialists, who were to be called throughout the church. The priesthood quorum employment specialists and a Relief Society counselor would help the ward employment specialist keep a roster of the ward members' occupations and identify any employment needs. The ward specialist should develop a log of employers in the ward, identify available job openings, help job searchers assess their capabilities, help prepare resumes, help improve job search skills, and refer the job seeker to openings, to public and private community resources, or to a church employment center if no appropriate job openings were known at the ward and stake level. The stake employment specialist would train ward specialists, coordinate with and share information among them, coordinate with any existing church employment centers (most stakes did not have access to one), and coordinate employment rehabilitation and career guidance activities within the stake.

As support services to the local priesthood structure, the one independent function of these centers (and not a minor one) was to solicit job opportunities from the business community. Beyond that, they were to coordinate job information on a multi-stake basis, maintain a library containing labor market information, training materials, and hints for job seekers, place applicants that the ward and stake level failed to place, provide technical information on request, and train priesthood leaders on request. Though the guidebook also described the church employment system's responsibilities as "counseling... for those in need of better employment or rehabilitation" and helping "parents... to counsel family members about employment and career planning," the guidelines did not include instructions for doing so.[75]

In short, the focus was not on job preparation but on finding openings for the job-ready. The manual assumed that most job seekers could find their own opportunities through friends, relatives, former employers, public agencies, or ward employment specialists. As something of a last resort, the church employment centers would seek job orders, primarily from LDS employers, for the candidates, advise them on job search methods briefly where necessary, set up interviews, and follow up with the candidate and employer to confirm the placement.

Rehabilitation Services

The 1980 *Welfare Services Resource Handbook* stated, "Employment Center personnel are not to be involved in career guidance or employment rehabilitative counseling."[76] Therefore, those not ready for employment were usually either referred to Deseret Industries or neglected, except for a note to their bishops explaining the policy.

During 1984, however, the Welfare Services Department decided to actively offer rehabilitation services outside the Deseret Industries

setting. Welfare services staff members with Deseret Industries backgrounds were assigned as area welfare specialists in the Washington,
D.C., and Boise, Idaho, areas. In both places, these supervisors asked
stake presidents and bishops to call retired couples as volunteers to
work one-on-one with the hard-to-employ, helping them use
community resources to overcome employment barriers. These
counselors persuaded those needing jobs to improve their dress and
grooming, instructed them in interview skills, guided them to apply
for training programs available in the community, accompanied them
to job interviews, and generally did whatever else was necessary to
improve their employability. The successes, considering the obsta-
cles, were sufficient to convince those involved that the effort was
worth extending to other regions. Gary Winters, a human resource
development specialist with a rehabilitation background, formerly
with Deseret Industries and director of the Washington, D.C., experiment, became staff specialist in the central Welfare Services office for
both Deseret Industries and employment centers.

Rehabilitation became an official program with its own manual at
all church employment centers in 1988.[77] The rehabilitation population
was defined as those with "no marketable skills, poor work habits and
histories, physical and mental disabilities, emotional problems, drug
and/or alcohol problems, cultural or language barriers, and chronic
dependency on welfare assistance." Clients might be referred by bishops or walk-ins, though in these cases, rehabilitation workers contacted the bishop for approval before providing services. Considering
each case was a rehabilitation team, chaired by the employment center
manager and consisting of representatives of each welfare services operation in the area, ward leaders, family members, and representatives
of appropriate community services. The team would meet weekly to
discuss needs and progress and plan for further action. The key resource was unpaid volunteer rehabilitation specialists, either individuals or married couples, willing and able to spend twenty to forty
hours a week guiding each client to church and community resources
until he or she achieved employment.

Because needs and resources vary widely and because of the system's essentially decentralized authority, the Welfare Services Department established no service quotas; however, local and supervisory
staff jointly set service targets and discussed rehabilitation success in
each annual performance review. The centers were eager to take on
the assignment, but finding enough volunteer specialists was difficult.
Employed members who could devote the required time were scarce;
retired volunteers were also in demand for proselyting, visitors' cen-

ters, genealogical, and temple assignments. Nevertheless, the system made 1,200 rehabilitation placements in 1989.

Church Employment Centers in the 1980s

The number of employment offices staffed with full-time professionals reached its plateau at thirty-six in the early 1980s, most of them in the western areas with denser LDS populations, but others in metropolitan areas like Chicago, New York City, and Atlanta. The system placed 35,000 in gainful employment during 1984. At that point, an intense internal debate arose over the appropriateness of spending church funds on private placement when public employment services were universally available. Alternatives included expansion to provide a comprehensive range of services throughout the United States and abroad, limiting services to rehabilitation candidates only, using the professional staffs only to train stake and ward leaders, staffing by church-service volunteers only, closing the entire operation, or continuing it on a self-supporting fee basis.

Those arguing for expansion were convinced that the savings in welfare assistance and the additional tithes and offerings paid by the otherwise unemployed were bringing returns to the church which were a substantial multiple of the annual employment system budget. Perhaps the lack of data on how long those same individuals would have remained out of work without the church employment system and the extent to which they would have found their own jobs or used public sources may account for the decision not to expand. However, arguments for contraction also failed to persuade. The thirty-six professionally staffed centers continued into 1991, but the system was supplemented by the addition of satellite centers operated by church service volunteers supervised by the professionals. Such satellite centers numbered fifty-one in the United States and Canada in 1991. These centers have theoretical jurisdiction over the entire United States, though members in many areas of limited Mormon population may be too far from a center for it to have any practical significance. In 1990, the system placed 54,000, the placements being split about half and half between the ward and stake specialists and the centers.[78]

Conceptually, the centers divide LDS clients into three categories: "easy to place candidates" who can find their own jobs with some advice from ward employment specialists, "self-help candidates" who need employment center assistance to prepare resumes, identify potential employers and job openings, set up interviews, and follow up with the candidate and employer, and "rehabilitation candidates" who require the most time but, because of the volunteer shortage, receive the least attention in most centers. Staff predilections and the membership population served by each center, more than policy, determine the client mix.

Most centers do little with career guidance counseling except for maintaining print and video-tape materials for self-help efforts or referring inquiring youth and job seekers to public agencies or professional counseling services in the community. The Church Education System experimented during 1966–74 with a vocational guidance program, "Gospel of Work for Youth," but abandoned it along with many other experimental educational programs in 1974.[79] In the mid-1980s when worker displacement was a major public policy concern in the United States, the Welfare Services Department contracted with a consulting firm to produce a series of six video tapes for self-directed training in job search skills for adults.[80] Those are the welfare system's only explicit ventures to date into vocational guidance. There are ample alternative sources for this important service in employment preparation in the United States, but international welfare services must surely consider it in greater depth.

A Central City Presence

Too new to fully judge its effectiveness in 1991 was a promising departure in Chicago, under consideration for other locations. Among the Latin American immigrants to the United States were many LDS members. Spanish-speaking missionaries also converted many in the Hispanic neighborhoods of American cities. In June 1978, a revelation announced by President Spencer W. Kimball extended priesthood opportunities to worthy black males, and proselyting began in black U.S. neighborhoods as well as in Africa. Rather than requiring central city residents to commute to white suburban meeting-houses, separate central city branches were formed in some locales.[81] Central city members were predominantly low income, intensifying welfare needs in those areas.

By late 1989, the Wilmette, Illinois, Stake had over a thousand Spanish-speaking members, most of them in Chicago central city wards along with other low-income members, while most of its more affluent membership was in the Chicago suburbs. The stake had a professionally staffed employment center located in a suburb. A satellite center was established in a central city chapel with easy access by subway. Multilingual volunteers staffed it at regular day and evening hours. Successful Hispanic members are among the job counselors on certain evenings. A professional staff member from the parent center spends one night per week at the satellite center to consult as needed. The staff makes placements to job openings emerging through the stake and ward employment specialists or developed by the parent center. In the same chapel, volunteers teach weekly English classes. During the first few months of operation, this center placed 51 percent of its applicants, and a similar satellite was opened in a black neighborhood. Data are not currently available on its progress nor that of the employment activities serving twelve inner-city branches organized in Philadelphia during 1991.[82] Welfare services officials are discussing the possibilities of similar installations in other large u.s. cities.

The Widening Focus of Welfare

LDS employment centers date back to the 1890s, but this revitalized conceptualization is one sign of a focus widening beyond commodity production, which dominated the LDS welfare system during 1936–60. It is as essential to self-reliance in a modern industrial economy where employment is the primary source of income as an agricultural infrastructure was in an agrarian economy. But self-reliance in an interdependent urban society also has social, emotional, and health requirements without which a system concerned with human welfare cannot be complete. In 1960–90, the LDS Church found itself increasingly involved in those efforts as well.

Health-related Activities

As the church sought to meet the health needs of its members in places where such facilities were absent, it gradually acquired hospitals—fourteen, by 1970, in Utah, Idaho, and Wyoming, without centralized budgeting, management, policy, or coordination with other personal welfare activities. Responsible for all church properties and recognizing a lack of logic in the current approach, the Presiding Bishopric in September 1970 created a Health Services Corporation and appointed Dr. James O. Mason, a specialist in public health working for the United States Public Health Service in Atlanta, as its first Commissioner of Health Services. The corporation combined all of the church's health-related facilities under a common management and budgeting system, not only for rationality of decision-making but to ease the challenge of complying with federal regulations.[83]

Upon Mason's arrival, Harold B. Lee, then first counselor in the First Presidency, asked him to study the possibility of providing health care to the international church, counseling him to remember that the primary church role was to provide concepts and principles rather than buildings and services. Mason found deplorable health standards among some members in emerging nations. For example, in Bolivia and Guatemala 50 percent of the children in LDS families died before age five. In February 1971, Mason proposed to the First Presidency the establishment of a health services missionary program in which young women and men with some experience in health care would teach members in selected area about health care, disease prevention, and the effective use of locally available health resources.[84] (See Chapter 9.)

Then a 1973–74 management study by the national consulting firm Cresap, Paget, and McCormick recommended that the church divest itself of its western-based hospitals and concentrate more fully on its worldwide mission, a conclusion toward which Mason and others had already been moving. From the worldwide perspective, there was little justification for pouring tithing into a service available only in a restricted area while areas of greater need lacked more basic services. On 6 September 1974, the First Presidency announced that the church was transferring its hospitals to a nonchurch, nonprofit organization, later named Intermountain Health Care, Inc. The net worth of the hospitals at the time was approximately $61 million, total indebtedness amounted to $28 million, and replacement cost of the physical facilities was estimated at $107 million. The church received no money from the transaction.[85]

The relevance of that story is the aftermath. Without hospitals to manage, Mason and his staff greatly enlarged the concept and program of health missionaries, called initially Worldwide Health Services but soon changed to Developing Welfare Services. This name essentially implied that the total welfare program would become operative in developing areas—not only directing health missionaries (soon called welfare services missionaries), but teaching health care, economic development, self-reliance, career planning, cooperation, and generosity.[86]

In August 1975 Mason announced a timetable for placing a professional welfare services representative in each of the globe's eighteen regions by the end of 1976. That individual would supervise as many as three hundred unpaid specialists who would teach and work with the local people. Once Developing Welfare Services prepared the local membership for the traditional program of projects and storehouses, the component of the welfare program responsible for that particular function would assume control.

In 1976, Mason became briefly the managing director of the entire welfare system; however, his vision apparently extended further than the church leadership was then prepared to support. The worldwide Developing Welfare Services regions were never created, and Mason later that year accepted an appointment as director of the federal Centers for Disease Control in Atlanta, later still becoming Assistant Secretary of the United States Department of Health and Social Services in the George Bush administration. But a modified welfare services missionary program survived (see Chapter 9), while the events during Mason's tenure were important in enlarging church social service activities.

Unified Social Services

The Relief Society provided the first Mormon social services as part of its compassionate mission. Between the 1920s and the 1930s, until the department was overwhelmed by the sheer magnitude of needs generated by the Great Depression, these caseworkers provided a variety of services to their client families. (See Chapter 5.) The advent of the Church Welfare Program, with its priesthood-structured services, relegated the Relief Society to a supportive, though hard-working and highly productive, role. It had, however, maintained three autonomous programs: Indian placement (fostering Indian students in Mormon homes during the school year), adoptive services, and youth guidance. All three services operated in Utah and, to a lesser extent, in Arizona, Idaho, and Nevada; Indian placement was the most widespread, functioning in a number of other states and provinces in western Canada.

These remaining social services were brought under the umbrella of a new department in 1969 called Unified Church Social Services. Marvin J. Ashton, a newly appointed Assistant to the Twelve, was named managing director, a position he held only until December 1971 when he was called to the Quorum of the Twelve. He then became chairman of the Social Services Advisory Committee, continuing as the major voice in policy-making.[87] He decided that coordination would allow professional upgrading and more effective management.[88] For example, each adoptive program had to be separately licensed in each state, but the new administration unified this procedure and placed one individual in charge of licensing for all social services. Relief Society President Belle S. Spafford supported the changes; and the transition, though not completely welcome to all concerned, occurred smoothly.

The reorganization increased the credibility and status of the church's social work among members and local leaders, involved ward and stake ecclesiastical committees and resource persons more intensively, made the program more visible, and provided a sound corporate foundation for expansion.[89] As Unified Social Services began hiring more professional personnel, many with graduate degrees, its status improved among other social workers. The salaries, benefits, and physical facilities of church-employed social workers improved significantly throughout the 1970s. These trends were not unique to Social Services but were part of a general introduction of professional personnel management throughout church administration during that period.

The former youth guidance program had focused on alcohol and drug abuse; but under the new unified program, youth guidance evolved into Clinical Services which dealt with many kinds of personal problems. Adoptive services split into two divisions, one working with the birth mother (or, rarely, both birth parents) and the other division with adoptive applicants.

The Indian Placement Program had begun operating on a very small scale unofficially shortly after World War II. With the encouragement of Spencer W. Kimball, then an apostle, it grew steadily, the numbers of students placed increasing from 68 in 1954 to a peak of 4,997 in 1972.[90] However, the zealous recruiting, primarily by church-employed social workers, at times violated the wishes of tribal leaders and Indian parents. In 1973, the responsibility for recruiting and interviewing prospective students shifted from the social service workers to branch presidents on Indian reservations, which led to an immediate decline in the number of participants. In 1972, 4,730 entered the program, in 1973 2,917, and in 1975 only 2,353. Thereafter, placements were limited to teenagers.[91] As education and living conditions improved among various reservations and as church units became stronger, applications continued to decline. Protest from Native American activists undoubtedly restricted applications as well. Currently, the Welfare Service Department coordinates applications with stakes and wards within reasonable distances; there assigned volunteers recruit host families. Of a total of 70,000 Native American youth who have been served by the program over the years, only 500 teenagers were involved in 1990.[92]

The program's stated intention is to maintain foster placement as an option in cases where it appears to be the best available alternative,

supplementing that effort with an aggressive Native American Educational Outreach Program at Brigham Young University to enhance
the higher education opportunities of American Indian youth.[93] Nevertheless, the church's international efforts and the death of Spencer
W. Kimball, the program's strong advocate, in 1985 led to a decline in
resources allocated to serving Native Americans; this issue led to the
disaffection and ultimate excommunication of the only Native American General Authority.[94]

LDS Social Services

The Cresap, Paget, and McCormick study of 1973–74 pointed
out legal and licensing requirements imposed by the various states,
the possibility of lawsuits by disgruntled clients, and the need to
protect church personal and financial records from government in-
spections. Their recommendation was to incorporate Unified Social
Services.[95] In late 1974 LDS Social Services was created with Victor L.
Brown, Jr., as its first commissioner. Another advantage of incorpo-
ration became rapidly apparent. It was easier for LDS Social Services to
collect fees as a corporation. Clients pay on a sliding scale related to
income, but this counseling arm has always done much of its work
free.[96]

In October 1976, Harold C. Brown (no relation) replaced Victor
L. Brown, Jr., as Commissioner of Social Services and Director of
LDS Social Services. Little adjustment followed except for increased
emphasis on management training and expanded services in stakes
away from the core Mormon area. Harold Brown considered the
training necessary because so many of the staff managing offices, supervising other personnel, and providing professional counseling had
come from social work backgrounds without management experience or education.

At the same time, another long-standing issue focused. Local
church leaders had often asked how to handle problems presented by
the deaf, the blind, the retarded, the mentally ill, the victims of family
breakup, the very elderly, and other troubled members. The Personal
Welfare Services Division had, in 1967, replaced the Employment,
Work Directors, and Rehabilitation Division to handle all noncommodity welfare functions. As originally conceptualized, it was
responsible for providing principle-oriented materials and programs
for local leaders, while LDS Social Services professionals worked with
personal cases—either directly or in consultation with local priesthood leaders.

From the beginning of Unified Social Services in 1969 until 1975, clinical counseling by Social Service personnel was the growing method of assistance for church members in need of such help. However, the apparently insatiable demand for such services led to greater restrictions on professional counseling and more emphasis on the counseling role of local priesthood leaders, who, if they felt the need, should draw on locally available resource people. Each ward and stake was supposed to create and maintain a list of doctors, nurses, social workers, counselors, and other professionals who could render volunteer service. If this process could not provide the needed help, the bishop should next consult with a Social Services representative, the two of them meeting jointly with the member to evaluate the problem. Then the bishop could continue counseling privately with the member or refer the case to LDS Social Services, still maintaining ultimate responsibility. Specialized professional help was thus allowed to be occasionally necessary, but most social and emotional problems were officially defined as spiritual in nature, best cured by repentance and best handled ecclesiastically, rather than professionally.

This reshaping of the relationship between ecclesiastical and professional services was given its capstone by a forceful address from Apostle Boyd K. Packer during the welfare session of April 1978 general conference. He acknowledged the need "in difficult and persistent cases" for specialized professional therapy but urged emotional self-reliance rather than dependence on continual counseling. In his analogy he explained that "if we lose our emotional and spiritual independence . . . we can be weakened quite as much, perhaps even more, than when we become dependent materially." Troubled members should seek personal revelation and, if necessary, counseling from priesthood leaders rather than professionals.[97]

Ecclesiastical leaders, in short, had access to the helping professions but were responsible for seeing that gospel standards and approaches were maintained. The church expected local priesthood leaders through their own efforts, study, and prayer to help members solve most social and emotional problems. Social Service leaders emphasized to their staff the need for a gospel approach to helping people without neglecting professional standards, approaches, and theories. Whether the current balance is successful can be judged only by individual cases.

The late 1970s brought two challenging assignments to LDS Social Services. Indicating a high degree of trust in the agency's competence and judgment, General Authorities began to refer to Social Services staff much of the immense volume of requests by troubled individuals for personal counsel and assistance. In 1978, for example, Social Services answered approximately four hundred letters sent to General Authorities, talked to some two hundred individuals who had come to see a General Authority, and conferred with an additional 150 people who had come to church headquarters to see either a General Authority or some other official. Second, in response to requests from the Presiding Bishopric, Social Services staff prepared a series of guidelines for perplexed local church leaders on homosexuality, suicide, child abuse, alcoholism, and unwed parenthood.[98]

By 1990, sixty Social Service offices had been established, positioned so that they nominally blanketed the United States and lapped over into Canada. There were also offices in Great Britain, Australia, and New Zealand, but no further extension was contemplated.[99] Adoption, foster care, and services to unwed parents remained the basic services; but a growing portion of staff time was devoted to the clinical services of consultation, evaluation, and therapy for a variety of mental health and personal needs. Realistically, outside the western U.S. areas of LDS concentration, distance prevented substantial service at the boundaries of any office's area and the demand for counseling services was overwhelming by any measure. That the staff of fewer than three hundred professionals, aides, and clerical employees handled 70,000 to 120,000 cases annually throughout the 1980s is an example.[100] The church has chosen not to increase services to match demand and is stabilizing the number of offices and professionals employed within the system.

Professionals are encouraged to make increasing use of nonprofessional volunteers to handle routine inquiries, involve LDS professionals on a voluntary and no-cost basis, and make increasing referrals to private counselors with LDS-compatible philosophies. LDS Social Services professionals tend to give higher priority to such cases as premarital pregnancies where abortion versus adoption might be an issue, homosexuality, child and spouse abuse, incest, and adultery, all conduct upon which the church has a firm doctrinal position and where certain behaviors may jeopardize church membership.[101]

Contributions to External Charities

Throughout its welfare history, the church has emphasized its responsibility to its own poor. But for many years within the limits of its resources, it has made ad hoc contributions outside its membership to alleviate distress. With broader exposure to the world and with more abundant resources, those occasions have become more frequent and more institutionalized.

Since the awareness as well as the requests are more likely to arise where church decision-makers are located, the recipients have historically been Utah charities.[102] As noted earlier, most floods, earthquakes, and other natural disasters in the western United States since the 1960s have received LDS welfare assistance. One example is 5,000 bags of flour and cereal grains and 120 tons of other foods given to the national Hunger Sabbath in November 1986, a contribution which has since become an annual event.

Rather than operate its own shelters and soup kitchens for the indigent and homeless, the church has assisted with continuing food, equipment, and cash those operated by the Catholic church, other private organizations, and government agencies in Salt Lake City and Ogden, Utah. The church has been by far the largest nongovernmental contributor to homeless shelters in those two cities. Salt Lake City's homeless, few of whom are LDS, are welcomed to a daily meal at Welfare Square, a few blocks from the city's homeless shelter, as long as they are willing to work for it. Fifteen hundred were thus fed during August 1991. The church has also supported Native American alcohol recovery centers in a number of western states, donated a church-owned building to the Salvation Army in Salt Lake City, donated a major portion of the church-owned Hotel Utah's furnishings, when it closed, to the Utah Boys' Ranch, to which it also makes ongoing food contributions, gave carpeting to a handicapped adult center, and made other contributions to Utah Girls' Village. Further afield, it shipped 700 tons of hay to drought-stricken farmers in the Southeastern United States in 1986; and, at the request of local LDS stake officers, donated food, clothing, and other assistance to a Los Angeles AIDS project and an Appalachian relief project. Continuing contributions go to such agencies as the American and International Red Cross and the Salt Lake Community Council, as well as ad hoc donations to lesser-known charities when special circumstances arise. All LDS missionaries, wherever they serve, are directed to devote one-half day each week to community service in addition to their proselyting activities. With increasing frequency, members are urged to participate individually in community service activities.

Throughout the United States, the canning facilities in every welfare storehouse are available for any interested community group; and where welfare farms exist nearby, the church also donates produce to fill the cans if the community group is working on a charitable project. In 1991, 200,000 cans of food for the needy were filled in Denver.[103] Speaking during a visit to the Salt Lake City homeless shelter but referring to more general policy, Thomas S. Monson, first counselor in the First Presidency, expressed, as his personal opinion, "Whether a man is of this faith or that faith or no faith, if he is hungry, he ought to be fed, and children should not go hungry; neither should their mothers."[104]

The church has generally been more generous with commodities than cash. The 1990 decision to give away Deseret Industries clothing surplus seems to be accelerating those contributions. Because of the special status attached to fast offerings, external contributions in cash come from either that source or from the earnings of church business investments, while tithing funds contribute to internal church operations.[105] In the spring of 1991, Welfare Services reportedly offered to supply vouchers to local charities and community action agencies in cities with Deseret Industries. The vouchers could be traded for clothing to needy individuals, particularly to groom them for job searches. Typically, the value of each individual contribution is not large, though some are, but the aggregate is substantial, though the church seldom makes the amounts public.

Of course, assuming major responsibility for the economic welfare of its members is, in effect, a contribution to taxpayers who would otherwise foot at least some part of the bill. A rare revelation of this contribution occurred in Salt Lake City in 1991 when church legal counsel revealed, in a service fee dispute, that the church had spent $4.6 million in 1990 for welfare services within Salt Lake City alone.[106] Although it is unlikely that such expenditure occurred proportionately throughout the state, such estimates would amount to more than $50 million. In another taxation dispute in 1971, the church revealed that it had spent $17.7 million in welfare aid in Utah during the previous twelve months, over $2 million of it in Salt Lake County.[107] Church members, of course, would have made contributions not only through taxes but also through fast offerings.

Reconsideration

The fiftieth anniversary of the 1936 welfare program sparked a deep discussion within the General Welfare Services Committee and central staff, reconsidering the value of refocusing church welfare-related activities. Questions included: Should the church be involved in agribusiness through its welfare farms? Why farm when it was cheaper to buy commodities commercially? Recipients were working

less than volunteers; could this be changed? Both volunteer and recipient labor was declining in proportion to paid employment; could or
should this change? What use should be made of external community
resources and programs? Should the church continue to provide services duplicated by the community to which Saints were contributing
as citizens and taxpayers? What was the appropriate balance between
teaching provident living and providing commodities and services?
What was the place of welfare-related activities within the overall mission of the church?

When two years of informal discussion had not resolved the issues,
three task forces of General Authorities and Welfare Services central
staff were assigned to consider such issues as the changing profile of
welfare recipients, church-state relationships, the administrative and
leadership structure of the program, the balance between fast offering
contributions and disbursement and between other resources and current and future needs, the implications of international growth, sensi-
tivities about the concept of consecration, and the role of welfare in
the overall mission of the church.

From those task force discussions emerged the first new welfare
handbook since 1980, *Providing in the Lord's Way: A Leader's Guide to
Welfare,* released at the April 1991 general conference. Because of the
growing diversity of the church membership and the varied welfare
conditions, the new handbook focused on principles rather than programs and resources. Designed for worldwide guidance throughout
the church, it was initially printed in nineteen languages. *Church Welfare Resources for Use in the United States and Canada,* a separate supplement, described policies, programs, and resources available only in
those areas. Further supplements for other areas may be produced as
needed.

The handbook is divided into three parts. The first, a one-page
statement of philosophy, emphasizes that welfare is an eternal obligation of all, not just a program limited in time, space, and application.
The statement begins:

> The responsibility to provide for ourselves, our families and the
> poor and needy has been part of the gospel since the beginning of
> time. As disciples of Christ, we should give of ourselves—our
> time, talent and resources—to care for those in need. We are better
> able to fulfill this responsibility if we are striving to become self-
> reliant, for we cannot give what we do not have. When we wisely
> use those things that the Lord gives us, we become more able to
> give to the Lord's work and provide for others.

After quotations from the New Testament, the Doctrine and Covenants, and recent church leaders advocating sacrifice on behalf of the needy, Part 1 concludes:

> The church is organized to help all members become more self-reliant and provide for the poor and needy in the Lord's way. The Lord's way embraces welfare. Welfare means temporal and spiritual well-being. As we apply welfare principles in our lives, we become more like God the Father and his Son, Jesus Christ, and we prepare ourselves to live with them eternally.[108]

Part 2, "Individual Responsibilities," contains two sections. The first begins with an exhortation to become self-reliant, quotations from scriptures, statements from church leaders, excerpts from earlier welfare pronouncements, and brief admonitions about the six components of personal preparedness: education, health, employment, home storage, resource management, and developing social, emotional, and spiritual strength. The second section addresses the individual's responsibility to care for the poor, to fast, to contribute fast offerings to support institutional efforts, and to personally manifest concern, charity, and service to others.[109] Parts 1 and 2 involve no policy changes, though they stress personal charity more than previous pronouncements.

Part 3, "Providing Church Welfare Assistance," outlines the duties of bishops, Melchizedek priesthood quorums, Relief Societies, stake and area presidencies, and ward, stake, and regional welfare committees and councils. This section reiterates most earlier directives but includes six policy changes, reflecting the church's new international diversity.

1. The historical term "Bishop's Storehouse" has become the "Lord's Storehouse," intended to shift expectations from a bricks-and-mortar warehouse filled with commodities to a more theologized concept:

> The Lord's storehouse receives, holds in trust, and dispenses consecrated offerings of the Saints. In form and operation, the storehouse is as simple or sophisticated as circumstances require. It may be a list of available services, money in an account, food in a pantry, or commodities in a building. A storehouse is established the moment faithful members give to the bishop of their time, talents, skills, compassion, materials, and financial means in caring for the poor and in building up the kingdom of God on the earth.[110]

As the bishop administers the affairs of this conceptual storehouse, he is to "ensure that organized church welfare assistance does not replace personal, compassionate caring of individuals for one another."

2. Church leaders are to "concentrate on helping people overcome those causes of welfare need which the individual or family can remedy" rather than seeking to "solve economic and political problems in their communities or nations."[111] In other words, though responsible to take appropriate political action, members cannot seek church sponsorship for them.

3. Though the bishop remains the primary decision-maker in determining who is to be helped and how, the stake president must see that the bishop is adequately trained and understands welfare principles.

4. "When fast-offering expenditures will exceed donations, the bishop and stake president should counsel together beforehand to assure that correct principles are being applied." Until 1988, the bishop could unilaterally call in funds from other wards or stakes to make up the deficit.[112]

5. Whereas previous U.S.-oriented admonitions had advised drawing on government only for individually earned assistance such as unemployment insurance, old age and survivors' insurance benefits, and Medicare, advice for the world church differs. After mobilizing resources from oneself, from the extended family, and from the ward, "individual members may decide to receive assistance from other sources, including government. In all such cases, members should avoid becoming dependent upon these sources and strive to become self-reliant. Where possible, they should work in return for assistance rendered."[113]

6. While the immediate needs of ward members are the bishop's responsibility, the priesthood quorums and the Relief Societies must teach members to live providently and help them achieve such prerequisites for self-reliance as education and skill training.

Items 3 and 4 recognize that many bishops in rapidly growing international areas are inexperienced and that the pressures of extended family obligations in many such settings can create psychological and social entanglements for bishops. Item 5 acknowledges that education, training, health care, housing, and other necessities are often government monopolies. Item 6 emphasizes a shifting focus from short-term emergency assistance, always the primary responsibility of bishops, to developing self-reliance, requiring much more basic and time-consuming assistance.

The United States-Canada supplement differs from the 1980 version in its emphasis on employment services as the new flagship of welfare assistance. Farms and other production projects receive one short paragraph; half of that single paragraph explains how to use them for work and on-the-job training opportunities. The same emphasis dominates two short paragraphs on bishops' storehouses, along with instructions to purchase commodities with fast offering funds when a storehouse is not available. The section on canneries spends more space describing how families and community charities may use them than in instructions to process the products of church welfare farms. Deseret Industries's two-page section is divided about equally between employment opportunities, including homecraft, and providing low-cost clothing and household goods. The section on LDS Social Services describes its services to the bishop as adoption, unwed parent counseling, foster care, refugee placement, Indian student placement, and individual, marriage, and family therapy.[114] No policy changes are apparent.

A long section directed at stake officers has one major innovation. Stake operating committees at their own initiative can contribute up to $500 per year worth of welfare commodities to local community charities—more, if they obtain area presidency permission.[115] The manual also reiterates the importance of relying on donated labor and church service volunteers, newly acknowledges the need for safety and environmental awareness, and includes a new section on emergency preparedness, including member training and a ward, stake, and area capability involving food, sanitation, housing, health, and medical care.[116] These latter instructions would be relevant to other areas of the world, except for the presumption of welfare services resources, currently available only in the United States and Canada.

Recipient Profiles

Changes in programs, resources, and administration sometimes refocus attention away from the critical question: who gets helped and how effectively? There is no objective way of determining how many LDS individuals and families remain self-reliant as a result of church instructions and encouragement who might otherwise be burdens upon the church and society. The bottom line for assessing the U.S.-based traditional church welfare system should be the nature of the needy population and how its needs are met. However, though the church maintains voluminous membership records, it has no standardized system for assembling socio-economic data concerning its members. Only fragmented data and personal observation are available for analyzing both need and response.

The United States public assistance system, within which the LDS welfare system operates, has been relatively parsimonious compared to many countries of Western Europe. It provides cash support, certain in-kind goods and services, and employment and training programs designed to return the poor to self-sufficiency. Of those Americans who were poor in 1986, 75 percent received some cash support from a variety of governmental programs.[117] For 23 percent, those payments were benefits provided through payroll taxes deducted during their working lives, which they would have received regardless of poverty. Over half of the poor received either cash or in-kind benefits from government programs designed for and limited to the poor. However, only the aged, the disabled, and single-headed households are supported at a subsistence level or above, and only the aged received support maintained above the official poverty threshold. Cash support comprises only 37 percent of the public assistance received by the poor, 73 percent involving in-kind services such as health care, food, and housing, again largely limited to the aged, the disabled, and single-headed households.

The LDS Church has gradually abandoned the Clark view of the 1930s that its members should be independent of government assistance. After various accommodations with the public welfare system, the essentially unspoken agreement, in effect since the 1940s, has been that the two systems would not mix. The political power of the elderly in the United States has assured their above-poverty income accompanied by significant health care and housing subsidies for many. The totally disabled receive social security programs of cash and in-kind income support. Public assistance for non-elderly female heads of household is primarily limited to women with children. No comparable public assistance is available to the family in which an employable adult male resides. Single mothers require a continuity of support which the church is unable to provide. Hence, a system has emerged in which, like the rest of the nation, the LDS aged and disabled rely on the Old Age and Survivors Health and Disability Income portion of the Social Security Act, in addition to their own private resources, while single mothers in need rely upon Aid to Families with Dependent Children (AFDC) and such in-kind services as food stamps, Medicaid, and public housing—to the limited extent that they are available. A high proportion of the poor who do not fit one of these three categories are either partially disabled or afflicted with substance abuse, the latter unlikely to be closely affiliated Latter-day Saints. Thus, the church deals primarily with those capable of self-support whose incomes have been temporarily interrupted and for whom unemployment compensation is either unavailable or inadequate. Church and public support are competitive primarily for those relative few who are eligible for the catchall Supplementary Security Income Program.

The United States government measures poverty by tripling the cost of a subsistence diet, varied by family size, and classifying all household units with family incomes below that level as in poverty. A survey of LDS households in the United States in 1981 when 14 percent of U.S. households were poor found 13 percent of LDS households poor by the same standard.[118] Since 14.5 percent of U.S. households were poor in 1990, it is not unreasonable to expect that about 13 percent of LDS households are also poor. However, the demographic mix is undoubtedly quite different.

The LDS membership in the United States includes relatively few of those minority groups which are highly impacted by poverty. For instance, 32 percent of blacks, 27 percent of Hispanics, and the majority of Native Americans in the United States were poor in 1988. In 1980 (the most recent year for which comparative data are available) blacks constituted 12 percent of the United States population but only 0.4 percent of the LDS population. Hispanics and Asians together made up 8 percent of the United States population compared to 3 percent among Latter-day Saints. Only with Native Americans did the LDS representation (1.1 percent) exceed that of the United States (0.6 percent).[119]

One-fourth of U.S. families with children are headed by a single parent and one-third of the persons in such households are poor. Singles head 31 percent of all LDS households in the United States, but that is true of only 5.2 percent of LDS households with children. In other words, 82.6 percent of LDS single-headed households in the United States include no children.[120] The average Mormon lifespan is unknown; but given the demonstrably healthier life-style, it is undoubtedly substantially higher than the national average, resulting in an extraordinary proportion of widows and widowers living alone, and probably providing the major explanation for the high proportion of childless singles. The infrequency among Mormons of out-of-wedlock births (25 percent of all U.S. births) is another factor. As in the nation at large, one-third of female-headed LDS families are poor, but relatively few children are involved. As of 1981, 16 percent of

Latter-day Saint adults were divorced compared to 23 percent of U.S. white adults, in part because three-quarters of LDS divorced persons remarry.[121]

However, poverty is directly related to family size; and LDS households are larger, on average, than their national counterparts, a factor which is counterbalanced by the LDS emphasis on education.[122] True to those patterns, the undereducated and larger families are over-represented among church welfare recipients, but those characteristics are not typical of LDS female-headed families. Given the long-term needs of the single mother, the short-term nature of LDS welfare, and the lack of substantial and continuous governmental support to men, it is not surprising that male-headed families comprise two-thirds of LDS Church welfare recipients and that one out of five of the female-headed recipient households contains no children.

The average period of church assistance is from three to four months, and the value of that assistance averages three to four hundred dollars. Temporary unemployment, low wages that require supplements, illness, family breakups, and excessive debt are the usual reasons why members apply for assistance. Hence, bishops perceive themselves as providing subsistence until a new or better job can be found, assisting while debt and money management problems are being solved, avoiding mortgage foreclosure or eviction, and averting crises during periods of ill health and other emergencies.

While education or training to qualify a candidate for a better job may be an appropriate recommendation in a particular case, such an approach would conflict with the emphasis on short-term emergency help. Most local leaders would probably encourage the individual to find resources in the extended family or community for that purpose. Ironically, the active member is more likely to follow principles of provident living, thus making the need greater among inactive members—who are precisely those with the least understanding of provident living and the least likelihood of following those principles. Though a bishop may now at his judgment assist inactive members, 70 percent of the recipient families are active, a category which includes an estimated 66 percent of all members.[123]

Assessment

By 1980, LDS welfare services in the United States had matured as a large, multi-faceted operation and continued with little change throughout the 1980s. Reflecting Joseph Smith's Nauvoo premise, "I teach them correct principles and they govern themselves," the Church Welfare Program focused on teaching LDS families to be self-reliant and provident, standing ready with significant practical assistance during interruptions to self-reliance. That assistance included not only the commodities that were program staples from the 1930s and cash from fast offerings, but also an extensive range of social and employment-related services. Bishops could refer the medically needy to local health care facilities and pay their bills. Both locally called volunteer ward and stake employment specialists and church employment centers could supply job search and job placement assistance. Deseret Industries offered sheltered employment to the handicapped, plus low-cost or no-cost household items. Both paid and volunteer LDS Social Services staff could provide personal and clinical counseling, licensed adoption and foster care, and services to unwed parents.

All of these formalized services are buttressed by an unreported abundance of neighborly service: shared meals, house cleaning and child care provided for the ill, yard work and snow and trash removal done for the aged and disabled, homes repaired and even built from scratch for those lacking physical health or financial means. Bishops, quorum leaders, Relief Society officers, and home and visiting teachers can initiate and/or carry out such services. No time limits or stringent eligibility requirements apply to these services, but they are all seen as temporary. The assumption is that the individual and family will promptly become self-reliant again.

The church does not expect to be the major source of social welfare assistance for its needy members. Applying the 1981 figure that approximately 13 percent of American Mormons are poor by U.S. government standards to America's 4.3 million Mormons at the beginning of 1990 would yield an estimate of 560,000 U.S. Mormons in the poverty ranks. If we assume that the number receiving cash and commodity assistance now represents approximately the same proportion as those receiving aid in 1985, the last year such statistics were made public, then only 150,000 received assistance—3.5 percent of all U.S. Mormons and 27 percent of the estimated number of poor among them.[124] In addition, that last report in 1985 shows that LDS Social Services assisted 82,804, and 34,552 were placed in gainful employment by church employment centers, most but not all within the United States.[125] There is no rule limiting assistance to those with family incomes below the United States government's official poverty threshold. We may assume that such poor received most of the cash and

commodity assistance while social service counseling and job placement found a broader audience but with the poor more than propor-
tionately represented.

Because the church operates its welfare program primarily in nations with extensive social welfare programs, it leaves longer-term financial support to government agencies, encouraging members to
take advantage of services to which they are legally entitled but to become self-reliant as rapidly as possible. Longer-term church assistance
is more advisory than substantive. It is a program designed to assist a
small minority of needy persons in a developed economy in which
most citizens at most times can earn a comfortable living, where public programs prevent widespread deprivation, and where the church's
major welfare role is a gap-filling one. It has not eliminated poverty
among its members, but it has reduced the number of poor among
them and made the penury of others less distressing.

Within that context, the Church Welfare Program as it functions
today in the United States and Canada reflects long-standing gospel
principles, many of which predate their specific project manifestations
of the 1930s. The changing society has not changed the principles, but
rather has prompted such innovations as an emphasis on urban employment, prevention of financial woes through provident living, and
therapy for individual and family ills. The goal of a Zion society still
has great emotional power as an ideal among Mormons, whatever its
realistic possibilities. Members loyally provide cash and labor contributions on request. Inactive members—those who do not heed the
encouragement for provident living—are most likely to be needy and
also most likely to escape church attention. Church assistance is potentially extensive and quite flexible, depending on the option of the
local bishop. Within those guidelines, help is substantial, personalized, and quick, provided with a maximum of compassion and confi-
dentiality and with a sincere effort to maintain the work ethic.

CHAPTER 9

The Welfare Program
in the International Church

JOSEPH SMITH prophesied in 1842 that Mormonism would "penetrate every continent, visit every clime and sweep every country."[1] Yet observers as long ago as Tolstoi have characterized it as a peculiarly American church. In some areas of the world, its U.S. origins and connections make it the target of violent attacks.[2] Not only did Mormonism originate in the United States, but for a century, the church Joseph Smith organized included, as part of its gospel message, at least an implicit appeal to immigrate to the United States. This official encouragement to "gather" ended at the turn of the century as overcrowding burdened the fragile economy of Mormon country.[3] The reversal of policy could not, however, overcome the natural attractions converts saw in Zion: life with coreligionists, temples, and the political and economic advantages offered by America. Emigration continued spontaneously and without the church's financial aid or relocation assistance until after World War I; then the stream slowed to a trickle. The United States offered little economic incentive during the 1930s. Conversions dropped precipitously during World War II, given the scarcity of missionaries; and the war effectively ended immigration for its duration.

Proselyting Patterns

The LDS Church sent missionaries into Canada during its first year, into Great Britain by 1837, and to Europe and Scandinavia by 1849.[4] Missionaries found heartening success in the South Pacific in the 1840s but, in the 1850s, found few converts in South America and the Far East.[5] Assuming that Mexico represented part of the ancestral lands of Book of Mormon peoples, Brigham Young sent missionaries into that country in 1876, and Utah expatriates established Mormon outposts in northern Mexico beginning in 1885 to avoid anti-polygamy persecution. Proselyting was slow, hampered by revolution, war, and internal conflict, until the 1960s, when baptisms skyrocketed.[6] Mormon colonies in western Canada, founded at the turn of the century, were largely motivated by population pressures in the LDS settlements of the Great Basin, although avoiding federal prosecution was also an element in some cases.[7]

In only four years prior to 1925 were the economically struggling Latter-day Saints able to send as many as a thousand missionaries into the field in one year; both the Great Depression (1929–41) and World War II were further checks, partly explaining why the church continued to allocate these scarce resources primarily in proven fields like the United States and Europe.[8] Serious and continuous proselyting in South America began among European immigrants in Argentina and Brazil in the 1920s. After the hiatus imposed by World War II, missionary activity spread to Uruguay in the 1940s, Chile in the 1950s, and the rest of the continent after 1960, a decade which saw soaring baptismal rates that paralleled the trend in Mexico.[9] Proselyting was extended to Central America and the Caribbean during the same period with similar results. The Latin American population went from 1.5 percent to 26 percent of the total LDS membership in just thirty years.

After a devoted but fruitless effort to interest Japanese in Mormonism (1901–24), sustained LDS growth began as LDS servicemen in the army of occupation organized small branches and proselyted among the conquered Japanese. A mission followed in 1948.[10] LDS servicemen also took Mormonism to the Republic of Korea in 1951; and missions followed in Hong Kong in 1955, in Korea in 1956, in Taiwan in 1959, in the Philippines in 1962, in Thailand in 1968, and in Singapore and Indonesia in 1969.[11] The Italian and Iberian peninsulas became formal mission areas in 1965 and 1968, respectively. The church had maintained missions in white South Africa and Rhodesia since 1903, after an earlier abortive effort during 1855–65; but after the priesthood revelation of 1978, missionaries took their message to native as well as European populations in selected areas of the African continent.[12]

The church sponsored cautious and low-profile "representatives" in Eastern Europe during the 1980s; but as the Soviet hegemony in Eastern Europe fragmented in 1990, new missions were opened in Czechoslovakia, Poland, Russia, and the Ukraine. That marked departure made more believable the 1979 prediction of LDS Church president Spencer W. Kimball: "We are turning our attention more diligently now to sharing the gospel with our Heavenly Father's children behind the so-called iron and bamboo curtains. We have need to prepare for that day. The urgency of that preparation weighs heavily upon us. That day may come with more swiftness than we realize."[13] Piercing the bamboo curtain remains a future but anticipated opportunity at this writing.

During the 1950s, church leaders explicitly counseled members abroad to build up the church in their own areas, provided enough missionary support to make critical nuclei of members in most nations, and began offering support services in a serious way: translations of scriptures and manuals, schools in the Pacific and Latin America between 1950 and 1970, a multi-million dollar building program that dotted three continents with Mormon chapels, and, during the late 1970s and 1980s, temples, which represented the final sign of spiritual equality. All of these elements of Mormon life and its proselyting mission came together in an expansion of the non-U.S. LDS membership from a quarter million in 1960 to 3.5 million by 1990 and from 16 percent to 44 percent of the membership total.

This explosion also compelled the church to deal systematically for the first time with the issue of how to meet its doctrinal responsibilities for the economic welfare of those millions in a multitude of nations. Until after World War II, international welfare was not a pressing problem, simply because there were so few members abroad; and in any case, no resources could be spared from the core church. The U.S. wards took care of their needy members on an ad hoc basis. The small LDS population centers in Europe, Canada, and Mexico were as well off as Utah members during the 1930s. The subsistence life-style in the South Pacific, where the only significant body of third world membership existed before the 1960s, apparently was not perceived as poverty, welfare assistance largely being limited to natural disasters.[14]

Since the U.S. Saints prospered during World War II and were spared physical destruction, they were well positioned to assist their suffering European brothers and sisters. Given its abundant human resources, Europe recovered rapidly with the assistance of U.S. capital through the postwar Marshall Plan. The LDS missionary force expanded as the U.S. military was demobilized and, thanks to the enlarged population and resource base, grew steadily thereafter. The number of missionaries in service surpassed 5,000 in 1950, neared 10,000 in 1960, had passed 20,000 by 1975, and topped 40,000 by 1990.[15]

By the time Japan, South Korea, Taiwan, Hong Kong, and Singapore had significant bodies of members, their initial postwar hard times were over. Government policies, disciplined work forces, and the expansion of world trade gave them stable economies. However, when LDS membership spurted in the poverty-stricken Philippines and Latin America during the 1960s, that was another matter. By 1970 the LDS Church had become a truly international organization. Although its membership was still clustered in the more affluent areas of Africa and Southeast Asia, it could not ignore the massive economic need of members in Latin America and the Philippines. For the first time, the church was challenged to meet its doctrinal responsibilities for the economic welfare of its members in a widely varied world economic context. (See Table 2.)

But the challenge was to become more compelling yet. Because of the historic priesthood ban, proselyting in the continent of Africa had been confined to Europeans in South Africa and Rhodesia; however, the church's explosive growth in Brazil with its mixed European, Indian, and black population challenged the church's belief that the gospel is universal in a way that civil rights protests in the United States had not. Racial policies had come into direct confrontation with proselyting responsibilities. In June 1978, President Spencer W. Kimball announced a revelation and policy change removing the racial restriction for worthy men.[16]

LDS missionaries immediately began teaching and baptizing among the blacks of South Africa and Zimbabwe (formerly Rhodesia). The change of priesthood policy also opened the way for proselyting in Nigeria and Ghana where, as early as 1946 in Nigeria and 1962 in Ghana, their people had learned LDS doctrines by informal contacts and through popular periodical literature. They had pressed the church to send missionaries to them but without success until 1961; then missionaries were denied visas, due to the priesthood ban. Meanwhile, interested parties in both nations had formed their own churches, teaching LDS doctrines and using the LDS name. Nigerian and Ghanian students had attended Brigham Young University. Thus, post-1978 missionaries—mature couples rather than young single men and women—had a foundation already in place.[17]

Despite an abundance of eager investigators, the missionaries were instructed to proceed carefully, balancing baptisms against training local leadership.[18] The same policy prevailed as missionary work began in Kenya, Uganda, Zaire, Swaziland, Namibia, Ivory Coast, Liberia, Botswana, Lesotho, and Sierra Leone during the 1980s, usually following upon the pioneering of some U.S., Canadian, or European members on government or business assignments.[19] By the end of 1990, there were 52,000 African Mormons, over one-third of them

TABLE 2 LDS Membership in Selected Latin American, Asian, and African Nations, 1950–90, by Numbers of Members

Nation	1950	1960	1970	1980	1990
Mexico	5,915	12,695	67,965	211,805	617,000
Brazil	648	2,644	33,104	54,410	368,000
Chile		614	9,416	42,033	298,000
Philippines		11	4,603	27,778	237,000
Peru		349	10,771	23,136	178,000
Argentina	1,031	3,456	19,454	45,988	171,000
Guatemala		1,807	12,252	17,822	125,000
Japan	211	2,502	11,868	34,969	96,000
Colombia			1,820	13,731	83,000
Ecuador				19,022	81,000
Bolivia			1,685	14,010	64,000
South Korea		537	4,245	12,966	59,000
Venezuela				4,963	53,000
Uruguay	252	2,555	15,311	22,801	52,000
Honduras		411	3,000	6,325	43,000
El Salvador		331	9,961	14,225	35,000
Panama				2,000	20,000
South Africa	1,372	2,901	5,637	7,712	19,000
Taiwan		371	3,509	7,494	18,000
Hong Kong	1	346	3,085	4,315	18,000
Nigeria					17,000
Costa Rica		214	1,698	4,100	16,000
Paraguay			1,644	2,232	12,000
Ghana					9,000
Nicaragua				3,185	8,600
Indonesia				1,418	4,200
Thailand				1,157	4,200
Zimbabwe				6,831	2,300
Zaire					2,000
Singapore				569	1,600
Totals (000)	1,111	1,693	2,931	4,640	7,762
Total non-US (000)	184	270	914	2,053	3,495
% of Total	16.6	15.9	31.2	44.2	44.1

Sources: *Deseret News 1991–1992 Church Almanac,* 328–31 and *Encyclopedia of Mormonism,* 4:1756–60.

white South Africans, in 7 stakes, 9 missions, 24 districts, and 232 wards and branches. A temple was dedicated in Johannesburg, South Africa, in 1985.[20] Only South Africa, Nigeria, Ghana, Zimbabwe, Zaire, and Liberia had more than a thousand LDS members by that date, but explosive growth on the world's poorest continent awaited only the go-ahead from church leaders.

The opening to LDS proselyting in 1989 and 1990 of the formerly closed communist countries of Eastern Europe, including remnants of the Soviet Union, represents the high tide of advance to date in the expanding world church. Church leaders anticipated permission to proselyte in China until its new repressions in 1989 but continue to encourage informal contacts while awaiting an appropriate entrée.[21] Only the Muslim world seems off limits for the immediate future, though Latter-day Saints interpret literally a Joseph Smith revelation that they must preach Mormonism to "every nation, kindred, tongue and people" (D&C 42:58).

The international welfare challenge varies greatly according to the number of members and the regional economies throughout the world. An area-by-area summary will provide a useful overview of the economic developments between 1950 and 1990.

Western Europe

Given the infusion of American capital and equipment and Europe's impressive human resources and economic infrastructure, Europe recovered quickly from the war's massive destruction and population dislocation. From the late 1940s until the early 1970s, previously industrialized countries flourished, absorbing the surplus labor of not-yet-industrialized Spain, Portugal, Italy, and Eastern European countries not aligned with the Soviet Union.

The first significant check came during the winter of 1972–73 when the Organization of Oil Exporting Countries (OPEC) enforced a severe oil embargo, restraining economic growth throughout Western Europe and creating substantial unemployment for the next two decades. But the extensive social welfare systems created after World War II equalized the shortages and prevented concentrations of poverty among groups in the essentially homogeneous populations. The guest workers, who were repatriated, suffered most, though their home countries had experienced substantial economic growth in the meantime. However, LDS membership was smaller in these countries; and economic deprivation was thus not a major concern among European Saints nor among church leaders in their behalf.

The Pacific Rim

War-devastated Japan, also rebuilt with American assistance, re-modeled both its economy and government.[22] Although suffering imme-diately after the war was severe, the economy was booming by the time conversions occurred in significant numbers during the 1950s.[23] Hong Kong and Singapore were conveniently located to become trading na-tions, had small populations and British assistance, and were also newly prosperous by the time LDS missionaries began having an impact.[24]

The Japanese-abandoned island of Formosa was forced to absorb 2 million mainland Chinese, in addition to its 6 million native population, after the triumph of the Chinese communists in 1949. But through a rig-orous policy of savings, investment, and export promotion during the 1950s, the new nation of Taiwan had experienced an "economic miracle" and was a model of prosperity before LDS proselyting began.[25] Similarly, South Korea emerged from poverty thanks to the combination of Ameri-can aid, Japanese reparations, a disciplined government, and expanding world trade that brought prosperity during the 1970s and 1980s. Some two decades earlier, U.S. Mormon soldiers followed by missionaries had begun preaching the LDS message.[26]

Thus, the LDS members in the newly industrializing Pacific Rim coun-tries were never a substantial welfare concern. As in the United States, fast offerings tided over the few who needed emergency assistance; but the church's major task was encouraging young people to position them-selves for good jobs through sufficient education and training.

The Philippines

LDS proselyting in the early 1960s found an almost overwhelming response in the Philippines and predicted the church's future in other newly industrializing Asian nations. The United States had governed its colony primarily in the interests of the American military and U.S. busi-ness before World War II. Japanese conquest, occupation, and U.S. recon-quest had devastated the nation, leaving political and economic power di-vided among a landed aristocracy, a "crony government" regulating business and industry to benefit a small group of supporters, and armed guerrillas in rural areas.[27] Though there are eighty-seven native languages and fewer than half of the Filipinos speak English, the labor force is highly literate and therefore potentially attractive to foreign investors. However, the nation lacks the discipline, incentive, and capital for inter-nally fostered development and is too politically chaotic to attract exter-nal investments.[28]

The Philippine government defines poverty as insufficient income to purchase 2,000 calories of food per day per person plus a minimum level of housing, fuel, clothing, and other amenities for a family of six.[29] By that standard, 49.3 percent of the population was poor in 1971—59 percent by 1985 as chaos accompanied the Aquino government after the Marcos regime.[30]

Since high-income Filipinos live sequestered behind guarded walls, LDS missionaries are highly unlikely to reach and teach many of them.[31] As a result, according to our personal observations, the poverty rate among LDS Filipinos is about 10 percent above the national average. Nearly 60 percent of Filipinos are rural and, on average, experience more poverty than their urban counterparts. Because of LDS proselyting practices, 60 percent of LDS Filipinos are urban, heightening the contrast between LDS members and urban Filipinos. Approximately 100,000 adult Mormons are in the labor market, most already employed or self-employed; but the LDS unemployment rate, 15 percent in the late 1980s, was also above the national average. Compared to 16 percent of all urban Filipinos, close to half of the Mormons there are self-employed, which primarily means home manufacture, street huckstering, and operating independent "jeepneys," combination bus/taxis. Housing quality reflects those income and employment handicaps.[32]

Under prevailing conditions, the Philippine economy has been unable to generate employment opportunities to keep pace with its rapidly growing and rapidly urbanizing population of 20 million. Its meager resources do not allow social programs like unemployment compensation, public welfare benefits, and old age pensions. Frequent floods, typhoons, and earthquakes have been cataclysmic drains on the economy. Political uncertainty discourages economic development.

Young Filipinos tend to make a mistake typical in most developing countries. Those who manage to obtain a secondary education ignore technical training in favor of high-prestige but low-demand college educations. The country cannot absorb them, creating the phenomenon of educated unemployment. Again based on personal observation, young Latter-day Saints, influenced by the church emphasis on education, are even more likely to seek only university educations. A further influence has been the example of the American missionaries with whom many of the young Filipinos serve. Four out of five LDS missionaries in the Philippines during the late 1980s were native Filipinos, most of them supported by contributions from church members abroad, living a standard above that of their families to whom some of them even sent home money, and companioned with college-bound Americans. The return to economic reality after missionary service is often difficult, yet they receive little career guidance or personal counseling.

Local church leaders are learning how to encourage fast offerings and to use those funds wisely for short-term emergency help. Health missionaries have provided excellent training in sanitation and nutrition that members usually follow carefully. Specially prepared lessons on self-reliance are taught often in church classes. In short, the transfer of principles has been generally successful, but practical help has been in short supply. A 1960s experiment with a welfare farm was short lived. Individual mission presidents have encouraged cottage crafts, but few such efforts have survived the mission president's tenure. Sewing machines placed in some chapels have developed some salable skills but have been more important for homemakers. There is an inherent interest in cooperatives and a few members have organized more stable family or group enterprises; but the concept has yet to provide substantial employment. Hoping that counseling and guidance for youth, appropriate training, and aggressive job development contacts with employers might reduce LDS unemployment, retired U.S. couples have been called to provide employment services.[33] If a permanent locally based program emerges, the church will have helped members take a major step toward self-reliance.

A logical, though difficult, second step is transforming the self-employed entrepreneurial activities engaged in by almost half of adult Filipino Mormons into successful enterprises. Most of them now earn only a bare subsistence. Both technical and financial assistance would be required, a thorny thicket that has generated more discussion than experimentation so far.

Latin America and the Caribbean

Political instability has traditionally been a long-term deterrent to economic development in Latin America. Their colonial masters treated these countries primarily as sources of raw materials and as captive markets, nor did conditions change much after nineteenth-century revolutions transferred the land to local oligarchs. Exports were limited to agricultural products and minerals to industrial nations, which then sold the manufactured products back. Their peoples received hand-labor earnings while customers and suppliers enjoyed the profits of mechanized production. World War II shortages offered increased outlets for the goods of some infant industries; and following the war, most countries prohibited foreign goods and produced their needs at home. These industries, however, were primarily inefficient, costly, and government controlled.

Coups and revolts traded power between rightist military regimes and leftist socialist-oriented ones, the former generally employing torture and death against dissidents and the latter guerrilla-fighting against the government in all the decades since World War II. Both sought to placate the people with industrial employment and subsidized necessities shielded from external competition. Latin American industries could seldom compete in export markets and, lacking effective tax systems, these nations suffered from rampant inflation, corruption, and grossly distorted income distributions.[34]

Despite those time bombs planted in their economic and political systems, most Latin economies grew rapidly between 1950 and 1980, achieving significant urbanization and social improvement. Rural populations shifted from more than two-thirds to less than one-third between 1960 and 1980. Life expectancy at birth jumped from fifty-six to sixty-four. Birth rates stayed high, leading to a growth rate of over 3 percent per year—doubling the population every two decades. Availability of clean water spread from 40 percent to more than two-thirds of the population. Primary education became almost universal. Income distributions remained extremely skewed throughout the 1960–80 period but did not generally get worse, and the entire income structure was rising.[35]

The 1973 oil embargo actually created a bonanza for Latin American oil exporters like Ecuador, Venezuela, and Mexico. The other Latin American countries had to pay higher energy prices; but the sparsely populated OPEC nations were so wealthy that Latin American oil importers could borrow, often at negative real interest rates, to maintain their rapid economic growth. For the next five years, Latin America borrowed freely, repaying with cheaper inflated currency.[36]

The bubble burst with the second oil shock of 1979. The industrial countries in recession cut back on their purchases of raw materials, spreading depression to their third-world suppliers. By the early 1980s, petroleum prices had collapsed. Most of the international loans, negotiated at variable interest rates, soared in real terms as well as nominally. With the end of world inflation, interest payments on the external debts of every Latin American country became a tremendous drain on their limited export earnings. World savings dropped, capital disappeared, and international lenders were reluctant to lend more to countries already behind in their commitments. A nation might meet its internal commitments with inflated money, but foreigners demanded hard currencies.

Having taken on debts beyond their long-term ability to pay, some Latin American nations defaulted. The International Monetary Fund bailed out others but demanded deflation of their monetary systems, creating deep regional depressions.[37] The economic chaos toppled military governments throughout the region, but the new democratic governments struggled with rising unemployment, uncontrolled inflation, and consequent falling real wages. They could do nothing but apply the brakes by deflating the currency and risking recession in the short run, hoping to achieve stability, privatize their inefficient industry, and thus build a foundation for long-term prosperity if the political system remained stable long enough.[38] In short, between 1960 and 1990, a period during which Mormon membership multiplied nearly five-fold, almost universal political and economic chaos racked Latin America.

Since the mid-1980s, reform pressures emanating from international agencies and discussions about hemispheric free-trade zones are raising hopes of economic recovery.[39] If reform fails, the survival of the new democracies is doubtful.[40] Closer views of three countries—Mexico, Brazil, and Peru—can give a better close-up of the economic plight of Latin American Saints.

Mexico

Mexico has enjoyed the stability but suffered the internal corruption of a one-party political system. Between 1950 and 1974, the country experienced a period of rapid economic growth (6.4 percent per year) with low inflation, moderate external debt accumulation, intense industrialization, and rapid urbanization.[41] By the mid-1980s, agriculture employed only 25 percent of the nation, manufacturing 12 percent, and services and government 40 percent.[42] Mexico City competed with São Paulo, Brazil, as the world's largest city, far outstripping housing. Most of the major industries developed under government ownership with the usual import substitution emphasis and consequent inefficiencies and high costs, although some private industries in the north could compete on the world market. Agriculture was heavily taxed to pay for industrial development, and unequal income distribution limited the gains for the average citizen, except for improvements in education and health services for the urban poor.[43]

Government borrowing and spending accelerated in 1973 to offset the oil embargo, while bank nationalization and land reform rhetoric frightened away private investors. Then Mexican oil was discovered and developed with continuous price increases. Both borrowing and spending, with accompanying inflation, accelerated in anticipation of oil profits. Then world oil prices fell in the early eighties, coinciding with the 1981 recession in the United States, Mexico's most important trading partner. Losing confidence, moneyed Mexicans began investing their capital abroad. Mexico could not meet its foreign debt payments in 1982. A new administration cut government spending, began privatizing industry, and devalued the currency. Unemployment rose, much existing work "went underground" as firms contracted with women to work at home at substandard wages, real wages fell, and the income distribution worsened.[44]

"Maquiladora" plants of American manufacturers just inside the northern border and u.s. investment in Mexican agriculture were the major sources of growth in the late 1980s. A proposed free-trade agreement with the United States was a major hope for export growth but many u.s. interests strongly opposed the proposal.[45] Trends in 1989 and 1990 were encouraging; but on almost every economic indicator, Mexico remained far short of where it had been in 1980.

Within that context, the LDS membership appears more prosperous than the population at large. No survey has been made of economic status, but knowledgeable observers place the majority of Mexican Mormons in the middle class.[46] Membership growth began in the villages but has urbanized with the nation's development. Even in the late 1950s, only 56 percent of Mexican children ever reached the second grade, 25 percent finished elementary school, 11 percent began high school, and 8 percent of those finished.[47] When the LDS Church introduced forty-three high-quality elementary and junior highs along with a preparatory and teacher training institution between 1959 and 1974, it catapulted a generation of its members far ahead of their peers, before phasing out most of those schools in the 1980s.[48] The church infrastructure is now sufficiently strong to pull lower-middle-class converts up rather than being pulled down by them. Studies by a non–Mormon scholar in the Puebla Valley of Mexico document this upward leverage for Mormons in comparison to other denominations.[49]

Perhaps that relatively benign condition accounts for the general lack of LDS welfare activity within the Mexico area. Nevertheless, the size of the Mexican membership, the pace of convert baptisms, and the deteriorating economy of the 1980s, despite recovery signs in the 1990s, virtually guarantee that Mexico has the largest number, though not the largest proportion, of Mormon poor, next to the United States.

Brazil

Brazil has the third largest LDS membership of any country and undoubtedly the third largest number of Mormon poor, even though LDS Brazilians, on the average, are also economically better off than the average of their countrymen.

Following World War II, Brazil undertook a deliberate policy of import substitution and exchange rate manipulation to turn the nation from a predominantly agricultural economy into an industrial and exporting nation. Its size gave it a potential internal market large enough for economies of scale in manufacturing sufficient to begin production for the home market and then, at least for a few products, to enter export competition.

High world commodity prices—especially for coffee—sustained rapid economic growth into the mid-fifties. Then falling coffee prices led to a decision to diversify in agriculture and to pursue industrialization simultaneously. Both decisions led to massive dislocations of labor. For instance, coffee production required eighty-three man-days of labor per hectare planted, soybeans only three. The ratio between seasonal and permanent labor was 2 to 1 in coffee production compared to 44 to 1 in cotton. As a result, land ownership, already concentrated, increased, accompanied by land speculation, declining rural wages, and forced out-migration. At present 70 percent of Brazil's land is owned by 5 percent of the agricultural establishments. Conversely, the gross output of 70 percent of the farming establishments in the poverty-stricken northeast region is less than the value of one minimum wage. The concentration on mechanized agriculture for export also led to neglected food production. Food prices rose sharply in real terms and per capita calorie consumption declined by 20 percent between 1967 and 1979.

The displaced rural workers went in three directions: (1) in search of new lands in the unsettled Amazon frontier, (2) into the impoverished life of a landless, casual rural labor force, and (3) into the industrializing southeast.[50] On the frontier they were no match for the expanding landowners who had access to credit and received both carte blanche and tax incentives for forcibly evicting previous settlers.[51] The result has been the devastation of the Amazon rain forest, with potentially fearful consequences for the global ecosystem.

Meanwhile, agriculture, which employed 67 percent of the labor force in 1940, accounted for only one-third in 1980. A housing stock which was 63 percent rural in 1950 was 69 percent urban by 1980. The out-migrants from agriculture concentrate primarily in the southeast, notably in São Paulo and Rio de Janiero which together, by 1980, contained 27 percent of the nation's population.[52] The southeast, with 10 percent of the land, contains nearly half of the total population. Social conditions are grim. Thousands of street children subsist by robbery while death squads of off-duty and retired police slaughter them at the behest of shopkeepers.[53]

Sixty percent of Brazil's exports had been coffee in 1950; by 1980, coffee had dropped to 13 percent. Instead, industrial products, of which it had essentially no exports in 1950, accounted for 57 percent in 1980. Economic growth was particularly rapid during the world-wide boom of 1967–73, with an emphasis on exports, not only of soybeans and other agricultural products, but also of steel, autos, industrial machinery, and aircraft—all capital-intensive activities with limited but high-skilled labor requirements. By 1985, manufacturing provided 24 percent of Brazil's employment with another 15 percent coming from related transportation and communication and 14 percent from commercial employment.[54]

Thus, in a few years, a rural country had become one of the ten most important industrial countries in the world in terms of output. But in contrast to other newly industrializing countries like South Korea and Taiwan, Brazil failed to improve the relative status of its overall population. Only twelve countries in the world have more distorted income distributions, among them South Africa, Iran, Mexico, and Peru.[55] The highest earning 10 percent of South Koreans, for instance, earned 27.5 percent of the total national income, 38.5 percent in the Philippines, and 50.6 percent in Brazil. The bottom 40 percent in these countries were receiving 16.9 percent, 14.2 percent, and 7.0 percent, respectively. Within Brazil, that income distortion was true regionally as well as among income groups.[56] Whereas 29 percent of all Brazilian households earned too little to provide 2000 calories per household member and related amenities in 1980, the figure had risen to 48 percent of households in the northeast but only 15 percent in the southeast.[57] Overall, 27 percent of Brazilians remained self-employed, usually a sign of inadequate employment opportunities rather than a preference for independence.[58]

Brazil, like other Latin American countries, survived the 1973 oil shock by borrowing the cheap international credit available in the Eurodollar market. However, the world-wide drop in demand following the 1979–80 quadrupling of oil prices, accompanied by higher real interest rates, finally pushed the Brazilian economy into recession in 1981–83. A high national rate of inflation, large public sector deficits, and a foreign debt four times greater than the nation's exports all followed. Urban unemployment doubled, despite the lack of any unemployment compensation. Bereft of any alternative income source, in the single year of 1984, jobs in the formal sector fell by 1 million while self-employment in the informal sector grew by 4 million.

The economy stuttered on through the rest of the 1980s under heavy pressure from the International Monetary Fund to reduce inflation and meet hard-money debts. Finally, in the spring of 1990, with the inflation rate at over 2000 percent per year, the newly inaugurated Brazilian government froze all bank accounts, cut back employment in government-owned industry, and began to privatize other industry. Inflation halted, but construction and the production of consumer durables plunged, and unemployment rose sharply. The decline had apparently halted at the end of 1990; but the congress refused to reduce government employment, cut public expenditure, or push privatization of industry, as a result of which inflation was again threatening in mid-1991.[59]

In this economic milieu, LDS policy makers must consider their obligation to their 368,000 Brazilian members. Because the great majority of Brazilian Latter-day Saints live in the relatively prosperous southeast cities, their average income exceeds national averages. However, the expansion of missionary activity throughout the rest of the country will almost certainly bring this average down, unless some action improves the economic progress of the membership. One-fifth to one-third of LDS Brazilians are employed in general office occupations, about 15 percent in service jobs, 10 percent in skilled and unskilled manual jobs, and a like number in technical employment. Ten to 15 percent are professional, if teachers and medical personnel are included. Most significantly, perhaps 30 percent in the north and 20 percent in the south, where there are more job opportunities, are self-employed.

To say that Brazilian Latter-day Saints are better off than the average Brazilian is not to say that they are well off. In 1990, an income of ten times the minimum wage or $670 per month was required to maintain a modest standard of housing, diet, clothing, and schooling for a family of four in a major Brazilian city like São Paulo or Rio de Janiero. It is our observation that 40 percent of LDS families had that income compared to 15 percent of Brazilians nationally. The median LDS household earned about $50 a month more than the $335 earned by the Brazilian household.

Education undoubtedly makes the difference. Only 16 percent of young Brazilians enter secondary education; although exact comparisons are not possible, half of Brazilian returned missionaries have apparently completed the secondary sequence; most also obtain additional schooling or occupational training after the mission. The education of those who do not serve missions is not as observable, but most probably cannot afford as much education as they would like; and it seems likely that the motivation for missions and education may be linked.

The major educational problem of the young Latter-day Saints in Brazil is typical throughout the developing world: unrealistic career expectations and too much of the wrong kind of education for the national labor market. Brazil has a few outstanding but very expensive and elitist universities; it also has many of lesser quality, also costly. Its primary and secondary education is generally poor—in some areas, abysmal.[60] On the other hand, employers faced with the skill demands of industrialization have created in cooperation with the government an outstanding nationwide system of tuition-free technical schools.[61] The nation is already over-supplied with professionals for its stage of development; yet Brazilian missionaries are, for the most part, church-supported during their missions, teamed with American companions, and dressed and treated with professional-level respect. Consequently, they set their career sights on levels of education they cannot afford to complete and which would leave them unemployed/ underemployed and frustrated if they did.

In short, relatively few Brazilian Latter-day Saints could be classified as poor, but the economic well-being of many could be improved and the prospects for the next generation assured by an effective combination of career guidance, education and training in demanded occupations, job development and placement, and assistance in enterprise development for the self-employed. However, few Brazilian Latter-day Saints can provide those services; practically none could do it as retired volunteers. At the same time, given the relative rarity of Portuguese language capability, few Mormons from other countries have the experience and language skills required. Therefore the LDS Church faces a dual challenge: whether to undertake the needed services, and, if so, whether to begin with an employed cadre or wait until unpaid volunteers can be recruited.

Peru

Peru is a nation plagued by geography. The country is divided into a dry narrow coastal plain with about one-tenth the land area, half of the population, and practically all of the industry, the *sierra* or highlands of the Andes with a quarter of the land area and 40 percent of the population, and the *selva* or tropical rain forest with two-thirds of the land area and one-tenth of the population. Only 15 percent of the land area is suitable for agriculture. That land produces 80 percent of the world's coca, though its drug profits are limited by the fact that Colombia markets its output. Peru's only additional resources are copper and a few other minerals, including some oil production. To their advantage, most Peruvian Latter-day Saints live in the coastal cities.

Peru's economic and political history follows the South American pattern. Until the 1960s, Peru was dominated by the landed oligarchy and foreign mining and industrial interests. Until 1940, most Peruvians were rural; but between then and 1970, they flooded into the coastal cities until they were half urban with 25 percent of the population in Lima alone. They hoped for industrial jobs, but the cities never had employment or housing for such numbers.

Military reformers, 1968–75, introduced state capitalism modeled after Peron's Argentina. They nationalized existing mines and industries and began new ones under government ownership. With public enterprises operating at a loss, no meaningful tax system, and rising public expenditures, it was no surprise that inflation, falling production, food shortages, and a large balance of payments deficit followed. A rightist military regime took over for the last half of the seventies, cutting food subsidies, raising food and gasoline prices, and restraining domestic credit. Production, employment, and real wages fell; unemployment, underemployment, and malnutrition increased. Strikes and riots stalled the economy.

In 1980, a moderate civilian government took over. The state was responsible for 36 percent of total production. Three foreign firms had survived (one in copper and two in petroleum) by taking in Peruvian partners and providing capital reinvestment. Powerful new domestic commercial consortia and a growing group of self-employed and small, unregistered enterprises made up the rest of the economy. The new regime pursued a schizophrenic policy; conservative economists tried to shrink the public sector, avoid subsidies, and attract foreign investment while the architect president undertook a massive public works program of highways and hydroelectric projects financed by borrowing. The projects, designed to develop the Amazon jungles, neglected the Andes where the guerrilla movement, *Sendero Luminoso,* or Shining Path, was forming. There was a brief resumption of economic growth with higher world raw materials prices and some foreign investment, but the 1981–82 U.S. recession, plunging copper prices, and natural disasters cracked the fragile economy. Unemployment and underemployment rose; foreign loans further inflated the economy and cut real wages. Foreign lenders demanded repayment while the International Monetary Fund insisted on further retrenchment. The government violently suppressed urban strikes while terrorist activities spread in the highlands.

Another civilian government coming to power in 1985 decided on a quick recovery, attained by boosting consumption demand which would in turn reactivate idle industrial capacity. It recklessly froze prices, increased wages, cut tax rates and interest, provided subsidies and preferential credit to agriculture, limited cash outflow with a complicated system of multiple exchange rates, cut off imports to force domestic purchases, and defaulted on foreign debts. An unparalleled economic expansion lasted only until 1987, then public revenues dropped and deficits climbed. Prices were being held below costs, encouraging consumption and discouraging production. Inflation zoomed to 650 percent in 1988 and 3000 percent in 1989. Peruvian products became expensive abroad, cutting exports and encouraging smuggling.

A new government in mid-1990 ended subsidies and privatized industry. The result: unemployment, underemployment, rapidly rising living costs, impoverishment, strikes, and violence. Food prices increased five-fold, public transportation 300 percent, and gasoline 3000 percent in one week. Then in the spring of 1991, a cholera epidemic swept the nation, infecting over 700,000, and killing at least 1,250 people by the end of April.[62] Nevertheless, though unemployment rose and real wages fell drastically, inflation for August 1990 to August 1991 held at 300 percent, important structural economic reforms began, and export sales rose.[63]

With continued discipline, the future looked hopeful; but Shining Path guerrillas entered the vast shantytowns surrounding Lima and other major centers, destroying infrastructure and assassinating not only public figures and opponents but Catholic priests, helpers in soup kitchens, foreign aid technicians, and anyone else who might diminish "the people's revolutionary ardor."[64] The government declared martial law in areas affecting over half the nation's population. With support for *Sendero Luminoso* widespread among the majority poor, the democracy's survival is currently in real doubt. As a conservative force for order and civility, the LDS Church is, of course, a potential target for guerrilla violence although, as of the close of 1991, no missionaries have been killed or chapels bombed as they have been in Bolivia and Chile.

Responding to the precipitous increase in food prices in August 1990, the LDS Church Welfare Service Committee shipped a community kitchen to Peru consisting of thirty stoves, sixty large soup kettles, and utensils for a charity feeding operation, plus forty tons of clothing as a gift to the Peruvian government and people.[65] But the most important welfare contribution to the Peruvian Latter-day Saints had already been made; hygienic training preserved them from the cholera epidemic.[66]

In 1990, at the prevailing exchange rates, a monthly household income equivalent to $110 was Peru's poverty threshold. In the urban centers where most Latter-day Saints lived, probably 60 percent of Peruvian households were below that level, as were about the same proportion of Latter-day Saints.[67] It was a rare LDS household which rose above the poverty line without multiple earners; and in a country where women earn 39 percent of family income, one-third of LDS women and four out of five LDS men were employed.[68] The income distribution of LDS households appeared significantly less unequal than that of their national counterparts, though still representing a wide range of family incomes—probably because few Mormons were wealthy.

Those Mormons earning more than a poverty income were business executives, skilled workers and technicians, professionals, civil servants, or households with numerous earners. The unskilled constituted the bulk of the unemployed. One-third of the LDS men and two out of five LDS women were self-employed or working in family enterprises, compared to the 43 percent of the national labor force in the informal economy.[69]

Education seemed decisive in determining which LDS households were in poverty but not which had the highest incomes. With very few exceptions, those with under secondary schooling had low incomes. For those with post-secondary education, type of occupational preparation and work experience seemed more important than the number of years in school. Being self-employed or employed by others did not appear to be a significant factor in determining income.

Few LDS households had incomes sufficient to keep them from being hard hit by the 1990 five-fold food price increase. Most probably had to cut back sharply on the quality of what they ate and many on the quantity, though relatively few suffered outright malnutrition. Sharing among stakes and wards certainly minimized actual suffering. The advantages of food storage were clear, though few of the urban Saints raised any of their own foodstuffs and their small homes have little storage capacity. Perhaps half have running water and flush toilets.

Peruvian Saints who have avoided poverty typically have multiple earners per family, have learned a demanded skill, and/or participate in reasonably successful small businesses. The church can do nothing about the Peruvian economy. It can only help its members adapt to those grim realities. Even with limited application, familiar programs like fast offerings, home storage, and home and visiting teaching proved relevant. The U.S. church can offer limited amounts of additional cash or commodities as short-term help. For the longer term, the most promising forms of assistance for urban Mormons are career guidance, occupational preparation, job development and placement, and small enterprise development. The same staffing stringencies and financing restraints that afflict the same programs in Brazil and the Philippines prevail but are not insurmountable. The Peruvian economy still has 36 percent of its economy in agriculture and only 12 percent in manufacturing, but most Latter-day Saints are urban and engaged among the 20 percent of the labor force in services and 15 percent in trade, suggesting that church employment services could serve a useful role.[70] But close to half of the Peruvian work force is self-employed or in family enterprises, with Latter-day Saints not far below those averages, suggesting a substantial need for micro-enterprise development.

Africa

With all of its chaos, the welfare challenge of Latin America is trivial compared to Africa's situation if church growth burgeons there. A

crescent of persistent drought aggravated by overgrazing and mismanagement spreads from West Africa across North Africa to the Horn of
Africa and then southward, including South Africa and Zimbabwe, the
area of greatest LDS membership.[71] Population growth rates exceed economic development throughout the continent. Since 1970 per capita agricultural production for the continent has fallen about 1 percent per year.[72]
One in three Africans is dependent upon imported food. Though four-
fifths of Africa's peoples depend upon agriculture for their livelihood,
governments average a meager 5 percent of annual expenditures in agricultural improvements, hold down prices, and distort markets to placate
the growing cities. Government extension, credit, and technical
assistance—where they exist—simply ignore women farmers who produce some 70 percent of the continent's food. International economic development agencies praise Africa's "informal sector" for its enterprise,
also primarily a female activity on that continent.[73]

The nineteenth-century colonialists monopolized managerial, technical, and skilled jobs but did not train a cadre capable of either governing
effectively or operating efficiently what remnants of transportation, communications, and industry survived the twentieth-century revolutions.
Native despots have plunged their countries into successive military
coups, and countries not ravaged by civil wars have all too often turned
on their neighbors.[74] European colonists set political boundaries, usually
arbitrarily and seldom reflecting the meaningful realities of ethnic and
tribal distinctions.

Despite this brutal history of political turbulence and oppression, the
winds of democracy stir across the continent.[75] But, as elsewhere, its
spread and survival depend upon economic improvements. The LDS involvement is too new (except in South Africa, where its members have
been relatively well-off) to have included significant welfare activities,
but church welfare leaders are well aware of the potential challenges.[76]
Among others, women produce more than half of the food in the developing world and as much as three-fourths in Africa. They comprise over
one-fourth of the industrial labor force in developing countries and head
from one-fifth to two-fifths of the households.[77] Those facts pose an interesting dilemma, given cultural differences and preconceptions. Should
the church accept this social reality and help LDS women in developing
countries meet their traditional economic challenges, or should it put its
efforts into training men to become primary breadwinners in accord with
the more familiar western model? When to accept and when to attempt to
change is a continuing issue of intercultural adaptation.

Against a chaotic but not hopeless economic background, the LDS

Church has established a significant presence in four countries and a beginning in several others.

South Africa

South Africa and Rhodesia (Zimbabwe since 1980) had the only substantial African LDS membership before the 1978 revelation and the consequent policy change that extended priesthood to all worthy males. Those early members were Europeans, among whom poverty was almost unknown. Now, after a decade, blacks constitute approximately 30 percent of South Africa's Mormons and a majority of Zimbabwe's.

Despite social and economic discrimination against blacks in South Africa and restrictive occupational laws, until the current prolonged recession, demands for their services were high in lower-level jobs. Though there were difficulties in obtaining convenient housing, unemployment was not a serious threat; and the average income of black South Africans rose far above blacks in other African countries. A more relevant comparison, then, is between black and white Mormons—not only in terms of income but in terms of apartheid congregations. With its immense natural resources, well-developed industry, and substantial human resources, the most serious handicap facing the South African economy is its pariah position among nations. As reduction in apartheid practices ends international sanctions, the long South African recession, which in the short run has probably hurt blacks more than whites economically, should turn again to prosperity. If the nation can avoid continued civil strife, the church should be able to help its black members prepare for better jobs and get access to them as they become available. However, it is currently difficult to do so, due to legal restraints, social customs, and inadequate employment opportunities.

Zimbabwe

Zimbabwe inherited the colonial-developed agriculture and mining in 1980 as black independents took over white-governed Rhodesia. The economy was well diversified with good growth potential and a well-developed administrative and physical infrastructure. It faced shortages of skilled manpower from the exodus of whites, war's devastation of the physical infrastructure, and the depletion of capital stock. The blacks expected immediate redress of inequalities in income, land-holding, and access to social services; however, the new government wisely honored the inherited structure of ownership, retained private enterprise, and encouraged foreign investment, while expanding education and health services, increasing minimum wages, introducing agricultural resettlement, encouraging communal farming, and rebuilding its damaged rail and road systems. Forty percent of the land is still owned by about 7,000 prosperous white farmers while 48 percent is worked communally by Africans on a primarily subsistence basis.[78]

Within that context, the government has struggled with balance of payments problems, restraining the growth of budget deficits and external debt, and combating inflation. With rapid population growth (3.6 percent per year), average per capita incomes fell during the 1980s and the widespread rural poverty persisted. On the other hand, the incomes of small landholders and communal farmers have risen, and higher minimum wages have raised the incomes of agricultural laborers, though probably fewer are employed as a result. Basic health services, education, family planning, and municipal organization have expanded substantially. But unemployment is a rising problem; sustained expansion of peasant agriculture and growth in rural and informal urban sectors seem to be the most promising solution.

A high proportion of LDS Rhodesians emigrated before independence. Proselyting among black Zimbabweans began in 1979, and they comprise the majority of Mormons in that country. Few Saints are well-to-do. White Mormons are reportedly lower middle class while black Saints are drivers, security guards, miners, farm laborers, clerks, and factory workers; a few are teachers. Black LDS families earn an estimated average monthly income of fifty dollars. Though black/white income differentials exist within the church, they appear less extreme than in South Africa; and as in the latter nation, black incomes are above those of most blacks in other areas of the continent. In that setting, though agriculture is still the base of the economy, economic betterment for Mormons is most likely to come through preparation for and access to higher levels of urban employment.

Other African nations where the LDS Church began low-key proselyting in the 1980s lack the economic base and, paradoxically, considering the racial strife, the relatively stable governments of South Africa and Zimbabwe. Nigeria, Ghana, and Zaire are more illustrative of those countries.

Nigeria

Nigeria is a major oil producer and has vast unexploited reserves of natural gas. Yet agriculture, mostly small-scale farming, employs over two-thirds of the labor force and constitutes 30 percent of the economic output.[79] Agricultural productivity is low with considerable scope for im-provement through small-scale irrigation and improved technology. Oil profits during the 1970s encouraged the government to expand expendi-tures and debt to unsustainable levels and to invest in public projects without sufficient attention to either their economic viability or the ca-pacity to implement and manage them. When oil prices fell, so did real wages, but public debt only grew. Urbanization has been rapid, particu-larly in Lagos, but the hope of the economy is in agriculture and the rural areas. Tribal divisions remain strong; and though there has been no repeat of the bloody Biafran civil war of the 1960s, coups and abrupt changes of governments have been frequent. Infant mortality is over 100 per 1000 live births, male life expectancy is 49 years and female 53, population is growing 3.2 percent per year, and calorie intake and safe water supplies are among the poorest in sub-Saharan Africa.[80]

Young people have sought college educations and white collar and professional jobs, contributing to educated unemployment even while the demand grows for farm laborers and skilled workers.[81] A structural adjustment program instituted with the assistance of international agen-cies in 1986 has slowly improved economic conditions but there is a long way to go.[82] While the earliest LDS members in the nation were predomi-nantly rural, formal proselyting has moved to urban centers among people of above-average incomes, suggesting some combination of agri-cultural development and employment preparation/placement as the dual emphases of any self-reliance effort undertaken.

Ghana

Prior to its independence in 1957, Ghana enjoyed one of the high-est standards of living in West Africa, but poor economic management, including forced industrialization and profligate government spending, aggravated by a prolonged and severe drought, and increased oil prices, along with the forced repatriation of a million Ghanians from Nigeria in 1981, led to a decline that lasted into the mid-1980s.[83] An estimated half of the population lives in absolute poverty. Only half have access to modern health services and safe water. Though free primary education is avail-able, only about 80 percent of the children are enrolled. Half of the men and two-thirds of the women have received no formal education. A new government took over in 1983, reducing subsidies, establishing more re-alistic price and interest policies, increasing health and education services, rehabilitating the natural resource and transportation infrastructure, improving public administration, restructuring and divesting itself of publicly owned enterprises, and increasing the production of its major export, cocoa. But despite improvements, poverty remains extreme and individual economic opportunities limited.

Mormonism entered both Nigeria and Ghana from indigenous efforts, as noted above. In contrast to Nigerian members, who were originally rural and low income, the earliest Ghanian members were urban professionals, civil servants, and executives. Though church membership is now spreading among the more general population, Mormons still tend to be urban and above average in socioeconomic class.

Zaire

Zaire is even further down the economic ladder and illustrates what the church will confront in Uganda, Kenya, Swaziland, and other African nations. Zaire has the third largest area and the fourth largest population in Africa; 40 percent live in squalid urban areas, the remaining 60 percent engage in subsistence agriculture.[84] In 1989, per capita income was $260, slightly over half that of Ghana.[85] It has considerable economic potential including an industrious population, fertile soil, ample rainfall, and mineral wealth. However, civil turmoil and economic decline followed its independence in 1960. Nationalization frightened off foreign investment in the 1970s followed by heavy external borrowing and excessive money creation to finance unsustainable public expenditures. The World Bank called its 1983–86 reforms "courageous," but they lapsed after the latter year. The nation's economic development obstacles are "inefficient management of public resources; a heavy debt burden; inadequate transport and other basic infrastructure and public services; insufficient attention to human capital development; unattractive investment conditions; and, last but not least, overwhelming governance issues."[86] Less diplomatic language would have called it governmental incompetence and corruption.[87]

Despite this less than perfect outlook, Mormon membership consists promisingly of mainly urban males ranging from the late teens to the early forties.[88] Three-quarters of the nation's labor force farms; 87 percent of the population is at the subsistence level.[89] But since the LDS members appear to be grouped in the urban one-quarter and the wage-earning 13 percent, their future is more hopeful than that of most of their compatriots.

These examples illustrate the church's African challenge. Mormonism cannot impact directly the daunting continental economy; instead, it must find niches within the national economies in which it can help its members earn adequate incomes. More than anywhere else in the world, Africa demands agricultural improvements for rural populations and self-employment opportunities for urban residents; and Latter-day Saints on that continent face the same challenges.

Eastern Europe

As Eastern European nations allow Mormon missionary work, welfare challenges follow. The issue will not be the absolute poverty of Africa, the Philippines, and some of Latin America but rather the stark contrasts with the economic well-being of prosperous Saints in Western Europe. The planned economies have long traded stability and no-risk for low standards of living and persistent shortages. Their inefficient and outmoded industries and shoddy goods cannot successfully compete in world markets nor with their own consumers.[90] Wealthy West Germany was confident it could promptly reintegrate East Germany in 1990, but the prognosis was less optimistic at the close of the following year.[91] Other countries are struggling to replace planned economies with market economies, but long periods of readjustment with high unemployment and falling incomes accompanied by possible civil unrest are likely.[92]

The Commonwealth of Independent States left behind by the disintegration of the Soviet Union was the originator and imposer of communist central planning rather than a reluctant victim; it will undoubtedly have the greatest economic and political difficulties in the transformation. The dual LDS traditions of sharing and self-reliance will face interesting local interpretations as membership spreads in that region. Meanwhile, the church has stepped forward, as part of its humanitarian effort discussed below, to assist nonmembers in Poland, Armenia, and Russia in response to natural calamities and food shortages.[93]

The Global Economic Challenge

Membership surveys that include economic information are needed to determine the financial status of Latter-day Saints throughout the world. As a rough surrogate, see the average status of all residents of countries with LDS members, listed in Table 3.

Sixteen of the thirty-five countries which international agencies classify as being in "absolute poverty" had at least a thousand members by the end of 1989. As noted earlier, proselyting has already begun or is being explored in another nine on the list. The LDS Church accepts as a divine mandate an obligation to reach every nation and people. But it must also answer some questions of far-reaching consequence. (1) Currently, the definition of "gospel" includes the scriptural admonitions to meet

TABLE 3 Relative Economic Status of Mormons in Nations
with at Least a Thousand Members in January 1990

LDS Membership by Country

Country	Members (000)	Penetration rate[a]	Urbanization	Calory Per Capita	Infant Mortality (per 1000 in first year)	Percent Literacy	Life Expectancy (years)	GNP per Capita US$	GNP Ranking
1. USA	4,175	1.70	74	3645	10	96	76	19,300	4
2. Mexico	570	0.65	71	3132	46	90	69	1,760	31
3. Brazil	302	0.20	75	2656	61	78	65	2,120	29
4. Chile	266	2.07	85	2579	20	94	72	1,510	33
5. Philippines	231	0.34	41	2372	44	86	64	630	46
6. Peru	159	0.73	69	2246	86	85	62	1,280	34
7. Argentina	153	0.72	86	3210	31	95	71	2,520	25
8. United Kingdom	149	0.25	92	3523	9	98	75	12,810	15
9. Canada	125	0.50	76	3462	7	97	77	16,960	8
10. Guatemala	99	1.05	33	2307	57	55	62	900	41
11. Japan	91	0.07	77	2864	8	99	78	21,020	2
12. New Zealand	76	2.24	84	3463	11	95	75	10,000	17

13. Colombia	76	0.24	69	2542	39	88	68	1,180	36
14. Australia	73	0.45	86	3326	9	95	76	12,340	16
15. Ecuador	70	0.67	55	2058	62	82	66	1,120	37
16. Bolivia	55	0.80	50	2143	108	74	53	570	47
17. South Korea	50	0.11	69	2907	24	96	70	3,600	23
18. Uruguay	49	1.64	85	2648	23	95	72	2,470	26
19. Venezuela	48	0.25	83	2494	35	87	70	3,250	24
20. W. Samoa	40	24.30	na	na	na	na	na	na	na
21. Germany	36	0.04	86	3528	8	98	75	18,480	7
22. El Salvador	32	0.58	44	2160	57	72	63	940	40
23. Tonga	31	28.70	na	na	na	na	na	na	na
24. Honduras	29	0.57	42	2068	68	59	64	860	42
25. Portugal	23	0.22	32	3151	14	84	74	3,650	22
26. France	21	0.04	74	3336	8	98	76	16,090	10
27. Dominican Republic	19	0.26	59	2477	63	72	66	720	44
28. Hong Kong	17	0.30	93	2859	7	99	77	9,220	18
29. Taiwan	17	0.08	na	na	na	na	na	na	na
30. Spain	17	0.04	77	3359	9	94	77	7,740	21
31. South Africa	17	0.05	58	2924	70	na	61	2,290	27
32. Puerto Rico	16	0.49	na	na	na	na	na	na	na
33. Panama	15	0.63	54	2446	22	88	72	2,120	30

TABLE 3 (*Continued*) Relative Economic Status of Mormons in Nations
with at Least a Thousand Members in January 1990

LDS Membership by Country

Country	Members (000)	Penetration rate[a]	Urbanization	Calory Per Capita	Infant Mortality (per 1000 in first year)	Percent Literacy	Life Expectancy (years)	GNP per Capita US$	GNP Ranking
34. Italy	14	0.02	68	3523	10	96	77	13,330	14
35. Costa Rica	13	0.44	45	2803	18	94	75	1,690	32
36. Nigeria	12	0.01	34	2146	103	42	51	290	51
37. Paraguay	11	0.24	46	2853	41	88	67	1,180	35
38. Tahiti	11	5.95	na	na	na	na	na	na	na
39. Ghana	8	0.06	33	1759	88	53	54	400	49
40. Samoa	8	18.30	na	na	na	na	na	na	na
41. Sweden	7	0.09	84	3064	6	99	77	19,300	5
42. Netherlands	6	0.05	88	3326	8	99	77	14,520	12
43. Fiji	6	0.88	na	na	na	na	na	na	
44. Switzerland	6	0.10	61	3436	7	99	77	27,500	1
45. Belgium	4	0.04	97	na	9	99	75	14,490	13
46. Denmark	4	0.08	86	3633	8	99	75	18,450	8

47. Finland	4	0.08	60	3122	6	98	75	18,590	6
48. Haiti	4	0.07	29	1902	116	38	55	380	50
49. Indonesia	4	0.00	27	2579	68	74	61	440	48
50. Norway	3	0.09	74	3223	8	99	77	19,990	3
51. Thailand	3	0.03	21	2331	30	91	65	1,000	39
52. Austria	3	0.05	57	3428	8	99	75	15,470	11
53. Ireland	2	0.07	58	3632	7	95	74	7,750	20
54. Papua Guinea	2	0.06	15	2205	61	45	65	810	43
55. Jamaica	2	0.09	51	2590	11	na	73	1,070	38
56. Nicaragua	2	0.06	59	na	na	na	na	na	na
57. Zimbabwe	1	0.02	27	2132	49	74	63	650	45
58. Singapore	1	0.05	100	2840	7	86	74	9,070	19
59. Zaire	1	0.00	39	2163	130	61	47	170	52

Source: *Deseret News 1991–1992 Church Almanac* and World Bank.

[a]Penetration rate is the LDS percentage of the nation's total population.

temporal as well as spiritual needs of members. Will this provision stand in the next generation of proselyting or will it, like the policy of the "gathering," be redefined? (2) If the church affirms its obligation to end destitution among its members, what standard will be used—the national norm or that familiar to its developed world majority?

In a constantly changing world, another day may bring a sharply different outlook. Despite the very real difficulties enumerated, the billion poor, the setbacks of the 1980s, and worsening conditions in Latin America and sub-Saharan Africa during the 1980s, the World Bank in 1990 concluded that "during the past three decades the developing world has made enormous economic progress."[94] The Worldwatch Institute, less sanguine, noted that world population continued to grow more rapidly than world food output and that world food prices were rising sharply; apparent progress, it claimed, was "illusory."[95] Whatever the actual path of world economic development, a worldwide church with a commitment to pursuing both the economic and spiritual well-being of its members will have to learn to adapt.

The vast differences in condition among nations with LDS populations make it obvious that no uniform plan of economic assistance, like the Welfare Plan of the homogeneous Mountain West in the 1930s, can fit all of the circumstances among which Latter-day Saints live in the 1990s. That observation sets the context for a review of recent LDS welfare experiments throughout the world.

International Welfare Experiments, 1970–1990

Just as the international challenge began in the 1960s and accelerated over the following twenty years before settling into a stable though high rate of international membership growth, there has been a corresponding crescendo of experimental response to the poverty of members in many lands. The welfare farms which were the base of the 1936 plan in the United States were tried and abandoned. LDS Social Services spread only to the United Kingdom, Australia, and New Zealand before the decision not to expand further in the United States was applied internationally as well. Deseret Industries products have made an international contribution, as noted below, but there will apparently be no new installations in the United States or abroad. So far the heart of the international welfare effort has been the health missionaries and church employment centers, but there have been many localized ad hoc experiments of other types, leaving open whether there will be a future international welfare program and what it will look like.

Production and Distribution

Though welfare farms and storehouses abroad did not continue, the early experiences with them are instructive. As noted in Chapters 7 and 8, a welfare production project was considered a characteristic of and a requirement for stakehood after 1936. No stakes existed outside the United States, western Canada, and the Anglo Mormon colonies in Mexico until 1958.[96] Most Mormons assumed that, as stakes were created abroad, they would adopt the entire church program, including welfare farms, processing facilities, and storehouses. As late as 1976, the Presiding Bishopric instructed ward and stake leaders to engage in a production project and have access to a storehouse, regardless of location.[97] In 1983, this trend reversed.

The first stakes outside the traditional "Mormon country" were in New Zealand in 1958 followed by Australia in 1960. England, Holland, West Germany, Switzerland, and other parts of Mexico followed in 1961 with Samoa and Scotland in 1962. South American stakes began their rapid expansion in 1966, with Central America following in 1967, South Africa, Japan, and Tonga in 1970, and the Philippines and South Korea in 1973.[98] New Zealand, Australia, Samoa, and Tonga, probably because of a rural and pioneer heritage something like Utah's, launched welfare farms as soon as they had stakes and were encouraged to do so by American leaders. Considering the limited areas of their island settings and their year-round growing seasons, extensive processing, storage, and distribution facilities were not necessary in Samoa and Tonga. In fact, most of the members had family lands which they could have farmed more intensively, so the major contribution of the church farms was organization and discipline. The welfare farms founded in Australia and New Zealand were more successful; master plans for storage and distribution facilities there were under way when a change of central church policy stopped the process in 1983.

The concept was less attractive in the United Kingdom and West Germany with their primarily urban history and membership. Small-scale agricultural production was tried in the former, along with small chapel-based storehouse facilities, but the distribution was more compatible than the production and neither spread widely.

One welfare farm each, primarily for rice production, was undertaken in the Philippines and South Korea in 1976, but without notable success.[99] Most of the Saints lived in cities, land was difficult to purchase, ownership titles were either unavailable or uncertain, few members owned automobiles, and getting to the farms was difficult. Nevertheless, despite difficulties and member reluctance, area and local leaders persisted until relieved of the burdensome responsibility by the 1983 policy change. By that time, there were over 400 stakes outside the u.s. and Canada, yet no additional welfare farms had been introduced. Those few stakes outside the u.s. and Canada with farms were instructed to sell or lease them.

Although the 1936 model will apparently extend no further, the expertise gained at home may export well. An advisory team from the production/distribution division of LDS Welfare Services visited Poland several times during 1991 to help local agricultural specialists break bottlenecks in their production and distribution systems as they shift from centralized government direction to decentralized private operation.[100] Intriguingly, related units may also find enlarged roles. Since the 1970s, the Ezra Taft Benson Institute for Food and Agriculture, a research group connected with Brigham Young University, has experimented with and taught improved methods of small-scale agriculture in Mexico, Guatemala, Peru, Bolivia, and other Latin American countries, often increasing yields by 300 to 500 percent.[101] The need is equally intense in other areas of the world, particularly Africa. Humanitarian service activities discussed later in the chapter open the possibility of a return to church-sponsored agriculture production in other nations, though under substantially different conditions and applications.

Welfare Services Missionaries

Given a charter of concern for members' health throughout the world, Dr. James O. Mason, Church Health Commissioner, established the health missionary program in 1972. Although it did not reach the magnitude he contemplated, it became a permanent and, at least through the 1980s, the most important component of LDS welfare activities abroad.

The first health missionaries were young women with nursing, sanitation, nutrition, and other relevant backgrounds, selected by the Church Missionary Department and assigned to serve in countries with health care and medical deficiencies. Their initial assignment was to combine teaching sanitation and nutrition with proselyting. Some difficulties emerged almost at once from their dual responsibilities. Mission presidents measured effectiveness primarily by converts per missionary and considered proselyting their highest priority. Naturally, they sought to maximize proselyting time per missionary. On the other hand, the health care needs of the members pressed upon the health missionaries' time available.

In 1976, calling health missionaries was transferred to the newly named Welfare Services Department and Clarence R. Bishop, a full-time Welfare Services employee, was put in charge. An enthusiastic proponent of the program, he traveled extensively, visiting the missions where the health missionaries were assigned and negotiating with their mission presidents to allow them to devote the maximum time to health and sanitation. They taught members about water purification, nutrition, food preparation, gardening, home preservation and storage, and how to construct sanitary privies. Member enthusiasm and anecdotal evidence of health improvement encouraged broader extension for the rest of the decade.[102] A manual that John M. Hill of Brigham Young University had developed in the Philippines in the 1970s was modified and distributed to other health services missionaries church-wide.[103]

The only statistical study of health missionary efforts fully supported the anecdotal reports. During the early 1980s, Hill made pre- and post-participation comparisons among twenty-two groups of Filipino Saints. With three-quarters following the water purification instructions and two-thirds the kitchen sanitation and gardening techniques, the average incidence of diarrhea and fever among children was reduced 70.0 percent and eye, ear, lung, skin, and scalp infections by 53.2 percent. A subgroup with higher participation rates showed 92.9 percent and 85 percent reductions, respectively.[104]

With their success in health care, Welfare Services began to press for more welfare services missionaries with additional expertise. Retired farm couples were called to serve, first among American Indians on reservations and then among rural LDS members abroad. The men taught farming skills and the women food storage, homemaking skills, and handicrafts. Next, in response to requests from area and local leaders, retired teachers were called to teach basic literacy, English as a second language, and even deaf signing in Spanish.[105]

Requests flowed in from areas in need. Many could not be fulfilled. But a well-driller from the deserts of the western United States took his portable equipment to Tonga and a mechanically minded Welfare Services missionary serving in the same country invented a machine to remove tapa bark for fabric production.[106] A mini-Peace Corps seemed to be emerging with 500 participants by 1979.[107] Simultaneously, available members were also being called to teach seminary, do genealogical research, and serve in temples.

The Missionary Department expressed serious concerns about the program in 1981, although Welfare Services staff argued that the health care and other practical instructional services would attract people who could then be taught Mormon doctrine and converted. Called by Welfare Services to do welfare services work, welfare missionaries were still as-

signed to the mission presidents in the field, thus representing a statistical
drain on their proselyting resources and convert/missionary ratios. But
more importantly, though mission presidents generally valued what was
being accomplished, supervising the unfamiliar and seemingly secondary
activities taxed the mission presidents' time and energy. Retired American couples in good health who were available and willing to serve these
self-financed missions were in limited supply, creating competition for
their assignment among proselyting, temple, welfare, and other activities.

After an internal debate at church headquarters, the decision was made
to return the calling of welfare services missionaries to the Missionary
Department. Thereafter, skills and assignments were narrowed more
closely to health care and they were required to perform standard proselyting duties part of the time. Exact figures of these ratios vary by mission; estimates from the Missionary Department and Welfare Services
range between 40 percent to 60 percent for each activity, depending upon
which department is making the estimate.

The numbers trended downward until, at the end of 1990, only 271
health missionaries were serving in seventeen missions in South America,
Central America, the South Pacific, and the Pacific Rim. Most of them
were young women, approximately one-third registered nurses or other
health professionals, with another third teachers, and the rest from a variety of backgrounds. They served either in specialist pairs or with proselyting companions at the mission presidents' discretion. An additional
twelve mature couples with medical or pharmaceutical specialties were
also serving.

In 1989, when the conflicts over the dual assignments increased, the
First Presidency directed that, at the request of area presidencies, individuals could be recruited and called through the Missionary Department
and assigned as "church service missionaries," not to the mission presidents for part-time proselyting, but to the area offices where they serve
full time in their specialties under the directors of temporal affairs. At the
end of 1990, five couples had been called to staff employment centers in
the Philippines; others had been tapped for similar assignments in Haiti
and Puerto Rico. An agricultural specialist was serving in the West Indies,
and two couples with social work specialties in child development were
being sought for other international assignments. Thirty other missionary couples were assigned to literacy programs. All in all, 1,417 retired
couples and 540 single women of retirement age were serving as unpaid
missionaries at the end of 1990, engaged in proselyting, leadership development, temple service, genealogical research, administrative and clerical
assignments, or welfare services assignments full time, 48 percent of
them in the United States and 52 percent abroad. However, statistics re-

veal priorities. Approximately 350 were doing welfare compared with nearly five times as many in administrative, proselyting, and temple assignments.

General Authorities and local leaders have increasingly preached that all Mormon couples should prepare financially for and anticipate this full-time post-retirement service—for the most part for minimum terms of twelve months in the United States and eighteen months abroad. Although it excludes single retirement-age men, such a policy taps a significant pool of potential missionaries; approximately 200,000 U.S. members are over sixty-five.[108] Many health-conscious Latter-day Saints approach their seventies with undiminished vigor, and the devout are schooled in the obligations of consecrated service.

Employment Centers

In contrast to the official reserve about extending social services to other settings, there has been much less reluctance to establish church employment centers internationally, though the numbers are still limited. They seem to have found general acceptance among church leaders and can be undertaken almost anywhere an area presidency can make a strong argument for their usefulness and where unpaid volunteers with the appropriate professional and language skills are available to operate them.

The first inquiries for a church employment center abroad came from Santiago, Chile, in 1978. H. Verlan Anderson, later a member of the First and Second Quorums of Seventy, and his wife, then serving as a post-retirement missionary couple, were assigned to open and staff the center. After a year or more of successful experience, they returned to the United States; the mission authorities then discovered that Chilean law allowed no unpaid staff for functions which could provide paid employment. Therefore, a Chilean member was hired as a full-time paid director and subsequently promoted to area welfare specialist, among other responsibilities supervising employment centers in Santiago, Viña del Mar, and Concepcion, Chile's three major cities. The Chilean economy in recent years has been the healthiest of the partially industrialized countries in South America; and by concentrating on job development and placement, the Chilean centers aggregated about 3,000 placements a year during the late 1980s.

Closely related to the Chilean employment center effort was a short-lived Deseret Industries-related job creation effort in 1983. Approximately forty otherwise unemployed Chilean members sorted bales of used clothing from overstocked U.S. Deseret Industries facilities, repaired what might be recycled, and cut up the rest into rags as stuffing for sleeping bags which they manufactured. The reconditioned clothing and sleeping bags were displayed and sold in LDS chapels or wholesaled to vendors. These employees also constructed hymnal racks, ping pong tables, and other simple furnishings on contract for chapels then under construction. Whether because of improvements in the Chilean economy or other reasons, the employment-creation effort did not continue.

The next request for an employment center came from Great Britain in 1980. A single center was established in Birmingham in 1981 with paid staff. However, the distances and the expense of transportation limited its access by members and also limited staff contacts with possible employers. Ward and stake employment specialists, called, beginning in 1981, according to the normal U.S. pattern, showed little enthusiasm for the assignment. After five years of inadequate response, a more successful "circuit rider" concept was substituted in 1986. Mini-centers were established in stake centers throughout England, Wales, Scotland, and North Ireland. The stake employment specialists, still volunteers, were transformed into stake employment managers and assigned to develop job contacts among local employers, ward specialists referring job seekers to their stake counterparts. A training manual was written to guide the managers. A director and an assistant director (full-time and paid) currently spend four days a week on the road, visiting each of the nineteen mini-centers every other week. There they train, motivate, and make job contact calls with the stake employment managers. The result has been a placement volume now averaging about 250 per year, considered sufficient to keep the centers in operation.

The success of the Chilean effort motivated the area presidency responsible for Argentina, Uruguay, and Paraguay to replicate the program. The first center in Montevideo, Uruguay, opened in 1982 and successfully placed 1,762 persons by 1988, primarily as a result of economic prosperity, including an expanding automobile assembly industry. Economic recession reduced the center's effectiveness: it placed 414 people in 1989 and 443 in 1990, primarily in service jobs and as household servants.

A center in Buenos Aires opened in 1983 with satellite centers in four other cities in subsequent years. The Buenos Aires center has a paid staff, and its director supervises part-time church service volunteers staffing the other centers. The Argentine experience was like Uruguay's, with an impressive placement record until recession took its toll. There were over 5,500 placements in Buenos Aires alone in 1988 compared to 1,300 in 1989 and 2,700 in 1990. The other four centers combined added from 300 to 400 placements per year over the same period. No employment center has been opened in Paraguay, which has comparatively few members and a weak economy.

An employment center established in the São Paulo Brazil Area office in the early 1980s concentrated on recruiting and screening applicants for internal employment in church administration. No employment centers that linked Mormons with jobs in the national economy were established during the 1980s, perhaps because the southeast's general prosperity and rapid industrialization were benefiting Brazilian Latter-day Saints without any special effort. But it may also have meant that opportunities to upgrade the employment of LDS members were being neglected, leaving them unnecessarily vulnerable during the recession that began in 1989.

In 1990, a new area presidency reassigned a member of the area office staff to spend full time developing an employment center program throughout the country. This individual, an Argentine of long residence in Brazil, faces the overwhelming obstacle of either finding competent volunteers or obtaining budget for paid staff. There are few retired members with adequate income to make full-time church service a possibility, and no general policy for hired staff outside of the United States yet exists. Furthermore, success will require more than just job development and placement, crucial though those services are, because Brazilian LDS youth are, by and large, educating themselves into unemployability.

The employment center effort spread into Central America in 1989. Sparked by Lynn Justice, an aggressive director of temporal affairs who had previously represented American firms throughout the entire region, a new area presidency launched a number of employment centers staffed by available volunteers. In Guatemala City, a retired Guatemalan couple with substantial business experience in that and adjacent countries was called in 1989 to manage an employment center in the building housing the area office. Despite high unemployment, employers found the services attractive. As they put it, to advertise for one job opening was to be deluged with applicants from whom they must select a capable employee. The church center guaranteed to select and deliver the capable employee without employer effort. Shortly thereafter, the retired city personnel director of Quetzaltenango, the nation's second largest city, opened a second employment center. His assignment included making job development calls in surrounding metropolitan areas as well. At the time of observation, part-year operation had resulted in ninety-eight placements between the two Guatemalan centers.

About the same time, a third employment center opened in Tegucigalpa, capital of Honduras, directed by a retired U.S. banker whose wife was Honduran. When, after a few months, they returned to New York City to live, no one could be found to replace them, and the promising center was closed. Another center has been discussed for La Ceiba, on the Caribbean coast of Honduras. A center in Panama City had been under discussion until the anti-Noriega U.S. invasion in December 1990 discouraged the effort. No more than modest success can be expected, given the current high unemployment in the Central American region.

A church employment center functioned briefly during 1990–91 in Haiti, where the economy was even more severely depressed; its paid director resigned for more favorable career opportunities. Between the devastated economy and the continual political unrest, he had made only thirty-five placements in a year. Search was under way for a church service volunteer as a replacement when the military coup overthrew the island nation's first democratically elected president in September 1991, adding to the economic chaos and ending interest for the present.[109] The opening of a center in Puerto Rico with volunteer staff was under discussion in 1991.

Welfare activities were not a high priority of the area presidencies assigned to Mexico during the 1980s and early 1990s and only one employment center had been established in that country by 1991. That center, established in Mexico City in 1989 and staffed by a retired Mexican couple, found jobs for 1,300 members in a wide range of occupations—accountants, secretaries, salespeople, and business managers—during their two years of service.[110] The search for replacements at their release in 1991 again illustrated the vulnerability of volunteer-dependent programs. Additional centers were under discussion for the Mexican cities of Puebla and Monterrey in 1991. We know of no employment centers in the Andean countries and across the northern tier of South America by that date.

In late 1990, the Welfare Services Department recruited five retired American couples to serve for eighteen months as employment specialists in the Philippines.[111] Each husband had long experience in either employment service operation, vocational education, or as administrators of employment and training programs in the United States. Wives participated in contacting employers, making presentations to leaders, and counseling applicants. The outgoing area presidency, George I. Cannon, George R. Hill III, and Phillip T. Sonntag, had made member self-reliance and economic well-being a high priority and had persistently lobbied the Church Welfare Services Committee for employment specialists. An earlier missionary couple (1989–90) had introduced employment concepts to regional, stake, and ward leaders, encouraging them to call stake and ward employment specialists. The newly called cadre, building on this foundation, energetically developed employer contacts and counseled job-seeking members in the Manila and Cebu City areas, though one couple had to leave shortly because of the ill health of the husband. Located in the two major metropolitan areas, they avoided the issue that fewer than half of Filipino members are English speaking, an even more intense problem in other countries.[112] Statistics were not yet available in mid-1991, but the effort seemed promising. The challenge is recruiting replacements to give the effort continuity.

Based on those experiences, it appeared at the end of 1991 that the church employment center was to be the key element of international welfare. But its challenges and limitations were already apparent:

1. Employment centers succeed only in an urban setting and a developing economy that offers substantial industrial and commercial employment.

2. Employment placement is obviously vulnerable to the host economy. It matches demand and supply; it does not create jobs.

3. Success, even in an expanding and healthy economy, depends on the aggressiveness, knowledgeability, and persuasiveness of the center's staff. Directors must establish good rapport with employers, understand their needs, and persuade them to accept referrals; they must simultaneously guide jobseekers to appropriate choices, teach job search skills, and select strong applicants for referral who will impress the employer and establish a reputation leading to further job orders. A fact of welfare life is that many of the people who need jobs most desperately are least qualified to be successful employees.

4. Directors must also provide career counseling for youth, returning missionaries, and displaced workers. These abilities are not widely available, especially when language facility and cultural expertise are also demanded.

5. Professional versus volunteer staffing remains a persistent issue. In the United States, volunteer centers function as satellites of professionally staffed centers, supported and supervised by a full-time area welfare specialist. Such a support system exists abroad only in Chile and Argentina. Generally speaking, most developing nations cannot afford professionals and cannot supply qualified volunteers. u.s. volunteers are not only scarce but limited in language skills and cultural adaptability. Professionals could be recruited, but not without a major policy departure. It appears anomalous that paid professionals undergird the system in the United States where the church system supplements the ubiquitous taxpayer-supported Job Service, yet international extension of the church system seems to be entirely dependent upon the availability of competent volunteers.

Humanitarian Services

Donating Deseret Industries surpluses to private charities, along with the domestic donations described in Chapter 8, illustrates a major change in Mormon welfare policies beginning in 1985. The church had historically made generous contributions to humanitarian causes, both internationally and domestically, but never as part of a continuing program. For example, between 1973 and 1985, the church provided medical supplies, building materials, clothing, and food as ad hoc responses to hurricanes in Tahiti and Tonga, tornados in South America, cholera outbreaks in Korea and Latin America, earthquakes in Nicaragua, Colombia, and Chile, and the expulsion of Ghanians from Nigeria.[113] However, the church focus was deliberately insular and its policy could be phrased as: "If we take care of our own, we will free the resources of other organizations to serve nonmembers."

A change of policy began after 1978; as a result of lifting the priesthood ban on black men, membership spurted in Ghana and Nigeria. At the urging of returned older missionary couples, the church, on an ad hoc basis, supported community projects in Ghana in 1982 and 1983, primarily because the members needed access to safe water, better agricultural methods, and nutrition and hygienic instruction.[114] Then, beginning in 1984, the crisis caused by the Ethiopian famine, exacerbated by political divisions and government ineptitude, captured the sympathy of Latter-day Saints as it did many groups throughout the world. In 1984, the LDS Church contributed food, clothing, and money to such organizations working in Africa as the International Red Cross, CARE, Africare, and Catholic Relief Services.[115] When it became apparent that the need was long term and more extensive than the church could supply from its ongoing internal programs, the First Presidency, turning to a long-standing tradition, declared a special fast for the last Sunday in January 1985, and appealed to Mormons in the United States and Canada to contribute generously "for the use of victims of famine and other causes resulting in hunger and privation among the people of Africa."[116] Members responded, contributing $6.6 million.[117] The church then contracted through those experienced organizations with staff already operating in Ethiopia. The relief consisted not only of food, the immediate requirement, but also small well drilling and other water projects for longer-term solutions to famine conditions.

At the time, Ethiopia's corrupt and inept government was Marxist in orientation. Perhaps responding to internal political criticism, Gordon B. Hinckley, second counselor in the First Presidency and the church's chief executive officer during the lengthy final illnesses of President Spencer W. Kimball and First Counselor Marion G. Romney, observed in the April 1985 general conference: "Where there is hunger, regardless of cause, I will not let political considerations dull my sense of mercy or thwart my responsibility to the sons and daughters of God wherever they may be or whatever their circumstances."[118]

Pleased with the response, the First Presidency declared a second special fast ten months later; it coincided with a national day of fasting for hunger relief called by President Ronald Reagan for Sunday, 24 November.[119] This fast, announced only to u.s. members, raised an additional $3.8 million for external relief.[120] Since the returns from the second fast were not designated for any particular country or project, the funds could be used more flexibly.

At first, Glenn L. Pace, second counselor in the Presiding Bishopric and former managing director of the Welfare Services Department, attempted to identify and negotiate uses for the funds personally. When that duty became too burdensome, a policy-making and administrative mechanism was developed. A Humanitarian Services Committee, so named to distinguish it from internal Welfare Services, was created. Its membership consisted of General Authorities, chaired by Apostle Joseph B. Wirthlin. Dr. Isaac Ferguson, a public health expert, former director of the health missionary program, and then an area welfare director in the Midwest, was named director. His assignment was to recruit/accept applications, screen them, and present worthy projects to the Humanitarian Services Committee for approval, then to supervise expenditures and execution of these projects.[121]

Based on the Ethiopian experience, the Humanitarian Services Committee, though it makes occasional grants, generally contracts with agencies experienced in international charity. By policy, the committee prefers to underwrite many small projects, rather than a few larger ones, especially if they can provide leverage by uniting with other funds. (See Table 4.) Pace summarized selection criteria in the October 1990 general conference: "Our resources are limited and the needs of the world are vast. . . . The Brethren closely monitor the multitude of crises throughout the world and give assistance to a wide range of countries. The assistance is given where the need seems to be the greatest, without consideration of the political or religious ideologies that exist in each country."[122]

TABLE 4—Humanitarian Services Projects, and
Contracting Agencies, 1982–90

Year	Country	Project	Contracting Agency
1982	Ghana	medical supplies	Friends of West Africa
1983	Ghana	corn/poultry farm medicine, food, farm equipment, well-drilling equipment	West Africa LDS mission

Year	Country	Project	Contracting Agency
1984	Ethiopia	food, medicine	International Red Cross
1985	Ethiopia	food, medicine blankets, tents	International Red Cross
		food, blankets, tents	Catholic Relief Services
		irrigation system	Africare
	Ghana	physicians	Friends of West Africa
	Africa	various relief efforts	CARE
	Sudan	disaster relief	International Red Cross
		credit, marketing	Catholic Relief Services
	Chad	irrigation development	CARE
1986	Ghana	water, agriculture	Ghana Accra Mission
	Ethiopia	irrigation	Africare
		disaster relief	International Red Cross
		commodity airlift	Catholic Relief Services
	Sudan	disaster relief	International Red Cross
	Nigeria	well-drilling	Nigeria Lagos Mission
		water, agriculture	Africare
	Chad	irrigation development	CARE
	Niger	agro-forestry project	CARE
	Cameroon	agro-forestry	CARE
1987	Bolivia	youth assistance	Bolivian government
		economic development	Andean Children Fund
	Ghana	agricultural development	Ghana Accra Mission
	Nigeria	water, agricultural development	Africare
1988	Guatemala	small plot agriculture	Benson Institute
	Hungary	medical equipment	Semmelweis University
	Zimbabwe	grinding mill, dam	Africare
	Kenya	community water	Technoserve
		polio immunization	Rotary International
	Ivory Coast	polio immunization	Rotary International
	Mozambique	relief assistance	Africare
	Poland	medical supplies	Europe Area Presidency
	Hungary	hospital beds	Hungarian government
	Philippines	resuscitation unit	emergency rescue unit
	Bolivia	village development	Andean Children Fund
	Ghana	demonstration farm	Africare
	Armenia	earthquake relief	USSR

Year	Country	Project	Contracting Agency
1989	China	earthquake relief	Peoples' Republic
	Nigeria	cassava processing	Aba Nigeria Stake
	Honduras	village banking	Katalysis
	Ghana	well-drilling	Ghana Accra Mission
	Armenia	children's relief	Armenian Relief Fund
	Nigeria	textbooks	BYU College of Nursing
	Haiti	literacy project	Laubach International
	Philippines	medical care	Mabuhay Deseret Foundation
	Venezuela	health fair	Venezuela Caracas Mission
	Mozambique	refugee relief	Zimbabwe Child Development
	Ghana	textbooks	Ghana Accra Mission
	Philippines	gardening training	area presidency
	Mexico	literacy project	Laubach International
	Puerto Rico	hurricane relief	governor's office
	Egypt	community development	Choice
	Mexico	village development	Andean Children Fund
	Peru	farm coop training	Technoserve
	Philippines	enterprise development	Enterprise Development Foundation
	Romania	general relief	area presidency
1990	South Africa	immunization	Homelands Health Department
	Portugal	flood relief	International Red Cross
	Zaire	self employment	Technoserve
	Honduras	community service	Katalysis
	Trinidad	boat repair	West Indies LDS Mission
	Mexico	used clothing	area presidency
	Guatemala	used clothing	area presidency
	Bulgaria	surgery	individual
	Uganda	dental program	Deseret International
	Mexico	fire damage repair	Beehive International
	Thailand	village bank	Freedom from Hunger
	Mali	village development	Ouelessebougou-Utah Alliance for Progress
	Romania	ear surgery	Volunteer medic team

Year	Country	Project	Contracting Agency
	India	literacy for women	Laubach International
	Nepal	literacy	Laubach International
	Dominican Republic	infant orphanage	orphanage
	Bulgaria	surgery	individual
	Philippines	earthquake relief	Philippine-American Foundation
	Bolivia	medicine, clothing	National Police Wives
	Nigeria	food production feasibility study	Technoserve
	Haiti	rice project	Ogla foundation
	Liberia	refugee assistance	area presidency
	Uganda	village development	women's organization

The community water project in a small Kenya village in 1988 can serve as an example of the leveraged results of small expenditures. A contract with Technoserve resulted in a well and piped culinary water. Revisiting the location in 1991, LDS Welfare Services and Humanitarian Services staff found that, because women and children no longer had to spend major parts of every day carrying water, the women could spend more time farming, reportedly augmenting production substantially. Because the children were no longer being water carriers, they had time to attend a school which was inaugurated by the Kenyan government in response to their availability.[123] Apparently, the men, in traditional fashion, had not altered their schedules.

After the success of the Deseret Industries baled-clothing experiment in Chile, similar projects were undertaken in Peru and Central America. But as part of its humanitarian outreach, the church has also made baled clothing available to nonmember groups in Appalachia, in the Peruvian crisis of 1990, in Africa, and in Eastern Europe, including to orphanages in Romania and Bulgaria.[124]

In the months immediately following the 1990 Desert Storm military action, the Humanitarian Services Committee presented 13,000 blankets, 80,000 pounds of clothing, and $100,000 worth of medicines to Iraqi refugees with impressive political sensitivity. To avoid appearances of partisanship, the church split its gift three ways: to the Turkish and Iranian branches of the Muslim Red Crescent on behalf of Kurdish refugees, to the American Red Cross to aid Shiite refugees in Southern Iraq, and to World Division, a group working in the hospitals of Baghdad and other cities in the control of the Iraqi government.[125] The church also responded to Chilean mud slides, Chinese earthquakes and floods, and Philippine volcano eruptions with food, clothing, medical supplies, and cash contributions during the summer of 1991.[126] Even though the United States government still maintained its embargo on Vietnam, the LDS Church donated medical supplies to aid Vietnamese needy in late 1991.[127] At the same time, parts of the former Soviet Union were the most recent recipients of LDS food donations, some from European congregations.[128] The church-wide requirement that LDS missionaries contribute half a day of community service per week was also making its international contributions.[129]

By mid-1991, all of the original donations to the two fasts had been exhausted along with the earned interest. However, church members had made unsolicited donations to the Humanitarian Services Fund of over $2 million, keeping the program alive.[130] This spontaneous generosity prompted the First Presidency to include a slot for humanitarian contributions on the preprinted donations form provided to every LDS ward; and a letter over the signatures of the First Presidency, read over all LDS pulpits in the United States and Canada during the 1991 Christmas season, urged contributions to the Humanitarian Services effort.[131] Thus, the fund was institutionalized as part of the regular giving program of the church, along with the fast offering and missionary contributions, though it is not yet clear whether it will prove more successful than special fasts.

The Church Education System (CES)

The contribution of the LDS Church to the economic well-being of its members cannot be adequately recorded without acknowledging the impact of its educational emphasis over the years and the contributions of that education to their self-sufficiency. Buttressed by such scriptural pronouncements as "the glory of God is intelligence" (D&C 93:36), "it is impossible for a man to be saved in ignorance" (D&C 131:6), and "if a person gains more knowledge and intelligence in this life . . . than another, he will have so much the advantage in the world to come" (D&C 130:19), Mormons have established schools and universities wherever they have gone until governments were prepared to take over the burden.[132] Not only has this commitment given U.S. Mormons a substantially higher average educational attainment than their national counterparts,[133] but it has also raised for them the question of their obligations to cobelievers in countries of limited education today.

The Mormon colonies in northern Mexico had their own schools beginning in 1887, but they served primarily transplanted American children.[134] Other Mexican LDS children profited when a wealthy member established a private school for his own children at San Marcos, Hidalgo, an area of membership concentration near Mexico City in 1944.[135] Then, with explosive church membership growth in the 1960s, the abysmal state of the Mexican education system became a concern to the educationally committed Mormons. Mexico had strict laws against parochial schools dating back to the anti-clerical Mexican Revolution, though they were not enforced in Mormon colonies. The Mexican government, also concerned about education, welcomed contributions to its meager resources and cooperated with the church in incorporating the Sociedad Educativa y Cultural, which owned and staffed the schools.[136]

Between 1960 and the late 1970s, the church established forty-three elementary and junior high schools throughout the nation, plus a college preparatory school and teacher training college, Benémerito, in the Mexico City area. At its peak in 1976, the system enrolled over 10,000 students. The schools, staffed by both Mormons from the United States and Mexican members, maintained high standards; influential nonmembers also eagerly enrolled their children. Those who passed through those schools served missions, went on to institutions of higher education, became the local ward and stake leaders, and created a middle class of substantial financial contributors to the church. Teachers trained in the LDS system staffed the church schools but also formed a cadre of well-prepared teachers and administrators when the Mormon schools were absorbed into the national school system after 1981.

However, by the late 1970s, rapid church growth and the schools' popularity produced applications far in excess of capacity. Acceptances and rejections involved member families in political problems. Discipline problems in the schools also affected spirituality in the local wards. Mexican authorities were becoming restive about Mormon rules of conduct and worried about the possibility of surreptitious proselyting. Simultaneously, the Mexican school system was improving, and the Church Commissioner of Education was receiving requests for church-funded schools from other areas of rapid church growth. All could not be accommodated, and it was difficult to come up with a rationale to support some and not others.

Considering all these factors—not the least of which was intense competition for church resources as world membership nearly doubled during the 1970s—church authorities decided in the late 1970s to establish no new schools in Mexico, began closing a few of them in 1981, and in 1983 decided to close all but the Juarez Academy, a historic institution in the northern colonies, and the Benémerito college preparatory school and teacher training college.[137] Shortly afterward, the Mexican government made teacher training a governmental monopoly; the church closed its teacher training college as well, leaving the 2,600-student Benémerito preparatory school and the Juarez Academy as the only remnants of the major 1960–80 Mormon educational investment in Mexican education.

Parallel developments occurred simultaneously in several Andean nations.[138] Seven primary schools and one secondary school functioned in and near Santiago, Chile, 1964–71, with a peak enrollment of 2,350. Primary schools enrolling approximately 180 students each were established in La Paz (Bolivia), Asuncion (Paraguay), and Lima (Peru), from the late 1960s to 1981.[139] All were closed or transferred to government control after 1981. The church retained its schools in Tonga, Samoa, Fiji, Tahiti, and among the Maoris of New Zealand, where church schools sometimes dated back to 1888, where LDS members constituted from one-fifth to one-third of the total populations, and where local education was otherwise inadequate. Some have since closed as alternatives became available to the members; but twenty-three elementary and secondary schools enrolling about 6,000 students were still in operation in 1991, even though state alternatives existed and applications routinely exceeded the places available.[140] No formal evaluations have been carried out of these schools' economic impact, but informed observers agree that church schools have contributed to better careers and better church leadership.

To compensate somewhat for fewer schools, the Church Education System in the 1980s inaugurated a student loan program for less developed countries. No-interest loans meet both educational and living costs while the student attends academic or vocational and technical schools near his or her home city. Church Education System representatives are periodically available to counsel with the students to make sure their education and career plans are realistic. Only candidates with recommendations from local priesthood leaders are eligible, thus limiting funding to active Latter-day Saints. The number of loan recipients has never been made public, and demand almost certainly exceeds supply; but CES officials, interviewed in the spring of 1991, reported that the funding was at least sufficient to meet requests from returned native missionaries, both men and women.[141] Some of them are among the 2,000 foreign scholarship students on the campuses of the Brigham Young University, its Hawaii campus, and Ricks College.

Volunteer literacy programs are a more recent innovation. In 1991 thirty retired couples, most of them former teachers, were serving full-time to administer and coordinate the efforts of part-time volunteer teachers. Seven served on U.S. Indian reservations, one couple in Chicago's central city, and the remainder in Latin America and the Caribbean. The local volunteers do most of the teaching in homes and church buildings. Instructional materials in Spanish are being duplicated for English- and French-speakers.[142] Participation is informal and fluid but was estimated at between 600 and 1,000 at the end of 1990. The program was aimed at teaching members to read the scriptures and church administrative materials, but literacy skills are unquestionably transferrable. On its 150th anniversary in early 1992, the LDS Relief Society announced its intention to undertake a more massive literacy effort among Mormon women throughout the world using CES materials.[143]

Curricular Instruction

The church's curriculum for international units includes instruction on the principles of provident living. An international manual has been available since at least as early as 1970, designed for small wards and branches. It assumes that the members will be newer, that the teachers will be less experienced, and that men and boys will meet together. All of the illustrations feature Latin Americans, Asians, or Micronesians. Lessons for men include "The Father's Responsibility for the Welfare of His Family," "Managing Family Finances," "Home Production and Storage," "Developing and Improving Employment Skills," "Keeping Physically Fit," "Involving Members with Disabilities," and "Serving the Community and Nation."[144] A supplement adds lessons on "Sharing Family Work," "Home Gardening," "Developing Our Talents," "Seeking Knowledge," "Tithes and Offerings," and "Building the Kingdom of God."[145]

Specialized manuals, largely for American members, explain the essentials of home production and storage; leadership manuals include instructions on emergency preparedness and services to unwed parents.[146] Individual missions and area offices have prepared additional lessons on self-reliance, primarily during the 1980s, reflecting local needs and conditions.

Certainly there is a great need for more region-specific materials. In fact, helping young people make the transition from childhood to adult family responsibilities and earning roles more easily may have a greater impact on economic well-being than any amount of direct services. Still, a beginning has been made in teaching "correct principles" of welfare in the arena where they are needed most.

Miscellaneous Activities

Possibly of more long-term significance than institutionalized activities are the numerous ad hoc and often short-lived assistance projects undertaken by various individuals and local leaders in many countries. As in the 1930s, it may be from these experimental efforts that a proven venue will emerge to be ultimately endorsed as official church programs. Insofar as we know, these efforts have never been centrally inventoried and recorded. We report those we have observed, been told about, or read about—almost certainly a limited sampling.

Personal loan programs were inaugurated in Argentina, Uruguay, Paraguay, and Chile around 1980. However, they proved unsuccessful and saddled local church leaders with the divisive problem of collecting unpaid loans when the program was abandoned a few years later. An area president in Mexico during the 1980s with banking background made personal loans to members to start businesses, but only he knows his success rate. A small-loan program undertaken by local members in one part of Uruguay during the same era caused internal strife when those managing it showed favoritism to family members, but a credit union in another part of the same country has succeeded under more neutral and business-like direction. A group of some sixty LDS families in Mexico, encouraged by BYU professors, participated in that country's abortive land reform movement of the early 1980s; half remained in urban employment to finance the other half in a cooperative farming venture. The project was described as having "worked remarkably well" but died out just the same.[147]

The Philippines has been a particularly fertile area for experimentation. Marion D. Hanks and William R. Bradford, serving as area presidents there in the mid-1980s, were responsible for the purchase and installation of commercial sewing machines in many chapels, apparently hoping that women could upgrade family clothing and acquire employable skills. The first objective has been better achieved than the second. A Philippine regional representative who owns handicraft stores buys and retails member-produced handicrafts. A marketing cooperative sells the output from member cottage industries, a stake consumer cooperative purchases and distributes food wholesale, another cooperative subcontracts stone-cutting, and a third produces paper and kimono materials for export to Japan. Church employees have established a credit union, and another group briefly tried a communal farming enterprise.[148] Using savings sent home by a Relief Society president's husband working in Saudi Arabia, members of a Manila ward established a successful small factory making shell lampshades. Women in one area received instructions on making soap for home use, an example of efforts to increase self-sufficiency in noncommercial ways.[149] None of these enterprises had been endorsed by the local and area leadership to become official church programs.

A medical doctor serving as Manila mission president arranged housing and the services of volunteer non-Mormon Philippine surgeons to undertake major restorative surgery for handicapped persons of all faiths. Mission presidents in the Philippines and elsewhere have encouraged home craft production and then attempted to market the output among friends in their home countries. However, the market is usually limited, and efforts rarely survive the mission president's three-year tenure. The Personal and Family Preparedness Program, including home storage as practiced in the United States, has been urged by local church units in a number of countries. However, subsistence incomes, small houses, the lack of storage facilities, and climate conditions shortening shelf life have made those principles difficult to apply. As a substitute for the bishops' storehouses of the U.S. program, Philippine bishops stock a meeting-house closet with emergency food, a generally successful system.

A retired professor of agriculture serving as a church representative in Nigeria obtained and persuaded LDS farmers to use appropriate fertilizers; substantial increases resulted. An LDS mission president with a mechanical background constructed a well-drilling apparatus for Nigerian members to use but the effort was unsuccessful until another American Mormon with well-drilling experience worked with an international agency to obtain more appropriate equipment. In another Nigerian effort, cassava seedlings of superior genetic stock increased the productivity of the major food crop. Member farmers were to replace the seedlings at harvest time to replenish the supply for the next crop but were not well enough organized to do so, and the project died out. A Nigerian petroleum engineer, now regional representative for West Africa, persuaded his company to accept some returned missionaries as apprentices and hopes to negotiate the same arrangement, both with other companies and in independent activities like concrete-block laying. The same Nigerian mission president who initiated well-drilling helped inaugurate a similar project on a Ghanian farm operated as a village cooperative by LDS members and nonmember residents. The possibilities of cooperative timber and lumber operations have been explored for the same area of Ghana but never undertaken. A Ghanian schoolteacher/branch president has encouraged pig-raising and pottery-making among his members.[150]

A Paris, France, stake established its own "drop of water" fund through voluntary fasts to relieve misery throughout the world. In response to the urgings of a former Relief Society president who contributes her own salary and spends three months each year working with the poor in India, the stake financed a pump, a fish pond, a vegetable garden, and a chicken-raising project for a Bengali *ashram* housing a hundred orphans. As part of the same effort, in 1988, thirty-five village families were chosen to receive two hens and a rooster. "After one year, the families that were patient enough not to eat their poultry right away had over thirty hens that could be sold to buy rice, medicine, books, and clothes. This is the start of self-reliance."[151]

Many examples of economic betterment emerged from the 1970s welfare missionary effort. For example, a small branch in Mexico was persuaded to plant gardens, which then required them to build fences to protect their crops and develop a village water system to water them. The latter led in turn to bathrooms and home storage rooms which in turn led to concrete floors, cooking stoves, and a whole new life-style.[152]

In early 1991, following the Peruvian economic crisis, priesthood quorums in Lima undertook a concrete-block manufacturing project, used for upgrading the housing of needy members in that city. Private individuals and groups of medical, dental, agricultural, and other Mormon professionals have contributed their professional expertise in many projects in many locations.[153]

Spread among 3.5 million non-u.s. members, this can hardly be described as an experimentational ferment. Nevertheless, it is out of such local efforts that innovations will emerge, fail, be modified, succeed, be proven in other locations, and adopted more broadly. From such a selection process, viable programs may emerge. On the way, although the total volume of poverty and deprivation is hardly dented, the lives of individuals and small groups are bettered; and those who serve are rewarded by that fact.

Micro-Enterprise Development

The troublesome personal loan experience in South America may have deterred LDS Church involvement with what has become the single most popular intervention currently employed by international agencies: micro- and small-enterprise development. The reasons behind such programs are clear. In underdeveloped economies without social welfare programs, those who have neither access to land nor paid employment must become self-employed if they are to survive. Therefore, self-employment and family employment generally involve from a quarter to over half of the employable population in less developed countries, compared to about 10 percent in the United States.[154]

Some buy and sell goods in small shops, but most are street hucksters, marketing produce or home crafts. The difference between grinding poverty and reasonable subsistence often lies in having enough capital for simple equipment, a sufficient stock of raw materials, some managerial know-how, and access to markets. International agencies and private foundations provide both capital and training through small-loan and technical-assistance programs. Often loans of fifty to a hundred dollars are enough, simple bookkeeping provides the most needed managerial skill, and cooperative marketing can be a substantial step toward profitability.[155] Many international programs concentrate their effort on economically empowering impoverished women. Some programs make loans to small groups, with all members equally responsible for repaying the loan, and each using the funds in turn in their individual micro-enterprises.

In Bangladesh, for instance, "bicycle bankers" make daily rounds, loaning cash in the morning to purchase raw materials or articles for sale during the day and collecting repayment in the evening.[156] Savings clubs and credit unions are often operated for the same purposes but with longer pay-back periods. Supervision by governments, international agencies, or private voluntary organizations prevent the more obvious forms of abuse. But all of these funding organizations have the advantage of an impersonal relationship with their beneficiaries.

LDS Church members have been at least as likely as their peers in underdeveloped countries to participate in the informal economy, some quite successfully but most eking out a survival income. Church leaders at the area and general church level, therefore, have not been unaware of micro-enterprise's possibility for helping its members; but they have been ambivalent about situations where local church authorities might have to refuse some applicants while accepting others or, more difficult still, collect delinquent loans from members. An alternative might be for the church to supply the money but leave loan decisions and collections to third-party entities. The issue has been frequently raised but never yet satisfactorily answered. An Enterprise Development Foundation combining skills from Brigham Young University's Marriott School of Management and experienced American LDS investment bankers established a center in Manila in 1990 to provide training and technical assistance for street vendors, family firms, and small businesses. This group intends to spread the effort elsewhere in the Philippines and to other countries.[157] But they have avoided the thorny thicket of small loans.

The most promising features of the LDS international welfare experience to date have been the welfare services missionaries and the church employment centers; but until some effective way is found to improve the performance and earnings of its many self-employed members in developing countries, the church's international welfare program will have a serious deficiency.

CHAPTER 10

The Future of
Welfare Services

THE MESSAGE of the past is clear. The Church of Jesus Christ of
Latter-day Saints has been motivated by three consistent objectives in
promoting the economic well-being of its members: (1) to care for the
needy, (2) to promote personal and family self-reliance and motivate
members to generate a surplus that can be used for aiding others, and
(3) to prepare psychologically and emotionally for the creation of a
Zion society, an ultimate association of unity, harmony, and equality.

But the Mormons have been no more successful than any other
idealistic society in winning its war on poverty. Alleviation, yes;
elimination, no. The two ecclesiastical exceptions are both in Mormon scriptures: Moses 7:18–20, 69 and 4 Nephi 1:3. Since poverty is
relative, only complete economic equality at a level above subsistence
can eradicate it. That is the claim of those two narratives but they give
no details on procedure or on the standards of living involved. With a
record of 160 years of persistent effort, however, few existing organizations have worked longer in the anti-poverty field than the Church
of Jesus Christ of Latter-day Saints and probably none has devoted
more per-capita effort toward that goal. But the church is a spiritual,
not an economic organization; it perceives its charge as the salvation
of human souls. In that context, economic well-being, as important as
it has been historically, has a lower priority and a lesser claim on the
resources of the church.

The Historical Record

The Ohio and Missouri periods (1830–39) were dominated by
the lack of external resources and the unremitting search for group
self-sufficiency. Unquestionably, the church's ambitions to create a

utopian economic system failed. The Ohio settlement collapsed from within; Mormon settlements in Missouri were destroyed from without. But more remarkable was the extent of the sharing and the survival under adverse circumstances. In Nauvoo, the same pattern of subordinating individual self-reliance to group self-sufficiency was repeated, making possible economic as well as religious survival until internal dissension and external violence again ended what had the portents of a viable community. The remainder of the nineteenth century played out the same drama of cooperation and group self-sufficiency as the Saints patiently settled and tended practically every viable plot no one else wanted between the Rocky Mountains and the Sierra Nevada, between Canada and Mexico.

By the turn of the century, the Mormon experiment in physical isolation had ended. They abandoned economic cooperation, political hegemony, and plural marriage. Joining the larger national economy, however, positioned them more effectively to carry out the institutional goals that, cast in the formulation of 1990, are

1. "To proclaim the gospel" to every nation,
2. "To perfect the Saints"—that is, to improve the moral performance of every member,
3. "To redeem the dead," by performing vicarious ordinances of baptism and the sealing of family groups in temples constructed for that purpose.[1]

The first and third assignments could not be accomplished without more resources than the isolated and struggling pioneers could command. The twentieth-century pattern for the church was to abandon group self-sufficiency and achieve individual self-reliance within the broader economies of, successively, the Mountain West, the United States, and the world. The church redefined its task from directing economic effort to teaching correct principles of education, training, frugality, diligence, initiative, and generosity in contributions. Families, neighbors, and wards met emergency needs, finally relegating to government care for the chronically needy. Willingness to consecrate time, talent, and means toward proselyting, temple building, genealogical research, and care of the poor were the continuing school for and test of Zion characteristics.

In that spirit, the church pioneered its 1920s social work and launched the commodity production and distribution plan of the 1930s. Its timing coincided with the emergence of a tax-supported welfare state. Everything the church did to care for its poor in developed nations after the end of the Great Depression was supplemental to and sometimes even in competition with available government programs. Church welfare programs might function with more loving warmth, immediate response, and flexibility but never with the ready cash of governmental programs. A territorial division left the church assuming responsibility for short-term emergency help for active members who were either not eligible for and/or not interested in government assistance. The permanently needy, such as the elderly, female-headed families, and the seriously handicapped, those unwilling to conform to church standards of personal conduct, and those eligible for unemployment compensation became clients of public programs.

Put another way, one might argue that the LDS welfare efforts in the Midwest during 1830–46 shared the means of production, those of the Great Basin era shared creation of the infrastructure of production, and the 1930s model shared both the production and the product but for only a margin of the membership. The 1980s model continued the marginal sharing but emphasized development of the individual capacity to produce. Thus, it reflected the changing bases of developed economies from natural to capital to human resources.

A Theology of Zion

As the church mobilized its members for welfare, it gave as much emphasis to service opportunities for the well-to-do as to commodities produced for the poor, a continuing indicator of the Zion consciousness. Certainly fast offering contributions, commodity distribution, sheltered employment through Deseret Industries, and employment placement services made substantial contributions to the members' well-being; but none were exclusive, all had their community counterparts, and no one would have been totally deprived of sustenance in their absence. Keeping the church aware of its spiritual responsibility to share, rather than abandoning charity to government, may have been one of the Welfare Program's major accomplishments. Presiding Bishop Robert D. Hales stressed this view at April general conference in 1986:

> The Welfare Plan builds a Zion people. Zion is characterized in scripture as a city in which the people "were of one heart and one mind, and dwelt in righteousness; and there was no poor among them" (Moses 7:18). Zion is "every man seeking the interest of his neighbor, and doing all things with an eye single to the glory of God" (D&C 82:19). This promised Zion always seems to be a little

beyond our reach. We need to understand that as much virtue can be gained in progressing toward Zion as in dwelling there. It is a process as well as a destination. We approach or withdraw from Zion through the manner in which we conduct our daily dealings, how we live within our families, whether we pay an honest tithe and generous fast offering, how we seize opportunities to serve and do so diligently. Many are perfected upon the road to Zion who will never see the city in mortality.

 . . . When we think of welfare, let us think of the plan revealed by the Lord for the eternal welfare of our souls. . . . It is a plan to build faith, love, compassion, self-reliance, and unity. When adapted to local needs throughout the world by vigorous priest-hood leaders, the plan sanctifies both givers and receivers and pre-pares a Zion people.

 With these basic welfare principles in mind, today we are being asked to teach and practice the doctrine of work, self-reliance, provident living, giving, and caring for the poor; to increase our generous fast offering donations to help those in need; to increase our compassionate service, involving the family in charitable acts of service to one another and to our neighbors.[2]

In short, the great contribution of the LDS Church seems to have been emphasizing certain teachings which, though spiritual in their intent, were also economically productive: family solidarity, educa-tion, frugality, diligence, avoidance of substance abuse, avoidance of debt, loyalty, and devotion to cause. Probably these principles explain why Latter-day Saints are generally disproportionately represented in professional occupations even though incomes usually approximate the average household incomes of the nations in which they reside.[3]

The economic accomplishments of Latter-day Saints who adhered to the discipline proved the premises—in fact, to such an extent that materialism has apparently replaced poverty as the chief economic challenge for American Mormons.[4] There is no consensus among Latter-day Saints about what the ideal of the Zion society will look like when and if it is realized.[5] Speculation is probably fruitless, since there is no scriptural description of its economic form—only the re-sults that the people will be of one heart and one mind and have no poor among them.

By that criterion, Latter-day Saints are obviously far from achiev-ing their Zionic ambitions. Individually, every kind of weakness can be identified among them, including economic disparities. What makes the ideal of Zion more than a pious hope is the record of service to each other and the high level of sharing. The history documented in previous chapters is the visible manifestation of profound theological commitments.

The Balance Between Resources and Needs

Contrasts between the standards of living of u.s. members and those in developing countries have presented American Mormons with a crisis of conscience.[6] Still an active part of the LDS canon is the injunction accepted as revelation: "It is not given that one man should possess that which is above another, wherefore the world lieth in sin" (D&C 49:20); but its conditions have never been pursued by the church in this century.

In the international context, what is the church's obligation to care for the needy when nearly all are needy? To what extent should church members in developed countries limit their own consumption and accumulation to support the poor in the developing world or to help them expand their earning power? And realistically, what church resources are available for increased international welfare? This last question deserves more detailed examination.

The LDS Church's income is, overwhelmingly, members' contributions. For the past three decades, the church has not disclosed budget information; and although some have estimated income, often giving imaginations free rein, few have attempted to measure outgo.[7] We are no more privy to knowledge of church income or expenditures than they, but it should be useful to illustrate the consequences of the probable relationship. If one were to assume that the average per capita income of LDS families in every nation is equal to the average per capita income of that nation (Table 3) and also assume that one-third of all Latter-day Saints paid a full tithing of 10 percent of their income, the tithing revenues of the church in 1990 would have been approximately $3 billion, 88 percent of it coming from members in the United States. To extend the annualized 1985 special fast offering estimate by the subsequent Consumer Price Index increases for u.s. members and attribute one-half that per capita amount to non-u.s. members would let us arrive at an annual offering of $120 million. If one also accepted the most exaggerated of the published estimates of the investment income of the church, the result would be an aggregate annual income of $3.5 billion.

Undoubtedly, the church has substantial real estate assets: chapels, temples, offices, welfare production units, and investment properties. In practical terms, however, these properties cannot be considered potential liquid assets. Rather, they are income drains. In 1990 there were approximately 18,000 congregations,[8] a few housed in rented facilities but the vast majority in meetinghouses which had to be maintained, heated, and lighted. Approximately 700 new congregations are formed each year, and approximately 500 new meetinghouses are completed annually.[9] An average cost of $1 million per chapel is a reasonable estimate, including real estate. Until 1990, members made additional contributions when it was necessary to build a new meetinghouse in their area, then made monthly contributions to the ward budget. Beginning January 1990, the church took over payment of both construction and maintenance costs in the United States and Canada from tithing revenues. (It had already been meeting most of those costs for international congregations.)[10]

The church maintains and staffs a twenty-seven-story office building and a three-story administration building in Salt Lake City. Eighteen area offices (1991) throughout the world are purchased or leased, maintained, equipped, and staffed with paid employees. Visitors' centers accommodate tourists at historical and current sites of church activity throughout the United States. In 1990, forty-three temples were in operation; six more were under construction.

Related to the temple purposes of vicarious baptisms and sealings is genealogical research. The church owns and maintains the world's largest collection of genealogical records with 1.5 million rolls of microfilm and 200,000 microfiche stored in Salt Lake City and accessible in 1,000 branch libraries in forty-three countries.[11] It underwrites an unspecified number of crews microfilming records throughout the world and finances an enormous computerized system to record, process, and recover the data.

There were 256 missions in 1991. Although the 44,000 missionaries of that year, their families, or other contributors pay their personal expenses and part of the cost of their proselyting materials, the church pays for medical care, some transportation, and proselyting materials. The church also pays for the mission office, a residence for the president and his family (both usually rented), furnishings, equipment, and maintenance. Most mission presidents receive a living allowance as do most of the General Authorities. A growing number of missionaries from third world countries are primarily or totally supported by the church, but from contributions earmarked for that purpose rather than from tithing funds.

The church pays all costs of housing, teacher salaries, and curriculum materials for 250,000 high-school-age seminary students, 125,000 college-age institute students, and 10,000 students enrolled in church-owned primary and secondary church schools. The tuition paid by nearly 40,000 students enrolled in church colleges and universities probably supported about one-fourth of the cost of their education.

Since the painful experiences with debt at the end of the nineteenth century (and one undiscussed period during the late 1950s and early 1960s which only reinforced the earlier decision),[12] the church has adhered rigidly to a policy of never spending beyond its revenues, never going into debt, and never allowing its subordinate units to do so, even temporarily. Nevertheless, it appears probable that the outgo from these financial responsibilities would exhaust an income of $3.5 billion. In short, the unbending law of economic scarcity remains in effect: every new activity or every expanded activity requires the elimination or curtailing of others.

In the early twentieth century, Joseph Smith's nephew and sixth president of the LDS Church, Joseph F. Smith, stated: "It has always been a cardinal teaching with the Latter-day Saints that a religion that has not the power to save people temporally and make them prosperous and happy here cannot be depended upon to save them spiritually and to exalt them in the life to come."[13]

Still, within the current definition of the church's tripartite mission, economic well-being can be defined only as an indirect contributor to the second goal—perfecting the Saints. Its primary justification in these terms is not that it relieves suffering, but that it frees the individual's mind from worries so pressing as to eliminate spiritual contemplation and that it offers opportunities for selfless service to others. But the Church of Jesus Christ of Latter-day Saints interprets its primary mission to be the salvation of souls, living and dead, through proselyting and ordinance work. Those activities take priority over all other responsibilities. Economic interests may have been essential to institutional survival in the past century, but they are not in this one and probably will not be in the next. It seems highly unlikely that either proselyting or ordinance work for the dead will ever be curtailed to commit more church resources to improving the economic well-being of members.

Only the fast offering, earmarked for the care of the poor, offers a source of augmentation for welfare expenditures. If more is to be done for the poor internationally, it must be supported by greater generosity in fast offerings, a reallocation of American welfare expenditures, or the direct contribution of time and talents by well-to-do members serving as welfare missionaries.

The Future of LDS Church Welfare

What happens to the Mormons' 160-year-old hot and cold war on poverty will, of course, depend upon the directions set by church leaders and members' responses and individual initiatives; but it is possible to make some informed guesses and to identify unresolved issues.

The program in the United States and Canada has reached a steady

state in which its activities, except for the contribution and expenditure of
fast offerings, will not expand as membership grows. The General Welfare Services Committee has already decided not to increase the number
of Deseret Industries and LDS Social Service offices. Expansion in
employment centers will likely be limited to inner cities where members
require rehabilitative services that go far beyond placement. Need for
commodities is unlikely to exceed current production and distribution
capacity; if it does, there is plenty of land in strategic reserve, though its
location may not coincide with the areas of need. The proportion of need
met in cash from fast offerings will continue to grow, making even less
likely any expansion of commodity production.

Quite clearly, the crucial challenge for the Church Welfare Program
lies in the international field. There prognostication is difficult. Though
there are inevitable differences in point of view, policy-making in the LDS
Church—at least in the present era—is a consensus process.[14] The president of the church can override his counselors and/or the Quorum of the
Twelve, but does so extremely rarely. The advanced age of most presidents of the church increases their dependence on counselors. (The average age of the six presidents who have assumed office since 1945 has been
eighty.) A revelation to Joseph Smith required that quorum decisions
"must be by the unanimous voice of the same" (D&C 107:27). This policy
takes the traditional form on all decision-making levels, from the First
Presidency to local bishoprics, of the presiding officer hearing all arguments, then announcing a decision. The counselors then shift their positions, if necessary, to make the decision unanimous. The same approach
could turn a majority vote into a unanimous one in the Quorum of the
Twelve. As a practical matter, however, it is ultimately less costly in
terms of harmony to achieve consensus than to enforce one in this manner; thus, decision-making is likely to be a lengthy process. No consensus
is currently apparent about international welfare; until it is, ad hoc experimentation driven by local need will prevail. But this same condition prevailed in the 1930s until mere months before the April 1936 announcement, and history may again repeat itself.

LDS missionary efforts and numbers of members will continue to
grow in Latin America, Asia, Africa, and Eastern Europe. The church
will almost certainly seize any openings for proselyting in China and the
Islamic nations. Consequently, international welfare will become more
pressing, not less; and neither doctrine nor tradition will allow the LDS
collective conscience to accept indefinitely a situation of massive economic need and gross income disparity among its members. But consensus on what to do will not be easily reached.

The 1936 solution resulted after some five years of local experimentation among a localized population with homogenous needs and solutions. In the 1990s and beyond, needs are world-wide and heterogeneous. Thus it seems most probable that the developments will be decentralized and that primary initiatives will continue to emerge from local efforts. Most welfare will always be member-to-member, through extended families and within local congregations, guided by bishops and carried out through priesthood quorums, Relief Societies, home teachers, and visiting teachers. A limited number of potential assistance measures can be centrally sanctioned and provisioned, but local leaders must design the local mix to match local conditions and needs. One suspects that future historians will identify among the decentralized experiments of the 1970s, 1980s, and early 1990s the seeds of a church-endorsed international program that should be in place before the turn of the twenty-first century. But such a program will have to be flexible, heterogeneous, and adaptable.

In fact, the most likely combination of functions appears to be taking shape already: fast offering funds will meet short-term emergency needs of actual hunger, lack of shelter, and medical crises. Church employment centers will probably continue to spread in countries with substantial industrial and commercial sectors, once a solution to the paid-versus-volunteer staff issue is found. When it is, vocational counseling and referral to education and training will be added to job search training, job development, and placement among its services. The percentage of members educated in church schools will inevitably decline, but the number of international members receiving scholarships from church-related sources will probably rise. Both technical and financial assistance for self-employment and micro-enterprise development—the latter in part agricultural—will emerge but slowly, given the pressing need to find an effective way to administer such funds. Demonstration farms with connected small-plot agriculture are likely developments for some parts of Central America and Africa.

These three components—fast offerings, employment centers, and micro-enterprise development—seem to be the logical cornerstones for a future international welfare program. Certainly this scenario amply accommodates other services such as credit unions and cooperatives for consumers, producers, and marketeers, developed and adapted to meet local conditions but not part of the central menu. The economies, political systems, and social structures around the world are so varied that there will never be one blueprint that fits all. Since the economies of less-developed countries offer only limited opportunities, Latter-day Saints in those countries must prepare to gain more than their proportionate share. As a result, research is urgently needed to ascertain the economic condition of members in each country, their prospects, trends in the national economy, and the identification of barriers and opportunities. Energetic area presidencies, who give member economic well-being high priority, are most likely to drive the system by channelling requests to church headquarters for assistance selected from the menu of approved services.

For American members, the encouragement to pay generous fast offerings, to contribute to humanitarian relief, and to make themselves available to serve in international welfare assignments after retirement will intensify. The competition will remain keen for eligible couples to serve in developing lay leadership among rapidly growing congregations, staffing temples, serving as guides in visitor centers, performing clerical duties in area and mission offices, engaging in genealogical research, and serving conventional proselyting missions.

Within the welfare realm, the need for specialized employment services may be partially met through retired volunteers, but at least a core of professionals to train the volunteers seems necessary. Volunteers with the competence and experience to foster micro-enterprise development and self-employment are even scarcer. Expertise will be required in both technical and financial assistance, once the church has overcome its reluctance and discovered a viable mechanism for providing the latter. The technical assistance function will require the knowledge and ability to teach the skills of production, accounting, and marketing for small-scale enterprises within the differing conditions of each developing country. Administration of the financial assistance function will require compassionate understanding, firm insistence on performance, and clear financial discipline within a structure separate from the ecclesiastical line. International experience will be essential for both; but American business people, accustomed to larger entities, even within what we here consider small business, will have a difficult time focusing on micro-enterprises. Native members with business experience will probably be the most useful but also the scarcest in terms of availability. Experience with employment centers has already created a sound foundation for further growth; but almost none of the essential research or experimentation necessary for micro-enterprise development has occurred. The activities of the Benson Institute should offer a nucleus of Latter-day Saints with experience in the promotion of small plot agriculture, supplemented by agricultural retirees.

Clearly, the LDS Church has abandoned its traditional American isolation and exclusionary focus on its own members. External humanitarian services are both emotionally and spiritually satisfying to Latter-day Saints, as they are to others who strive to make a difference in the world. Institutionally, the church has an interest in continuing its humanitarian effort, not only as an exercise in Christian service, but also because such aid may be the political price for proselyting permission. Furthermore, such activities offer practical research laboratories for developing services needed by LDS members in those and similar countries.

Reprise

Looking back at over 160 years of LDS anti-poverty activity, the dominant characteristic is its persistence. The goals have been consistent:

short-term emergency help for those most in need
pursuit of self-reliance for the many
consciousness of the need to develop the oneness and
    selflessness considered to be characteristic of a Zion people.

Intensity of effort has waxed and waned, and strategies of attack have varied according to need and condition. Economic well-being has never held first priority. That position has been reserved for spiritual salvation pursued through proselyting, temple ordinances, and religious instruction. Thus, welfare efforts have never had prior claim on resources and have often given way to the higher priorities, as documented by the pull-backs in education, social services, and Deseret Industries and by the restrained expansion of employment centers. Decision-making has been slow in international welfare because the needs appear overwhelming and the techniques unfamiliar and unsure, but experimentation has never been abandoned and the philosophical commitment has only deepened. Within that set of priorities, economic welfare has never been neglected.

Individual LDS members have consistently contributed time, effort, and money. They have never given all that they could, but it is doubtful whether any group of comparable size gives as much or as consistently on a per capita basis. Latter-day Saints have never won their war on poverty and only in the most dire circumstances have even pursued it full tilt; but the skirmishes have been continual. Both member and nonmember have benefited, economically and spiritually, from the perpetual crusade.

NOTES

Introduction

1. Marc A. Rose, "The Mormons March Off Relief," *Reader's Digest,* June 1937, 43–44.

2. James B. Allen and Glen M. Leonard, *The Story of the Latter-day Saints* (Salt Lake City: Deseret Book Company, 1976), 550–53.

3. Bruce B. Blumell, "The Latter-day Saint Response to the Teton, Idaho, Flood, 1976," *Task Papers in LDS History, No. 16* (Salt Lake City: Historical Department of the Church of Jesus Christ of Latter-day Saints, 1976).

4. *Church News* articles: "Relief Effort Gets Church Funding," 18 November 1984; "Fast for World Hunger Nets $3.5 Million," 29 December 1985, 3, 10; *Ensign,* Isaac C. Ferguson, "Freely Given: How Church Members' Donations and Special Fasts Are Helping Those in Need," August 1988, 10–15; Thomas S. Monson, "A Royal Priesthood," May 1991, 48.

5. In Albert E. Bowen, *The Church Welfare Plan* (Independence, Mo.: Zion's Printing and Publishing Company, 1946), 36.

6. The phrases "perfecting the Saints," "proclaiming the gospel," and "redeeming the dead" are from *Melchizedek Priesthood Leadership Handbook* (Salt Lake City: Church of Jesus Christ of Latter-day Saints, 1990), 348. However, the tripartite formulation in different words first appeared in *Melchizedek Priesthood Handbook,* 1962, 19–20. The concepts themselves of course, permeate LDS beliefs and systems.

7. James E. Talmage, *The House of the Lord* (Salt Lake City: Deseret Book Company, 1968), 84.

8. For instance see Spencer W. Kimball, "The False Gods We Worship," *Ensign,* June 1976, 4–5.

Chapter 1 Economic Welfare in Ohio and Missouri, 1831–1839

1. Richard Bushman, *Joseph Smith and the Beginnings of Mormonism* (Champaign: University of Illinois Press, 1984), 40–49, 172–73; Lucy Mack Smith, *History of Joseph Smith by His Mother* (Salt Lake City: Bookcraft, 1954), 179–86.

2. Merritt Ierley, *With Charity for All: Welfare and Society, Ancient Times to the Present* (New York: Praeger, 1984), 39–86 and Robert Morris, *Rethinking Social Welfare: Why Care for the Stranger?* (New York and London: Longman, Inc., 1986), 145–62; Charles Nordhoff, *The Communistic Societies of the United States* (1875; reprint. ed., New York: Hillary House, 1960), 70–78.

3. Bushman, *Joseph Smith and the Beginnings of Mormonism,* 40–49, 172–73.

4. Smith, *History of Joseph Smith by His Mother,* 179–86.

5. Bushman, *Joseph Smith and the Beginnings of Mormonism,* 76–78.

6. Lewis Bernard Schmidt and Earle Dudley Ross, eds., *Readings in the History of American Agriculture* (New York: Macmillan Company, 1925), 153–62; Jimmy M. Skaggs, *An Interpretive History of the American Economy* (New York: Grid, Inc., 1975), 94.

7. James F. Willis and Martin L. Primak, *An Economic History of the United States* (Englewood Cliffs, N.J.: Prentice-Hall, Inc., 1989), 146–50.

8. Bushman, *Joseph Smith and the Beginnings of Mormonism,* 143–54.

9. See also William G. Hartley, "Coming to Zion: Saga of the Gathering," *Ensign,* July 1975, 14.

10. Milton V. Backman, Jr., *The Heavens Resound: A History of the Latter-day Saints in Ohio, 1830–38* (Salt Lake City: Deseret Book Company, 1983), 1–8.

11. Milton V. Backman, Jr., "The Quest for a Restoration: The Birth of Mormonism in Ohio," *Brigham Young University Studies* 12 (Summer 1972): 347.

12. Backman, *The Heavens Resound,* 64; Marvin S. Hill, *Quest for Refuge: The Mormon Flight from American Pluralism* (Salt Lake City: Signature Books, 1989), 351, 361.

13. Leonard J. Arrington, *Great Basin Kingdom: An Economic History of the Latter-day Saints, 1830–1900* (Cambridge, Mass.: Harvard University Press, 1958), 7–10; Leonard J. Arrington, Feramorz Y. Fox, and Dean L. May, *Building the City of God: Community and Cooperation Among the Mormons* (Salt Lake City: Deseret Book Company, 1976), 15–40.

14. Leonard J. Arrington, "Joseph Smith, Builder of Ideal Communities," in *The Prophet Joseph: Essays on the Life and Mission of Joseph Smith,* edited by Larry C. Porter and Susan Easton Black (Salt Lake City: Deseret Book Company, 1988), 117.

15. Hill, *Quest for Refuge,* 207–08; Smith, *History of Joseph Smith by His Mother,* 209–37.

16. Backman, *The Heavens Resound,* 70, 137.

17. Hill, *Quest for Refuge,* 37.

18. Backman, *The Heavens Resound,* 71–73.

19. Ibid., 313.

20. Joseph Smith, Jr., *History of the Church of Jesus Christ of Latter-day Saints,* edited by B. H. Roberts, 7 vols., 2d ed. rev. (Salt Lake City: Deseret Book, 1948 printing), 3:231; hereafter cited as *History of the Church.*

21. Backman, *The Heavens Resound,* 138–39.

22. Ibid., 141.

23. *History of the Church,* 2:468–69.

24. Ibid., 3:231.

25. Marvin S. Hill, C. Keith Rooker, and Larry T. Wimmer, *The Kirtland Economy Revisited: A Market Critique of Sectarian Economics* (Provo, Utah: Brigham Young University Press, 1974), 15.

26. Ibid., 43–44.

27. Ibid., 21.

28. Davis Bitton, "The Waning of Kirtland," *Brigham Young University Studies* 12 (Summer 1972): 455.

29. Henry L. Ellsworth, ed., *Washington Irving on the Prairie, or the Tour of the Southwest in the Year 1812* (New York: American Book Company, 1937), 61.

30. Hill, Rooker, and Wimmer, *Kirtland Economy Revisited*, 21.

31. Max H. Parkin, "A History of the Latter-day Saints in Clay County, Missouri" (Ph.D. diss., Brigham Young University, 1976), 25.

32. Ibid., 126.

33. Ibid., 26; Joseph A. Geddes, *The United Order Among the Mormons: The Missouri Phase* (Salt Lake City: Deseret News Press, 1924), 49.

34. Parkin, "A History of the Latter-day Saints in Clay County," 263.

35. Leland H. Gentry, "A History of the Latter-day Saints in Northern Missouri from 1836 to 1839" (Ph.D. diss., Brigham Young University, 1965), 47–48.

36. Ibid., 33–40.

37. Ibid., 54.

38. Ibid. This figure appears inconsistent with his own statement (p. 53) that the farms were limited to forty acres because the Saints lacked money to purchase more acreage.

39. Ibid., 123; Arrington, *Great Basin Kingdom*, 15–16.

40. Arrington, *Great Basin Kingdom*, 128–29.

41. *History of the Church*, 3:251.

42. Alma P. Burton, *Toward the New Jerusalem* (Salt Lake City: Deseret Book, 1985), 82.

43. William G. Hartley, "'Almost Too Intolerable a Burthen': The Winter Exodus from Missouri, 1838–39," *Journal of Mormon History* 18 (Fall 1992): 1–33.

Chapter 2 Resettlement and Relief in Nauvoo, 1839–1846

1. Historians do not agree on Mormon population during this period. The most recent estimate of eight thousand comes from William G. Hartley, "'Almost Too Intolerable a Burthen': The Winter Exodus from Missouri, 1838–39," *Journal of Mormon History* 18 (Fall 1992): 1–33. B. H. Roberts, *A Comprehensive History of the Church of Jesus Christ of Latter-day Saints,* 6 vols. (Salt Lake City: Deseret Book, 1930), 1:511, claims that between twelve and fifteen thousand Mormons were driven from Missouri during the winter of 1838–39. This figure is almost certainly too high. Robert Bruce Flanders, *Nauvoo: Kingdom on the Mississippi* (Urbana: University of Illinois Press, 1965), 1, records that five thousand straggled into the Quincy area in the spring of 1839.

2. Flanders, *Nauvoo: Kingdom on the Mississippi*, 15–18.

3. Ibid., 27–30.

4. Joseph Smith, Jr., *History of the Church of Jesus Christ of Latter-day Saints,* edited by B. H. Roberts, 7 vols. 2nd ed. rev. (Salt Lake City: Deseret Book, 1948 printing), 3:375; hereafter cited as *History of the Church.*

5. Flanders, *Nauvoo: Kingdom on the Mississippi*, 39–46.

6. *History of the Church*, 3:301–02.

7. In Flanders, *Nauvoo: Kingdom on the Mississippi*, 55–56.

8. James B. Allen and Glen M. Leonard, *The Story of the Latter-day Saints* (Salt

Lake City: Deseret Book Co., 1976), 139–42; David E. Miller and Della S. Miller, *Nauvoo: The City of Joseph* (Salt Lake City: Peregrine Smith, Inc., 1974), 33–35.

9. Miller and Miller, *Nauvoo: The City of Joseph*, 45–47, 207.

10. *History of the Church*, 4:472–75. No mention was made of the responsibility or contributions of women; but the household was considered the earning unit.

11. Miller and Miller, *Nauvoo: The City of Joseph*, 149; Flanders, *Nauvoo: Kingdom on the Mississippi*, 147.

12. Richard L. Jensen, "Transplanted to Zion: The Impact of British Latter-day Saint Immigration Upon Nauvoo," *Brigham Young University Studies* 31 (Winter 1991): 77–85.

13. *History of the Church*, 5:44.

14. Ibid., 7:251.

15. Flanders, *Nauvoo: Kingdom on the Mississippi*, 80.

16. George W. Givens, *In Old Nauvoo: Everyday Life in the City of Joseph* (Salt Lake City: Deseret Book Company, 1990), 66; *History of the Church*, 7:437–38.

17. Dean C. Jessee, "The John Taylor Nauvoo Journal," *Brigham Young University Studies* 23, no. 3 (Summer 1983): 87.

18. Leonard J. Arrington, *Great Basin Kingdom: An Economic History of the Latter-day Saints, 1830–1900* (Cambridge, Mass.: Harvard University Press, 1958), 10, 17.

19. Edwin De Leon, *Thirty Years of My Life on Three Continents*, 2 vols. (London: Ward and Downey, 1890), 1:65.

20. *History of the Church*, 6:58–59.

21. Flanders, *Nauvoo: Kingdom on the Mississippi*, 209; *History of the Church*, 4:474, 5:44, 6:350, 376.

22. Flanders, *Nauvoo: Kingdom on the Mississippi*, 45–46, 126, 167–68.

23. Miller and Miller, *Nauvoo: The City of Joseph*, 30–31; Flanders, *Nauvoo: Kingdom on the Mississippi*, 45–46, 144, 166–67; Allen and Leonard, *The Story of the Latter-day Saints* 141–42, 155.

24. Givens, *In Old Nauvoo*, 84–85.

25. Flanders, *Nauvoo: Kingdom on the Mississippi*, 150–53.

26. Allen and Leonard, *The Story of the Latter-day Saints*, 139–42, 161–63.

27. H. W. Mills, "De Tal Palo Tal Astilla," *Historical Society of Southern California* 10 (1917): 118–19; this is a reproduction in part of the journal of George Miller plus some of his correspondence.

28. Ibid.

29. *History of the Church*, 4:402–43.

30. *Nauvoo Neighbor*, 31 January 1844.

31. A. Dean Wengreen, "The Origin and History of the Fast Day in the Church of Jesus Christ of Latter-day Saints, 1830–96" (M.A. thesis, Brigham Young University, 1955), 23–27.

32. *History of the Church*, 7:41. Either the supply was overestimated or the need underestimated; at least Hunter continued to receive and disburse donations to his ward's needy throughout the summer.

33. *Times and Seasons*, 1 November 1844.

34. *History of the Church*, 7:325.

35. *History of the Relief Society, 1842–1966* (Salt Lake City: General Board of the Relief Society, 1969), 15.

36. *History of the Church,* 4:602-7.
37. See Jill Mulvay Derr, Janath Russell Cannon, and Maureen Ursenbach Beecher, *Women of Covenant: The Story of Relief Society* (Salt Lake City: Deseret Book, 1992), chap. 2.; and *Woman's Exponent* 9 (1 September 1980): 53-54.
38. *Times and Seasons,* 1 April 1843, 154-57.
39. Journal History, 2 July 1844, 1.
40. De Leon, *Thirty Years of My Life,* 1:63.
41. See Edith Abbott, *Public Assistance* (Chicago: University of Chicago Press, 1940), 5; Joseph Chapin Brown, *Public Relief, 1929-39* (New York: Henry Holt and Company, 1940), 6-10; Grace Abbott, *From Relief to Social Security* (Chicago: University of Chicago Press, 1941), 6; R. Clyde White, *Administration of Public Welfare* (New York: American Book Company, 1940), 36.
42. Bruce R. McConkie, "Obedience, Consecration, and Sacrifice," *Ensign,* May 1975, 51; James E. Talmage, *The House of the Lord* (Salt Lake City: Deseret Book Company, 1968), 84.

Chapter 3 The Economics of the Exodus, 1846-1887

1. Joseph Smith, Jr., *History of the Church of Jesus Christ of Latter-day Saints,* edited by B. H. Roberts, 7 vols., 2d ed. rev. (Salt Lake City: Deseret Book, 1948 printing), 7:465; hereafter cited as *History of the Church.*
2. In Leonard J. Arrington, *Brigham Young, American Moses* (New York: Alfred A. Knopf, 1985), 456.
3. Lewis Clark Christian, "Mormon Foreknowledge of the West," *Brigham Young University Studies* 21, no. 4 (Fall 1981): 404-6.
4. Arrington, *Brigham Young,* 123.
5. In Leland H. Creer, *The Founding of an Empire: The Exploration and Colonization of Utah* (Salt Lake City: Bookcraft, 1947), 225.
6. David E. Miller and Della S. Miller, *Nauvoo: The City of Joseph* (Salt Lake City: Peregrine Smith, Inc., 1974), 199-208.
7. Dallin H. Oaks and Joseph I. Bentley, "Joseph Smith and the Legal Process: In the Wake of the Steamboat *Nauvoo,*" *Brigham Young University Studies* 19, no. 2 (Winter 1979): 192, 198.
8. In Creer, *Founding of an Empire,* 230.
9. B. H. Roberts, *A Comprehensive History of the Church of Jesus Christ of Latter-day Saints,* 6 vols. (Salt Lake City: Deseret News Press, 1930), 3:41.
10. Carol Lynn Pearson, "Nine Children Were Born: A Historical Problem from the Sugar Creek Episode," *Brigham Young University Studies* 21, no. 4 (Fall 1981): 443.
11. Creer, *Founding of an Empire,* 229-30.
12. See Stanley B. Kimball, "The Saints and St. Louis, 1831-57: An Oasis of Tolerance and Security," *Brigham Young University Studies* 13, no. 4 (Summer 1973): 506; Richard E. Bennett, "Mormons and Missourians: The Uneasy Truce," *Midwest Review* 9 (Spring 1987): 12-21.
13. Leland H. Gentry, "The Mormon Way Stations: Garden Grove and Mt. Pisgah," *Brigham Young University Studies* 21 (Fall 1981): 445-61.
14. Creer, *Founding of an Empire,* 230; Leonard J. Arrington, *Great Basin Kingdom: An Economic History of the Latter-day Saints, 1830-1900* (Cambridge, Mass.: Harvard University Press, 1958), 20.
15. Arrington, *Great Basin Kingdom,* 21.

16. Ibid., 21; James B. Allen and Glen M. Leonard, *The Story of the Latter-day Saints* (Salt Lake City: Deseret Book Co., 1976), 225–33.

17. Dale Beecher, "The Office of Bishop," *Dialogue: A Journal of Mormon Thought* 15, no. 4 (Winter 1982): 104; Historical Department Staff, "Early Development of the Office of Bishop as It Relates to Wards, Stakes, and to the General Church," Special Report Prepared for Marvin R. VanDam, 16 August 1976, typescript, LDS Church Historical Department Library.

18. Beecher, "The Office of Bishop," 105–6; S. George Ellsworth, *Dear Ellen: Two Mormon Women and Their Letters* (Salt Lake City: University of Utah Tanner Fund, 1974), 6–9.

19. Ibid., 13, 15 December 1846; 21 February 1847; 21 March 1847.

20. This figure is Arrington's estimate of the number who made the trek from 1847 to 1869. *Great Basin Kingdom,* 82, 99, n. 38. It combines the 20,000 who departed from Iowa with the 51,000 assisted from Europe by the Perpetual Emigration Fund by 1869.

21. Ibid., 77, 97.

22. Ibid., 98–99; See also Gustive O. Larson, "History of the Perpetual Emigrating Fund Company" (M.A. thesis, University of Utah, 1926); Lily Pritchard, "Across the Waves: Mormon Emigration of British Saints, 1840–1870" (Undergraduate diss., University of Bradford, England, 1959); Richard L. Jensen, "Steaming Through: Arrangements for Mormon Emigration from Europe," *Journal of Mormon History* 9 (1982): 3–24; Leonard J. Arrington, "Gather Ye Together... Upon the Land of Zion," *The Instructor,* April 1967, 148–49; P. A. M. Taylor, *Expectations Westward: The Mormons and the Emigration of Their British Converts in the Nineteenth Century* (Edinburgh and London: Olson and Boyd, 1965), 113–42.

23. Brigham Young, *Journal of Discourses,* 14 April 1867, 27 vols. (London and Liverpool: LDS Booksellers Depot, 1855–86), 12:36.

24. Ibid., 97–98; Pritchard, *Across the Waves,* 37.

25. Arrington, *Great Basin Kingdom,* 155–60.

26. Ibid., 205–11; James B. Allen and Glen M. Leonard, *The Story of the Latter-day Saints* (Salt Lake City: Deseret Book Co., 1976), 327.

27. *Great Basin Kingdom,* 381–82.

28. Ibid., 157.

29. Letter to Orson Pratt, 30 September 1856, ibid., 158.

Chapter 4 Economic Welfare in the Mountain West, 1847–1900

1. Leonard J. Arrington, *Great Basin Kingdom: An Economic History of the Latter-day Saints, 1830–1900* (Cambridge, Mass.: Harvard University Press, 1958), 283–322.

2. Ibid., 33.

3. J. Kenneth Davies, *Mormon Gold, The Story of California's Mormon Argonauts* (Salt Lake City: Olympus Publishing Company, 1984), xv. The church's central collection and use of these funds caused considerable dissatisfaction among some battalion members who felt, with some cause, that they should have had first claim on these earnings.

4. Ibid. For example, Henry Bigler, a Mormon Battalion member whose journal dates the discovery of gold in Sutter's trace, reluctantly accepted a mission

call from Patriarch John Smith to mine on "shares" to establish an "inheritance" for the elderly man. See M. Guy Bishop, *Footsoldier for Mormonism: The Life of Henry W. Bigler, 1815–1900*, chap. 5, "Reluctant Argonaut, 1849–50," forthcoming.

5. Arrington, *Great Basin Kingdom*, 66–71.

6. Eugene E. Campbell, *Establishing Zion: The Mormon Church in the American West, 1847–69* (Salt Lake City: Signature Books, 1988), 2.

7. Robert Heilbroner, *The Economic Transformation of America* (New York: Harcourt Brace Jovanovich, 1984), 155–57.

8. Arrington, *Great Basin Kingdom*, 97.

9. The best source on the origin and purpose of the Council of Fifty and its role in the exodus and colonization is Klaus J. Hansen, *Quest for Empire: The Political Kingdom of God and the Council of Fifty in Mormon History* (Lansing: Michigan State University Press, 1970).

10. Beecher, "The Office of Bishop," *Dialogue: A Journal of Mormon Thought* 15 (Autumn 1982): 80; Arrington, *Great Basin Kingdom*, 48.

11. In Arrington, *Great Basin Kingdom*, 60, and Campbell, *Establishing Zion*, 34.

12. Davis, *Mormon Gold*, 109–28; Campbell, *Establishing Zion*, 41–55.

13. Campbell, *Establishing Zion*, 34; Arrington, *Great Basin Kingdom*, 58–60; Beecher, "The Office of Bishop," 80.

14. Brigham Young, *Journal of Discourses*, 7 June 1863, 27 vols. (London and Liverpool: LDS Booksellers Depot, 1855–86), 10:206; Arrington, *Great Basin Kingdom*, 108–12.

15. Brigham Young, *Journal of Discourses*, 5 March 1860, 8:11–12.

16. Ibid., 3 February 1867, 11:293.

17. Arrington, *Great Basin Kingdom*, 155, 228, 270–90.

18. William H. Dixon, *New America* (Philadelphia: J. B. Lippincott & Co., 1867), 182.

19. Edwin Brown Firmage and Richard Collin Mangrum, *Zion in the Courts: A Legal History of the Church of Jesus Christ of Latter-day Saints, 1830–1900* (Urbana: University of Illinois Press, 1988), 293–98. Certificates of ownership were issued from 1847 until 1869, but they had no standing outside the community since they were disbursing federal lands.

20. Lowell "Ben" Bennion, "A Geographer's Discovery of *Great Basin Kingdom*," in *Great Basin Kingdom Revisited: Contemporary Perspectives*, edited by Thomas G. Alexander, 109–32 (Logan: Utah State University Press, 1991).

21. Ibid., 51–53; Leonard J. Arrington, *Brigham Young, American Moses* (New York: Alfred A. Knopf, 1985), 168–69.

22. Arrington, *Great Basin Kingdom*, 90–92.

23. Ibid., 91, 93.

24. Many observers have commented on the Mormons' achievement in cooperatively developing and operating irrigation systems and, conversely, irrigation's contributions to Mormon cooperativeness. For an excellent overview and bibliography, see Donald Worster, "The Kingdom, the Power, and the Water," in Alexander, *Great Basin Kingdom Revisited*, 28–30.

25. Campbell, *Establishing Zion*, 57–91; Arrington, *Great Basin Kingdom*, 88.

26. Bennion, "A Geographer's Discovery," 116.

27. For some of the economic consequences of Mormon Indian policy, see Campbell, *Establishing Zion*, 93–111, 113–33, 303; Nels Anderson, *Deseret*

Saints: The Mormon Frontier in Utah (Chicago: University of Chicago Press, 1942), 105–7, 117, 124–32; S. George Ellsworth, *Utah's Heritage* (Santa Barbara and Salt Lake City: Peregrine Smith, Inc., 1972), 210–13; Eugene E. Campbell, "Brigham Young's Outer Cordon—A Reappraisal," *Utah Historical Quarterly* 41 (Summer 1973): 220–53; Charles Peterson, "Jacob Hamblin: Apostle to the Lamanites and the Indian Mission," *Journal of Mormon History* 2 (1975): 21–34; Ronald W. Walker, "Toward a Reconstruction of Mormon and Indian Relations, 1847–77," *Brigham Young University Studies* 29, no. 4 (Autumn 1989): 23–42; Lawrence George Coates, "A History of Indian Education by the Mormons" (Ed.D. diss., Ball State University, Muncie, Indiana, 1969).

28. Arrington, *Great Basin Kingdom*, 94–95; James B. Allen, "The Development of County Government in the Territory of Utah, 1850–96," M.A. thesis, Brigham Young University, 1965; Leonard J. Arrington and Dean L. May, "Irrigation and Society in Nineteenth Century Utah," *Agricultural History* 49 (January 1975): 181; Firmage and Mangrum, *Zion in the Courts*, 323–75.

29. Leonard J. Arrington, *Brigham Young: American Moses* (New York: Alfred A. Knopf, 1985), 174–75; Campbell, *Establishing Zion*, 118, 122.

30. Arrington, *Great Basin Kingdom*, 354, 383.

31. Ibid., 55–57, 66–67; Arrington, *Brigham Young, American Moses*, 174–75; Davies, *Mormon Gold*.

32. Arrington, *Great Basin Kingdom*, 116–20, 122–29, 227–28.

33. Ibid., 149.

34. Ibid., 149–56.

35. Arrington, *Great Basin Kingdom*, 153; A. Dean Wengreen, "The Origin and History of the Fast Day in the Church of Jesus Christ of Latter-day Saints, 1830–96" (M.A. thesis, Brigham Young University, 1955), chap. 4.

36. *Journal of Discourses*, 8 October 1855, 27 vols. (London and Liverpool: LDS Booksellers Depot, 1855–86), 3:122.

37. Arrington, *Great Basin Kingdom*, 148–56.

38. William G. Hartley, "Ward Bishops and the Localization of LDS Tithing, 1847–1856," in *New Views of Mormon History: Essays in Honor of Leonard J. Arrington*, edited by Davis Bitton and Maureen Ursenbach Beecher, 94–114 (Salt Lake City: University of Utah Press, 1987); "Early Development of the Office of Bishop as it Relates to Wards, Stakes and to the General Church," Unpublished Special Report Prepared for Marvin R. VanDam by the Staff of the Historical Department of the Church, August 1976, typescript, LDS Church Historical Department Library; William G. Hartley, "Edward Hunter: Pioneer Presiding Bishop," in *Supporting Saints: Life Stories of Nineteenth-Century Mormons*, edited by Donald Q. Cannon and David J. Whittaker, 275–304 (Provo, Utah: Religious Studies Center, Brigham Young University, 1985).

39. Dixon, *New America*, 177.

40. Ibid., 183.

41. Ibid., 182.

42. Brigham Young, *Journal of Discourses*, 19 August 1860, 8:145–46.

43. Ibid., 6 April 1857, 4:312–20.

44. *New America*, 149–50.

45. Heber C. Kimball, *Journal of Discourses*, 6 April 1857, 5:19–22; Jessie L. Embry, "The Relief Society Grain Storage Program, 1876–1940" (M.A. thesis, Brigham Young University, 1974).

46. See sermons by Grant, *Journal of Discourses*, 3 August 1856, 4:19–20; 12

October 1856, 4:152–53, and by Young, *Journal of Discourses*, 26 January 1862, 9:171.

47. Linda King Newell, "Gifts of the Spirit: Women's Share," in *Sisters in Spirit: Mormon Women in Historical and Cultural Perspective*, edited by Maureen Ursenbach Beecher and Lavina Fielding Anderson, 111–50 (Urbana: University of Illinois Press, 1987).

48. Brigham Young, *Journal of Discourses*, 8 December 1867, 12:114–16.

49. Richard Hofstadter, *Social Darwinism in American Thought* (Boston: Beacon Press, 1955), 144.

50. Beecher, "The Office of the Bishop," 111.

51. Young, *Journal of Discourses*, 8 December 1867, 12:115.

52. Ibid., 8 August 1869, 13:109.

53. Arrington, *Great Basin Kingdom*, 354–56. See also Jill Mulvay Derr, Janath Russell Cannon, and Maureen Ursenbach Beecher, *Women of Covenant: The Story of Relief Society* (Salt Lake City: Deseret Book Co., 1992), chap. 3.

54. Leonard J. Arrington, Feramorz Y. Fox, and Dean L. May, *Building the City of God: Community and Cooperation Among the Mormons* (Salt Lake City: Deseret Book Company, 1976), 72–77; Arrington, *Great Basin Kingdom*, 148–56.

55. Arrington, *Great Basin Kingdom*, 145–47; Arrington, Fox, and May, *Building the City of God*, 63–70, 75–77.

56. Clayne L. Pope, "Households on the American Frontier: The Distribution of Income and Wealth in Utah, 1850–1900," in David W. Galenson, ed., *Markets in History: Economic Studies of the Past* (New York: Cambridge University Press, 1989), 148–49.

57. Arrington, *Great Basin Kingdom*, 251–53.

58. Ibid., 243–44.

59. Ibid., 247–49, 298–334.

60. Ibid., 330–37; Arrington, Fox, and May, *Building the City of God*, 79–310.

61. Dean L. May, "Brigham Young and the Bishops: The United Order," in *New Views of Mormon History: Essays in Honor of Leonard J. Arrington* (Salt Lake City: University of Utah Press, 1987), 115–35.

62. Arrington, Fox, and May, *Building the City of God*, 311–13.

63. In Arrington, *Great Basin Kingdom*, 338–39.

64. Ibid., 338–49.

65. For discussions of Woodruff's role, see Thomas G. Alexander, *Things in Heaven and Earth: The Life and Times of Wilford Woodruff, a Mormon Prophet* (Salt Lake City: Signature Books, 1991), and B. Carmon Hardy, *Solemn Covenant: The Mormon Polygamous Passage* (Urbana: University of Illinois Press, 1992). For economic information, see Arrington, *Great Basin Kingdom*, 397–90; Gustive O. Larson and Richard D. Poll, "The Forty-Fifth State," in *Utah's History*, edited by Richard D. Poll, Thomas G. Alexander, Eugene E. Campbell, and David E. Miller (Provo: Brigham Young University Press, 1978), 387–93.

66. The welfare activities described in this section are drawn from Leonard J. Arrington, "Utah and the Depression of the 1890s," *Utah Historical Quarterly* 24 (1961): 3–19.

67. Richard Sherlock, "Mormon Migration and Settlement after 1875," *Journal of Mormon History* 2 (1975): 53–68.

68. Thomas G. Alexander, *Mormonism in Transition: A History of the Latter-day Saints, 1890–1930* (Urbana: University of Illinois Press, 1986), 78–92.

69. Arrington, *Great Basin Kingdom*, 384–408.

70. Leonard J. Arrington, "Blessed Damozels: Women in Mormon History," *Dialogue* 6 (Summer 1971): 25; Cheryll Lynn May, "Charitable Sisters," in *Mormon Sisters*, edited by Claudia L. Bushman (Salt Lake City: Olympus Publishing Company, 1976), 228.

71. See the financial reports in the April issues of *Report of the Semi-Annual Conference of the Church of Jesus Christ of Latter-day Saints* (Salt Lake City: Church of Jesus Christ of Latter-day Saints, semi-annual), throughout this period.

72. Thomas G. Alexander, "The Manifesto: Mormondom's Watershed," *This People*, Fall 1990, 21–27.

Chapter 5 Twentieth-Century Welfare, 1900–1930

1. Much of this chapter was earlier published as Bruce R. Blumell, "Welfare before Welfare: Twentieth-Century LDS Church Charity before the Great Depression," *Journal of Mormon History* 6 (1979): 89–106. Some of the documentation in this chapter has been consolidated from the original references.

2. Harold Underwood Faulkner, *American Economic History* (New York: Harper and Brothers, 1960), 625–30.

3. For an excellent summary of Utah's economic conditions during this era, see Leonard J. Arrington, "The Commercialization of Utah's Economy: Trends and Developments from Statehood to 1910," and Thomas G. Alexander, "The Burgeoning of Utah's Economy, 1900–20," and Thomas G. Alexander, "The Economic Consequences of War: Utah and the Depression of the Early 1920s," all in *Charles Redd Monograph Series in Western History, No. 14*, edited by Dean May (Provo, Utah: Brigham Young University Press, 1974).

4. *Annual Instructions No. 5 to Presidents of Stakes and . . . Bishops and Counselors* (Salt Lake City: Church of Jesus Christ of Latter-day Saints, 1903–04), 13–14. This is one of a consecutively numbered series of handbooks (variously titled) prepared by the First Presidency and Presiding Bishopric beginning in 1899; hereafter cited as *Handbook of Instructions*, by series number and year of issue. Also of importance in showing Salt Lake City's welfare problems are *Handbook of Instructions*, No. 11, 1910, 23–24; No. 12, 1913, 39; and No. 14, 1928, 9. The discussion later in this chapter contains statistics illustrating the larger relief problems in Salt Lake City. See also Richard Sherlock, "Mormon Migration and Settlement after 1875," *Journal of Mormon History* 2 (1975): 53–68, documenting the problem of rural Mormon overpopulation during the last quarter of the nineteenth century.

5. *Handbook of Instructions*, No. 9, 1908, 13.

6. *Report of the Semi-Annual Conference of the Church of Jesus Christ of Latter-day Saints*, 6 October 1916 (Salt Lake City: Church of Jesus Christ of Latter-day Saints, semi-annual), 4–5; hereafter cited as *Conference Report*.

7. See all of the issues of *Handbook of Instructions* beginning with 1900. *Handbook of Instructions*, No. 5, 1903–04, 12, asked members to donate at least an amount equal to what they saved by fasting. *Handbook of Instructions*, No. 4, 1902, 11, asked bishops to send in surplus fast offerings to the Presiding Bishopric for use in other wards.

8. *Handbook of Instructions*, No. 14, 1928, 30–34.

9. *Handbook of Instructions*, No. 3, 1901, 13; No. 5, 1903–04, 13–14; see also

subsequent handbooks through 1928 and Leonard J. Arrington, "Utah and the Depression of the 1890s," *Utah Historical Quarterly* 24 (January 1961): 9–12.

10. Thomas G. Alexander, *Mormonism in Transition: A History of the Latter-day Saints, 1890–1930* (Urbana: University of Illinois Press, 1986), 93–114.

11. William G. Hartley, "The Priesthood Reform Movement, 1908–22," *Brigham Young University Studies* 13 (Winter 1973): 137–56; see also issues of the *Handbook of Instructions* beginning with No. 3, 1901.

12. Blumell, "Welfare before Welfare," 92–93.

13. William G. Hartley, "Saints and the San Francisco Earthquake," *Brigham Young University Studies* 23 (Fall 1983): 450–52. *Handbook of the Relief Society of the Church of Jesus Christ of Latter-day Saints* (Salt Lake City: General Board of the Relief Society, 1931), 43–48; *Conference Report*, 4 April 1915, 8 and 3 April 1921, 13.

14. Alexander, *Mormonism in Transition*, 193.

15. Ibid., 180–203.

16. Ibid., 129–35.

17. Ibid., 129.

18. James B. Allen and Glen M. Leonard, *The Story of the Latter-day Saints* (Salt Lake City: Deseret Book Co., 1976), 452–53; *Handbook of the Relief Society*, 1931, 35, 42–43. See issues of *Handbook of Instructions* beginning with No. 3, 1901; *Handbook of Instructions*, No. 12, 1913, 45; Amy Brown Lyman, "In Retrospect: Relief Society Welfare Work and Related Activities," *Relief Society Magazine* 29 (July 1942): 468; and *A Centenary of Relief Society, 1842–1942* (Salt Lake City: General Board of the Relief Society, 1942), 46; Jill Mulvay Derr, Janath Russell Cannon, and Maureen Ursenbach Beecher, *Women of the Covenant: The Story of the Relief Society* (Salt Lake City: Deseret Book Co., 1992) chaps. 5–7.

19. *A Centenary of Relief Society*, 41; Lyman, "In Retrospect," 463–64; Lyman, "Social Service Work in the Relief Society, 1917–28," 3–4, in Blumell, "Welfare before Welfare," 97.

20. Lyman, "In Retrospect," 469–70; Lyman, "Social Service Work," 3–6; and *Handbook of the Relief Society*, 1931, 52–53.

21. In Lyman, "Social Service Work," 9.

22. Ibid., 3–6, 27.

23. Ibid.; and *Handbook of the Relief Society*, 1931, 52–53.

24. Jessie L. Embry, "Relief Society Grain Storage Program, 1876–1940," (M.A. thesis, Brigham Young University, 1974), 42–48; *A Centenary of Relief Society*, 30.

25. *A Centenary of Relief Society*, 46–49; Lyman, "In Retrospect," 467–70; Lyman, "Social Service Work," 20; *Children's Friend*, 21 (July 1922): 371; Carol Cornwall Madsen and Susan Staker Oman, *Sisters and Little Saints: One Hundred Years of Primary* (Salt Lake City: Deseret Book Company, 1979), chap. 4.

26. Clark A. Chambers, *Seedtime of Reform: American Social Service and Social Action* (Minneapolis: University of Minnesota Press, 1963), especially 99–100.

27. Lyman, "Social Service Work," 8, 12–14.

28. Ibid.

29. Ibid., 5, 15, 21–22, 24; *Handbook of Instructions*, No. 13, 1921.

30. *Laws of the State of Utah*, 1919, chaps. 77 and 12, Special Session in 1919.

31. Lyman, "Social Service Work," 2, 8, 13–14.

32. Ibid., 1–2, 8, 13–14, 21; "Relief Society Social Service Department Annual Report," 1929, 7–11, in Blumell, "Welfare before Welfare."

33. Lyman, "Social Service Work," 19; Lyman, "In Retrospect," 468–70; "Relief Society Social Service Department Annual Report," 1929, 15–16.

34. "Relief Society Social Service Department Annual Report," 1929, 5, 8, 15; Lyman, "Social Service Work," 16.

35. "Relief Society Social Service Department Annual Report," 1929, 11–13; Genevieve Thornton, "The Relief Society Social Service Department," *Relief Society Magazine* 18 (January 1931): 14–17; Lyman, "Social Service Work," 17–18.

36. "Relief Society Social Service Department Annual Report," 1929, 1; Lyman, "In Retrospect," 466; Lyman, "Social Service Work," 15.

37. Lyman, "Social Service Work," 18–20; Mayola Rogers Miltenberger, "Some Aspects of the Welfare Activities of the Church of Jesus Christ of Latter-day Saints" (M.A. thesis, Tulane University, 1938), 39–40. "Relief Society Social Service Department Annual Report," 1929, 1 contains a response to a Presiding Bishopric letter questioning the administrative costs of the Relief Society Social Services Department.

38. Lyman, "Social Service Work," 17, 23, 25–27, and passim.

39. Ibid., 30–33; *Handbook of the Relief Society,* 1931, 53–56. The social relations lessons, taught one Sunday per month in today's Relief Society curriculum, are descendants of this original emphasis on social work.

40. *Handbook of Instructions,* No. 13, 1921, 25–28; Lyman, "Social Service Work," 15.

41. Lyman, "In Retrospect," 464; *A Centenary of Relief Society,* 44–45; *Handbook of the Relief Society,* 1931, 54; Lyman, "Social Service Work," 10, 20; see also Emmaretta G. Brown, "History of Church Welfare Work in Granite Stake, Church of Jesus Christ of Latter-day Saints, 1929, 1933," in Blumell, "Welfare before Welfare," n. 56.

42. In Blumell, "Welfare before Welfare," 103.

43. This change in emphasis reflected national trends. There were only five college-level schools of social work in the nation in 1915; by 1930 there were at least forty. See Chambers, *Seedtime of Reform,* 92–96, and Roy Lubove, *The Professional Altruist* (Cambridge: Harvard University Press, 1965).

44. *Handbook of Instructions,* No. 14, 1928, 30; No. 13, 1921, 9, 26.

45. Ibid.

46. *Conference Report,* April 1931, 3.

47. Josephine Chapin Brown, *Public Relief, 1929–39* (New York: Henry Holt and Company, 1940), 51, 55, 57.

48. See Hazel M. Peterson, "Administration of Public Welfare in Utah" (M.A. thesis, University of Chicago, 1928), ii, 6, 93–105.

49. In Lyman, "Social Service Work," 19–20.

50. In Blumell, "Welfare before Welfare," 106.

Chapter 6 Response to the Great Depression, 1929–1935

1. Betty Barton, "Mormon Poor Relief: A Social Welfare Interlude," *Brigham Young University Studies* 18 (Fall 1977): 66–88; especially 76–77, 88.

2. Dean Brimhall to Harry Hopkins, 14 July 1936, Memorandum, "The Mormon Relief Plan," p. 5, box 62, fd. 8, The Papers of Dean R. Brimhall, Special Collections, Marriott Library, University of Utah, Salt Lake City, Utah; hereafter cited as the Brimhall Papers. Brimhall, born 11 December 1886 in Provo, Utah, was a son of Brigham Young University's third president, George

H. Brimhall. After serving a mission in Germany (1907–09), he obtained a bachelor's degree in psychology from Brigham Young University (1913) and a master's and Ph.D. in the same discipline from Columbia (1916, 1920). After teaching intermittently at BYU and Columbia and serving as executive secretary of the Psychological Corporation, he and Robert H. Hinckley launched Utah Pacific Airways. That enterprise and his political connections led to his appointment as Utah Director of Aviation for the Civil Works Administration (1933) in charge of building municipal and emergency landing fields throughout the state under that early work relief program. In 1934, he became state director of planning for the Federal Emergency Relief Administration and, in 1935, also became director of the Utah State Planning Board for all federal work-relief programs and advisor on labor relations to the Works Progress Administration for Utah. Taking strong exception to LDS criticism of the federal relief effort, he became a vitriolic critic of the Church Welfare Program in 1936. When Hinckley became chairman of the federal Civil Aeronautics Authority in 1939, Brimhall left Utah to become his assistant, then served the CAA in other capacities until he retired to Utah in 1951. The seventy-six boxes of official papers and personal correspondence include items cited in this chapter and the next from his years as relief administrator.

3. See, for example, Thomas F. O'Dea, *The Mormons* (Chicago: University of Chicago Press, 1957), 216; William E. Berrett and Alma P. Burton, *Readings in LDS Church History*, 3 vols. (Salt Lake City: Deseret Book Company, 1958), 3:357–404.

4. Lester V. Chandler, *America's Greatest Depression, 1929–41* (New York: Harper and Row Publishers, 1970), 25–29.

5. Ibid., 193–98.

6. Leonard J. Arrington and Thomas G. Alexander, "The Dependent Commonwealth: Utah's Economy from Statehood to the Great Depression," in *Charles Redd Monographs in Western History, No. 4,* edited by Dean L. May (Provo, Utah: Brigham Young University Press, 1974), 57–89.

7. E. P. Staudt, Letter to Howard Myers, 23 June 1934, box 62, fd. 8, Brimhall Papers.

8. George H. Hansen, Letter to Dean Brimhall, 4 November 1938, box 34, fd. 1, Brimhall Papers.

9. Ibid.; George H. Hansen, Memorandum to Dean Brimhall, 20 August 1937, Brimhall Papers.

10. Dean Brimhall, Memorandum to Louis Wirth, 29 March 1939, box 34, fd. 12, Brimhall Papers.

11. Paul Child, "Physical Beginning of the Church Welfare Program," *Brigham Young University Studies* 14 (Spring 1974): 383; Leonard J. Arrington, "Harold B. Lee," in *The Presidents of the Church: Biographical Essays,* edited by Leonard J. Arrington (Salt Lake City: Deseret Book Company, 1986), 357–58. Though Preston Nibley originally authored this book, after his death in 1966 the publisher, which had been turning out subsequent editions, adding each new president, since 1947, continued to do so under Nibley's name through the 1975 edition, after which editorship of the continuing publication was taken over by Leonard J. Arrington.

12. Leonard J. Arrington, "Economy in the Modern Era," in *The History of a Valley: Cache Valley, Utah-Idaho,* edited by Joel Ricks (Logan, Utah: Centennial Commission, 1956), 242.

13. Interspersed throughout the papers of John Mills Whitaker, director of

the Deseret Employment Bureau during this period, are numerous examples of this reaction. See especially boxes 21–22 containing 1931–32 correspondence, John Mills Whitaker Papers, Special Collections, Marriott Library, University of Utah. Born in Centerville, Utah, in 1863, Whitaker married a daughter of LDS Church President John Taylor, taught himself Pittman shorthand, and became assistant to Church Historian Franklin D. Richards, private secretary to several Salt Lake businessmen, secretary and treasurer of the First Council of the Seventy, secretary of the Deseret Sunday School Union, a reporter for Utah's Constitutional Convention, deputy treasurer of Salt Lake County, and manager of a number of businesses before retiring as an LDS seminary teacher in 1929 at age sixty-five. He was then appointed manager of the Deseret Employment Bureau and, in addition, was "loaned" by the church to head a city/county-sponsored Civil Employment Bureau during the winters of 1930–31 and 1931–32. He served as the paymaster of the Civil Works Administration during 1933 and continued in his Deseret Employment Bureau responsibilities until 1939. He died in 1960 at age ninety-six. In addition to voluminous official papers and personal and official correspondence, the Whitaker Papers include an original diary in shorthand covering 1878–1959. Boxes 21–26 of the collection are those most relevant to the Deseret Employment Bureau and the Church Welfare Program.

14. Apostle Melvin J. Ballard advised farmers: "If you will be patient and stay by the enterprises you have undertaken and practice self-denial God will deliver you," and to others he counseled, "patience and self control" because "I am looking for greater progress in the alleviation of economic distress in the next 10 years than the last hundred years have seen." Whether that was a prediction of the advent of modern macroeconomic demand management or World War II, both having the signified impact, he never later identified. *Semi-Annual Conference Report of the Church of Jesus Christ of Latter-day Saints,* 9 April 1932 (Salt Lake City: Church of Jesus Christ of Latter-day Saints, semi-annual), 60–61; hereafter cited as *Conference Report.*

15. Jill Mulvay Derr, "Changing Relief Society Charity to Make Way for Welfare," in *New Views of Mormon History: Essays in Honor of Leonard Arrington,* edited by Davis Bitton and Maureen Ursenbach Beecher (Salt Lake City: University of Utah Press, 1987), 257.

16. Henry D. Taylor, "The Church Welfare Plan," typescript, 1984, 2, LDS Church Historical Department Library, Salt Lake City, Utah.

17. Presiding Bishopric, *Ward Charity: Details of Administration,* 10 February 1930; see also Church of Jesus Christ of Latter-day Saints, *Handbook of Instructions to Presidents of Stakes and...Bishops and Counselors,* No. 14 (Salt Lake City: Church of Jesus Christ of Latter-day Saints, 1928); titles of handbooks vary; hereafter cited as *Handbook of Instructions,* by series number and year of issue.

18. *Conference Report,* 5 October 1930, 104–5.

19. Ibid., 103.

20. Derr, "Changing Relief Society Charity," 246–48.

21. Albert E. Bowen, *The Church Welfare Plan,* Gospel Doctrine Course of Study, 1946 (Salt Lake City: Deseret Sunday School Union, 1945), 27.

22. In *Conference Report:* Melvin J. Ballard, 4 October 1930, 50; Sylvester Q. Cannon, 5 October 1930, 103–4; Charles W. Nibley, 5 October 1930, 96–97.

23. Heber J. Grant, "Financial Report," *Conference Report,* 4 April 1931, 3.

24. Ibid.

25. Ibid.; see also the *Deseret News 1991–92 Church Almanac* (Salt Lake City: Deseret News, 1990), 334. This figure represents the membership in stakes and wards, but excludes missions; it is 10.6 percent of the total 1930 Church membership.

26. Report of the Community Chest, 1 June 1931; authors' files.

27. Derr, "Changing Relief Society Charity," 249.

28. *A Centenary of the Relief Society, 1842–1942* (Salt Lake City: General Board of the Relief Society, 1942), 39–45. See also Jill Mulvay Derr, Janath Russell Cannon and Maureen Ursenbach Beecher, *Women of the Covenant: The Story of the Relief Society* (Salt Lake City: Deseret Book Co., 1992), chap. 8.

29. Leonard J. Arrington, Feramorz Y. Fox, and Dean L. May, *Building the City of God: Community and Cooperation Among the Mormons* (Salt Lake City: Deseret Book Company, 1976), 341; Derr, "Changing Relief Society Charity," 250.

30. *Conference Report,* 4 October 1931, 97.

31. Ibid., 124–25.

32. Ibid., 107–10. Only one figure was reported for this year.

33. *Conference Report,* 6 April 1932, 2–3.

34. B. F. Quinn, "Cooperation Between Salt Lake County Charity Department and L.D.S. Relief Society," *Relief Society Magazine* 18 (June 1931): 326–27.

35. "Three Named as Committee on Job Finding: Governor Dern Appoints Head of Job Board, Sylvester Q. Cannon Assigned Task of Leading Job Policy," *Deseret News,* 12 August 1931, B-1.

36. Bowen, *The Church Welfare Plan,* 26, 27, 43.

37. Taylor, "The Church Welfare Plan," 2.

38. Sylvester Q. Cannon, *Conference Report,* 7 October 1932, 14–15; Emmaretta G. Brown, "History of Church Welfare Work in Granite Stake, 1929–33," 14; John Mills Whitaker, Letter to Presiding Bishopric, 30 July 1931, box 21; Child, "Physical Beginnings of the Church Welfare Program," 383.

39. Only one figure was reported for this year. See *Conference Report,* David O. McKay, 9 April 1932, 61–62; Joseph F. Merrill, 10 April 1932, 112–16; Sylvester Q. Cannon, 7 October 1932, 11–16; George F. Richards, 8 October 1932, 44–48; Richard R. Lyman, 8 October 1932, 51–57.

40. Bowen, *The Church Welfare Plan,* 26–27. This June 1932 survey prefigured one taken in the summer of 1933, which is popularly seen as the church's first step in creating the 1936 Welfare Plan. See J. Richard Clarke, "The Storehouse Resource System," *Ensign,* May 1978, 82, and Berrett and Burton, *Readings in LDS Church History,* 3:359–61.

41. Brown, "History of Church Welfare Work in Granite Stake, 1929–33."

42. *Conference Report,* 7 October 1932, 14.

43. Taylor, "The Church Welfare Plan," 10. Liberty Stake also established, in 1939, the Deseret Soap Factory, which in 1991 still produced soap for distribution throughout the welfare system. Ibid., 11.

44. Ibid., 13.

45. Child, "Physical Beginnings," 383.

46. *Deseret News,* 25, 26 April 1933, 23 November 1935; Child, "Physical Beginnings," 383–86; Arrington, Fox, and May, *Building the City of God,* 341–42; Arrington, "Harold B. Lee," 356–57.

47. Whitaker to Presiding Bishopric, 20 August 1932, box 24, fd. 2, Whitaker Papers.

48. "Liberty Stake Increases Activities to Aid 2500 Jobless Prepare for Winter: Men Cut Wood and Plan to Assist Farmers in Harvesting," *Deseret News,* 4 September 1933, Section 2, p. 1.

49. For example, Cache Valley wards had established storehouses to collect and distribute food and clothing by 1932. By the early spring of 1933, the three Uintah Basin stakes in eastern Utah were cooperatively adopting self-help programs with the optimistic goal of becoming independent of public assistance. Arrington, Fox, and May, *Building the City of God,* 341.

50. Annual Report of the Executive Secretary of the Community Chest, 5 June 1932; William Wallace to members of the Salt Lake City and County Relief Committee, 9 May 1932; Albert U. Romasco, *The Poverty of Abundance* (New York: Oxford University Press, 1965), 222–23; *Emergency Relief and Construction Act of 1932, Statutes at Large of the United States,* XLVII, Part I (1932), Title I, Sec. I. (a); Engineering Department, Work Division, comp., *Statistical Summary of Expenditures and Accomplishments, Utah Emergency Relief Program,* authors' files.

51. "The Poor," *Deseret News,* 26 March 1932, 12.

52. *Conference Report,* 9 April 1932, 84–85.

53. *Conference Report,* 7, 9 October 1932, 40, 100.

54. John Mills Whitaker to the Presiding Bishopric, 20 October and 17 November 1932, box 24, fd. 2, Whitaker Papers; Sylvester Q. Cannon to bishops, Circular, 27 January 1933, and reiterative memorandum, "Suggestions for Reducing the Amounts Drawn by Bishops from the Tithing Funds for Charity Purposes," 30 January 1933, ibid.

55. Whitaker to the Presiding Bishopric, 20 October and 17 November 1932; and Memorandum, 30 January 1933, box 24, fd. 2, Whitaker Papers.

56. *Conference Report,* 6 April 1933, 4–5.

57. Ibid., 6 April 1934, 4–5; 5 April 1935, 2–3; and 4 April 1936, 2–3.

58. "State Body for Social Work Urged, LDS Relief Society Starts Plan to Create Central Bureau," *Salt Lake Tribune,* 5 April 1933, 1; Hazel M. Peterson, "Administration of Public Welfare in Utah" (M.A. thesis, University of Chicago, 1938), 100–5.

59. *Conference Report,* 6 October 1933, 35.

60. Ibid., October 1933, 34–35.

61. "Utah Given Small Part in Projects, Legislature Begins to Act On State Recovery Plan," *Salt Lake Tribune,* 18 July 1933, 1.

62. Salt Lake County Expenditures, 1934, authors' files.

63. Chandler, *America's Greatest Depression,* 189–208.

64. John F. Bluth and Wayne K. Hinton, "The Great Depression," in Richard D. Poll, Thomas G. Alexander, Eugene E. Campbell, and David E. Miller, eds., *Utah's History* (Provo, Utah: Brigham Young University Press, 1978), 486–89.

65. For example, see Bruce Blumell, "The Development of Public Assistance in the State of Washington During the Great Depression" (Ph.D. diss., University of Washington, 1973), chaps. 3, 4; James T. Patterson, *The New Deal and the States: Federalism in Transition* (Princeton, N.J.: Princeton University Press, 1969).

66. "Rules and Regulations Governing Expenditures of Federal Emergency Relief Funds," No. 1, 23 June 1933.

67. James R. Clark, comp., *Messages of the First Presidency,* 6 vols. (Salt Lake

City: Bookcraft, Inc., 1971), 5:330–36. This messsage was originally published in the *Deseret News,* 2 September 1933.

68. Ibid., 5:331–32.

69. Ibid., 5:334–38.

70. Derr, "Changing Relief Society Charity," 255–56.

71. Brown, "History of Church Welfare Work in Granite Stake, 1929–33," 15.

72. Derr, "Changing Relief Society Charity," 257.

73. Derr, "Changing Relief Society Charity," 256–57; Blumell, "The Development of Public Assistance," 155, describes similar developments in Washington state.

74. In Derr, "Changing Relief Society Charity," 255.

75. Ibid., 256.

76. A few signs of this divergence were apparent when the first handbook to stake presidencies and ward bishoprics since 1928 came out in 1934. Its instructions about caring for the poor were almost identical to those of earlier manuals. The few differences, relating almost exclusively to changes in governmental welfare programs since the beginning of the depression, had already been dealt with in circular letters. Members were urged to take advantage of public work projects, and the handbook suggested that each stake appoint a special employment representative. The handbook also instructed ward and stake relief officials to cooperate with county relief personnel through a designated representative "so that any of our people in need of either direct or unemployment relief may receive proper consideration from the county." Those "who hardly ever enter a meetinghouse and have little interest in the Church except when in need of aid . . . should be referred to the County Welfare Department. . . . Faithful, active Latter-day Saints in need of direct relief should not be referred to the County Welfare Department, but should be taken care of directly by the bishoprics and ward Relief Society officers." However, when federal and local "make-work" projects were available, "every possible effort should be exercised toward placing members of the Church who are in need of work on such projects," even (or especially) active members. The handbook also counseled bishops to remind eligible members to take advantage of widows' and old-age pensions. *Handbook of Instructions,* No. 15, 15 November 1934, 41–46. Furthermore, the relative absence of welfare as an April conference topic was conspicuous in 1934. Relief administration within the church had apparently stabilized, at least for the moment. See comments of Cannon, Lyman, and Widstoe, *Conference Report,* 6–8 April 1934, 76, 110, 115–16.

77. "Social Work: Outline Summary for Relief Society Social Service Institute," January 1934, mimeograph with handwritten marginal notes by Amy Brown Lyman, Topic 7, pp, 11–12. Amy Brown Lyman Papers, University Archives and Manuscripts, Harold B. Lee Library, Brigham Young University.

78. *Salt Lake Tribune,* 5 October 1934.

79. Frank W. Fox, *J. Reuben Clark: The Public Years* (Provo, Utah: Brigham Young University Press, 1980); D. Michael Quinn, *J. Reuben Clark: The Church Years* (Provo: Brigham Young University Press, 1983), 251–78.

80. J. Reuben Clark, Jr., "Suggestive Directions for Church Relief Activities," 30 June 1933, unpublished manuscript, binder 1, box 196, J. Reuben Clark Papers, Special Collections, Harold B. Lee Library, Brigham Young University, Provo, Utah; Quinn, *J. Reuben Clark: The Church Years,* 260–61.

81. Taylor, "The Church Welfare Plan," 27.

82. In Quinn, *J. Reuben Clark: The Church Years*, 260.

83. *Conference Report*, 9 April 1933, 103.

84. "Pres. Clark Urges Use of Local Aid: Former Envoy Decries Falling Back on US Funds, *Deseret News*, 20 June 1933, 8.

85. *Conference Report*, 8 October 1933, 102.

86. Quinn, *J. Reuben Clark: The Church Years*, 259.

87. Ibid., 261–62.

88. Ibid., 262.

89. Ibid., 263.

90. *Care of the Poor* (Salt Lake City: Presiding Bishopric, 1934), 1, 12. This pamphlet is excerpted directly from Section 6, pp. 40–52, of *Handbook of Instructions*, No. 15, 1934, which would guide church relief activities until the advent of the 1936 program.

91. Quinn, *J. Reuben Clark: The Church Years*, 261.

92. *Conference Report*, 7 October 1934, 97, 99.

93. Ibid., 6 October 1933, 5.

94. Ibid., 7 October 1933, 64–65.

95. Ibid., 5 October 1934, 36.

96. Derr, "Changing Relief Society Charity," 257.

97. In Quinn, *J. Reuben Clark: The Church Years*, 256.

98. Ibid., 264; Clark, *Messages of the First Presidency* 6:10; Leonard J. Arrington and Wayne K. Hinton, "Origin of the Welfare Plan of the Church of Jesus Christ of Latter-day Saints," *Brigham Young University Studies* 5 (Winter 1964): 67.

99. In Mayola Rogers Miltenberger, "Some Aspects of the Welfare Activities of the Church of Jesus Christ of Latter-day Saints" (M.A. thesis, Tulane University, 1983), 52.

100. Derr, "Changing Relief Society Charity," 257.

101. Caroline Bird, *The Invisible Scar: The Great Depression and What It Did to American Life* (New York: David McKay Company, Inc., 1966), 131, 197–99; Chandler, *America's Greatest Depression*, 191–94; Arthur M. Schlesinger, *The Age of Roosevelt: The Politics of Upheaval* (Boston: Houghton Mifflin Company, 1960), 632–36. *Deseret News* editorials sounded remarkably similar to newspaper editorials across the nation cited in these sources. For instance, see its attack on "the dole" in the editorial of 1 April 1933, 2.

102. *The Public Papers and Addresses of Franklin D. Roosevelt; Volume 4: The Court Disapproves* (New York: Random House, 1938), 19–20.

103. *Conference Report*, Richards, 5 October 1934, 37; Ballard, 4 October 1935, 27.

104. *The Public Papers and Addresses of Franklin D. Roosevelt*, 4:20.

105. Arrington and Hinton, "Origins of the Welfare Plan," 67–85.

106. Taylor, "The Church Welfare Plan," 27.

107. *Conference Report*, 6 October 1935, 112.

108. Taylor, "The Church Welfare Plan," 28.

109. Bowen, *The Church Welfare Plan*, 27; Arrington and Hinton, "Origin of the Welfare Plan," 67.

110. Clark, *Messages of the First Presidency*, 7:10. There is some confusion over the source of the 17.9 percent cited as the proportion of the church membership on relief. The 88,460 was only 11.9 percent of the church's total 746,384 member-

ship. At the same time, the survey summary indicates that 495,000 persons were surveyed in Utah and surrounding states, of whom 88,460 would have been 19.9 percent. No doubt the haste and the lack of professional personnel to conduct the survey and analyze its findings accounts for the error which, however, is not of a magnitude to compromise the conclusions. More questionable was the conclusion that 13,455 were receiving assistance because they were unemployed since the families of those breadwinners were on relief for the same reason. The conclusion that between 11,500 and 16,500 were receiving unmerited relief because they did not need it or had farms which, if worked, could have supported them is obviously subjective, especially in light of the fact that the survey summary also reveals that an offsetting number needed assistance, in the judgment of the surveyors, but were not receiving it, in part because they were reluctant to apply. See *Deseret News,* 7 April 1936, 1, 3.

   111. Arrington, "Harold B. Lee," 444.

Chapter 7 The Church Welfare Plan, 1935–1960

   1. Henry D. Taylor, "The Church Welfare Plan," typescript, 1984, 113, LDS Church Historical Department Library; "Important Message from the First Presidency," *Deseret News,* 7 April 1936, 1, 3; reprinted in *Improvement Era,* May 1936, 305–6 and James R. Clark, comp., *Messages of the First Presidency,* 6 vols. (Salt Lake City: Bookcraft, Inc., 1971), 6:9–13. The new plan was originally called the Church Security Plan but was renamed the Church Welfare Plan in 1938 to avoid confusion with the governmental programs under the Social Security Act of 1935. Apostle John A. Widtsoe gave the name change a theological justification: "Only the Lord can give security to human kind. Men can only advance one another's welfare. Therefore, the name Church Welfare Plan is preferable to Church Security Program." *Improvement Era,* June 1938, 352. For simplicity, we use Church Welfare Plan/Program/Committee for 1936–38, as well as thereafter.

   2. The message indicated that the church was spending "approximately a quarter of a million dollars during the year 1935," an apparently inadvertent understatement. According to the Church Financial Statement, ward and stake charity expenditures amounted to $183,810 and unspecified "charities" stood at $402,939 for a total of $586,749. *Semi-Annual Conference Report of the Church of Jesus Christ of Latter-day Saints,* 4 April 1936 (Salt Lake City: Church of Jesus Christ of Latter-day Saints, semi-annual), 3; hereafter cited as *Conference Report.*

   3. As noted in Chapter 6, what was being curtailed was federal support of direct relief, except that which would be subsequently provided under the Social Security Act. In fact, the combination of the Social Security Act public assistance, the WPA, and the continuance of the NYA and CCC youth programs constituted a substantial multiplication of federal resources allocated to the poor and unemployed. But that may not have been clear to church decision-makers at the time.

   4. *Handbook of Instructions for Stake Presidencies, Bishops and Counselors, Stake and Ward Clerks,* No. 15, (Salt Lake City: Church of Jesus Christ of Latter-day Saints, 1934), 49. Titles of handbooks vary; hereafter cited as *Handbook of Instructions,* by series number and year of issue.

   5. Clark, *Messages of the First Presidency,* 6:10–13.

   6. "Launching of a Great Church Objective, New Relief Project Begins with Creation of Regional Organization," *Deseret News,* Church Section, 25 April

1936, 1, 4; *Improvement Era,* May 1936, 305; Leonard J. Arrington, "Harold B. Lee," in *Presidents of the Church,* edited by Leonard J. Arrington (Salt Lake City: Deseret Book Company, 1986), 360.

7. *Deseret News 1991–1992 Church Almanac* (Salt Lake City: Deseret News, 1990), 51.

8. J. Reuben Clark, Jr., "Suggestive Directions for Church Relief Activities," unpublished manuscript, pp. 10–11, binder 1, box 196, J. Reuben Clark Papers, Special Collections, Harold B. Lee Library, Brigham Young University, Provo, Utah; also cited in D. Michael Quinn, *J. Reuben Clark: The Church Years* (Provo, Utah: Brigham Young University Press, 1983), 260–61.

9. Arrington, "Harold B. Lee," 358.

10. Ibid., 359.

11. Henry A. Smith, "Church-wide Security Program Organized," *Improvement Era,* June 1936, 337.

12. William E. Berrett, "Revelation," An Address Given to the Seminary and Institute Instructors at Brigham Young University, 27 June 1956, quoted in Richard O. Cowan, *The Church in the Twentieth Century* (Salt Lake City: Bookcraft, 1985), 151–52. See also James B. Allen and Richard O. Cowan, *Mormonism in the Twentieth Century,* 2d printing, rev. (Provo, Utah: Brigham Young University Press, 1969), 91.

13. *Conference Report,* 4 October 1936, 114–15.

14. *Building the City of God: Community and Cooperation Among the Mormons* (Salt Lake City: Deseret Book Company, 1976), 346.

15. As reported in the *Deseret News,* Church Section, 25 April 1936, 4.

16. "Church Security Program Endorsed by President Roosevelt," *Deseret News,* 9 June 1936, 11.

17. "LDS to Take 88,000 from the Relief Rolls, Clark Outlines Program," *Salt Lake Tribune,* 25 May 1936, 1.

18. Leonard J. Arrington, Feramorz Y. Fox, and Dean L. May, *Building the City of God: Community and Cooperation Among the Mormons* (Salt Lake City: Deseret Book Company, 1976), 347–48; Leonard J. Arrington and Wayne K. Hinton, "Origin of the Welfare Plan of the Church of Jesus Christ of Latter-day Saints," *Brigham Young University Studies* 5 (Winter 1964): 68; Marc A. Rose, "The Mormons March Off Relief," *Reader's Digest,* June 1937, 43–44; Martha Emery, "Mormon Security," *Nation,* 12 February 1938, 182–83. Other articles appeared in *Cosmopolitan, Saturday Evening Post,* and *American Banker.*

19. For example, see Dean Brimhall to Harry Hopkins, Memorandum, 14 July 1936, "The Mormon Relief Plan," box 62, fd. 8, Brimhall Papers, Special Collections, Marriott Library, University of Utah, Salt Lake City; hereafter cited as Brimhall Papers. Then federal relief administrator for the state of Utah, Brimhall sent to federal relief administrator Harry Hopkins a diatribe against Mormon leaders and their welfare plan. Some of his ill feeling may be understood in light of direct and implied criticisms that some church leaders, notably Grant and Clark, were making of federal relief policies and programs; but his wrathful document contains serious misrepresentations. Brimhall was well acquainted with the church survey made during the fall of 1935 and the figures for Salt Lake County which showed that at least 60 percent of those receiving public charity were LDS. He bitterly declared that "Church officials apparently became panic stricken," and, deciding "something must be done," announced their own welfare program "after more than six years of inaction during the depression."

Brimhall knew this last statement was inaccurate. His own report in another context contained statistics on church help. Moreover, he neglected to mention that church relief response to the depression was well ahead of that of any governmental unit, including Roosevelt's leadership as governor of New York. The event and others like it continued to rankle; even after he had left Utah to serve in Washington, D.C., with the Civil Aeronautics Authority, he wrote to Albert E. Bowen objecting to an alleged statement in Bowen's 1946 Sunday School manual, *The Church Welfare Plan,* Gospel Doctrine Course of Study, 1946 (Salt Lake City: Deseret Sunday School Union, 1945), that the church had successfully taken all of its members off the public relief rolls. Bowen correctly replied that he had not made that claim but had only cited the declared policy. Brimhall, Letter to Bowen, 29 July 1946; Bowen, Letter to Brimhall, 6 August 1946, box 12, fd. 21, Brimhall Papers.

20. See, e.g., Cannon, *Conference Report,* 5 October 1933, 31–33; James H. Moyle to Dean R. Brimhall, 14 November 1936, box 34, fd. 1, Brimhall Papers; Edwin B. Firmage, ed., *An Abundant Life: The Memoirs of Hugh B. Brown* (Salt Lake City: Signature Books, 1988) 84. Ballard also reported that Roosevelt responded favorably to his description of the church program. "Church Security Program Endorsed by President Roosevelt," *Deseret News,* 9 June 1936, 11. Roosevelt's reported endorsement is hardly astonishing given the plight of the poor, the needs that had surpassed any resources up to that point, and the fact that it was an election year.

21. See also Arrington and Hinton, "Origin of the Welfare Plan," 67–85; Arrington, Fox, and May, *Building the City of God,* chap. 15; Leonard J. Arrington and Davis Bitton, *The Mormon Experience* (New York: Alfred A. Knopf, 1979), 272–78.

22. *Conference Report,* 2 October 1936, 3.

23. *Deseret News,* Church Section, 25 April 1936; "An Important Message from the First Presidency to the Presidents of Stakes and Bishoprics of the Church," *Improvement Era,* May 1936, 305; "A Message from the President of the Church to the Presidencies of Stakes and Bishoprics of Wards," 21 April 1936, *Improvement Era,* June 1936, 332; Henry A. Smith, "Churchwide Security Program Organized," *Improvement Era,* June 1936, 333–38.

24. Smith, "Church-wide Security Program Organized," 337.

25. *Deseret News* Church Section, 25 April 1936, 3. As discussed in Chapter 5, the church had promoted sugar beets since the 1890s and was controlling stockholder in the Utah and Idaho Sugar Company. More importantly, under federal agricultural policy, sugar enjoyed a guaranteed market at supported prices highly attractive to southern and western farmers. "Committee in House Gives Tentative Okeh to Sugar Quota Setup," *Deseret News,* 22 April 1937, 1.

26. *Conference Report,* 2 October 1936, 3–4.

27. Smith, "Church-wide Security Program Organized," 332, 337; Harold B. Lee, "Church Security: Retrospect, Introspect, Prospect," *Improvement Era,* April 1937, 206–10; Bowen, *The Church Welfare Program,* 34; Alfred Urhan, "Welfare in the Church," *Improvement Era,* November 1956, 810.

28. Bowen, *The Church Welfare Program,* 30–34; *Handbook of Instructions for Welfare Workers of the Church of Jesus Christ of Latter-day Saints* (Salt Lake City: General Church Welfare Committee of the Church of Jesus Christ of Latter-day Saints, 1940), 26–27. This pamphlet is reprinted from the *Handbook of Instructions,* No. 16, 1940, with revisions.

29. Taylor, "The Church Welfare Plan," 112.

30. Ibid., 121.

31. See the statistical report for each April conference, *Conference Report,* 1932–37.

32. "Corporation Formed to Aid Church Plan," *Deseret News,* 22 April 1937, 1, 3; Frank Dunn, "A Description and Evaluation of the Welfare Plan of the Church of Jesus Christ of Latter-day Saints" (M.A. thesis, Colorado College, Colorado City, Colo., 1938), 3. Probably because the title fit, this name was not changed when the Church Security Program became the Church Welfare Program in 1938; it continues today as Zion Securities Corporation with responsibility for church real estate and other holdings.

33. Irvin T. Nelson, "Looking Toward Church-wide Beautification," *Improvement Era* 40 (April 1937); Marvin O. Ashton, "A Thousand Wards Join the Church-wide Improvement Procession," *Improvement Era,* June 1937, 348–49.

34. Melvin J. Ballard, "Temple Work in Connection with the Church Security Program," 13–17, in *Addresses Delivered at a Special Meeting of the Presidencies of Stakes, Bishops of Wards and Other Officers Conducting the Church Security Program, 5 April 1937;* authors' files.

35. Urhan, "Welfare in the Church," 811.

36. Clark, *Messages of the First Presidency,* 6:12.

37. *Conference Report,* 3 October 1936, 80–86.

38. *Deseret News 1991–1992 Church Almanac,* 51.

39. *Conference Report,* 6 April 1938, 96.

40. Jill Mulvay Derr, "Changing Relief Society Charity to Make Way for Welfare," in *New Views of Mormon History: Essays in Honor of Leonard Arrington,* edited by Davis Bitton and Maureen Ursenbach Beecher (Provo, Utah: Brigham Young University Press, 1987), 259–65; Jill Mulvay Derr, Janath Russell Cannon, and Maureen Ursenbach Beecher, *Women of the Covenant: The Story of the Relief Society* (Salt Lake City: Deseret Book Co., 1992), chap. 8.

41. Derr, "Changing Relief Society Charity," 258–59.

42. Derr, ibid., 259.

43. In Ibid., 260. The Relief Society Charity Fund which was maintained through donations from women at the ward level was dissolved during World War II (p. 263).

44. Ibid., 259–61.

45. Ibid., 261–64.

46. Arrington and Hinton, "Origin of the Welfare Plan," 76–77.

47. Louis Wirth, Letter to Dean Brimhall, 29 March 1939, box 34, fd. 12, Brimhall Papers; Arrington and Hinton, "Origin of the Welfare Plan," 80. Brimhall, the federal relief administrator, employed Wirth, a sociologist from the University of Chicago, to conduct a study to determine the proportion of Utah relief recipients who were Mormons.

48. See *Handbook of Instructions,* 1934, 49–50; and *Handbook of Instructions,* 1940, 48, 50, 60–61.

49. In Arrington and Hinton, "Origin of the Welfare Plan," 76.

50. Lee, "Church Security: Retrospect, Introspect, Prospect," 206.

51. Quinn, *J. Reuben Clark: The Church Years,* 268–69; Arrington and Hinton, "Origin of the Welfare Plan," 84–85.

52. *Salt Lake Tribune*, 18 September 1987, 4A.

53. In 1943, when there were 145 stakes, there were 50 church-owned welfare farms. With postwar prosperity, stakes and wards were able to buy welfare projects. By 1950 there were over 400 church-owned welfare farms in the United States, even though there were only 180 stakes. See statistical report sections of *Conference Report* for those years.

54. Bowen, *The Church Welfare Plan*, 98; *Handbook of Instructions*, No. 16, 1940, 34, 57–58. The general committee appointed a number of subcommittees to take advantage of special expertise with the guidance and assistance of paid staff. The agricultural committee not only assisted in selecting stake welfare farms and advised on their operation but also counseled LDS farmers and helped those who wanted to increase their self-sufficiency through agriculture relocate and buy new farms.

55. Franklin S. Harris, "Agriculture: A Foundation of Welfare," *Improvement Era*, April 1938, 207.

56. Bowen, *the Church Welfare Plan*, 98–99; C. Orval Scott, "The Agricultural Program of the Church Welfare Plan," *Improvement Era*, October 1939, 586, 634; *What Is the "Mormon" Security Program?*, pamphlet (Independence, Mo.: Zion's Printing and Publishing Company, n.d.), 8; *Handbook of Instructions for Welfare Workers*, 5–6, 30–31.

57. Bowen, *The Church Welfare Plan*, 96.

58. *Handbook of Instructions for Welfare Workers*, 5–6; Bowen, *The Church Welfare Plan*, 96.

59. Bowen, *The Church Welfare Plan*, 47–48; George Stewart, Dilworth Walker, and E. Cecil McGavin, *Priesthood and Church Welfare: A Study Course for the Quorums of the Melchizedek Priesthood for the Year 1939* (Salt Lake City: Deseret Book Company, 1939), 28–38, 50–53.

60. Don L. Searle, "Deseret Industries at 50," *Ensign*, July 1988, 32–37.

61. Bowen, *The Church Welfare Program*, 102–3.

62. Ibid., 105; Urhan, "Welfare in the Church," 811; William Mulder, "Helping Others to Help Themselves," *Improvement Era*, December 1938, 734, 737.

63. *Handbook of Instructions*, 5–6, 30–31.

64. Urhan, "Welfare in the Church," 811; Mulder, "Helping Others to Help Themselves," 734, 737.

65. Urhan, "Welfare in the Church," 811; "Administration Building Rising on Central Storehouse Building Project," *Improvement Era*, December 1938, 734, 737.

66. *Conference Report*, 6 April 1942, 89.

67. Arrington, Fox, and May, *Building the City of God*, 352–53.

68. Urhan, "Welfare in the Church," 811.

69. *Conference Report*, 1 October 1943, 24.

70. *LDS Church Welfare Handbook of Instructions* (Salt Lake City: Church of Jesus Christ of Latter-day Saints, January 1944), 12–14.

71. James B. Allen and Glen M. Leonard, *The Story of the Latter-day Saints* (Salt Lake City: Deseret Book Co., 1976), 550; "LDS Welfare Sends Food to Japanese Families" and "LDS Donations for Europe Total 85 Cars," *Salt Lake Tribune*, 26 October 1947, B20; Arrington and Bitton, *The Mormon Experience*, 275–76.

72. Allen and Leonard, *The Story of the Latter-day Saints,* 350–51.

73. Sheri L. Dew, *Ezra Taft Benson: A Biography* (Salt Lake City: Deseret Book Company, 1987), 198–227. See also excerpts from Benson's journal and letters to his family in *A Labor of Love: The 1946 European Mission of Ezra Taft Benson* (Salt Lake City: Deseret Book, 1989), and the account of his personal secretary, Frederick W. Babbel, in *On Wings of Faith* (Salt Lake City: Bookcraft, Inc., 1972).

74. David Lawrence McKay, *My Father, David O. McKay* (Salt Lake City: Deseret Book Company, 1989), 229.

75. Allen and Leonard, *The Story of the Latter-day Saints,* 550–53.

76. See statistical summaries announced at each April general conference and published in *Conference Report.*

77. *Helping Others to Help Themselves: The Story of the Church Welfare Program* (Salt Lake City: Church of Jesus Christ of Latter-day Saints, 1941), 12.

78. See Bowen, *The Church Welfare Plan;* Stewart, Walker, and McGavin, *Priesthood and Church Welfare;* Lee, "Church Security: Retrospect, Introspect and Prospect," *Deseret News,* Church Section, 15 May 1937; Lee, "What Is the Church Welfare Plan?" *Instructor,* July 1946, 313–16; and selected addresses in *Conference Report:* David O. McKay, 4 October 1941; Harold B. Lee, 6 April 1942; J. Reuben Clark, 3 October 1942.

Chapter 8 The Maturing of Welfare Services in the United States and Canada, 1960–1990

1. For useful summaries of economic developments in the United States during the period 1960–90, see Herbert Stein, *Presidential Economics: Economic Policymaking from Roosevelt to Reagan and Beyond,* 2d. ed. rev. (Washington, D.C.: American Enterprise Institute for Public Policy, 1988) and Paul Krugman, *The Age of Diminishing Expectations* (Cambridge, Mass.: MIT Press, 1990). For descriptions of the anti-poverty policies responding to some of those events see Garth L. Mangum, *The Emergence of Manpower Policy* (New York: Harper and Row, 1969); Sar A. Levitan, Garth L. Mangum, and F. Ray Marshall, *Human Resources and Labor Markets* (New York: Harper and Row, 1981); and Sar A. Levitan, *Programs in Aid of the Poor,* 6th ed. (Baltimore: The Johns Hopkins University Press, 1990).

2. Levitan, *Programs in Aid of the Poor,* 13–14.

3. *Report of the Semi-Annual Conference of the Church of Jesus Christ of Latter-day Saints,* 5 April 1975 (Salt Lake City: Church of Jesus Christ of Latter-day Saints, semi-annual), 163; hereafter cited as *Conference Report.*

4. "An Overview of Church Welfare Services," *Ensign,* November 1975, 114.

5. Vaughn J. Featherstone, "Food Storage," *Ensign,* May 1976, 116–17. See also two other addresses given in the same welfare session of the 3 April 1976 conference: Victor L. Brown, Sr., "The Church and Family Welfare Services," and Relief Society President Barbara B. Smith, "Teach LDS Women Self-Sufficiency."

6. H. Burke Peterson, "The Welfare Production/Distribution Department," *Ensign,* November 1975, 116.

7. Nathan Eldon Tanner, "Constancy Amid Change," *Ensign,* November 1979, 80–82.

8. *Welfare Services Resource Handbook* (Salt Lake City: Church of Jesus Christ of Latter-day Saints, 1980).

9. *Providing in the Lord's Way: A Leader's Guide to Welfare* (Salt Lake City: Church of Jesus Christ of Latter-day Saints, 1990).

10. *Welfare Services Resource Handbook,* 18.

11. Ibid., 21. This rule is not enforced outside the United States and Canada.

12. *Deacons Course A, 1984,* contains lessons titled "Self Mastery," 31–34, "Work," 74–76, and "Using Time Wisely"; *Deacons Course B, 1985,* has lessons entitled "Decision Making," 116–18, "Goals," 119–22, and "The Value and Purpose of Education," 123–25 (Salt Lake City: Corporation of the President of the Church of Jesus Christ of Latter-day Saints, years as cited).

13. *Teachers Course A* (1984), "The Blessings of Work," 111–14; *Teachers Course B* (1985), "Preparing for a Career," 105–8; *Priests Course A* (1983), "Acquiring True Manhood," 34–37; *Priests Course B, 1983,* "Consecration and Sacrifice," 72–75, (Salt Lake City: Corporation of the President of the Church of Jesus Christ of Latter-day Saints, years as cited).

14. *Laurels Manual 1* (1989), "Service in the Community," 137–40, "Avoiding Crisis Living," 202–5, "Choosing a Vocation," 206–10, "Money Management," 211–14; *Laurels Manual 2* (1988), "Developing Yourself," 190–95, "Learning Throughout Our Lives," 194–95, "Value of a Vocation," 198–200, "Financial Management," 201–4 (Salt Lake City: Corporation of the President of the Church of Jesus Christ of Latter-day Saints, years as cited).

15. Address at October conference 1975, quoted in *Laurels Manual 1,* 206 and *Laurels Manual 2,* 199.

16. Address at the Paris, France, Area Conference, 1979, quoted in *Laurels Manual 1,* 198.

17. *To Make Thee a Minister and a Witness,* Melchizedek Priesthood Personal Study Guide 2 (Salt Lake City: Church of Jesus Christ of Latter-day Saints, n.d.), 22–26, 31–34, 115–18.

18. *Learn of Me,* Relief Society Personal Study Guide 2 (Salt Lake City: Church of Jesus Christ of Latter-day Saints, n.d.), 40–49, 154–60, 212–29.

19. Ibid., 25–42.

20. Henry D. Taylor, "The Church Welfare Plan," typescript, 1984, 96; LDS Church Historical Department Library, Salt Lake City, Utah.

21. Ibid., 114; "Changes in Welfare Program," *Church News,* 8 April 1972, 4; *Deseret News 1979 Church Almanac* (Salt Lake City: Deseret News, 1979), 71, 80.

22. *LDS Church Welfare Handbook of Instructions* (Salt Lake City: General Church Welfare Committee, 1944), 68; *Handbook of Instructions for Welfare Workers of the Church of Jesus Christ of Latter-day Saints: Official Handbook of Instructions No. 19* (Salt Lake City: General Church Welfare Committee, 1940), 6.

23. Frank O. May, Jr., "Correlation of the Church Administration," *Encyclopedia of Mormonism,* 4 vols. (New York: Macmillan Publishing Company, 1991) 1:323–25; James B. Allen and Glen M. Leonard, *The Story of the Latter-day Saints* (Salt Lake City: Deseret Book Company, 1976), 599–609.

24. Taylor, "The Church Welfare Plan," 111–12.

25. *Welfare Plan of the Church of Jesus Christ of Latter-day Saints,* rev. 10 February 1969 and reprinted 1972 (Salt Lake City: Deseret News Press, 1969 and 1972, p. 9 in both); *Deseret News Church Almanac, 1979* (Salt Lake City: Deseret News, [1978]), 71.

26. *Melchizedek Priesthood Handbook* (Salt Lake City: Church of Jesus Christ of Latter-day Saints, 1964), 28–29. This concept was still evident in the 1970 *Handbook* (p. 31) but had disappeared by 1974.

27. Harold B. Lee, *Conference Report,* 104–5; Henry A. Smith, "An Eventful Conference," *Church News,* 7 October 1967, 3; Harold B. Lee, "The Church Faces the Future," *Church News,* 21 October 1967, 7–10.

28. Stephen W. Gibson, "Welfare Services Go Worldwide," *Church News,* 7 October 1972, 8–9.

29. "Changes in Welfare Program," *Church News,* 8 April 1972, 4; Gibson, "Welfare Services Go Worldwide," 8–9.

30. Brown, "An Overview of Church Welfare Services," 113; *Church News,* 7 April 1973, 4.

31. "Area Supervisory Program Announced," *Church News,* 3 May 1975; "General Authorities as Area Supervisors," *Church News,* 1 July 1977; "Area Presidencies Called as Church Modifies Geographical Administration," *Ensign,* August 1984, 75; "New Presidencies Announced for 13 Geographical Areas," *Church News,* 24 June 1984, 3, 14.

32. *Welfare Services Resource Handbook,* 6–8.

33. See "Financial and Statistical Reports" given at April general conference, 1936–50, in *Conference Report.* Taylor, "The Church Welfare Plan," 121, reports the 1936 fast offering at 22 cents per capita. Inflation, which increased the cost of the meals, no doubt accounted for some of the rise.

34. Welfare Agricultural Meeting, 3 April 1971, 1, quoted in *Come Unto the Father in the Name of Jesus,* Melchizedek Priesthood Personal Study Guide 3 (Salt Lake City: The Church of Jesus Christ of Latter-day Saints, 1992), 118.

35. *Conference Report,* 6 April 1974, 184. He made a similar plea in October 1977 general conference.

36. J. M. Heslop, "Welfare Services Worldwide," *Church News,* 11 October 1975, 10–11; Taylor, "The Church Welfare Plan," 121.

37. "Fast for World Hunger Raises $3.8 Million," *Church News,* 29 December 1985, 3, 10; see also Introduction and Chapter 9.

38. *Providing in the Lord's Way,* 13.

39. Quoted, for example, in Albert E. Bowen, *The Church Welfare Plan* (Salt Lake City: Deseret Book Company, 1946), 130, and Spencer W. Kimball, "And the Lord Called His People Zion," *Ensign,* August 1984, 3.

40. *Welfare Resource Handbook,* 21.

41. That directive has not prevented government/church cooperation during emergencies. For instance, the LDS home teaching system, reaching directly into each home, has been used with spectacular effect to recruit volunteer labor to combat floods and for similar public emergencies in Utah cities. See Introduction.

42. Statistical reports, April conference, *Conference Report,* for the years cited.

43. *Welfare Services Resource Handbook,* 34.

44. Heslop, "Welfare Services Worldwide," 10–11; Peterson, "The Welfare Production/Distribution Department," 117.

45. Heslop, "Welfare Services Worldwide," 10; Marion G. Romney, *Conference Report,* 5 October 1975, 172; Peterson, "The Welfare Production/Distribution Department," 117.

46. Heslop, "Welfare Services Worldwide," 11. The seventy-eight facilities were a 1975 figure; the 1977 number was not given.

47. Garth L. Mangum, "Welfare Services," *Encyclopedia of Mormonism,* 4 vols. (New York: Macmillan Publishing Company, 1991), 4:1557.

48. Expenditures and number of persons assisted are from the statistical and financial reports, April general conference, *Conference Report,* for the years

named; membership figures are from *Deseret News 1991–92 Church Almanac,* 335.

49. Junior Wright Child, "Welfare in the Church," *Ensign,* September 1973, 68–71; "Welfare Program Broadened," *Church News,* 9 June 1973, 3.

50. Welfare Services Department, "Agronometric Study," 25 vols., 1 July 1977.

51. Marion G. Romney, *Conference Report,* 5 October 1975, 171, quoted and reiterated the 1936 policy, "The implementing of this charge requires that every ward, by itself or in cooperation with other wards, acquire a production facility." H. Burke Peterson, "Acquiring and Managing Production Projects," *Ensign,* November 1976, 114–18, urged every ward and stake to "become involved in a welfare services production project at the earliest possible time."

52. R. Quinn Gardner, "Welfare Services in Perspective," *Ensign,* February 1979, 12–18.

53. Statistical reports, April general conference, *Conference Report* of the years cited.

54. Ibid.

55. Taylor, "The Church Welfare Plan," 123.

56. "Church Reducing the Number of Welfare Projects," *Ensign,* February 1985, 80.

57. "Major Changes in the Funding of Welfare," *Church News,* 10 April 1983, 2–6.

58. Mangum, "Welfare Services," 4:1557.

59. "Manage Resources Efficiently, Church Counseled," *Ensign,* May 1981, 96–97.

60. Statistical reports, April conference, *Conference Report* for the years cited.

61. Romney, *Conference Report,* 5 October 1975, 171; Peterson, "The Welfare Production/Distribution Department," 117.

62. "Welfare Plan in Action in Fairbanks, Alaska, Flood," *Church News,* 2 September 1967, 10; "Stephen W. Gibson, "Welfare Plan in Full Swing in Quake Area," *Church News,* 13 February 1971, 3, 11; "Flood Shows Value of Welfare Planning," *Church News,* 2 October 1973, 13; Terry Green, "LDS Assist in Clean-up of Flood in Arizona," *Church News,* 30 December 1978, 3; Barbara Bernstein, "Flood Help Was Sermon Put in Action," *Church News,* 25 August 1979, 3; Gerry Avant, "Members Aid Stricken Flood Victims," *Church News,* 1 March 1980, 3, 8–9; Vernice W. Pere and Rubina Forester, "Folks Are Knee Deep in Service after Flood," *Church News,* 20 October 1982, 4; Golden A. Buchmiller, "National Media Lauds Utah Flood Volunteers," *Church News,* 3 July 1983, 7; Graham W. Kirby, "Hurricane Diana Blows Members, Non-LDS Together," *Church News,* 23 September 1984, 6; "They're Picking Up Pieces after Elena," *Church News,* 15 September 1985, 3; Donna Morgan, "Quake's Disaster Offset by Preparedness, Faith," *Church News,* 15 May 1983, 7; "System Working in California Floods," *Church News,* 9 March 1986, 15; "Missionaries Assist During Hurricane," *Church News,* 31 October 1987, 5; Elayne Wells, "Fury of Hurricane Hugo Unites LDS in Midst of Overwhelming Ruin," *Church News,* 30 September 1989, 7; John L. Hart, "'Great Group' Pitches in at Disaster Sites: Wins Praise for Work," *Church News,* 4 November 1989, 9; "'Flood' of Support Given in Washington," *Church News,* 29 December 1990, 5; Laurel MacDonald, "Hurricane Hugo and High Rise Helpers," *Ensign,* June 1991, 59–60; Lorin Hunsaker and Ludeen Hunsaker, "Angels in White Shirts Come to Help after Flood," *Church News,* 24 August 1991, 11.

63. The narrative that follows is drawn from Bruce D. Blumell, "The Latter-day Saint Response to the Teton, Idaho, Flood, 1976," *Task Papers in LDS History, No. 16* (Salt Lake City: Historical Department of the Church of Jesus Christ of Latter-day Saints, 1976); Blumell, "The LDS Response to the Teton Dam Disaster in Idaho," *Sunstone* 5, no. 2 (March-April 1980): 35–42; and "Assistance Rendered Idaho, 1976," a compilation of welfare statistics, files in the Joseph Fielding Smith Institute for Church History, Brigham Young University, Provo, Utah.

64. See addresses at welfare session of general conference 31 March 1979, published in *Ensign*, May 1979: N. Eldon Tanner, "New Emphasis on Church Councils," 85–86; Ezra Taft Benson, "Church Government Through Councils," 86–89; and Victor L. Brown, Sr., "Develop Temporal Plan and Priorities," 89–92. In 1989, agent stake presidents were assigned to supervise regional welfare activities, rotating each three to five years.

65. Michael C. Cannon, "Deseret Industries," *Encyclopedia of Mormonism*, 1:375–77.

66. Doyle L. Green, "The Privilege to Work Is a Gift," *Improvement Era*, July 1963, 584.

67. "Worldwide Clothing Distribution," *Church News*, 15 December 1990, 3, 6.

68. Cannon, "Deseret Industries," 1:376.

69. Don L. Searle, "Deseret Industries at 50," *Ensign*, August 1988, 32–37.

70. Otelia B. Hale, "History of the Employment System," unpublished memorandum, 31 December 1961, authors' files.

71. Glenn L. Pace, Director of Financial and Management Services, "LDS Church Assistance to the Unemployed—A Historical Perspective," address to the Employment Center Managers' Seminar, 11 July 1979; photocopy of typescript in authors' files.

72. Statistical reports, April conference, in *Conference Report* for 1950–86.

73. Fyans, "Employment Challenges in the 1980s," *Ensign*, May 1982, 82–84; Packer, "The Gospel—Foundation of Our Career," ibid., 86.

74. *Church Employment System Guidebook* (Salt Lake City: Corporation of the President, 1982), 3.

75. Ibid., 1.

76. *Welfare Services Resources Handbook*, 28.

77. *Providing Vocational Rehabilitation Through Church Employment Centers*, Supplement to *Church Employment Center Operational Procedures* (Salt Lake City: Church of Jesus Christ of Latter-day Saints, May 1988).

78. *Conference Report*, April 1985, 26; Tucker Carlson, "Holy Dolers: The Secular Lessons of Mormon Charity," *Policy Review*, Winter 1992, 30.

79. Hugh B. Brown, "After High School What?" *New Era*, June 1968, 32–33; *Church News*, 9 November 1968; *Gospel of Work for Youth* (Salt Lake City: Corporation of the President, 1971).

80. *Job Search: The Inside Track*, six-tape video program, prepared for the Church of Jesus Christ of Latter-day Saints by Eclecon Commercial, Salt Lake City, n.d.

81. Gerry Avant and Angela Bennett, "Milwaukee City Branch: Gospel Light Shines through Urban Blight for Growth, Progress," *Church News*, 23 February 1991, 8–9, 13; Carolyn Sessions Allen, "Inner City Angels," *New Era*, 21 April 1991, 28–31; LaRene Gaunt, "Testimonies from the Inner City, Can the Gospel *Really* Change Lives on the Streets of Harlem?" *Ensign*, April 1992,

36–43; "Bringing Blessings to Those in Need: Church Infuses Gospel Truths in Lives of Central-City Residents," *Church News*, 25 July 1992, 8, 14; Jessie L. Embry, "Separate But Equal?: Black Branches, Genesis Groups, or Integrated Wards?" *Dialogue: A Journal of Mormon Thought* 23 (Spring 1990) 11–37; see also Embry's forthcoming book-length study on the integration and social adjustment of LDS blacks.

82. "Bringing Blessings to Those in Need," *Church News*, 25 July 1992, 8, 14.

83. "3 Welfare Units Joined," *Church News*, 7 April 1973, 4. Prior to this time these church-owned hospitals had operated with little centralized supervision.

84. Gibson, "Welfare Services Go Worldwide," 8–9.

85. David Croft, "Church Divests Itself of Hospitals," *Church News*, 14 September 1974, 3, and "Health Care President Named," 11 January 1975, 3.

86. "3 Welfare Units Formed"; Brown, "An Overview of Church Welfare Services," 113.

87. Jay M. Todd, "Marvin J. Ashton, Assistant to the Twelve," *Improvement Era*, December 1969, 4–6.

88. Marvin J. Ashton, "The Church Focuses on Social and Emotional Problems," *Ensign*, January 1971, 30–31; Marvin J. Ashton, "You Can Get There from Here," *Ensign*, December 1971, 99–101.

89. C. Ross Clement, "Social Services," *Encyclopedia of Mormonism*, 3:1387.

90. Brown, "An Overview of Church Welfare Services," 113–15; Clarence R. Bishop, "A History of the Indian Student Placement Program of the Church of Jesus Christ of Latter-day Saints" (Master's thesis, University of Utah, 1967), chaps. 2 and 3; Genevieve De Hoyos, "Indian Student Placement Services," *Encyclopedia of Mormonism* 2:679–80.

91. De Hoyos, "Indian Student Placement Program," 2:679.

92. "Indian Placement Modified," *Ensign*, February 1985, 80; Bruce A. Chadwick and Thomas Garrow, "Native Americans," *Encyclopedia of Mormonism*, 3:984; Genevieve De Hoyos, "Indian Student Placement Services," 2:679–80.

93. Chadwick and Garrow, "Native Americans," 3:984–85.

94. Katherine Kapos, "Graduates Urge BYU to Open Doors for American Indian Education," *Salt Lake Tribune*, 12 April 1992, B1; Chadwick and Barrow, "Native Americans," 3:985.

95. Clement, "Social Services," 3:1387.

96. "3 Welfare Units Joined"; *Welfare Services Resource Handbook*, 35–38.

97. Boyd K. Packer, "Solving Emotional Problems in the Lord's Own Way," *Ensign*, May 1978, 92.

98. *Identification of Suicidal Behavior*, 1974; *Services for Unwed Parents*, 1981, 1985; *Facts on Infertility*, 1982; *Interpreting for Deaf Members*, 1982; *Resource Manual for Helping Families with Alcohol Problems*, 1984; *Child Abuse: Helps for Ecclesiastical Leaders*, 1985; *Guidebook for Parents and Guardians of Handicapped Children*, 1988; *Concerning Gambling*, 1988; *Preventing and Responding to Child Abuse*, 1991; *Understanding and Helping Those Who Have Homosexual Problems: Suggestions for Ecclesiastical Leaders*, 1992 (Salt Lake City: Church of Jesus Christ of Latter-day Saints, years as cited).

99. Clement, "Social Services," 3:1387.

100. Statistical reports, April conference, *Conference Report* for 1980–89.

101. Clement, "Social Services," 3:1387.

102. Sources for the services described include authors' files; "Church Donates 100,000 Pounds of Food to Salt Lake Food Bank," *Ensign*, December 1991, 68; Lois M. Collins, "Church Helps to Replenish Food Bank," *Salt Lake Tribune*, 11 September 1991, B1-B2; Isaac C. Ferguson, "Humanitarian Services," *Encyclopedia of Mormonism*, 2:661-63. Giles H. Florence, Jr., "Called to Serve," *Ensign*, September 1991, 12-16; "Red Cross Thanks Church for Hunger Fund Donation," *Church News*, 9 April 1988, 23; Peter Scarlet, "Homeless Find New Cafe For 'Square Meal' Daily," *Salt Lake Tribune*, 7 September 1991, A8; Lloyd R. Scott, "Church Boosts Hay Drive," *Church News*, 17 August 1986, 3; "Serve Simply Where You Live," *Ensign*, January 1992, 65; Peggy Fletcher Stack, "Famine, Flood? LDS Humanitarian Agency Supplies International, Local Helping Hand," *Salt Lake Tribune*, 31 August 1991, A10; audio tape-recording of statement by Richard Winters, director, Salt Lake Community Services Council, Sunstone Theological Symposium, 9 August 1991; Carol Sisco, "Hunger Sabbath Set to Fill Food Banks," *Salt Lake Tribune*, 16 May 1991, C1.

103. Twila Bird, "A Charitable Partnership," *Church News*, 13 July 1991, 11.

104. Mike Cannon, "Helping the Needy Isn't a Start and Stop Thing," *Church News*, 23 March 1991, 7.

105. Rodney H. Brady, "Church Participation in Business," *Encyclopedia of Mormonism*, 1:241.

106. "Tribune Corrects AP Story on LDS Welfare," *Salt Lake Tribune*, 4 June 1991, B1.

107. "$17 Million Given in Welfare Aid," *Church News*, 13 February 1971, 3, 11.

108. *Providing in the Lord's Way*, 3.

109. Ibid., 5-9.

110. Ibid., 11.

111. Ibid.

112. Ibid., 12-13.

113. Ibid., 15.

114. *Church Welfare Resources for Use in the United States and Canada*, 3-9.

115. Ibid., 10-13.

116. Ibid., 14-17.

117. Levitan, *Programs in Aid of the Poor*, 35-36. For a general discussion of services, see pp. 40-113.

118. Tim B. Heaton, "Vital Statistics: Demographic Characteristics," *Encyclopedia of Mormonism*, 4:1536. This information comes from a sample survey of U.S. members in 1981. It seems strange that the church average exceeded substantially that of all of the states with large LDS populations at the time, Utah having 9.5 percent poor in 1980, for instance. Utah's poverty rate for 1990 was 11.4 percent. U.S. Bureau of Census, "A First Look at 1990 Census Sample Data," *Summary Tape File (STF) 3*, Table 3, Income and Poverty Status in 1989: 1990, Utah. Applying the 1981 proportion to 1990 members in the United States, the number in poverty would have been 560,000 and the proportion served by the LDS welfare system, assuming all of those served were poor, would have been 27 percent. We suspect the 1981 survey was in error; however, it is the best information available and is useful for comparing the number of LDS poor and the number served within the LDS welfare program.

119. The poverty proportions are from Levitan, *Programs in Aid of the Poor*, 9-18; the population proportions are from Heaton, "Vital Statistics," 4:1530-36.

120. Heaton, "Vital Statistics," 4:1533.

121. Kristen L. Goodman, "Divorce," *Encyclopedia of Mormonism* 1:391–93.

122. Terrell H. Bell, "Educational Attainment," *Encyclopedia of Mormonism,* 2:447.

123. Heaton, "Vital Statistics," 4:1527.

124. "She Served At, Ate From the Lord's Table," *Church News,* 6 April 1986, 10. This article includes a graph of the number of individuals served by the LDS Welfare Program for selected years, 1950–85. The 150,000 shown in that graph for 1985 is the number of individuals receiving welfare assistance at least once during that year; but any individual may have received assistance numerous times, making the incidents of service some unknown multiple of that number. The 350,000 bishop's storehouse orders reported for 1987 is an indication of the total volume of services rendered. Mangum, "Welfare Services," 4:1557.

125. *Conference Report,* 6 April 1985, 26.

Chapter 9 The Welfare Program in the International Church

1. Joseph Smith, Jr., *History of the Church of Jesus Christ of Latter-day Saints,* edited by B. H. Roberts, 7 vols., 2d ed. rev. (Salt Lake City: Deseret Book, 1948 printing), 4:540.

2. Thomas J. Yates, "Count Tolstoi and the 'American Religion,'" *Improvement Era,* January 1939, 94. Yates reports a conversation between Alexander Tolstoi and an American ambassador, Andrew White, in which Tolstoi allegedly classified Mormonism as *the* American religion because it originated in the New World. Recently, the connection between the United States and the church has resulted in terrorist attacks on LDS properties and missionaries in Latin America. See, e.g., David Knowlton, "Missionaries and Terror: The Assassination of Two Elders in Bolivia," *Sunstone* 13, no. 4 (August 1989): 10–15; Michael Phillips, "Amid Bombs, LDS Church Reshaping Its Image in Chile," *Salt Lake Tribune,* 17 January 1992, A1, A17.

3. William Mulder, *Homeward to Zion: The Mormon Migration from Scandinavia* (Minneapolis: University of Minnesota Press, 1957); Gustive O. Larsen, "The Mormon Gathering," in Richard D. Poll, Thomas G. Alexander, Eugene E. Campbell, and David E. Miller, eds., *Utah's History* (Provo, Utah: Brigham Young University Press, 1978), 175–92; James B. Allen and Glen M. Leonard, *The Story of the Latter-day Saints* (Salt Lake City: Deseret Book, 1976), 314; B. H. Roberts, *A Comprehensive History of the Church of Jesus Christ of Latter-day Saints,* 6 vols. (Salt Lake City: Deseret News Press, 1930), 5:111–12; "Advice to Intending Emigrants," *Millennial Star* 69 (23 May 1907): 329; William G. Hartley, "Coming to Zion: Saga of the Gathering," *Ensign,* July 1975, 18; Leonard J. Arrington and Davis Bitton, *The Mormon Experience: A History of the Latter-day Saints* (New York: Alfred A. Knopf, 1979), 127–44.

4. Brief histories of missionary activity and church development by nation are contained in *Deseret News 1991–92 Church Almanac* (Salt Lake City: Deseret News, 1990), 114–74; hereafter annual editions are cited by year and page.

5. R. Lanier Britsch, *Unto the Islands of the Sea: A History of the Latter-day Saints in the Pacific* (Salt Lake City: Deseret Book, 1986).

6. F. LaMond Tullis, *Mormons in Mexico: The Dynamics of Faith and Culture* (Logan: Utah State University Press, 1987).

7. Brigham Y. Card, "Charles Ora Card and the Founding of the Mormon Settlements in Southwestern Alberta, Northwest Territories," in *The Mormon Presence in Canada,* Brigham Y. Card, Herbert C. Northcott, John E. Foster, Howard Palmer, and George K. Jarvis, eds. (Edmonton: University of Alberta Press, 1990), 77–99; Jessie L. Embry, "Exiles for the Principle: LDS Polygamy in Canada," *Dialogue: A Journal of Mormon Thought* 18 (Autumn 1985): 108–22.

8. *Deseret News 1991–1992 Church Almanac,* 336–37.

9. F. LaMond Tullis, "Church Development Issues Among Latin Americans," in *Mormonism: A Faith for All Cultures,* edited by F. LaMond Tullis, 85–150 (Provo, Utah: Brigham Young University Press, 1978).

10. Spencer J. Palmer, *The Church Encounters Asia* (Salt Lake City: Deseret Book Company, 1970), 53–88.

11. Ibid., 44–49, 89–124, 155; Tullis, *Mormonism: A Faith for All Cultures,* 151–80.

12. Allen and Leonard, *The Story of the Latter-day Saints,* 455; E. Dale LeBaron, "The Church in Africa," *Encyclopedia of Mormonism,* 4 vols. (New York: Macmillan Publishing Company, 1992), 1:22–23; Rendall N. Mabey and Gordon T. Allred, *Brother to Brother: The Story of the Latter-day Saint Missionaries Who Took the Gospel to Black Africa* (Salt Lake City: Bookcraft, 1984); and Alexander B. Morrison, *The Dawning of a Brighter Day: The Church in Black Africa* (Salt Lake City: Deseret Book Company, 1990).

13. *Report of the Semi-Annual Conference of the Church of Jesus Christ of Latter-day Saints,* 31 March 1979 (Salt Lake City: Church of Jesus Christ of Latter-day Saints, semi-annual), 3; hereafter cited as *Conference Report.*

14. Britsch, *Unto the Isles of the Sea,* 22, 34, 161.

15. *Deseret News 1991–1992 Church Almanac,* 336–37.

16. Mark L. Grover, "Religious Accommodation in the Land of Racial Democracy: Mormon Priesthood and Black Brazilians," *Dialogue: A Journal of Mormon Thought* 17 (Autumn 1984): 23–34.

17. James B. Allen, "Would-Be Saints: West Africa before the 1978 Priesthood Revelation," *Journal of Mormon History* 17 (1991): 207–47.

18. Mabey and Allred, *Brother to Brother.*

19. LeBaron, "The Church in Africa," 23–25; Morrison, *The Dawning of a Brighter Day,* 25–26.

20. "Gospel Pioneers Still Making Inroads on Diverse Continent," *Church News,* 26 January 1991, 8–10; "Church Membership Figures," *Encyclopedia of Mormonism,* 4:1756–63.

21. "Open Minds, Hearts to People of China," *Church News,* 16 March 1991, 5.

22. Robert Guillan, *The Japanese Challenge* (New York: J. P. Lippincott Company, 1970), 96–119.

23. Palmer, *The Church Encounters Asia,* 70.

24. Brian Kelley and Mark London, *The Four Little Dragons: A Primer for the Pacific Century* (New York: Simon and Schuster, 1989), 241–322.

25. S. C. Tsiang, "Taiwan's Economic Miracle: Lessons in Economic Development," in *World Economic Growth: Case Studies of Developed and Developing Nations,* edited by Arnold C. Harberger, 301–32 (San Francisco: Institute for Contemporary Studies Press, 1984).

26. Michael E. Porter, *The Competitive Advantage of Nations* (New York: Free Press, 1990), 453–79.

27. Manuel Montes, "The Philippine Economy in 1990: Recovery and Restoration," in *Problems of Developing Countries in the 1990s,* edited by F. Desmond McCarthy, 151–81; Vol. 2 in *Country Studies, World Bank Discussion Papers No. 98* (Washington, D.C.: World Bank, 1990).

28. World Bank, *Aspects of Poverty in the Philippines: A Review and Assessment,* Country Programs Department, East Asia and Pacific Regional Office, Report No. 2984-PH, 1 December 1980; Marvin K. Gardner, "Philippine Saints: A Believing People," *Ensign,* July 1991, 37. Before December 1989, it seemed likely that the Philippines could attract significant investments from Japan, Taiwan, and Hong Kong. Montes, "The Philippine Economy," 155. Another attempt to overthrow the Aquino government that month cast doubt on the nation's political stability, and prospective investors decided to wait.

29. Ruperto P. Alonzo, "Trends in Poverty and Labor Market Outcomes in the Metro Manila Area," in *Urban Poverty and the Labour Market: Access to Jobs and Incomes in Asian and Latin American Cities,* edited by Gerry Rodgers, 173–99 (Geneva: International Labor Office, 1989).

30. *Medium-Term Philippine Development Plan, 1987–92,* November 1986, 11.

31. "Lifting Filipino Members from Poverty," *Church News,* 9 February 1992, 12; Augusto Lim, "The Church in the Philippines," in Tullis, *Mormonism: A Faith For All Cultures,* 160–63.

32. Lim, "The Church in the Philippines," 160–63.

33. "Lifting Filipino Members from Poverty," 13–14.

34. *Poverty in Latin America* (Washington, D.C.: World Bank, September 1986); Economic Commission for Latin America and the Caribbean, *Economic Panorama of Latin America 1991* (Santiago, Chile: United Nations, September 1991); Margaret E. Grosh, *Social Spending in Latin America: The Story of the 1980s* (Washington, D.C.: World Bank, 1990), 4–14.

35. *Poverty in Latin America,* 1–25.

36. Seiji Naya, Miguel Urrutia, Shelley Mark, and Alfredo Fuentes, eds., *Lessons in Development: A Comparative Study of Asia and Latin America* (San Francisco: International Center for Economic Growth, 1989).

37. Ibid., 39–54, 77–92.

38. Eliana A. Cardoso, "Privatization Fever in Latin America," *Challenge: The Magazine of Economic Affairs* 34, no. 5 (September/October 1991): 35–41; Felipe Larrain and Marcelo Selowsky, eds., *The Public Sector and the Latin American Crisis* (San Francisco: International Center for Economic Growth, 1992).

39. William Glade, ed., *Privatization of Public Enterprises in Latin America* (San Francisco: Institute of the Americas and Center for U.S.-Mexican Studies, 1991); "Can Latin America Move from the Third World to the First?" *Business Week,* 21 October 1991, 54–56; "Unity Finally on the Horizon for Latin America?" *Salt Lake Tribune,* 11 August 1991, A-4.

40. "New Democracies in Peril," *Salt Lake Tribune,* 1 March 1992, A1-A3.

41. *Trends in Developing Economies, 1990* (Washington, D.C.: World Bank, 1990), 358–61.

42. George Thomas Kurian, *Encyclopedia of the Third World* (New York: Facts on File, Inc., 1987), 2:1356.

43. Nora Lustig, "The Mexican Economy in the Eighties: An Overview," in McCarthy, *Problems of Developing Countries in the 1990s,* 75–91.

44. Lourdes Beneria, "Subcontracting and Employment Dynamics in Mexico City," in *The Informal Economy: Studies in Advanced and Less Developed*

Countries, edited by Alejandro Portes, Manuel Castells, and Lauren A. Benton, 173–88 (Baltimore: Johns Hopkins University Press, 1989).

45. Sidney Weintraub, *Free Trade Between Mexico and the United States* (Washington, D.C.: Brookings Institution, 1984); "Labor Cites Mexico Trade Pact Peril," *AFL-CIO News,* 18 February 1991, 3; Walter R. Mead, *The Low-wage Challenge to Global Growth: The Labor Cost-Productivity Imbalance in Newly Industrialized Countries* (Armonk, N.Y.: M. E. Sharpe, Inc., 1991).

46. Tullis, *Mormons in Mexico,* 171–95; Tim B. Heaton, "Vital Statistics: Demographic Characteristics," *Encyclopedia of Mormonism,* 4:1536.

47. Tullis, *Mormons in Mexico,* 187.

48. Ibid., 189–91.

49. David L. Clawson, "Changing Religious Patterns in Mexico," in *Latin America: Case Studies,* edited by Richard G. Boehm and Sant Visser (Dubuque, Ia.: Kendall/Hunt Publishing Company for the National Council for Geographic Education, 1984), 39–56; and David L. Clawson, "Religious Allegiance and Economic Development in Rural Latin America," *Journal of Interamerican Studies and World Affairs* 26, no. 4 (November 1984): 499–524.

50. *Brazil: Integrated Development of the Northwest Frontier* (Washington, D.C.: World Bank, 1981).

51. "How Brazil Subsidises the Destruction of the Amazon," *The Economist,* 18 March 1989, 69.

52. *Brazil: Human Resources Special Report* (Washington, D.C.: World Bank, 1979, 1983).

53. "Death Squads Stalking Brazil's Street Kids," *Salt Lake Tribune,* 30 November 1991, A1.

54. Kurian, *Encyclopedia of the Third World,* 1:258.

55. Guy Pierre Pufferman and Richard Webb, *The Distribution of Income in Brazil,* World Bank Working Paper No. 356 (Washington, D.C.: World Bank, 1979).

56. Vinod Thomas, *Differences in Income, Nutrition and Poverty Within Brazil,* World Bank Staff Working Paper, No. 505 (Washington, D.C.: World Bank, 1982).

57. Jorge Jatoba, "Urban Poverty, Labour Markets and Regional Differentiation in Brazil," in Rodgers, *Urban Poverty and the Labour Market,* 35–64.

58. Kurian, *Encyclopedia of the Third World,* 1:258.

59. United Nations Economic Commission for Latin America and the Caribbean, *Preliminary Overview of the Economy of Latin America and the Caribbean 1990* (Santiago, Chile: United Nations, December 1990), 5; United Nations Economic Commission for Latin America and the Caribbean, *Economic Panorama of Latin America 1991* (Santiago, Chile: United Nations, September 1991), 24–25.

60. See for instance, Robert E. Verhine and Ana Maria Pita de Melo, "Causes of School Failure: The Case of the State of Bahia in Brazil," *Prospects* 18, no. 4 (1988): 558–68.

61. *Brazil: Human Resources Special Report,* 35.

62. "Doctors Believe Cholera Could Claim Tens of Thousands More in South America," *Salt Lake Tribune,* 28 April 1991, A12.

63. *Economic Panorama of Latin America 1991,* 64–65.

64. Gordon H. McCormick, *The Shining Path and the Future of Peru* (Santa Monica, Calif.: Rand Corporation, March 1990); "Guerrillas See Rebellion as Peru's Shining Light," *Salt Lake Tribune,* 16 February 1992, A31.

65. "Officials in Peru Receive supplies from Church for Community Kitchen," *Church News*, 15 December 1990, 6.

66. "LDS Healthy Despite Epidemic," *Church News*, 25 May 1991, 12.

67. Richard Webb and Graciela Fernandez Baca, *Almanaque Estadistico: Peru en Numeros 1990* (Lima: Cuanto S.A., 1990), 107, 298–99.

68. Barbara K. Herz and Shahidur R. Khandker, *Women's Work, Education, and Family Welfare in Peru* (Washington, D.C.: World Bank, 1991), 39.

69. Ibid., 203–6.

70. Kurian, *Encyclopedia of the Third World*, 3:1600.

71. Rick Lyman, "Drought Expected to Bring Famine to Southern Africa," *Salt Lake Tribune*, 7 June 1992, A10-A11.

72. Robert J. Berg and Jennifer Seymour Whitaker, eds., *Strategies for African Development* (Berkeley, Calif.: University of California Press, 1986), 2–7.

73. Leila Webster, *World Bank Lending for Small and Medium Enterprises: Fifteen Years Experience* (Washington, D.C.: World Bank, 1991), 60–63.

74. David Lamb, *The Africans: Encounters from the Sudan to the Cape* (New York: Random House, 1983), 108–33.

75. Robert M. Press, "Africa's Turn," *World Monitor*, 5, no. 2 (February 1992): 36–43; "Democracy: From Algeria to Zambia," *Salt Lake Tribune*, 1 December 1991, A17.

76. Michael A. Hiltzik, "Hearty Informal Sector Helping to Nourish African Economies," *Salt Lake Tribune*, 14 June 1991, A12; Julie A. Dockstader, "Video Tells Story of Church in Africa," *Church News*, 17 August 1991, 4.

77. *Women in Development: A Progress Report on the World Bank Initiative* (Washington, D.C.: World Bank, 1990), 1–4.

78. Kurian, *Encyclopedia of the Third World*, 2:617–19.

79. World Bank, *Trends in Developing Economies 1990*, 395–400.

80. Ibid., 395.

81. Macleans A. Geo-JaJa, "Manpower Planning with Occupational Choice," *International Journal of Manpower* 8, no. 3 (1987): 18–24.

82. "Structural adjustment" is the term the World Bank and the International Monetary Fund use to encompass the reforms considered necessary to get developing countries on a sustainable growth track. It includes privatizing industry, bringing government budgets into balance by both restraining social welfare spending and creating viable taxation systems, restraining inflation by restrictive monetary policies, yet containing civil unrest through investment in human resources and the creation of employment and earning opportunities through small enterprise development and the rejuvenation of agriculture. See *The Challenge of Development: World Development Report 1991* (Washington, D.C.: World Bank, 1991).

83. World Bank, *Trends in Developing Economies 1990*, 222–27.

84. Kurian, *Encyclopedia of the Third World*, 2:2186.

85. World Bank, *Trends in Developing Economies 1990*, 603–6.

86. Ibid., 603.

87. Robert Weller, "Collapse, Chaos Rule Zaire," *Salt Lake Tribune*, 30 June 1991, A15.

88. David E. Wright, "Orderly Growth Marks Church in Zaire," *Ensign*, April 1991, 75–77.

89. Kurian, *Encyclopedia of the Third World*, 2:2186.

90. *World Economic Outlook: A Survey by the Staff of the International Monetary*

Fund (Washington, D.C.: International Monetary Fund, October 1990), 22–25, 83–86.

91. "Europe Gets in Shape by Pushing Out Pink Slips," *Business Week*, 2 March 1992, 52–53.

92. "Reawakening: A Market Economy Takes Root in Eastern Europe," *Business Week*, 15 April 1991, 46–58.

93. "Food Shipment Eases Soviet Hunger," *Church News*, 30 March 1991, 3; "LDS Food Shipment Bound for Russia," *Church News*, 21 December 1991, 3.

94. World Bank, *Poverty: World Development Report 1990* (New York: Oxford University Press, 1990), 1–6.

95. Lester R. Brown, "The Illusion of Progress," in *The State of the World 1990*, edited by Lester Brown et. al. (New York: W. W. Norton and Company, 1990), 3–16.

96. *Deseret News 1991–1992 Church Almanac*, 187.

97. H. Burke Peterson, "Acquiring and Managing Production Projects," *Ensign*, November 1976, 114; Victor L. Brown, Sr., "Welfare Overview," ibid., 116.

98. Ibid., 224.

99. "First Stake Welfare Farm in Asia Established in Korea," *Church News*, 1 May 1976, 14.

100. "A New Bridge: LDS Humanitarian Efforts Help Poland's Farmers Help Selves," *Church News*, 26 October 1991, 8–10.

101. James P. Bell, "The Poor Among Us," *BYU Today*, September 1991, 36–46.

102. See the following *Church News* articles: "Mission Message Goes to Work," 16 July 1977, 13; "Hong Kong Cancer Display Sparks Interest in the Church," 6 August 1977, 10; "Missionaries Help Families Plant Own Gardens in El Salvador," 24 September 1977, 7; "Sign Language in Spanish," 8 July 1978, 14; "Church's Health Team Teaches Maternal Care," 3 March 1979, 13, 15; "Membership Soaring in Asia," 18 August 1979, 3, 8–9; "Thailand Family Upgrades Lifestyle," 3 May 1980, 15; "Marcus Walks with Help of Bridge," 1 November 1980, 12; "Nigerian Members Share Testimonies, Grow in Knowledge," 14 June 1980, 10, 19. See also the following *Ensign* articles: "Crucial Health Need Gives Missionaries Opportunity," December 1978, 46; James E. Faust, "Establishing the Church: Welfare Services Missionaries Are on an Important Mission," May 1979, 79; "Missionaries Fill Different Needs," November 1979, 91–93. It is interesting and not surprising in the context of long-standing LDS traditions that many of these stories either justify welfare services as door-openers to proselyting or take a defensive stance in maintaining that meeting health and social needs is justified in its own right.

103. *Basic Self Reliance* (Salt Lake City: Corporation of the President of the Church of Jesus Christ of Latter-day Saints, 1982, 1989).

104. John M. Hill, M. E. Woods, and Steven D. Dorsey, "A Human Development Intervention in the Philippines: Effect on Child Morbidity," *Social Science Medicine* 27, no. 11 (1988): 11183–88.

105. "Sign Language in Spanish," *Church News*, 8 July 1978, 14.

106. Reed L. Madsen, "Elder's Machine Saves Time, Labor in Tonga," *Church News*, 3 March 1979, 15.

107. *Welfare Services* (Salt Lake City: Church of Jesus Christ of Latter-day Saints, 1979), 9.

108. Tim B. Heaton, "Vital Statistics: Demographic Characteristics," *Encyclopedia of Mormonism*, 4:1530.

109. "Haiti's Military Assumes Power after Troops Arrest President," *New York Times*, 1 October 1991, A1.

110. "Employment Success in Mexico," *Church News*, 16 March 1991, 7.

111. "Lifting Filipino Members from Poverty: Church Program is 'Inspired Answer' to Employment Woes," *Church News*, 29 February 1992, 6, 13.

112. Lim, "The Church in the Philippines," 160.

113. See, for example, the following *Ensign* articles: "Agricultural and Health Services Missions: A New Way to Serve the Whole Man," September 1973, 68–71; "Tonga Cyclone Brings Destruction, Strengthens Faith," May 1982, 111–12; "Church Aids Three Distressed Nations," June 1983, 77; "Friendships, Testimonies Grow during Arizona Cleanup," December 1983, 69; and the following *Church News* articles: "Welfare in the Church: A Conversation With Junior Wright Child," 12 December 1963, 6; "Mission Gives Aid to Korean Needy" 11 October 1969, 15; "Church Ships Relief Supplies to 3 Countries," 1 May 1983, 5; "Chile Leaders Give Thanks for Aid in Quake Aftermath," 2 June 1985, 10.

114. Reed L. Clegg, "Friends of West Africa: An Opportunity for Service," *Dialogue: A Journal of Mormon Thought* 19 (Spring 1986): 94.

115. "Relief Efforts Get Church Funding," *Church News*, 18 November 1984, 11.

116. First Presidency, "Fast Day and Donation to the Needy of Africa," 11 January 1985, *Encyclopedia of Mormonism*, 4:1730. Similar fasts had been declared a generation earlier, in 1921 for Armenian relief after the massacres in Turkey, and in 1947 to raise $210,000 for European postwar relief, distributed through a non-LDS agency. Thomas G. Alexander, *Mormonism in Transition: A History of the Latter-day Saints, 1890–1930* (Urbana: University of Illinois Press, 1986), 193; *Deseret News 1991–1992 Church Almanac*, 295.

117. Isaac C. Ferguson, "Humanitarian Services," *Encyclopedia of Mormonism*, 2:662; Thomas S. Monson, "A Royal Priesthood," *Ensign*, May 1991, 48.

118. Hinckley, "The Victory Over Death," *Ensign*, May 1985, 51.

119. First Presidency, "National Day of Fasting to Be Observed, November 15, 1985," *Encyclopedia of Mormonism*, 4:1731.

120. "Fast for World Hunger Raises $3.8 Million," *Church News*, 29 December 1985, 3, 10.

121. Isaac C. Ferguson, "Freely Given: How Church Members, Donations and Special Fasts Are Helping Those in Need," *Ensign*, August 1988, 10–15; Peggy Stack Fletcher, "Famine, Flood? LDS Humanitarian Agency Supplies International, Local Helping Hand," *Salt Lake Tribune*, 31 August 1991, A10.

122. Pace, "A Thousand Times," *Ensign*, November 1990, 9.

123. "Humanitarian Projects in Africa Bearing Fruit," *Ensign*, November 1991, 111.

124. "African Clothing Project Is Double Blessing," *Church News*, 23 March 1991, 7; Pace, "A Thousand Times," 9; "Officials in Peru Receive Supplies from Church for Community Kitchen," *Church News*, 15 December 1990, 4.

125. Stack, "Famine, Flood?" A10.

126. See the following *Church News* articles: "Five LDS Die in Chilean Mudslides," 20 July 1991, 7; "Members in Guam Aid Volcano Victims from the Philippines," 20 July 1991, 12; "Donation to Help Flood Victims in China," 17

August 1991, 11; "Church Donates Funds for Filipino Relief," 28 September 1991, 4. See also "Church Donates Aid for Victims of Quake in China," *Ensign,* May 1989, 109.

127. "Church Donates Medical Gift to Vietnam," *Church News,* 11 January 1992, 3.

128. "LDS Food Shipment Bound for Russia," *Church News,* 21 December 1991, 3; "Humanitarian Relief in Europe: LDS Transcend Boundaries to Serve Needy in Neighboring Nations," *Church News,* 29 February 1992, 3.

129. "Missionaries Perform Humanitarian Service," *Church News,* 7 December 1991, 10. In addition to routine home repairs and clean-up for the elderly and handicapped and similar ad hoc service projects, this story describes the efforts of a post-retirement missionary couple spending a year in a Romanian orphanage to conduct a Special Olympics for the handicapped of that country.

130. Monson, "A Royal Priesthood," 48.

131. First Presidency, Letter to All General Authorities; Regional Representatives; Stake, Mission, and District Presidents; Bishops and Branch Presidents in the United States and Canada, 13 December 1991.

132. David P. Gardner, "Attitudes Toward Education," *Encyclopedia of Mormonism,* 2:441–46.

133. Terrell H. Bell, "Educational Attainment," *Encyclopedia of Mormonism,* 2:446–47.

134. Efraín Villalobos Vásquez, "Church Schools in Mexico," in Tullis, *Mormonism: A Faith for All Cultures,* 126.

135. Ibid., 126–35; Tullis, *Mormons in Mexico,* 186.

136. Clark V. Johnson, "Mormon Education in Mexico: The Rise of the Sociedad Educativa y Cultural" (Ph.D. diss., Brigham Young University, 1977).

137. Tullis, *Mormons in Mexico,* 191.

138. Ibid., 192.

139. J. Stephen Jones, "Church Schools," Memorandum to Garth L. Mangum, 18 March 1991.

140. CES News Release, January 1991; Jones to Mangum, 18 March 1991, authors' files.

141. CES News Release, January 1991. Probably of no direct economic significance but possibly encouraging school retention is the weekday religious instruction program which establishes seminaries near high schools and institutes adjacent to college campuses or conducts early-morning programs in church facilities in the U.S. and abroad. The seminaries enrolled 320,000 in 1990, 92,000 of them outside the United States, and the institutes 130,000, 69,000 of them abroad, teaching in 20 languages.

142. *Lecciones De Lectura,* Preparado Por El Sistema Education de La Iglesia de Jesucristo de los Santos de los últimos Días, 1990.

143. Sheridan R. Sheffield, "After 150 Years, Relief Society Remains Deeply Rooted in Charity," *Church News,* 7 March 1992, 10.

144. *Duties and Blessings of the Priesthood, Basic Manual for Priesthood Holders, Part A* (Salt Lake City: Church of Jesus Christ of Latter-day Saints, 1970, 1979, 1986).

145. *Duties and Blessings of the Priesthood, Basic Manual for Priesthood Holders, Part B* (Salt Lake City: Church of Jesus Christ of Latter-day Saints, 1979, 1987).

146. *Essentials of Home Production and Storage* (Salt Lake City: Church of Jesus

Christ of Latter-day Saints, 1978); *Preparing for and Responding to Emergencies: Guidelines for Church Leaders* (Salt Lake City: Church of Jesus Christ of Latter-day Saints, 1981, 1987); and *Services for Unwed Parents* (Salt Lake City: Church of Jesus Christ of Latter-day Saints, 1981, 1985).

147. Warner Woodworth, "Third World Strategies Toward Zion," *Sunstone* 14, no. 5 (October 1990): 17–18.

148. Ibid., 18–19, and authors' files.

149. Fred Nielsen, "Self Sufficiency with Soap—Naga Philippine Stake," *Church News,* 16 March 1991, 7.

150. Clegg, "Friends of West Africa," 94–105.

151. Thierry Crucy, "Cécile Pelous: Love and Friendship in India," *Tambuli* (official Philippine publication of the Church of Jesus Christ of Latter-day Saints), March 1992, 8–15.

152. Victor L. Brown, Sr., "The Remarkable Example of the Bermejillo, Mexico, Branch," *Ensign,* November 1978, 79–81.

153. "Church Focuses on Everyone's Welfare, President Hinckley Says," *Church News,* 7 April 1991, A5.

154. Portes, Calstells, and Benton, *The Informal Economy,* 17.

155. Ruperto P. Alonzo, "The Informal Sector in the Philippines," in *The Silent Revolution: The Information Sector in Five Asian and Near Eastern Countries,* edited by A. Lawrence Chickering and Mohamed Salahdine (San Francisco: ICS Press, 1991), 39–70.

156. *World Development Report 1990: Poverty* (Washington, D.C.: World Bank, 1990), 67; Webster, *World Bank Lending;* Andreas Fuglesang and Dale Chandler, *What We Can Learn from the Grameen Bank, Bangladesh* (Oslo: Nordic Consulting Group, October 1986).

157. Woodworth, "Third World Strategies," 22–23.

Chapter 10 The Future of LDS Welfare Services

1. *Melchizedek Priesthood Leadership Handbook* (Salt Lake City: Church of Jesus Christ of Latter-day Saints, 1990), 3–8.

2. "Welfare Principles to Guide Our Lives: An Eternal Plan for the Welfare of Men's Souls," *Ensign,* May 1986, 30.

3. Tim B. Heaton, "Vital Statistics: Demographic Characteristics," *Encyclopedia of Mormonism,* 4 vols. (New York: Macmillan Publishing Company, 1991), 4:1536.

4. Spencer W. Kimball, "The False Gods We Worship," *Ensign,* June 1976, 4–5; Ezra Taft Benson, "Beware of Pride," *Ensign,* May 1989, 4–6.

5. For different views, see Dean L. May, "The Economics of Zion," *Sunstone,* August 1990, 15–23; Lyndon W. Cook, *Joseph Smith and the Law of Consecration* (Provo, Utah: Grandin Book Company, 1985); Kent W. Huff, *Joseph Smith's United Order, Instrument of the Gathering and Forerunner of the Corporation of the President: A Noncommunist Interpretation of Early Church History and Policy* (N.p.: Kent W. Huff, ca. 1985).

6. For various views encouraging more generosity from the institutional church, see audio-taped presentations from "Plotting Zion," a symposium sponsored by the Sunstone Foundation, August 1990, available at 331 S. Rio Grande Street, Suite 30, Salt Lake City 84101–1136. For a view that reflects no criticism

of the church or its leadership but instead challenges members to abandon materialism and become more generous with others, see Hugh Nibley, *Approaching Zion* (Salt Lake City: Deseret Book Company, 1989).

7. John Heineman and Anson Shupe, *The Mormon Corporate Empire* (Boston: Beacon Press, 1985), 116, 125, estimated 1983 income at $2 billion and estimated total assets at $8 billion in accumulated wealth. Membership then stood at 5 million, approximately two-thirds of the 1991 membership. James Coates, *In Mormon Circles: Gentiles, Jack Mormons, and Latter-day Saints* (Reading, Mass.: Addison-Wesley Publishing Company, 1991), 116–17, repeated the estimate of $2 billion but attributed only $1 billion to tithing from the 7.5 million members, an improbably low figure. An extensive investigative report by the *Arizona Republic* ("LDS Financial Empire Puts Church at Fortune 500 Level," *Salt Lake Tribune,* 30 June 1991, A1), probably overestimated members' contributions at $4.3 billion with an additional $400 million in investment income. We have no access to information that would correct these figures.

8. *Deseret News 1991–1992 Church Almanac* (Salt Lake City: Deseret News, 1990), 328.

9. Gordon B. Hinckley, "The State of the Church," *Ensign,* May 1991, 51–54.

10. Presiding Bishopric, "Implementing the Budget Allowance Program; Sacred Nature of Tithing Funds," *Encyclopedia of Mormonism,* 4:1737.

11. Marvin K. Gardner, "Genealogy," *Encyclopedia of Mormonism* 2:538–39.

12. D. Michael Quinn, "Church Finances from Joseph Smith Up to the Ascendency of President N. Eldon Tanner," audio-tape, Sunstone Symposium West, 7 March 1992, Burbank, California, Sunstone Foundation, 331 Rio Grande Street, Suite 30, Salt Lake City, UT 84101–1136.

13. In Albert E. Bowen, *The Church Welfare Plan* (Independence, Mo.: Zion's Printing and Publishing Company, 1946), 36.

14. D. Michael Quinn, "Decision-Making and Tensions within the LDS Church's Presiding Quorums," audio-tape, Sunstone Symposium, 10 April 1992, Washington, D.C., Sunstone Foundation, 331 S. Rio Grande, Suite 30, Salt Lake City, UT 84101–1136.

INDEX